Politics of Security

In this critique of security studies, with insights into the thinking of Heidegger, Foucault, Derrida, Levinas and Arendt, **Michael Dillon** contributes to the rethinking of some of the fundamentals of international politics, developing what might be called a political philosophy of continental thought.

Drawing especially on the work of Martin Heidegger, *Politics of Security* establishes the relationship between Heidegger's radical hermeneutical phenomenology and politics and the fundamental link between politics, the tragic and the ethical. It breaks new ground by providing an etymology of security, tracing the word back to the Greek *asphaleia* (not to trip up or fall down), and a unique political reading of *Oedipus Rex*. Michael Dillon traces the roots of desire for security to the metaphysical desire for certitude, and points out that our way of seeking security is embedded in technology.

Accessible and lucid, *Politics of Security* will be invaluable to both political theorists and philosophers, and to anyone concerned with international relations, continental philosophy or the work of Martin Heidegger.

Michael Dillon is Senior Lecturer in Politics and International Relations at the University of Lancaster. He has held visiting positions at The Johns Hopkins University and the Australian National University, and has written extensively on the structures and processes of post-war defence decision-making. He has also written on the onto-political underpinnings of modern international politics in *The Political Subject of Violence* (1993, co-edited with David Campbell).

'Michael Dillon engages the problem of security not as a mere matter of geopolitical boundary maintenance, but as the dark heart of the western *logos*. Dillon knows that in the late modern era, we come closer to comprehending the limit-experience of danger in the realisation of our deepest desire for certitude – a desire that can never be filled, except in total destruction. Providing us with a new way to think about the ontological underpinnings of security and insecurity is but the first major accomplishment of *Politics of Security*. But Dillon does more than this: he asks us to rethink the tragic as a way of evading the fate of security. This is a challenging and important book.'

Thomas Dumm, Amherst College

'Dillon has done both political theory and international theory a great service, not least by collapsing the traditional foundations of the two fields through a genealogy of security that turns metaphysical, political and disciplinary boundaries inside out. This could well be disquieting for readers – as I suspect Dillon intends. But it is a disquiet that aptly captures the globalised anxieties of insecure times.'

James Der Derian, Professor of Political Science, University of Massachusetts

'Although I do not share the author's commitment to a Heideggerean mode of thinking, with its residual anthropocentrism and philosophical idealism, I am impressed by the earnestness and boldness with which Michael Dillon seeks to rethink and revitalise the question of the political in Heidegger's wake. In particular, his reading of the tragic and Greek tragedy to illuminate his problematic of security/insecurity is genuinely brilliant and compelling.'

Keith Ansell Pearson, Senior Lecturer in Philosophy, University of Warwick

Politics of Security

Towards a political philosophy of
continental thought

Michael Dillon

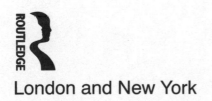

London and New York

First published 1996
by Routledge
11 New Fetter Lane, London EC4P 4EE

Simultaneously published in the USA and Canada
by Routledge
29 West 35th Street, New York, NY 10001

Routledge is an International Thomson Publishing company

© 1996 Michael Dillon

Typeset in Times by
Ponting–Green Publishing Services, Chesham, Bucks
Printed and bound in Great Britain by
Clays Ltd, St Ives PLC

British Library Cataloguing in Publication Data
A catalogue record for this book is available from the
British Library

Library of Congress Cataloguing in Publication Data
Dillon, Michael, 1945–
 The politics of security: towards a political philosophy of
 continental thought / Michael Dillon.
 Includes bibliographical references and index.
 1. Security, International–Philosophy.
 2. International relations–Philosophy.
 3. Political science–Philosophy.
 I. Title.
 JX1952.D58   1996
 327.1'01–dc20   96–3435–CIP

ISBN 0–415–12960–5 (hbk)
ISBN 0–415–12961–3 (pbk)

For

Jayne and Sarah

Contents

Acknowledgements

I would like to thank the following for the intellectual and moral support they provided in the writing of this book: Keith Ansell Pearson; Alastair Black; Robert Bernasconi; David Campbell; Howard Caygill; William Connolly; Costas Constantinou; Simon Critchley; James Der Derian; Peter Euben; Richard Kearney; Michael McKinley; Michael Shapiro; Rob Walker; Sam Weber. I am also very grateful to the graduate students at Lancaster University, and at The Johns Hopkins University, for suffering the thought that has gone into it. Thanks as well to Jeannette, for always being there.

The book is dedicated with love to the two people for whom it was most written: my daughters, Jayne and Sarah.

Introduction

The other is the future. The very relationship with the other is the relationship with the future.

(Emmanuel Levinas)

International Relations is a discipline concerned with observing how the political project of *living-out* the modern emerged, and how it continues to operate globally. I am concerned with how we might *out-live* the modern politically. I think of *out-living* here as surpassing the modern political imagination, not merely surviving its dereliction.

In making its contribution to out-living the modern, politics must be an art capable not only of applying existing moral and economic codes, or of administering the interests of existing subjectivities. It must be capable, also, of allowing new possibilities of political being to emerge out of the unstable, unjust and violently defended sediment of modern political existence. In the development of such a project, International Relations becomes more rather than less important. For the question of whether or not human being does out-live the modern is one posed in and through the interstitial politics of (inter)national politics.

To conceive of politics as being concerned with making way for new possibilities of being requires reimagining politics itself. Specifically, it requires that politics be thought as something which arises from human being as a possibility. To understand human being as a possibility, however, means understanding that it consists in the improbable feat of always already containing more than it is possible to contain; understanding that there is always already in human being an excess of being over appearance and identity.

Thought as a possibility rather than a fixed and determinate actuality, human being must necessarily also be thought as free; free to take-up the difficult and inescapable challenge it encounters in itself as a possibility, and make that possibility its own. For if the human were not free, in the condition of having its being as a possibility to be, there would be no action to take, no decisions to make, no dilemmas to face, no relations to relate, no loves to love, no fears to fear, no laws to make and no laws to break. There would, in short, be no politics. Consequently, the very project of politics is made possible by human being as a possibility. A possibility engendered by the freedom of human being as a possibility, the project of politics must then be the making way for the taking place of human being's freedom as possibility. Such an account of politics would also make International Relations more rather than less important: albeit, it would make International Relations something which its orthodox proponents would not recognise.

Reimagining politics is, of course, easier said than done. Resistance to it – especially in International Relations – nonetheless gives us a clue to one of the places where we may begin. For although I think of this project as a kind of political project, resistance to it does not arise from a political conservatism. Modern exponents of political modernity pride themselves on their realistic radicalism. Opposition always arises, instead, from an extraordinarily deep and profound conservatism of thought. Indeed, conservatism of thought in respect of the modern political imagination is required of the modern political subject. Reimagining politics therefore means thinking differently. Moreover, the project of that thinking differently leads to thinking 'difference' itself.

Thought is therefore required if politics is to contribute to out-living the modern; specifically, political thought. The challenge to out-live the modern issues from the faltering of modern thought, however, and the suspicion now of its very own project of thought, as much as it does from the spread of weapons of mass destruction, the industrialisation and ecological despoliation of the planet, or the genocidal dynamics of new nationalisms. The challenge to out-live the modern issues, therefore, from the modern condition of both politics and thought. This so-called suspicion of thought – I would rather call it a transformation of the project of thought which has disclosed the faltering of the modern project of thought – is what has come to distinguish continental thought in the last century. I draw on that thought in order to think the freedom of human being against the defining political thought of modernity; that ontological preoccupation with the subject of security which commits its politics to securing the subject.

Motivated, therefore, by a certain sense of crisis in both philosophy and politics, and by the conviction that there is an intimate relation between the two which is most violently and materially exhibited globally in (inter)national politics, the aim of this book is to make a contribution towards rethinking some of the fundamentals of International Relations through what I would call the political philosophy of contemporary continental thought. Its ultimate intention is, therefore, to make a contribution toward the reconstruction of International Relations as a site of political thought, by departing from the very commitment to the politics of subjectivity upon which International Relations is premised. This is a tall order, and not least because the political philosophy of continental thought cannot be brought to bear upon International Relations if the political thought of that thought remains largely unthought.

The continental thought upon which I draw is that concerned with the way in which the entire tradition of Western thinking, and the very understanding of how it is thought and functions as a metaphysical tradition, has been questioned since

Nietzsche. It primarily comprises also that recent triangulation of thinking specifically composed of Heidegger, Levinas and Derrida, whose basis, I would argue, is Heidegger; because of the way in which, operating at the limit of the Western tradition of thought, he effected a 'destruction' of metaphysics which opened-up the ground of questioning for the other two thinkers.

The political philosophy of this continental thought, however, remains in many ways to be thought. By that I mean that none of its principal thinkers has produced – or is ever likely to produce – a political philosophy. Moreover, none of them ever expressed, or has expressed, an interest in doing so. Rather, each of them has been concerned, in related, but also very significantly different, ways, to bring traditional philosophy itself into question. To talk of a political philosophy of continental thought, when the thought is their thought, is to talk, therefore, of something in many ways yet to be accomplished, rather than something which is already available as an established body of political problematics, or a set of political maxims and assumptions, widely disseminated and shared in a common political vocabulary.

The political philosophy of this continental thought is not only yet to be thought, however, it is also there to be thought in a different way. Because philosophy as such is in question, politics is in question. For that very reason, it is something of a misnomer therefore to refer to the political philosophy of such continental thought at all. For the political philosophy of continental thought is now a matter of having to rethink the question of the political in response to the rethinking of thought itself; rather than appropriating precepts and concepts from an area that is already a fundamentally shared tradition of thinking, in order to apply them to some other region of it.

Consequently, when I refer to the political philosophy of continental thought I am not referring to a canon. Rather, I am referring to a thought which poses a particular kind of challenge to thinking about politics. I am referring also to the way in which such a challenge requires a form of political philosophising in which the project of thought (politics) is in question because the very form of thinking (philosophy) is itself at issue. In the process, the identity of both politics and philosophy is necessarily modified. For the one cannot be allied to the other here, and the relationships between them fruitfully explored, without loosening the ties which each of them has to their current identities. As William Connolly wisely observed:

> to redefine its relation to others, a constituency must also modify the shape of its own identity.[1]

To invoke the political philosophy of continental thought here and now is to reply, then, to a demand to produce a political vocabulary capable of articulating a different political imagination. Embracing that project can leave neither the enterprise of contemporary continental thought, nor that of contemporary political philosophy, unchanged.

In its turn, such a reimagination invites new forms of (inter)national political analysis and political interventions. Their task, also, is newly to disclose the political character of human freedom in and for late modern times, against what is otherwise in danger of becoming a project of global technological ordering. I also think that there is no greater need for this thought than on the political site of what I will be calling our (inter)national politics of security, which is why I also think International Relations is capable of being rethought as the place where this thinking may take place. Moreover, I think there is no greater opportunity to engage in this project than on the site of International Relations. In order to capitalise upon that opportunity, however, we have to take the 'inter' of International Relations seriously. To do that, we have to ally it closely to the way in which the philosophical resources upon which I draw alert us to the political significance of the between as such; where plurality is insinuated into the very existing of beings, so that being, at all, is itself plural and not merely composed of a plurality of beings.

In as much as we think the political in the way that we do because of the way that we think, therefore, contemporary continental thought has called the way that we traditionally think in the 'West' so profoundly into question that we cannot avoid rethinking the political in response to its questioning of thought itself. There are several reasons why this project is of direct relevance to International Relations. I do not claim to list all of them, but these, it seems to me, are some of the more obvious ones.

First, even when it has aspired merely to be an epistemic mastery of the technology of power, rather than a theory of politics, indeed most then, International Relations has in fact always been a very definite kind of political thought. One, I would argue, that has constituted the very citadel of the metaphysical thought of the political. Orthodox International Relations became the epitome of the closure of political thought, by reliance upon a technologised instrumentalisation of it as representative–calculative thought, whose threat is precisely what any political philosophy of continental thought would now primarily concern itself with.

Second, I refer to the continental thought upon which I draw as a philosophy of the limit. I do so because it is a body of thought that is intensely preoccupied with the way in which the limit of anything – that which gives it identity as the very thing that it is – nonetheless continuously also betrays an excess, or surplus, to which the very existence of that thing remains irremissibly indebted. As a philosophy of the limit, however, continental thought is not simply concerned merely with the difference between things, nor with the relationship between existing things. For example, it would be less concerned with intersubjectivity as with the operation of the 'inter' – the very relationality – which gives subjects definition. That relationality always betrays identity's indebtedness not just to other identities, but to the operation of an unassimilable difference or Otherness as such.

To put the point another way. The philosophy of the limit is concerned with the operation of boundary. Not just the human making of boundaries, but the making of the human through the advent of boundary or difference as such: fundamentally, that between being and not-being which is signalled by the limit of human mortality itself. Within the open space of that limit all other delineation takes place for human being. Thus the philosophy of the limit consequently sets itself to think the very 'inter' of the interval of being and not-being.

From this perspective, always already relational, taking place also in a world of time and motion, all identity is not only plural but is continuously also being pluralised by its very delimited circumstances of existence. As a possibility of being, the human way of being is disclosed as always already engaged in that operation of limits which brings new possibilities of being into being. As such, it cannot but itself also disclose the irredeemable debt which it owes to the difference – radical alterity, or Otherness – that can never become the same. In short, as a possibility, human being appears as always already indebted to a surplus, indelibly traced in its own being, that it can nonetheless never master and make its own. It thus inevitably traces that difference in itself, often despite itself. The 'inter' – relationality or between – is what therefore accounts not only for the plural, but the continuously pluralising character of all identity as it necessarily both summons and is summonsed by that which always exceeds it. Human being, its politics and its freedom, thereby arise for this thinking within, and as a discrete manifestation of, a donation to which they are challenged to remain hospitable.

The issue, then, is how the political is to be thought in the light of this philosophy of the limit. It seems to follow naturally, at least to me, that this issue should become *the* issue of thought for that domain of political thought which already has 'inter' and 'relation' in its title because these are claimed to be definitive of it. In taking the 'inter', relationality or the between seriously this philosophy of the limit would insist, therefore, that we should take the cognate 'inter' of International Relations equally seriously. For 'inter' is the vantage point of estrangement, which is the vantage point of human beings as such.

International Relations is, of course, no stranger to limits. Classically, its very definition is dependent upon limits. Indeed, it is dependent upon what is said to be the limit of political order itself; namely that limit prescribed by the juridically and territorially defined boundary of the sovereign State. Once more, it is not a matter of a simple gap, here, between International Relations and the political philosophy of continental thought. Neither is it a matter of pointing-out something that orthodox International Relations has overlooked; which may then be assimilated into its paradigms of thought.

Rather, it is a basic attunement of thought which separates International Relations from the political philosophy of continental thought. International Relations is more concerned with the fixing and policing of stringent limits. It is preoccupied, also, with the matrices and dynamics of power associated with what it thinks of as existing – and, sometimes, even universal – political being. Such limits, it insists, are not just limits to political existence, but limits to what it is allowable to think as reasonable and realistic political analysis. And so, it instinctively allies itself to the project of delineating and enforcing limits. That, too, is why its basic political and intellectual sympathies have always predisposed it towards Princes and States. It is International Relations' fundamental attunement to limits, therefore, which fundamentally limits it as a mode of political thought. This book is intended radically to exceed those limits.

It does so, first, by thinking about politics through foregrounding the re-opening of the question of the limit as such. It does so, second, by reconfiguring the political as a necessarily plural 'how', rather than a singular 'what'. A how, moreover, that is intimately related to the intrinsic relationality, and therefore excessiveness, of the human way of being as a possibility. As a possibility, human being is obliged to bring the possibility of its way of being into new possibilities of being. Its freedom as possibility is not only a difficult, it is therefore also an obligatory, freedom. There is no escaping it; because the human way of being is a responsive way of being, shared with others in Otherness, challenged by its very responsiveness as a being to assume its possibility of being. The political is the plural 'how' dedicated to keeping the taking place of that possibility open.

Re-attuned to limits, International Relations may, however, progress beyond its fixation with the ways in which political subjectivities are currently thought to exist before the operation of the (inter)national political practices materially responsible for constituting them. It may become, instead, the place where championing the cause of the very possibility of new possibilities of political being takes place. Takes place, that is to say, as a project of thought critically responsive to the challenge of out-living the modern – which modern (inter)national politics itself poses – precisely because of the different way in which it is attuned to the liminality of the political moment of human being.

Third, we not only think the political in the way that we do because of the way that we think, we necessarily also, of course, think International Relations in the way that we do because of the way that we think. Hence, International Relations is a tradition of (political) thought within a tradition of thought whose very foundational – ontological, epistemological and ethical – structures of thought are profoundly in question. Indeed, it is a tradition within a tradition whose very modern definition of thinking, as that which can ground itself, has realised its own failure.

What has been happening to this failed project of thought is consequently of direct significance to the thought of International Relations as well, because it directly impacts upon the thought of the political as such. Hence, debates about Modernity and Post-modernity have now entered into the discourse of International Relations about International Relations. Although I see it as part of that movement of thought, this book is not, however, an introduction to those debates. Neither is it designed to champion one school of thought, there, over another.

That is not to say, however, that the book is not partisan. Anybody who has read this far will already have recognised that it is. But, it exercises its partisanship in a particular way. It does not seek, for example, to persuade by entering into a debate which has already taken-on a certain shape. Rather, it tries to engage in a certain kind of thinking, that which I have called the political philosophy of continental thought. And it does so in a way that focuses very powerfully upon a critical conceptual orthodoxy not just of International Relations, but of the tradition of thinking about politics within which International Relations has always stood.

The book does not proceed, therefore, by surveying different schools of thought. Instead, it pursues a suspicion about security which develops into a particular thought. That thought is not, however, any thought. It is a thought with very considerable, and disturbing, potential. It is one which I also pursue doggedly until it develops into the very widest of arguments about the political itself. It is as a certain kind of exercise in thinking, therefore, that the book is offered as a contribution to a debate in which I have already taken sides, by virtue of electing to think in this way.

It is precisely the way that we habitually think which has been most challenged by the philosophical resources upon which I draw. These have called the foundational assumptions of Western thinking as metaphysics into question, and sought deconstructively to contest the closure of thought always threatened by metaphysics. This is a closure effected more as a movement of thought integral to thought, than a moment in thought; although some argue it is that as well. Here, too, I would note, the foreclosure of politics which so distinguishes International Relations' attunement to the limits of politics is not, first, a political response, but a closure of thought derived from the tradition within which it is very firmly located. One could even say that what most distinguishes International Relations is the way in which it so intimately allies itself to that closure of thought, in order to develop a highly technologised and instrumentalised account of (inter)national politics.

Now, if we think the political in the way that we do because of the way that we think, and if the project of thought has taken a significantly different turn, then the entire range of our political concerns must take a different turn as well. The scope of that turn is such that it must traverse all of our traditional political concerns. It re-raises, for example, the thought of the political itself, in what I would call the politics of the thought of the political. It necessarily, also, re-poses the ancient concern with forms of government, in as much as it raises the question of the public space. It has direct purchase, also, upon what most preoccupies everyday politics; namely 'policy', or the moment of decision and judgement.

In respect of the question of public space, the turn of thought insists upon a bi-focal interpretation of the limits set by the institutional delineation of public space, and the necessary play of both presence and absence which takes place there. For its borders both separate and join − differentiate as they individuate − constitute the politically abject as they constitute the politically subject. That bi-focality, alert to their relationality, emphasises also the undecidability of borders. Necessary but contingent, material but mutable, precise but porous, they are prone to violent foreclosure which excites its own resistance. This is not a question of refusing people individual or collective identity, enframed and sustained by institutional practices. Rather, it is a matter of construing the institutional question of the political in a way, consistent with the openness of human being, that cultivates its freedom to be. A freedom to be that can only be enjoyed within mutably habitable, rather than viciously and unsustainably circumscribed, limits. Limits, too, which are on terms with the ineradicable and irreducible Otherness human beings encounter within themselves as well as with others, because they are indebted to it.

This turn of thought also re-poses the question of policy. It does so as the moment of ethical encounter for human beings; beings which, however rooted they may think that they are, are always already *en route*, out in the open and on the move. Exposed to, and constituted by, an Otherness they share with others, human beings are always already both decided, and in a position of having to decide, in respect of themselves with others in that Otherness. Their mode of decision *en route* (simultaneously deciding and being decided) is consequently their ethos.

However much this moment is rendered, politically, as a technologised decisional administration of things, there is, in fact, no escape from encountering it as an ethical encounter. For a way of being that is gratuitously given its being to be, that being is a free being which has responsibly to assume its taking place in the world as a responsive being. Short of death, there is no way out of this predicament, other than to immerse ourselves in the routinised everyday in the hope that we will never have to confront it. Ironically, because the everyday has a disturbing habit of breaking-down, such a recourse is always unsafe. Generalised routines never satisfactorily fit the singular case, old habits are continuously overwhelmed by the new, or the body inevitably begins to age and crack-up. We are temporal beings and temporality is a motility which treats the everyday like a vagrant. Given no peace, it is continuously told to move-on.

This book is very clearly devoted to a very small part only, however, of what the turn in continental thought requires of political thought and analysis. It is committed to exploring some of the ways in which this turn of thought re-poses – and in William Connolly's terms pluralises – the question of the political as such. The politics of the thought of the political, here, is then waged against the conceptual apparatus of traditional political philosophy. That is one of the reasons why that struggle is a struggle over Language, engaged specifically in a contest about, and for, a political vocabulary which would assist in the reimagining of the political itself.

The political philosophy of continental thought not only calls the unreconstructed ontological, epistemological and ethical foundations of International Relations into question. Contrary to received opinion, it is also capable of providing a powerful alternative account of both the ethical and the political. Indeed, it is capable of advancing its own distinct account of how an intimate alliance necessarily obtains between the two of them. In short, it leads to understanding politics differently. The issue, then, is not one of refining the technologies of power with which politics is currently identified, but of refashioning political imagination. Consequently, there is very much less about orthodox International Relations in this book than there is about how (inter)national politics appears in the light of continental thought, and how we might think beyond the fixation with security.

The book is thus very much part of a beginning, one best described as an exercise in rather than simply a description of, the political philosophy of continental thought. But, it is nonetheless one that contributes to a beginning that is already well underway, both in the political theory of International Relations and elsewhere in the theorisation of politics.

Its contribution to that beginning derives, however, from a point of entry into the crisis of philosophy and politics – namely security – that is not only foundational to their respective and related enterprises. It is one which is also crucial to the foundation of International Relations as well. For no discipline is more explicitly preoccupied with the modern practices of security, nor as preoccupied with the axiomatics of an understanding of politics that is principially based upon security, than that of International Relations. Security, then, my most substantial point of intersection with orthodox International Relations, nonetheless figures as the start of my point of departure from the limits that International Relations sets for itself and for politics. That start-point of departure is also worked in a traditionally non-traditional way, by invoking the poetic – specifically the tragic – rather than the metaphysical imagination.

Here, too, the means by which I effect my point of departure, and explore its ramifications, is not as foreign to International Relations as its techno-orthodoxies might suggest. Although I would disagree with his interpretation of it, one of the designated high-priests of political realism, Hans Morgenthau, for example, amongst others in the International Relations canon, displayed a profound interest in the tragic. We ought not to be as fazed by this as we might be. One way of disrupting the closure of thought by those who insist that the canon of International Relations goes back to Thucydides, is to insist that it also goes back to Aeschylus, Sophocles, Aristophanes and Euripides as well. This is a good conference retort, but, in practice, it entails taking the poetic seriously. It also entails taking the tragic away from the way in which it has tended to be thought as 'mourning play' in realist thought.

The poetic disrupts traditional thinking because it was the historical other to metaphysical thought. It is a natural recourse, therefore, for those troubled by the closure of metaphysics. It is not an escape from confrontation with the difficulties of human freedom, however, but a different point of entry into them. Specifically, in the form of the tragic, the poetic was a means of staging, and exploring the dynamics of the staging of, the political possibilities of human being; possibilities possessed in virtue of its freedom. In this respect, the rift between poetry and thought was the original site of contest with metaphysical thought. It was a site of contest, also, which was fought precisely over the very possibility of politics and its practice as a form of life. The turn in thought which questions the foundational assumptions of metaphysical thought not only, thereby, questions the foundational assumptions of traditional political thought. It does so, in addition, by returning, also, to the rift between poetry and thought. A rift which, from the beginning, was a site of profound political conflict.

I begin the process of exceeding the limits set by security to our modern political imagination, however, by showing how security, itself exceeding those limits, challenges us to out-live the modern. For modern politics calls its own foundations into question by the very ways in which, securing, it nonetheless profoundly threatens human being. If this is the end of modern politics, we are compelled to ask: what must its origins have been? Here, we are propelled beyond International Relations' observation of a mere security paradox deep into the very way in which modern politics has been discursively constituted and thought. Once more, we are re-introduced to a certain crisis of both philosophy and politics.

In taking security as its focus of concern, this study not only reflects my background as a student of foreign and defence policy making within the discipline of International Relations. It also reflects a wider concern, prompted initially by International Relations' security preoccupation, with the way in which modern understandings of politics as such seem to be so generally reliant, foundationally, upon security. Without security, we are taught by Hobbes for example amongst others, there can be no political subject whatsoever. Without security, moreover, there can be no discourse of the rights of those subjects. Without the discourse of the rights of subjects – whether individual or collective – there can be no modern conception, either, of freedom and emancipation through the advancement of the knowledge and understanding of subjects, by which they not only secure their rights, but also resolve conflicts between them over the enjoyment of those rights. For the very right to be – more precisely the right to begin and to endure by having that right secured, somehow – is not simply the axiomatic foundation of any other right whatsoever. It is constitutive of the rights-bearing subject as such. This applies whether one is speaking of the right of an individual (born or unborn), of the right of a State, or of the right of a so-called Nation or People.

And yet, we are nevertheless free before we are secured. The book therefore concentrates on exploring the character of that freedom. It does so, in particular, by drawing on the thought of Martin Heidegger. Heidegger, a long-time member of the Nazi Party, is a deeply controversial figure. He is also most controversial in precisely that area – politics and freedom – where I intend to draw upon him. Use of Heidegger should, therefore, come equipped with a government health warning. His thought is dangerous. As it happens, any thought is dangerous in its own particular way. It is a question, then, of being on watch for the dangers in the thought one employs. I am not primarily interested, here, however, with charting such dangers in Heidegger. Much better cartographers than I will ever be have done that. I am more concerned, instead, aided by other bearings, to navigate past those hazards while plotting an account of the ethico-political character of human freedom which is nonetheless indebted, in some measure, to his original chart work.

Heidegger's thought is also treacherous, in the sense that it offers no secure ground; another reason why one has to traverse it with extreme care. But I think it is nonetheless also an inescapable terrain of thought which has to be crossed. In making this passage, I find that Heidegger's monstrous political fallibility is, ironically, an asset. It insists that, in pursuit of the question of the political possibilities entailed by human freedom, you proceed with caution when traversing this thinking. And it also forces you to supplement what Heidegger gives you – politically and ethically – to think about. When therefore drawing upon Heidegger's thought, to develop and extend the account of human freedom which I find there, I do so by allying it also to that amplification of the question of the ethical which I find in Derrida and Levinas; two thinkers deeply influenced by, but also profoundly at odds with, Heidegger.

The tragic irony of modern politics is that it is not only often compelled to take away human freedom in the effort to secure it. In the process we are also led to the brink of destruction. This tragedy is, nonetheless, a classic one. It has been played-out before; specifically, in the tragedy of *Oedipus Rex*. I therefore offer this tragedy as a political allegory of modern times, when I play it out again at the end of the book. In doing so, I insist that the message of tragedy is generally misunderstood when it is treated as an account of inevitability. That message remains, instead, the best available account of the aporetic difficulties of human freedom. Even more to the point, tragedy is a political art distinguished most not only by the way it insists on the fact of human freedom. It also celebrates that freedom. Moreover, it does so without resorting either to the nostalgia for a pristine state that never was, or to the fearful desire to have freedom commanded away.

In tragedy I find a superior sensibility to the operation of limits, to the very relationality of all identity, to the plural and pluralising character of the human way of being as possibility, and to the excessiveness and peculiar difficulties posed by this condition. All this I find played-out as a political struggle to articulate the political life itself. I find, also, a superior account of the ethical responsibility that the human way of being owes both to itself and to the Otherness to which it is indebted in the obligatory freedom into which it is thrown. In short, I simply find a superior account of human freedom as a responsiveness to its own possibility of being. In what follows, I plunder that account scandalously to reimagine the political in a time struggling also to out-live its time.

Chapter 1

Security, philosophy and politics

> What might be called a society's threshold of modernity has been reached when the life
> of the species is wagered on its own political strategies.
>
> (Michel Foucault, *The History of Sexuality*)

INTRODUCTION

There is a preoccupation which links both the beginning and the end of
metaphysics, and so also the beginning and the end of metaphysical politics. It is
something which, because it furnishes the fundamental link between politics and
metaphysics, affords me my entry into the relationship which obtains between
them. That something is security. If the question of the political is to be recovered
from metaphysical thinking, therefore, then security has to be brought into
question first.

Security, of course, saturates the language of modern politics. Our political
vocabularies reek of it and our political imagination is confined by it. The
hypocrisy of our rulers (whosoever 'we' are) consistently hides behind it. It would,
therefore, be an easy task to establish that security is the first and foundational
requirement of the State, of modern understandings of politics, and of International
Relations, not only by reference to specific political theorists but also by reference
to the discourses of States. But I want to explore the thought that modern politics
is a security project for reasons which are antecedent to, and account for, the
axioms and propositions of (inter)national political theorists, the platitudes of
political discourse, and the practices of States, their political classes and leaders.
Consequently, to conceive of our politics as a politics of security is not to advance
a view held by particular thinkers or even by particular disciplines. It is to draw
attention to a necessity (which Heidegger's history of metaphysics will later allow
us to note and explore) to which all thinkers of politics in the metaphysical
tradition are subject.

In pursuing this thought it follows that security turns-out to have a much wider
register – has always and necessarily had a much wider register, something which
modern international security studies have begun to register – than that merely of
preserving our so-called basic values, or even our mortal bodies. That it has, in

fact, always been concerned with securing the very grounds of what the political itself is; specifying what the essence of politics is thought to be. The reason is that the thought within which political thought occurs – metaphysics – and specifically its conception of truth, is itself a security project.

For metaphysics is a tradition of thought defined in terms of the pursuit of security; with the securing, in fact, of a secure *arche*, determining principle, beginning or ground, for which its under-standing of truth and its quest for certainty calls. Security, then, finds its expression as the principle, ground or *arche* – for which metaphysical thought is a search – upon which something stands, pervading and guiding it in its whole structure and essence. Hence, as Leibniz wrote:

> If one builds a house in a sandy place, one must continue digging until one meets solid rock or firm foundations; if one wants to unravel a tangled thread one must look for the beginning of the thread; if the greatest weights are to be moved, Archimedes demanded only a stable place. In the same way, if one is to establish the elements of human knowledge some fixed point is required, *on which we can safely rest and from which we can set out without fear*.[1]
>
> (emphasis added)

It is for this reason, therefore, that metaphysics first allows security to impress itself upon political thought as a self-evident condition for the very existence of life – both individual and social. One of those impulses which it is said appears like an inner command to be instinctive (in the form, for example, of the instinct for survival), or axiomatic (in the form of the principle of self-preservation, the right to life, or the right to self defence), security thereby became the value which modern understandings of the political and modern practices of politics have come to put beyond question, precisely because they derived its very requirement from the requirements of metaphysical truth itself. In consequence, security became the predicate upon which the architectonic political discourses of modernity were constructed; upon which the vernacular architecture of modern political power, exemplified in the State, was based; and from which the institutions and practices of modern (inter)national politics, including modern democratic politics, ulti-mately seek to derive their grounding and foundational legitimacy.

Thus, for example, and in a time other than our own, the security of an ecumene of belief in the ground of a divinely ordained universe promising salvation for human beings – something that, constituting the Christian Church, provided an ideal of community which continues to pervade the Western tradition – insisted: '*extra ecclesiam nulla salus*'[2] (no salvation outside the Church). Salvation was the ultimate form of spiritual security. And that security was to be acquired through being gathered back into where we belong; a belonging, in other words, to God. What is crucial here is not what happens to us after death, but salvation as the expression of the longing for the return to a pure and unadulterated form of belonging; a final closing-up of the wound of existence by returning to a lost oneness that never was. The reverse of Cyprian's dictum was, of course, equally true. No Church without salvation. The outcome of this project was a rejection of the world through the constitution of an ideal world which – not least because of the model it offered, the resentment which it fostered and the economy of salvation and cruelty which it instantiated – acted in the world to constitute a form of redeeming politics.[3] In a way that indicates the continuity of the metaphysical tradition, however, this slogan can be, and was, easily adjusted to furnish the defining maxim of modern politics: no security outside the State; no State without security. And this, in its turn, has given rise to powerful forms of what I would call the disciplinary politics of Hobbesian thought and the actuarial politics of technologised thought. Each of these is also concerned to specify the principle, ground or rule that would satisfy the metaphysically sequestered compulsion for security; thus relieving human being of the dilemmas and challenges it faces to discover, in its changing circumstances, what it is to be – to act and live – as humans.

The basic thought to be pursued is one which, in simultaneously drawing both our current politics and our tradition of political thought into question by challenging their mutual foundation in security, serves, in addition, to illustrate and explore some important aspects of the political implications of Heidegger's thought. My thought, then, is that modern politics is a security project in the widest possible – ontological – sense of the term because it was destined to become so by virtue of the very character or nature of the thinking of truth within which, through which, and by continuous and intimate reference to which, politics itself has always been thought. What is at issue first of all, for me, therefore, is not whether one says yes or no to our modern (inter)national regimes of security, but what Foucault would have called the overall discursive fact that security is spoken about at all, the way in which it is put into political discourse and how it circulates throughout politics and other discourses. I think Heidegger's account of metaphysics provides a means of addressing that fundamental question.

MUST WE SECURE SECURITY?

The way of sharpening and focusing this thought into a precise question is first provided, however, by referring back to Foucault; for whom Heidegger was *the* philosopher. Of all recent thinkers, Foucault was amongst the most committed to the task of writing the history of the present in the light of the history of philosophy as metaphysics.[4] That is why, when first thinking about the prominence of security in modern politics, I first found Foucault's mode of questioning so stimulating. There was, it seemed to me, a parallel to be drawn between what he saw the technology of disciplinary power/knowledge doing to the body and what the principle of security does to politics.

What truths about the human condition, he therefore prompted me to ask, are thought to be secreted in security? What work does securing security do for and upon us? What power-effects issue out of the regimes of truth of security? If the truth of security compels us to secure security, why, how and where is that grounding compulsion grounded? How was it that seeking security became such an insistent and relentless (inter)national preoccupation for humankind? What sort of project is the pursuit of security, and how does it relate to other modern human concerns and enterprises, such as seeking freedom and knowledge through representative–calculative thought, technology and subjectification? Above all, how are we to account – amongst all the manifest contradictions of our current (inter)national systems of security: which incarcerate rather than liberate; radically endanger rather than make safe; and engender fear rather than create assurance – for that terminal paradox of our modern (inter)national politics of security which Foucault captured so well in the quotation that heads this chapter.[5] A terminal paradox which not only subverts its own predicate of security, most spectacularly by rendering the future of terrestrial existence conditional on the strategies and calculations of its hybrid regime of sovereignty and governmentality, but which also seems to furnish a new predicate of global life, a new experience in the context of which the political has to be recovered and to which it must then address itself: the globalisation of politics of security in the global extension of nihilism and technology, and the advent of the real prospect of human species extinction.

A logical way of pursuing this Foucauldian impulse would, therefore, have been to document the discursive facticity of security by discovering how security is spoken about, and who or what does the speaking. To consider historically, again *a là* Foucault, the propositions, viewpoints and assumptions from which they speak: to specify the institutions, and detail the various interlocking discursive practices, which produce, store and distribute the bulk of what is said (assembling it in great archives and policing what is true about it): to note as well the tensions and conflicts within the plural regime of security as it weaves the tight (inter)national/intertextual[6] discursive economics which comprise the texture of modern global life: including those, for example, of the state; (inter)national organisations; parasitic public media; economic corporations; para-statal research institutions; teaching academies; and medical, informational, communicational, pedagogic and academic disciplines. For Foucault's genealogical method was concerned to show how the

> theme of struggle only really becomes operative if one establishes concretely – in each particular case – who is engaged in struggle, what the struggle is about, and how, where, by what means and according to what rationality it evolves. In other words if one wants to take seriously the assertion that struggle is the core of relations of power, one must take into account the fact that the good old logic of 'contradiction' is no longer sufficient, far from it, for the unravelling of actual processes.[7]

Pursuing such a genealogical line of enquiry would have the virtue of enabling us to see that security is employable in any and every circumstance, and is invested with a plurality of meanings. It would reveal the extent, too, of the work that security does for and imposes upon us, and serve effectively to excite suspicion about the extraordinary valency and velocity which it has in the production and preoccupations of our forms of (inter)national life. We could not then escape noticing the way security impresses itself upon us as a kind of floating and radically inter-textual signifier which, by constant reference to all other signs of the times, transgresses disciplinary, political, corporeal and geographical boundaries as it courses throughout the defining technologically inspired discourses of Modernity: state security; national security; political security; global security; regional security; territorial security; economic security; financial security; individual security; collective security; personal security; physical security; psychological security; sexual security; social security; environmental security; food security. . . .

These, then, would be some of the central considerations to which a genealogy would draw attention. For security, the genealogist would insist, is not a fact of nature but a fact of civilisation. It is not a noun that names something, it is a principle of formation that does things. It is neither an ontological predicate of being, nor an objective need, but the progenitor instead of a proliferating array of discourses of danger within whose brutal and brutalising networks of power–knowledge modern human being is increasingly ensnared and, ironically, radically endangered. Security is the word under which the manifold rationalities of the modern age march together – witness the serried ranks of security listed above – in a struggle which continuously threatens to overwhelm any other understanding of the political – and of the obligatory freedom of human being – than that concerned, one way or another, with securing security.

Hence we are not only users of language, we are used, the genealogist would argue, by the language we use. We are not simply the people who employ discourses of security, we are the people who are ensnared in and used by them. Just as there therefore could be no history of security without a history of the (inter)national politics that seeks to define, pursue and prosecute order under the various names of security, so also any individual political formation would manifest its own particular order of fear. Don't ask what a people is, the genealogist of security might say, ask how an order of fear forms a people. And, in particular, bearing the imprint of the way determinations of what is political have originated in fear, s/he would emphasise that security is a principal device for constituting political order and for confining political imagination within the laws of necessity of the specific rationalities thrown-up by their equally manifold discourses of danger.

My initial inclination, therefore, was to interpret the defining and now threateningly terminal paradox of security genealogically. That way one could more easily resist the call, now regularly made, to interpret the 'concept' of security more clearly, as if it somehow existed outside of language and time, and to extend its range and register so as to make its *telos* more encompassing. Security does not need a larger domain and it is not my intention to argue for an extension of its remit. Neither do I think that we need to recover security's 'true' meaning through historical elucidation. A genealogical approach therefore offered the additional virtue of avoiding an historiographical history of the 'concept' of security in the *Begriffsgeschichte* tradition, where political theory has tended to neglect political reality and the reality of rule for the formal analysis of political concepts.[8] Such an analysis of the concept of security, for example, would tell us nothing about the deep philosophical impulses that lie behind the urge to secure security. Nor would they tell us very much about the vast and widely different experiences of rule human beings have enjoyed, or suffered, under various regimes of security. As a rough rule of thumb one might even say to the conceptual analyst that the more a political theory makes security axiomatic for (inter)national politics, the less it is likely to tell us about any particular experience of rule under any particular discourse of danger propagated by any specific regime of security.

I do not think that it is a matter, therefore, as both these approaches suggest, of overcoming any kind of limitation of seeing, or of broadening the horizons belonging to the scheme in which security appears, so as to thematise a more total and encompassing understanding of it. And so I will not be arguing for a refinement of the concept of security nor for a more total immersion in the conventional world of security in order to help make us even more theoretically and empirically knowledgeable about security. Quite the contrary.

The very alliance of security and knowledge, so characteristic of modern (inter)national politics, is what excites my suspicion most, and generates my sympathy for the genealogist.[9] 'Look,' insisted the first genealogist, 'isn't our need for knowledge precisely this need for the familiar, the will to uncover under everything strange, unusual, and questionable, something that no longer disturbs us?' 'Is it not the *instinct of fear*', he asked – making explicit the crucial connection between the will to truth and the will to secure – 'that bids us to know?':

> And is the jubilation of those who attain knowledge not the jubilation over the restoration of a sense of security.[10]

Hence: security as knowledge (certainty); security's reliance upon knowledge (surveillance); security's astonishing production of knowledge in response to its will to know (calculability); and the claim of knowledge which gives security its licence to render all aspects of life transparent (totality). All these constitutive elements of our contemporary manifold politics of security excited my suspicion because they comprise a monumental enterprise of power–knowledge whose insatiable maw threatens to consume not only all thought, and not only that relating to the question of the political, but of what it is to be human.

Rather, and by first noting and questioning the already hypertrophic register of security, I want to call the entire scheme of security into question. For that way lies a modest contribution to making 'our way back from the world to the life already betrayed by knowledge; knowledge that delights in its theme and is absorbed in the object to the point of losing its soul and its name there, of becoming mute and anonymous'.[11]

'Foucault's genius is evidenced not in the pasting together of unrelated anecdotes', a recent Foucault commentator noted, but in illustrating that historical coherences are formed from the confluence of multiple strategies and tactics of power and knowledge. History, he shows, is not the product of grand narratives with teleological movements but of diverse struggles that nonetheless become organised into coherent (that is to say, more or less continuous) patterns of domination, subjectification, and government.[12]

One of those constellations of struggles, however, indeed the one which informs all others, is the recurring struggle for the political itself. For whatever politics is allowed or taken to be – how it is captured, fixed and determined in its foundations; in short secured – is a decisive element in all power struggles. And yet I think that the very surfeit of information about politics which academic and media techno-logies create has made us so ignorant of the political, and the way that it is secured, that we are hardly even capable of formulating, much less posing and pursuing, the question of the political itself.

Genealogy therefore allows me to formulate my preliminary question in respect of the political. But I am not interested in posing that question because I am interested in pursuing a genealogy. Instead, because it is an interrogatory disposition – a way of questioning, or even a life of questioning – genealogy allows me to stimulate a kind of pre-philosophical as well as a pre-political perplexity about security and politics. It does so because it immediately alerts us to the radically historical, ubiquitous, ambiguous, contradictory, generative and con-stitutive character of security and its relation to both philosophy and politics. Echoing and compacting Foucault, therefore, my question is: '*Must we secure security?*'[13] As it focuses this pre-philosophical and pre-political perplexity, this question puts us in the mood to think about the political anew; or, rather, announces the mood expressed in a related question – '*Is security the secure foundation of Justice it is claimed to be?*' – which demands that we think about the political anew. For a mood can express itself in a question, just as a question can excite a mood, and I want to do both; express and excite a mood through a question. But we can only approach the political anew after the question concerning security has been explored, and a path towards a recovery of the question of the political itself cleared, because I do not think that we are in a position yet even to formulate this, the primary question. For the moment then I remain confined within the scope of the question of security.

But, because the project is one concerned with what is required in order to recover the question of the political, by asking must we secure security I refrain from any engagement with the enormous and secondary literature surrounding security – particularly the explosion of such literature in the last fifty years – because none of it can help me with this project. On the contrary, that literature proves a fundamental obstacle because it does not ask the question of security as such. It invokes security as a ground and seeks largely to specify what security is; how security might be attained; and which are the most basic, effective, or cost-effective means of doing so. Along the way, it occasionally notes a so-called security paradox; that my security project may excite your insecurity. What it does not do is realise that there is never security without insecurity and that the one always occurs in whatever form with the other. Indeed, of course, our politics of security does not ask after its own ground in terms of the question of the political either. We have, instead, to make security questionable, and go through that questioning process, in order to arrive at the threshold of the question of the political itself. Once we recognise that we have to think security and insecurity together, we have already moved beyond security thinking towards posing the thought of the obligatory freedom of human being itself. In short, it is only at that point that we find ourselves on the path of beginning to think the *aporia* of obligatory human freedom as it manifests itself in our own times, and have begun to think politically again.

All this, then, necessarily points beyond genealogy. That security has a genealogy, and that this genealogy reveals how security variously and diversely operates in the production and dissemination of (inter)national political order and identity, is a thought which provokes me. It is, in turn, one of the thoughts which I want to provoke in others. That this genealogy further amounts to being the political genealogy of the political tradition of the 'West' is the additional, much broader and more ambitious thought, which I want to provoke. This last thought follows from the way in which posing the security question necessarily calls into question the way thought itself has been thought. Hence, if one has to account for security's entry into discourse at all, one has to address the very terms in which the political has been thought within the tradition of the 'West'. It is that which points beyond genealogy towards the vexed but fundamental relationship between politics and philosophy.

Hence, just as political thought has its inception in metaphysics, so metaphysics has its inception in the *polis*. Each – metaphysics and traditional political thought – is an enterprise concerned with securing foundations because each has its inception in a question – whose Leibnizian formulation is: 'Why is there something rather than nothing?' – which imbues it with an endless security imperative. To pose our puzzlement about existence, and our desire for the truth of it, this way requires that it be shown how something is wrested from nothing and is prevented somehow against falling back into nothingness. In other words, it requires us to discover how secure (certain) things are – what secures them and how they can be secured – so that we can confidently take them to be the very things that we take them to be; or resolve disputes between us in respect of what they really are. A ground is sought that will explain the emergence of some-thing, allow us to judge exactly what it is, and measure the inevitable variation in its appearance against how that ground tells us it 'really' is. And, of course, if this is done, if we can securely determine how something is something rather than nothing, then we have mastered it. Naturally, the reverse also applies. We are driven to mastery of the world because of the way that we have expressed puzzlement about it, and comported ourselves towards it in search of a certain kind of truth about it, and each other within it. This is what directs us to make the world secure. If this is our question – the question in fact that makes us the 'we' of the 'West' – then we must secure security.

In securing security of all things, therefore, we must also, of course, secure the political as well; that is to say, not only make it certain and unquestionable, but also make of it an enterprise which is itself preoccupied with realising the securing of security. It comes to maturity as just that in the subjectivised and technologised theory and practice of the modern State. To recover the political, to repose the question of the political, does not, however, suppose that it was once properly understood but lost in the midst of time, so that we would have to travel back through those mists in order to rediscover it. To recover the political means to respond to that very subjectivising technologisation of politics as a security project, which has reached its apogee in the (inter)national security politics of the modern State system, by calling into question the security imperative itself through recalling the obligatory freedom of human being. The question 'Must we secure security?' politicises the technologising anti-politics of our current (inter)national politics of security, therefore, grounded as it is in the insistence upon secure subjectivities of every invented description, because it responds to the absence of the political through the triumph of calculation in our current politics of security.

The reduction of metaphysics, and so also of political understanding, to calculation, results from the very inception of metaphysical thought. Because the appearance of things is inevitably various, because we ourselves always encounter them from a manifold of perspectives and because, finally, we ourselves are also mortal and fallible creatures, whatever the secure ground of things is that metaphysics seeks, it cannot actually be the sensible world of the appearance of things themselves. For they are too . . . well, insecure. It has, ultimately, to be supra-sensible, situated outside the realm of the appearance of things, otherwise the ground that is sought would be as mutable (read insecure) as the coming and going, and apparently endless variation, of the world itself. It could not serve, therefore, as the guarantor which the answer to metaphysics' guiding question requires. Literally, it could not offer any security for the sensible world of appearances if it were already located within, and therefore also contaminated by, the very insecurity of the comings and goings of that world.

Metaphysics, then, is the masque of mastery; securing some foundation upon which to establish the sum total of what is knowable with certainty, and conforming one's everyday conduct – public and private – to the foundation so secured. Such foundations may go by different names but that of the project itself does not. Hence, the responsibility, traditionally incumbent upon the philosopher – his 'true' mission – consisted in securing ultimate referents or principles. Philosophy was, as Nietzsche put it, a matter of valuation, 'that is, establishment of the uppermost value in terms of which and according to which all beings are to be'.[14] In as much as these were precisely what were to be secured, for without them no beings would be, without them, it was said, where would we be? The philosopher therefore spoke as a security expert. A security expert not merely in respect of what the substantial values were, but increasingly only in terms of how they were to be secured, whatever they were to be taken to be; hence the rise of theory and of method.

The philosopher became a security expert, then, in the sense of being able to tell you how to secure security. He or she was someone skilled in determining the means by which the invariable standards to establish meaning in discourse, soundness in mind, goodness in action, objectivity in knowledge, beauty in art, or value in life were to be secured (guaranteed). In such wise, whatever was said – meant; done; understood; esteemed; or valued – was authorised and secured by reference to such a standard, principle or reference. The philosopher's task had to be to tell you how to secure such a thing even after they had come-up with an essential value of one description or another. Their security project could not then cease, but only intensify. For having secured this secure value, the value then had to be located securely, and securely policed, so that it could never be forgotten or lost again. Even with Nietzsche, in order for the will to power, as the essence of the Being of beings, to secure itself it has continuously to extend itself; that is to say, it secures itself in its essence as never-ending increase continuously extending itself. Hence, though Nietzsche's will to power may be differentiated as self-overcoming – against the Darwinian, or even Spinozan, principle of self-preservation – it is arguable that this represents the security project *à l'outrance*.

The charge levelled at philosophy at the end of metaphysics – the 'end of philosophy' thesis which has consequently turned philosophical thought into a contemplation of the limit; where limit is, however, thought liminally and not terminally – is that the philosopher has simply run out of things to say. It is that the philosopher cannot, in fact, secure any particular value for you and is, therefore, confronted with the manifest impossibility of discharging the traditional security function, other than to insist upon securing security itself. All that remains of the great project of Western philosophy, then, is the continuing, increasingly violent, insistence upon the need to secure security; hence its nihilism. The savage irony is that the more this insistence is complied with, the greater is the violence licensed and the insecurity engendered.

The essence of metaphysics, then, is nihilistic, as the best of the realists fear that it is, precisely because it does not matter what you secure so long as security itself is secured. That is to say, so long as things are made certain, mastered and thereby controllable. Securing security does not simply create values. In essence indifferent to any particular value, and committed as it must ultimately be merely to rendering things calculable so that the political arithmetic of securing security can operate, it must relentlessly also destroy values when they conflict with the fundamental mathesis required of the imperative to secure. Its *raison d'être*, in other words, masquerading as the preservation of values, is ultimately not valuation at all but calculation. For without calculation how could security be secured? And calculation requires calculability. Whatever is must thereby be rendered calculable – whatever other value might once have been placed upon it – if we are to be as certain of it as metaphysics insists that we have to be if we are to secure the world.

Western understanding of the political is, therefore, continuously suborned by metaphysics' will to the calculative truth of correspondence, and its various regimes of power and knowledge to which Foucauldian genealogy alerts us. It is consequently Foucault's indebtedness not only to Nietzsche but also to Heidegger which antecedes, while it remains nonetheless integrally related to, the task of genealogy.[15] In order to pursue the recovery of the question of the political from metaphysics, therefore, I not only have to be able to pose the question which I have used Foucault to pose, I have to use it to bring security into question and explore that question through the sources which Foucault himself drew upon. Metaphysics is itself unwittingly an aid here, for it bears its own deconstruction within itself. Consider the outcome of the guiding question – why is there something rather than nothing? – for with its closure we are challenged to rethink the question.

Contesting our politics of security, therefore, not only requires more than a technical engagement over the meaning, range, efficiency, effectiveness, morality or accountability of conventional and nuclear, military and political, technologies of security, it also requires something in addition to genealogy as well; because genealogy, however politicising it might be – Foucault arguing, powerfully, that this politicising takes place for, or rather around, the battle over truth as 'the ensemble of rules according to which the true and the false are separated and specific effects of power attached to the true'[16] – does not directly pose and seek to think the question of the political as such.[17]

However much it is therefore stimulated by the interrogatory disposition of the genealogist, my question, like any question, sets something else, or at least in addition, in train. It opens-up another world of thought and discloses the prospect also of another form of life, because that is how all questioning works. Such a world goes beyond the project which allowed the question to be posed in the first place. In the world that a question opens-up, the question itself multiplies and plurifies. It divides and sub-divides demanding more of you and provoking you to other thought. That is the way the world of a question builds. And in this burgeoning world not only do new considerations arise but all manner of other established issues are amplified and intensified in different ways.

Not least of these is the way in which the question alerts us to that which is prior to the question, the source of the question itself to which the question is in fact responding. That which is prior here is that in which we are already immersed, the obligatory freedom of human being; what has happened to it, what might happen to it in the effort to secure it, and what might become of it now it is so secured by and within the security problematic. Hence, what ultimately concerns me is the very thought of security, rather than just its history or its genealogy, and how to let ourselves into the struggle of the duality which is entailed in security – that is to say, the indissoluble relation between security and insecurity which is, as you shall see, even contained within the word itself – from access to which we are secured for the moment, however, by security. This movement, integral to questioning, consequently carries us beyond the genealogical. That is another reason why the question I have derived from it ('Must we secure security?') offers a way – I think, perhaps, *the* way – of opening-up the question of the political.

'Must we secure security?' is, then, not one question amongst many others. Neither is it a question that allows us to confine the response which it demands to genealogy or to the debates about the status of the International Relations of political Modernity. To embrace this question directs us towards an exploration of the link between the philosophical and the political in Western thought. It forces us to consider their current and shared predicament. It situates us right in the midst of the travails of the Western tradition, of the very differentiation between thought and action, and of all the questions which that separation poses. 'Must we secure security?' is therefore a question within whose realm the crisis of modern global politics reverberates and resonates with that of the crisis of modern thought. It forces us to think about the political at a time when the Western understanding of the political, having been globalised, has contributed to the formation of a world that it can no longer comprehend or command – to a world in which it is incapable of realising the very values which it is said to comprise – and that means thinking once more about the belonging together of security and insecurity.[18]

THE CRITICAL CONJUNCTION OF THE PHILOSOPHICAL AND THE POLITICAL

While philosophy and the *polis* were deeply implicated in one another from the outset of Western thought – the question of the Being of beings materialised and developed in the space of the *polis* just as much as in the sayings of Heraclitus, the poems of Parmenides, the teaching of Socrates, Plato and Aristotle, or the history of Thucydides[19] – modern philosophy and politics continue to remain deeply implicated in one another.[20] But now differently. During the course of the last hundred years it not only became impossible to continue to subscribe to the metaphysics of presence that has constituted Western thinking, it has become equally impossible to subscribe to an (inter)national politics predicated upon the securing of security.[21] This coincidence was not merely coincidental, but neither does it offer itself to simple diagnosis.

On the one hand, the very lethality and globality, and the potentially terminal paradox, of the modern political condition have not only called into question the specific institutional structures, vocabularies and practices which comprise our contemporary (inter)national politics of security. The late modern apprehension of danger also calls into question the entire political imagination that underpins that politics of security, the very limits provided by the grounds of its thinking. Our contemporary (inter)national politics of security drive us back, in other words, to the very presuppositions of the political itself. This metaphysical politics is at an end in the sense that it is now gathered – in the technology of our modern politics of security – into its own extreme possibilities.[22]

On the other hand, post-Nietzschean thought has called into question the metaphysical reserve of philosophy from which our political thinking has traditionally derived its very suppositional support. Consequently, while sensibility to the dangers which our contemporary civilisation has engendered demands that we ask how we came to be in the now terminal paradox of security, post-Nietzschean thought, responding to somewhat different impulses, complements this regress and pushes it one stage further. In asking directly about the Being in virtue of which there are beings at all, and without always falling into the metaphysical trap of representing it as a being (even a supreme Being, hence onto-theology, the other name for metaphysics) – recalling, in other words the ontological difference between Being and beings – it calls into question not simply the vocabulary or institutions of (inter)national politics as such, but the very metaphysical grammar, or scheme, according to which the political has come to be variously thematised and schematised. The provocation for my question is, therefore, furnished both by material and philosophical concerns; by the conjunction of an ontic with an ontological crisis in which the one compounds the other, and a renewed violence, pertinency and urgency is lent to the conjunction of philosophy and politics.

To put it crudely, and ignoring for the moment Heidegger's so-called 'anti-humanist' (he thought 'humanism' was not uncannily human enough) hostility to the anthropocentrism of Western thought.[23] As the real prospect of human species extinction is a function of how human being has come to dwell in the world, then human being has a pressing reason to reconsider, in the most originary way possible, notwithstanding other arguments that may be advanced for doing so,[24] the derivation of its understanding of what it is to dwell in the world, and how it should comport itself if it is to continue to do so. Such a predicament ineluctably poses two fundamental and inescapable questions about both philosophy and politics back to philosophy and politics and of the relation between them: first, if such is their end, what must their origins have been?[25] Second, in the midst of all that is, in precisely what does the creativity of new beginnings inhere and how can it be preserved, celebrated and extended?

No matter how much we may want to elide these questions, or, alternatively, provide a whole series of edifying answers to them, human beings cannot ignore them, ironically, even if they remain anthropocentric in their concerns, if they wish to survive. Our present does not allow it. This joint regress of the philosophical and the political to the very limits of their thinking and of their possibility therefore brings the question of Being (which has been *the* question of philosophy, even though it has always been directed towards beings in the answers it has offered) into explicit conjunction with the question of the political once more through the attention it draws to the ontological difference between Being and beings, and emphasises the abiding reciprocity that exists between them.

We now know that neither metaphysics nor our politics of security can secure the security of truth and of life which was their reciprocating *raison d'être* (and, *raison d'état*[26]). More importantly, we now know that the very will to security –

the will to power of sovereign presence in both metaphysics and modern politics – is not only a prime incitement to violence in the Western tradition of thought, and to the globalisation of its (inter)national politics, but also self-defeating;[27] in that it does not in its turn merely endanger, but actually engenders danger in response to its own discursive dynamic. One does not have to be persuaded of the destinal sending of Being, therefore, to be persuaded of the profundity – and of the profound danger – of this the modern human condition.

That, then, is why the crisis of Western thought is as much a fundamental crisis of (inter)national politics, as the crisis of (inter)national politics is a crisis of thought. Moreover, that is why in doubting the value of security, and doubting in a Nietzschean mode better than Descartes,[28] we are also enjoined by the circumstances of this critical conjunction of the philosophical and the political to doubt metaphysical truth. For the political truth of security is the metaphysical truth of correspondence and adequation in declension to mathesis; the mere, but rigorously insistent, mensuration of calculability. To bring the value of security into question in the radical way required by the way it now, ironically, radically endangers us, correspondingly requires that we attend to metaphysics' own continuous process of deconstruction. In doing this, however, we go beyond mere doubting – which, after all, is the mere counterpart of the desire for certainty – and find non-apocalyptic ways of affirming and so continuing to enjoy and celebrate (in)security; that is to say human being's own obligatory freedom.

Ultimately, now, our (inter)national politics of security is no longer even distinguished or driven by humanistic considerations. It is a security simply ordering to order. But it is only by virtue of the fact that our (inter)national politics of security has come to this end that we can in fact begin to consider the relationship between its end and its beginning. Through this we do not, in a sense, go back to anything at all. Neither does this turn disguise some covert nostalgia for a phantom past. Rather, attention is turned towards consideration of what is entailed in the preparation and inception of continuous new political growth. This is also why, at the limit, it is useful to think about these origins and limits again. Not because they hold an answer that is now lost but because, antecedent to metaphysics, they make us think about the very liminal character of origins and limits, of the relationship which obtains between them, and of what proceeds from them, in ways that are not utterly determined by metaphysics. That way we may get some clues to some ways of thinking that are not metaphysical; nor, indeed, pre-metaphysical, because we cannot be pre-metaphysical at the end of meta-physics. What happens, instead, is that the whole question of emergence and origination, of the very possibility of repeating ourselves, opens-up again; specifically in the sense of the historical possibilities of the obligatory freedom of human being now terminally endangered globally by its very own (inter)national 'civilising' practices.

There is no going back, but there is also no stepping outside of this condition. Humankind has attained a certain limit here in our time and our thinking. And this limit, by virtue of the globalisation of Western thought and politics, now increasingly conditions the future of human being. Politics at the end, or rather in the *extremis*, of security consequently confronts the same tasks as philosophy at the end, or in the *extremis*, of metaphysics. That *extremis*, or limit, is the insecurity of security itself. Because there is no overcoming this limit, modern thought and modern politics are each an encounter, therefore, with that limit. An encounter that has to be designed to defer both the closure of thought and the termination of politics threatened by the terminal construal of limits in general, and of this limit in particular.[29] That, critically, means thinking limits differently.

This global conjunction of the limit of the philosophical and the political, therefore itself, constitutes a new political experience. It is one which compounds the deconstruction of the way political experience, or rather the understanding of political life, has hitherto been thought, because that new experience cannot be addressed – much less 'resolved' – in the traditional terms and categories of political philosophy.

Everything, for example, has now become possible. But what human being seems most impelled to do with the power of its actions is to turn itself into a species; not merely an animal species, nor even a species of currency or consumption (which amount to the same thing), but a mere species of calculation. For only by reducing itself to an index of calculation does it seem capable of constructing that political arithmetic by which it can secure the security globalised Western thought insists upon, and which a world made increasingly unpredictable by the very way human being acts into it now seems to require. Yet, the very rage for calculability which securing security incites is precisely also what reduces human freedom, inducing either despair or the surrender of what is human to the de-humanising calculative logic of what seems to be necessary to secure security. I think, then, that Hannah Arendt was right when she saw late modern humankind caught in a dangerous world-destroying cleft between a belief that everything is possible and a willingness to surrender itself to so-called laws of necessity (calculability itself) which would make everything possible. That it was, in short, characterised by a combination of reckless omnipotence and reckless despair. But I also think that things have gone one stage further – the surrender to the necessity of realising everything that is possible – and that this found its paradigmatic expression, for example, in the deterrent security policies of the Cold War; where everything up to and including self-immolation not only became possible but actually necessary in the interests of (inter)national security. This logic persists in the metaphysical core of modern politics – the axioms of inter-State security relations, popularised, for example, through strategic discourse – even if the details have changed.

What is most at issue here, then, is the question of the limit and of how to finesse the closure of the fatally deterministic or apocalyptic thinking to which the issue of limits ordinarily gives rise in onto-theological thought: as the authoritative specification of an eschaton; as the invocation of our submission to it; or in terms of the closure of what it is possible for us to say, do and be in virtue of the oper-ation of it. The question of the limit has therefore to be posed in a way that invokes a thinking which resists the siren calls of fatal philosophers and historians alike. That is why limits have to be thought differently, and why the question concerning limits has to be posed, instead, in terms of that which keeps things in play (for '[w]here demarcation is lacking nothing can come to presence as it is'[30]); exciting a thinking, in particular, which seeks continuously to keep 'open the play of [political] possibility by subtracting the sense of necessity, completeness, and smugness from established organ-izations of life',[31] all of which are promoted by an insistence upon security.

Metaphysics, therefore, becomes material in politics of security because metaphysically determined being has a foundational requirement to secure security. Hence our (inter)national politics of security are the municipal metaphysics of the Western tradition. That is why the fate of metaphysics and the fate of that politics of security are so inextricably intertwined.

There is more than an academic interest at stake, therefore, in this modern conjunction between the philosophical and the political. How we think and what we do, what we think and how we are doing, condition one another. There is clearly more than a coincidence also in relying upon post-Nietzschean thought to argue for that reappraisal of both which requires a recovery of the question of the political. For between Hegel and Heidegger metaphysics exposed itself to its own deconstructive impulses. After Marx 'one finds Schopenhauer, Kierkegaard, Freud, and Nietzsche turning philosophy upon itself, thereby unmasking its own taboos and twisted roots';[32] realising and exhausting its potential, according to Heidegger, in the advent of the epoch of technology.

The same period also witnessed the exhaustion of the European State system's modern metaphysical resolution of the question of the political – its profoundly ambiguous and deeply problematic inauguration as both a State of emergency and a certain kind of democratic project – through the very globalisation of the language, forms and practices of the politics of security upon which it was based. The advent of the globalised industrial nuclear age exhibits not only the hollowness of that system's foundational promises to secure order, identity and freedom – hence the reason why the disciplines which promise to tell the truth about the operation of its orders and identities appear to be so peculiarly limited and unreal in their vaunted realistic representation of reality – but also, in the gulf that exists between what its (inter)national political prospectus offers and what its (inter)national politics provides; the exhaustion of its political imagination.[33] For this was a period, in which World War One was critical, when that (inter)national politics of security finally realised the full potential of the self-immolative dynamic pre-figured in its very inception; the real prospect of human species extinction.[34]

Although fundamental to that axiomatic privileging of security upon which Western understanding of the political relies, although fundamental to its common sense, fundamental questions concerning security nonetheless seem never to be pressed. When asked, especially by those branches of the study of politics that currently assert particular disciplinary claims on the word – political philosophy, whose modern inaugural moment paradigmatically occurs with Hobbes, and International Relations and Strategic Studies (currently the popular twin citadels of the metaphysical determination of the political), whose inaugural moment occurs in the global technologisation of the political that began once the idea of politics articulated in the post-Westphalian European state system exhausted its pre-figured possibilities in global militarisation and conquest[35] – they are never pursued beyond that point where its function as a ground is precisely what is at issue.[36]

There is, then, an exquisite paradox at work here. Our (inter)national politics of security hide what they most depend upon, by making it most obvious. The metaphysical dynamics and demands that determine them are securely secured – locked away and forgotten – by means of the very insistence upon security itself. The engagement with security has not, therefore, even begun. Securing security is, it seems, too immediate and too pervasive a preoccupation within our world. We have not, yet, been sufficiently separated from it. Locked in an intensely technologised epistemic preoccupation with it, we lack the dramatic distance needed for re-thinking the belonging together of security and insecurity and so, therefore, of a politics which operates in an understanding of their indissoluble, and indissolubly agonistic, connection in the condition of obligatory freedom.

For some, the very pursuit of security is misguided, for others it is, inevitably, a first order priority. But I do not want to pose the question of whether we must secure security through this dichotomy, and the invitation it inevitably issues finally to resolve the relation between security and insecurity one way or another. But that does not mean that I think it is possible to settle, either, for a macho insouciance that would accept the so-called security paradox, as if this were the end of the matter rather than its beginning. Instead, I want to approach the question through the primordial and inescapable relation which adheres between the two of them.

The questions about security, which the tradition ordinarily takes as its guide, ask: What ultimately secures us? What do we ultimately wish to secure? How can we secure security? or, What is the most secure way of securing security? The grounding question – What is the essence of security? – simply does not unfold in our politics of security at all; because it is taken to be the very ground of things itself, that unquestionable thing which anybody and anything needs in order for it to be at all. Neither then does the answer which begins to emerge from that question – that security and insecurity are inherently related – begin to be addressed.

Rather, throughout the course of its successive transformations, Western political thought has been impelled by its metaphysical determination to secure the appropriate theoretical grounds and instrumental means by which security itself could be secured. The politics of Western thought has, therefore, been a security project in the fullest sense of the term. Driven by the requirement to secure security, it not only constituted an escape from politics but also, for reasons and in ways I will elaborate later, a form of tragic denial. Preoccupied with command and rule, rather than with politics, it has been substantially concerned in the modern period with specifying the conditions under which rulers can guarantee their subjects a secure private existence. Along with that preoccupation, it has further found itself concerned to figure-out what price, in terms of obligations and duties, subjects ought to pay for this privilege; and with whether, and under what terms and conditions, they might determine that this utilitarian security contract has been rendered null and void, so leaving them free to conclude another.

I, therefore, intend to examine the link between political thought and metaphysics by looking back at it from the vantage point at the end of metaphysics – that is to say, at the limit of what has so far made Western political thought possible – but to do so specifically from the vantage point which is afforded by my preliminary question concerning security. For the question concerning security is itself, of course, fundamentally a question concerning limits as well, specifically the limit of what it means to be mortal. Mortality, then, is where the questions both of security and of politics first arise.

CONCLUSION

While, therefore, not denying that modern (inter)national political discourses and practices have also sought to derive and provide a politics of rights, freedoms and interests out of metaphysics, and that these are in certain ways definitive of the modern condition, all such (inter)national politics are always already subject to a process of reduction to the determinants of security – foremost amongst which is calculability – in as much as they remain metaphysically conceived. This reduction arises not merely because of the way the exigencies of war and danger always acquire a powerful dynamic and logic of their own;[37] something which Alexander Hamilton noted long before strategic theorists sought to make a political technology out of it *via* the principles of strategic thought or the rubrics of crisis management.[38] 'The violent destruction of life and property incident to war', Hamilton observed,

> the continual effect and alarm attendant on a state of continual danger, will compel nations the most attached to liberty to resort for repose and security to institutions which have a tendency to destroy their civil and political rights. To be more safe, they at length become more willing to run the risk of being less free.[39]

But, more than this, because freedom is largely conceived in modern liberal democratic thought, indeed also with Hamilton himself, as something that can be secured ultimately only outside of the public realm of appearance, and is thus separated from politics itself.

Thus, as Arendt notes:

> We need go no further than the political thinkers of the seventeenth and eighteenth centuries, who more often than not simply identified political freedom with security. The highest purpose of politics, 'the end of government', was the guarantee of security; security in turn made freedom possible, and the

word freedom designated a quintessence of activities which occurred outside the political realm.[40]

For Arendt, in contrast, freedom is a 'form' of Heideggerian freedom. That freedom,

> to call something into being which did not exist before, which was not given, not even as an object of cognition or imagination, and which therefore, strictly speaking, could not be known,[41]

is something which is experienced and realised in the action allowed by the freedom of the (in)security of mortal life.

It is precisely because it is conceived in subjectivist and utilitarian terms that modern liberal democratic thought can always be trumped by the super-utilitarian – and super-subjectivist – claims of security. This is perhaps part of the explanation why liberal humanism displayed such an inability during the inter-war period of the twentieth century to understand what Claude Lefort calls 'the drama that was unfolding in the world, and in particular, its inability to understand the depths from which the collective identifications and death wishes sprang'. Its inability, then, to grasp 'the link between the unbridled pursuit of individualism and economic competition, on the one hand, and the attractions of communist or fascist collectivism, on the other',[42] is something which, in its triumphalism over the dissolution of the Soviet empire, it is in danger of repeating; and not because of some simple policy omission, but because of the very way in which it seeks to ground itself through and through in representative–calculative thought.

The more the dissociation of freedom from politics becomes pronounced, however, the more security is embraced as the foundation of politics; and the more obligatory freedom is suborned by security. Whereas the condition of the political is the freedom of (in)security, being thrown into a world which is determined neither by a unified *logos* nor a transcendental *telos*, security insists, instead, on being the condition which has to be secured so that freedom can be enjoyed; or even that it can release us altogether from the burden of freedom itself. It was not the celebration of this freedom which, therefore, stimulated and fuelled the desire of liberal revolutions for participation in government, but the fundamental lack of trust in the capacity and probity of government when it came to fulfilling what the dissociation of freedom from politics had established as its higher purpose; that *raison d'être*, as Spinoza defined it, which knew 'no higher law than the safety of [its] own realm'.[43]

Hence our (inter)national politics of security are not merely concerned to document and detail that, and how, the exigencies of necessity operate. (We would not need the entire edifice of (inter)national security to tell us this, we confront necessity one way and another every day in our everyday lives. There is nothing especially realistic about the (inter)national security-mongers who trade in telling us so.) Nor do they merely claim to offer just another picture of political life. The point is that they claim utilitarianly to be most true of it.

Why? Referring back to my earlier point about politics and limits, and directly recalling the mathesis that governs the technological mode of being. It is not only because of the way freedom has been construed by them – something which Arendt has detailed so persuasively – but also because they claim to articulate the bottom line, the single figures and universal numbers, the final calculus (the limit condition conceived in terms of terminality and calculability – indeed the calculability of terminality, and the terminality of calculability – rather than liminality) that makes politics possible. They make a determinate claim both on the construal and the answering of the question of the political, because, in virtue of the mortal danger which it is their self-appointed distinctive competence to articulate, they claim to have found, and therefore possess, the mandate for the political. (Inter)national politics of security are, therefore, essentially a form of eschatology; politics thought in the light of the last things, the limit situation as a determinable and determining terminus. But because eschatology is ineluctably linked also, through diverse idioms (essence, cause, *telos* and revelation) to the beginning of things, this terminus also articulates the natality, the first cause, the ultimate goal, defining essence or revelatory initiation and fulfilment of the political as well. Specifying the end (the limit condition as the terminal and not the liminal),[44] politics of security claim also to have discerned the advent of the political.[45] That understanding of the political ultimately construes the political realm as a domain of calculability in which political practices become exercises in the political arithmetic of representation of the things to be secured and of the calculuses which will secure them. This makes of human being not merely an index of (inter)national security, but an index whose very indexicality has to be secured first if there is to be any (inter)national political arithmetic at all.

Most theorists who are, however, critical of liberal individualism and who want to understand freedom in public rather than private terms tend to think of it as participation in collective decision making: taking decisions, that is, on an agenda which is somehow already set. The point about Arendt's concept of freedom, then, and the reason why I think it has relevance to the globalised (inter)national politics of security which now dominate world politics, is that, by contrast, she stresses that politics is not confined to choice between prescribed alternatives but essentially entails action in concert with others to call entirely new possibilities into being.[46] Such a new possibility might be a novel engendering of the political itself – a new *mise en forme* in response to the new experience of politics engendered by the globalisation of the technicity and nihilism of our (inter)national politics of security itself.

Security cannot be taken as an unproblematic ontological predicate of the political because the question of ontology has itself become so problematical since the radical problematisation of the very tradition in which it has hitherto been thought. That problematisation, and its implications for thinking politics, is what I want to explore next. Consequently we cannot understand the inception and operation of (inter)national politics of security by reference to the expression of that predicate in self-consciousness, the biological individual, the comunity/

nation/people, or the egotistical subject. Just as certainty is never certain of itself, (inter)national security never succeeds in securing itself. For each consists in exactly the same demand, which redoubles with any act that might satisfy it.

One of the virtues of approaching security through a philosophy of the limit lies in the way such thinking is concerned not with the discernment of meta-physical truth but the decipherment of value, not with the production of reliable knowledge but the exposure of the processes of valuation and the foreclosure of possibilities effected by regimes of truth as power–knowledge. Such a posture emphasises that (inter)national security names a process of valuation and so alerts us to what is being devalued as well. And that such a process is not a simple monolithic determination of values, but sets in motion a dynamic play of (de)valuation in its preoccupation with calculation.

While we have no greater provocation than the terminal paradox of our (inter)national politics of security to doubt the truth and the value (the truth-value) of security, it is perfectly obvious also that thinking the limit is itself, however, a dangerous game. For to doubt the truth and value of security seems to deny us the very means of survival in the most lethal of circumstances; particularly when it does not come equipped with a promise that we can secure an escape from (in)security, danger or a final overcoming of the violence which threatens, and is always threatened by, the agonal mortal life of human being.

'There are no dangerous thoughts', said one of the very few contemporary political philosophers – Hannah Arendt – whose work was deeply influenced by Heidegger.[47] 'Thinking itself', she concluded, 'is dangerous'.[48] Heidegger, too, called the ontological difference – which is the very thought that re-opens the question of the political – 'the most dangerous matter for thought'.[49] But 'non-thinking', Arendt nonetheless also cautioned, 'which seems so recommendable a state for political and moral affairs, also has its perils'.[50] To think and not to think, especially where the matter for thought is the question of the political, are therefore equally dangerous things to do. All this, then, is very dangerous talk.[51] However, even if it is inevitably dangerous, it is dangerous in different ways and for different reasons.

It is dangerous first of all because it is the product of, and requires a certain kind of, thinking; one which challenges the very assumptions of thought itself. And is, therefore, not merely thought but a wager with the wager of human being itself. 'To work in Heidegger's choppy wake', as Dennis Schmidt put it,

> is both to take a risk and to set oneself at odds with oneself. One takes the risk of radical error if one is less than vigilant when answering the call for questioning without restraint, even questioning our capacity to question at all today.[52]

Worse, vigilance itself is no ultimate guarantee of security against such error. The very possibility of such error is ineradicable precisely because our mortal condition is a free one.

It is dangerous, second, because, of course, any consideration of security is concerned with danger. 'Everything "anti" thinks in the spirit of that against which it is anti.'[53] How, in other words, would you know what security was without its being differentiated as such from what it is not. All security, however defined, is consequently a relationship towards insecurity, and *vice versa*. Security and insecurity belong together. (In)security is, therefore, humanity's share.

This talk is dangerous, thirdly, in that the very thinking from which it draws its inspiration is not only thought to be dangerous but has also been appropriated, in the past, to service the totalitarianism which has given political form to the nihilistic impulses of modern life. It is also dangerous, finally, in that this dangerous thinking is itself ultimately preoccupied with the global danger of the nihilism of the (inter)national politics of late modern times. Danger does not merely stalk all of this talk and its thought, danger is its very *métier*.

Nothing, then, is without danger. Certainly not, of course, the *traditional* thought of the political upon which our modern (inter)national politics of security rely. Dealing with dangerous discourses of danger should, therefore, encourage caution, but there is simply no escaping the risk. For this risk is the risk which mortal freedom necessarily entails. Here, Heidegger, not only the leading philosopher of the philosophy of the limit but also the most controversial, himself provides one of the best guides. He does so not simply because his own thought is a model of deliberate and careful questioning, specifically designed to impose a brake upon the sheer velocity, and effect a break with, the imperatives of the tradition in an effort to disrupt its ballistic trajectory. He is a good guide because he seems to have proved fatefully fallible in his commitment to his own project at the very point in which he directly encountered the question of the political. Ordinarily taken to be the decisive reason for dismissing Heidegger, I think that this fallibility has a crucial value in the recovery of political thought,[54] precisely because in the pursuit of the question of the political one can never rest easy with Heidegger's thinking, or adopt him as a political mentor.[55] In addition, then, to his model of questioning, his very conduct keeps political questioning alive within you.

In the thought of the limit there is therefore no escape from danger, no new programmatic schema or template for politics, no promise of final resolution of the human condition. But what it does offer in the *caesura* that announces the 'end' of metaphysical politics, includes the following.

First, it alerts us to the inescapable violence and the dogmatic imperatives deeply sequestered within the most foundational valuing practices of our (inter)national political thought, as well as of our systems of rule. That includes, preeminently, security itself, of course. But it also includes security's cognates. For security is a package which tells you what you are as it tells you what to die for; which tells you what to love as it tells you what to defend (*dulce et decorum est pro patria mori*); and which tells you what is right as it tells you what is wrong. Its cognates consequently include individual and collective identity, evil, goodness and justice.

Most of all, and most neglected of all, however, its cognates include certain related understandings of love. Any love, that is to say, which proclaims an imperial yes to conceal a violent no. All those loves whose affirmative denials, denying the denials upon which we feed, so form and inform the space of our (inter)national politics of security: love of liberty; love of order; love of country; love of church; love of one god; love of the people; love of the leader; love of the party; love of the nation; love of the individual; love of the very cult of the subject. Security always seems to come crenellated in the form of some obligatory, denying and self-denying love masquing the spirit of revenge. Chief amongst them is the so-called political realists' narcissistic 'primeval "love"' of the real:

> Every feeling and sensation contains a piece of this old love; and some fantasy, some prejudice, some unreason, some ignorance, some fear, and ever so much else has contributed to it and worked on it.[56]

In consequence, the thought of the limit teaches us that our (inter)national politics of security are not only always already a politics of identity and difference[57] but also a politics of desire. For in the process of saying what we are menaced by, and in the course of harnessing means for dealing with whatever that is said to be, a politics of security, constituting and mobilising difference, imparts form and character to human being and to its forms of life. It specifies who we are, and what we are allowed to be, by teaching us what to fear about what we are not. This is by no means a negative affair. Fear is an education in what we are not, what we do not have, what we are supposed to care for and to care about, whose lack, or the fear of it, is so integral to the pursuit of security. Ironically, such a course in fear and danger betrays the fact that difference is integral to what we are. A discursive economy of security is consequently not only a discursive economy of danger, it is also a discursive economy of the absence which invokes desire. Through the alliance of *eros* and *thanatos* effected by the politics of identity and difference integral to (inter)national security, we are therefore struck by accounts of ontological danger into postures of policing love.

Second, the thought of the limit promotes a radically hermeneutic application of a critical phenomenology of presencing to the practices and institutions of politics. Because security does things rather than merely names things, we have to pose questions about it in the active interrogatory voice of genealogy and hermeneutics in the pursuit of the peculiar phenomenon that it is. From whence does the demand for security arise? How does security secure? What does security secure? What is securing? Who is secured? Similarly, because they are alive to the excess of Being over appearance,[58] as well as concerned with how things come to be rather than operating upon assumptions about what they are already exhaustively or determinately supposed to be, genealogy, hermeneutics[59] and deconstruction encourage us to reverse the usual order of political questioning and, in so doing, while looking for the supplement which security requires but denies in the ordering of (inter)national politics – insecurity itself – disturbs the established truths of a regime of security and loosens 'the sense of necessity, lawfulness, unity, or intrinsic purpose', which attaches to them.[60]

Third, it pursues the invention and exploration of those political strategies, that

William Connolly, for example, calls for, which are capable of folding 'agonistic generosity more deeply into the cultural ethos of a democratic society'.[61] In doing so it does not address the question 'What is to be done?' according to the way security so rigidly enframes it (with or without 'man'; and now increasingly indifferent to 'man'). Rather, it seeks to formulate that question in a way that is consonant with the limits of modern thought and politics – What could the political practice of mortals, now globally endangered by their own (inter)national politics of security, possibly be?

Finally, and in these ways amongst others, it contributes to that continuous recovery of the question of the political which might relax the grip which the insistences and claims of (inter)national security exercise upon our political imagination.

This then would be how I would begin to formulate a new agenda of 'security' questions. Not by asking how effective are our political regimes at satisfying their foundational claim to legitimacy by furnishing us with security? But by asking how must the concept of the political be construed, how must the political universe be determined, and what has to be rigorously policed, warred-against and excluded, to secure security? Not by asking what is dangerous? But by asking what does a representation of danger make of 'us' and of those who are not 'us'? Not by asking who or what is threatened, or what is doing the threatening? But by asking how does the specification of threat and its discourse of danger determine the 'who', the 'we', and the 'what' that is said on the one hand to be endangered, and on the other to be doing the endangering? Not by asking what are we endangered by? But by asking how does a representation of danger make 'us' what we are? Not by asking what is danger? But by asking from whence does the anger in (d)anger arise? And, finally, not by asking how to secure security? But, by enquiring about what is lost and forgotten, and who or what pays the inevitable price, for the way that 'we' are thus habited in fear?

According to these thoughts, security does not reflect what a 'people' are, and seek to protect it. Rather, it discloses how, in tragic denials of the (in)security of mortal life, people – and 'a people' – are actually formed by attempts to extirpate the 'foreign, strange, uncanny, [and] outlandish'[62] which inevitably constitute their very own free [(in)secure] mortal existence. The character of that obligatory, mortal freedom always already lived with others in Otherness, and the ethical charge which it carries, is something I try to disclose first by following Heidegger's account of radical hermeneutical phenomenology and, second, by amplifying the tragic sensibility which I find there.

Chapter 2

Radical hermeneutical phenomenology

An age whose objective conditions of existence have been radically transformed by the possibility of nuclear death evades the need for a radical transformation of its thought and action by thinking and acting as though nothing of radical import had happened.[1]

(Hans J. Morgenthau, 'Death in the Nuclear Age')

The political tradition of the 'West' is a tradition of thought within a tradition of thought which is metaphysical. Because Western political thought is conditioned by the tradition within which it is located, and in whose assumptions it is steeped, it receives its very ambitions, terms and categories of thinking from metaphysics. The essence of the different ways in which politics is understood within the Western tradition is intimately connected, therefore, with metaphysics. It follows, moreover, that political thought parallels the career of metaphysical thought; of the narrowing of thought to metaphysics; and, within metaphysics, not only of the narrowing of thought to the *ratio* of a subject but also to the technologisation of thought itself. The politics of the 'West' in the modern period, therefore, also first became subjectivised then technologised. Any account of the political within the Western tradition must consequently also take account of metaphysics. The one philosopher who has called metaphysics itself to account in the most profound of ways, however, is Martin Heidegger. It further follows, therefore, that the question of the political can no longer be adequately posed and addressed without taking Heidegger's thinking into account as well.

Through his sustained questioning of its philosophical foundations, few philosophers this century have issued as profound and comprehensive a challenge to the entire tradition of the 'West' as Heidegger has done. Few have challenged its contemporary technologically dominated way of life more deeply. Arguably no such challenge has had the influence, over contemporary Continental Thought in particular, which Heidegger's has had, and none remains more pertinent to a time so distinguished by the globalisation of a securing technologisation of human being that radically endangers it. Neither has any thinker this century been regarded, however, as more politically reprehensible in his actions nor more politically dangerous in his thought. Indeed, as someone in whom the crises of modern philosophy and politics were joined, Heidegger is perhaps the most thought-provoking figure of the political and philosophical crisis of our times.

For me, Heidegger is deeply challenging, therefore, not simply because of his philosophy and not simply because of his 'politics' (by which I mean, for the moment, the political commitments which he once expressed). Rather, his challenge is a profoundly important and inescapable one precisely because of the way politics and philosophy – the twinned dreams of knowledge and freedom which comprise the tradition of the 'West' – come together with him. The question of philosophy (that is to say, the question of Being) and the question of the political (that is to say, the question of human freedom) collided with enormous impact in Heidegger, as they have throughout this century, in ways that challenge us to address the fundamental relation between philosophy and politics once more in pursuit of the question of the political itself. And to do so not only *via* a thinker but also for a domain of conduct, the (inter)national politics of political Modernity, in which that relationship was and remains most forcefully at issue.

This is no easy task. Its difficulty, however, goes far beyond establishing the point that there is an essential relationship between Heidegger's philosophy and his 'politics', and the corresponding implication that if we can somehow finesse his philosophy we can escape his 'politics'.[2] Heidegger's philosophy cannot be separated from his 'politics'. But that is not a problem peculiar to Heidegger. Heidegger's philosophy cannot be separated from his 'politics' because philosophy and politics were never separate, are never separate and can never be separated.[3] What is always at issue, instead, and this is what makes the task not only so difficult but one that goes beyond the mere question of Heidegger's politics, is the original and ineradicable belonging together of philosophy and politics – that is to say, of thinking and of freedom – in the (inter)national politics of political Modernity.

PHILOSOPHY AND POLITICS

Heidegger's thought and life occurred as European politics – plunged from 1914 onwards into unprecedented political violence, technological intensification and holocaustal extermination – itself re-opened the question of the relationship between the philosophy of the 'West' and its very understanding of politics; and precisely because the violence of both rather than merely being directed outwards at Europe's subject empires erupted at the epicentre of the 'West' and called the grounds of its entire enlightened subjective self-possession into question. Heidegger was a deeply thoughtful and active participant in the forceful renewal, and failure, of the *Auseinandersetzung* between philosophy and politics which has characterised European thought since the end of the nineteenth century. He not only addressed himself to its deepest levels and widest implications, but at one time he also sought, and was prepared to make, the most direct of personal political commitments to it. He consequently joined the Nazi Party. If there is an escape not only from Heidegger's 'politics', therefore, but also the Fascism to which he was drawn, it can only come through pursuing the reopening of the question of the political itself as it is made possible through his philosophy. But this applies not only because his philosophy evidently contributed to his own fateful commitment. Despite his monstrous silence in respect of the Holocaust, his thinking also led Heidegger into an elaborate investigation of the Western nihilism which gave, and continues to give, rise to Fascism.[4]

It is not a matter here, therefore, of testing either Heidegger, or his thinking, for their political incorrectness. His thought offers a major resource, instead, for continuously interrogating the indissoluble relationship between philosophy and politics, the character of the political thought of the 'West', and the crisis of politics which the age of global technology inaugurated by the 'West' now poses. All three are critically important to the reconfiguration of the International Relations of political Modernity as site for rethinking the advent of the political.

That crisis of philosophy and politics is foremost a political crisis of democratic politics, however, rather than the crisis of a mere discipline. Hence one of the features that would distinguish the reconfiguration of International Relations would be a renewed concern with the question of democratic thought. For Heidegger – with Levinas, Derrida, Foucault, Nancy and others – is prominent amongst those who would take the measure of the radical insufficiency of subjectivised freedom upon which modern democratic politics relies. He forcefully explored, in addition, how modern human being has become a mortal danger to itself in its obligatory freedom without, increasingly, knowing how to think that danger while preserving this freedom.

Specifically, Heidegger's account of truth as disclosure, together with his existential analytic of *Dasein*, separates the theme of freedom – from out of which politics itself arises as a possibility – from the modern metaphysics of subjectivity and the thought of truth as correspondence. But, at the same time, as Michel Haar has argued, it appears also, especially in the later work, to subjugate human freedom to the sending of Being.[5] Hence, as Jean-Luc Nancy in particular has shown, human freedom has also to be thought differently after, with and against, Heidegger.[6] Since freedom is to be thought differently, so also must the politics of freedom. The issue is, therefore, not whether politics is to be democratic. For, if the human condition is free, and if this freedom is that from which the political arises, then politics can only be democratic. Rather, the compound question of the political is: Given that politics is possible only in virtue of human freedom, how is freedom to be thought? How is politics continuously to attend and adhere to this the obligatory freedom of the human condition? What is the *demos*? What is the relation of the *demos* to that freedom? How, in other words, is the politics of free being to be democratic without betraying this freedom to the rule of some totalitarian idea of subjectivity?[7]

Whereas Heidegger was contemptuous of modern democratic politics, and of the Liberal understanding of freedom, Heidegger's thought may nonetheless also provide a means of opening-up the very register of the democratic precisely because it poses the fundamental and intimately related questions of freedom, responsibility and the political for all of human being. That, in turn, poses the question: How might modern democratic politics, therefore, exceed its contemporary reliance upon the heritage of onto-theology, in general, and the philosophy of subjectivity in particular? I do not claim to be able to provide definitive answers to these questions, nor to address all of them here. But that, it seems to me, is the extent of the agenda of political thinking required in the wake of Heidegger's thought. Moreover, it is an agenda that is neither merely local nor global. Rather, it is one that concerns the very interplay between the global and the local that has in fact, often despite itself, always concerned International Relations, but which is now such a distinguishing feature of the (inter)national politics of late modern times.

What follows is less about Heidegger or International Relations, therefore, than it is about the question of the political, and how it looks and stands after Heidegger for the purpose ultimately of rethinking (inter)national politics. Because the question of the political cannot now be pursued without going through the trial of Heidegger's thought, however, 'after Heidegger' therefore means both 'since Heidegger' and 'informed by the character of Heidegger's philosophical questioning'.

By radically questioning the dominant conception of philosophy as metaphysics, Martin Heidegger also put in question the conception of politics contained in traditional political thought as well. By radically questioning the dominant conception of philosophy, however, Heidegger also opened the way to reinventions of philosophical history other than his own. Consequently, and crucially given his one-time political commitment to National Socialism, by radically challenging the dominant conception of philosophy in a way that allowed a radical challenge to the dominant ways in which politics is thought, Heidegger nevertheless may open the way to a recovery of politics which entails comportments and commitments different from the ones which he once displayed. As his thinking therefore offers resources which invite us creatively to re-engage a tradition, the exhaustion of whose thinking and politics are intimately connected and dangerously evident in the globalisation of what I have been calling our (inter)national politics of security, so it also offers resources which may free us from certain conclusions which, at one time, he seems to have drawn from that history.

In as much as Heidegger himself both politicises and polemicises the Western tradition, even as he contributes towards the idea of there being such a thing, he thereby radically problematises it and opens it to further polemicisation and politicisation. His thinking consequently recalls us to the creative re-inheritance of that which we are already undergoing in our (inter)national politics; what he calls 'the tradition'. But Heidegger does not hand creative re-inheritance over to us on a plate; nor, at least in politics, does he offer us much by way of a good example. By exposing you, instead, to the very limits of the Western tradition – which is in fact where he thinks we are at – Heidegger's thought makes you work very hard indeed at those limits and in a way in which the liminality rather than the finality, or terminality, of the limits becomes the matter at issue. For a world at its limits as well as for a discipline traditionally concerned with limits – of the State, of politics, of law and justice, and of peace and war – Heidegger's thinking could be no more relevant. Its relevance, however, lies precisely in the way that Heidegger reinterprets and therefore disrupts traditional thought of limit.

Limiting thought liminally, rather than as mere closure, is what Heidegger's thinking continuously pursues. Hence the notion of limit is 'not that at which something stops, but that in which something originates, precisely by originating therein as being "formed" in this way or that, i.e., allowed to rest in a form and as such to come into presence as that which it is'.[8] This philosophy of the limit does not invoke limit as an iron law of necessity, therefore, but as the very liminal medium of the finite mortal freedom of human being as such.

The 'tradition' which his own thought partly helps us to understand as a tradition is one in crisis. But it is in crisis in the dual sense of the word *krisis*. That is to say, Heidegger diagnoses a condition which must always already have been circumscribed by limits to have been anything definable at all, but which has now also exhausted the very possibilities inherent in those limits; while simultaneously recognising that this limit itself is also a critical moment of decision, rather than foreclosure, from which other possibilities consequently arise.[9] This is something which Heidegger writes about as 'the end of philosophy'.[10] But it is no end in the sense of something ceasing to be. 'We understand end', he says, 'in a double sense'. On the one hand:

> The end, insofar as it gathers into itself all essential possibilities of the history of a beginning, is not the cessation of something over and done, but, quite to the contrary, it is an affirmation of the beginning by way of a completion of its possibilities, ones which grew out of what followed the beginning.[11]

On the other hand:

> At the same time, however, and above all, we are standing within the twilight of the end of Western thinking especially in a second sense, according to which end means running out and running astray of the confusion of the various basic positions, valuations, concepts and systems as they have been prepared and formed throughout the centuries. This end . . . has its own duration, presumably one which is still to last a long time.[12]

If Heidegger's sense of 'end' is, therefore, one which encompasses the fulfilment as well as the ultimate dissolution of the possibilities contained within the origins of Western thinking, so also it is one which anticipates an extended working-out of this complex relationship between beginning and end. Hence:

> In the protracted expiration of the end, former 'modes of thought' will presumably be taken up again and again, and the end will characteristically be a succession of 'renaissances'.[13]

What has to be carefully understood, therefore, is that just as we never simply begin at the beginning for Heidegger so we never simply end at the end. Through his thought we see that particular beginnings and ends always already belong together as the liminal horizon which constitutes a specific historical temporality of the creative event of existence itself. The conclusion he draws from this in respect of his and our relation to the tradition is de-constructive. That is to say, it is both a questioning into the ground and a rebuilding from the ground up; although, of course, for Heidegger, 'ground' is no mere foundation, as the tradition understands foundation, but the abyssal freedom of temporality itself. Consequently,

> destruction or deconstruction are not in themselves terms which prophesy the 'end' of a historico-metaphysical temporal structure, a going beyond metaphysics, but terms which address the destiny of thought which through translation and reinscription allow us to consider and even perform those textual enactments of menacing limits whose effect is to counter the premises upon which an authority of the self-givenness of meaning is established.[14]

In short, for him we have no option but to go through the tradition deconstructively – which is itself, of course, a certain critical invention of tradition – if we are to find any release from the technologisation both of thought and of human being, which he argues constitutes the end of the tradition, if we are to recover the responsiveness of human being to its very mode of being; its free existential constitution as responsive possibility defined and singularised by death as the absolute end of that possibility.

No flat commentaries or summaries of the 'relevance' of Heidegger's work, which ordinarily provide ways out of engaging with the challenging thought of a difficult thinker, will, therefore, suffice to respond to a thinker who has made the very responsiveness of human being – or, rather, human being as responsiveness – one of the definitional features of his questioning and thinking. Flat commentary pales, for example, because it sometimes seems that in almost everything he said and did Heidegger provoked not only admiration, worry and concern but also puzzlement and outrage. If it is conceded, as I think it must be, that Heidegger's questions are so well framed and pertinent that they raise difficulties so fundamental (for the ways in which we both think and act) that they cannot be ignored or elided, one has to find a way of remaining open to that challenge as one struggles within and against it.

It also makes little sense to attempt to summarise Heidegger's 'relevance', precisely because the whole of his thought makes us suspect the sense of contemporary thought, and the very limits through, and within which, such thought and politics currently define what is relevant and sensible. Albeit he proclaimed the 'uselessness' of philosophy and the centrality of 'destiny' we can never take Heidegger's words at their face or conventional value. He is notorious for the way he struggles with, by inventing and punning within, Language. For the limit of Language was also integral to the philosophical point he was dedicated to making. Hence philosophy was nonetheless also for him the sovereign knowledge. As a kind of 'radical' philosophy, therefore, Heidegger's thinking also holds out the prospect of a 'radical' politics relevant to the modern human condition. In a very particular sense – that of an understanding of how the question of the political would appear in the light of his way of thinking – that is exactly, I would argue, how Heidegger himself conceived of the very purpose of his philosophical questioning:

> For the decisive intention of our questioning is precisely to free us from the past. . . . We want to raise questions on the basis of our own present and future necessities.[15]

Moreover, he insisted upon the radicality of the relationship between his own thought and that of the tradition, the destructuring of which, on behalf of human 'freedom' in its relation to the event of Being, he made his project of thought:

> the original and genuine relation to the beginning is revolutionary, which, through the upheaval of the habitual, once again liberates the hidden law of the beginning.[16]

He was, therefore, entirely dismissive of the conservative relation to origins and to history:

> the conservative does not preserve the beginning – it does not even reach the beginning. For the conservative attitude transforms what has already become into the regular and the ideal, which is then sought ever anew in historio-graphical considerations.[17]

But herein lies the source of some of the deepest mistrust of, as well as the greatest frustration with, Heidegger; not to say of the confounding of his thought.

Mistrust, because when he chose his own radical politics he chose disastrously. If we cannot escape his philosophy neither can we escape his politics. That he seems to have recognised what a disastrous choice he had made, has not detracted from the terrible fact that he made it; neither has the fact that in thinking about technology or technicity, he devoted much of the rest of his work to thinking through that nihilism of which Nazism was an expression in a way that consequently remains a powerful resource for critical political thinking in the age of technology.

Frustration, on the other hand, arises most amongst those who expect their politics to arrive ready-made, in self-assembly packs or, at least, as an intelligible set of instructions. Such is not on offer with Heidegger. Instead, his call to think anew about the established ways in which we have come to think at all, makes us think anew about the very limits of politics, and about the political as the liminal operation of limit in the assumption by human beings of their peculiar mode of free being. It is not politics, as it has come to be understood in an increasingly technologised global life, which arises as a positive concern through Heidegger's thinking, therefore, but what he would no doubt have called the very essence of the political. There are no instructions, however, especially after his association with the Nazis, as to how this may resolve itself in terms of specific political commitments. Quite the contrary. Given the character of his thought, such commitments cannot, however, be determined in advance of the particular circumstances in which human being, at determinate times and in determinate places, is challenged to free itself from the closures which are threatened by such specific historical circumstances. For Heidegger, what distinguishes the predicament of contemporary human being is the determinate technological emplacing of late modern times.

In necessarily broaching the question of the essence of the political once more, because he questions the thought in which it was first thought,[18] I find that there is a sensibility in Heidegger's thought which thoroughly informs the very structure of it. That sensibility has a very special purchase on, and provides a very particular means of disclosing the entire question of, the political. Although he speaks of it rarely and with restraint – 'even in his reading of Nietzsche',[19] and of Hölderlin – this sensibility and structure is that of what he also referred to as the highest form of 'Saying' the tragic.[20] But we cannot begin to appreciate the character and the significance of this sensibility without making our way to it, however summarily, via the route of that radical phenomenology of hermeneutical questioning by which means Heidegger opened-up philosophy's question of Being; and disclosed the mutually disclosive relationship between Being and human being as the there of Being (*Dasein*) in a way that has so profoundly influenced the thought of the freedom of human being.

THE TRUTH OF HERMENEUTICAL PHENOMENOLOGY

In all of his thinking Heidegger remained for the most part a phenomenologist. He effected a hermeneutical transformation of Husserlian phenomenology, however, and thus effected an escape from its desire for a cognitive security and certainty that was even more intense than Descartes'.[21] In this he was not only emphasising and exploring the capacity for attending to, and so necessarily interpreting, what is both said and unsaid within the texts and sayings of the tradition.[22] He was, in addition, referring again to the radically situated being of human being and its existential character as a being in the midst of meaning. The hermeneutical dimension he brought to phenomenology was, therefore, no mere add-on to it. Neither was that hermeneutics traditional hermeneutics, an auxiliary discipline of the human sciences dealing with the rules of the interpretation of texts and, later, the interpretive plumbing of the truth of human being.[23] If the human way of being is always already to be in the midst of the meaning which attaches to itself and other beings, and to always be in the position of having to interrogate that meaning in order to assume its own being as a project for itself, its very being is hermeneutical. That is to say, understanding and interpretation are part of its primary structure. Heidegger's hermeneutics was instead, therefore, and of course, an ontologised hermeneutics precisely because it arose out of his pursuit of the Being question through an existential analytic of that (hermeneutical way of) being which asks the question of Being itself of itself.

Phenomenology on the other hand, and as he explains in *Being and Time*, means 'to let that which shows itself be seen from itself in the very way in which it shows itself from itself'. This is, Heidegger says, 'the formal meaning of that branch of research which calls itself "phenomenology"'.[24] But rather than rest with the formal conception of phenomenon he radicalises it into a phenomenological one, insisting that we must also ask:

> What is it that phenomenology is to 'let us see'? What is it that must be called a 'phenomenon' in a distinctive sense? What is it that by its very essence is *necessarily* the theme whenever we exhibit something *explicitly*?[25]

Husserlian phenomenology effectively confined itself to an investigation of the constituting acts of transcendental consciousness. It did so by suspending assertions about Being. Whereas phenomenology had discovered intentionality, categorial intuition and the original sense of the *a priori*, it had left undetermined the Being of the intentional being. This being Husserl had distinguished as consciousness, but without raising the ontologial differentiation upon which the distinction of consciousness from reality was dependent. What was therefore required and offered by Heidegger was an analysis of the being that was intentional (designated *Dasein* rather than consciousness) as the means of raising the question of Being as such, and as a means also of radicalising phenomenology. In the process, of course, the understanding of human being itself was also radically revised.

The answer he gave to the questions which he posed above was thus a startlingly obvious and irresistible one. What is it that phenomenology must let us see?

> Manifestly, it is something that proximately and for the most part does *not* show itself at all; it is something that lies hidden, in contrast to that which proximally and for the most part does show itself; but at the same time it is something that belongs to what thus shows itself, and it belongs to it so essentially as to constitute its meaning and its ground.[26]

What it must let us see is that which, integral to everything, 'not just this entity or that, but rather the *Being* of entities',[27] is that which is never to be seen as such. For Heidegger, the *Sache* or thing which phenomenology must let us see, therefore, became Being. Consequently, his phenomenology is primarily a phenomenology neither of what is merely manifest, nor even, if we are to be absolutely precise, of what is hidden, for the disclosure of Being is inherently dualistic, both revealing and concealing. His phenomenology is, therefore, a phenomenology of the play of the two; namely of the event of un-concealment, or dis-closure, in which what is hidden appears as hidden. This uncanny phenomenon refuses Husserlian phenomenologisation precisely because it withdraws, continuously retreats from the gaze, as it phenomenolises. Ultimately that raises the question of whether there can, strictly speaking, be a phenomenology of it at all – which is no doubt why Heidegger eventually abandoned the term phenomenology – unless such a 'phenomenology' while realising its impossibility as a science expresses its intuition in a form which does justice to what Derrida later calls, in a Levinasian mutation of this Heideggerian insight, the appearance of the inapparent.[28]

Although all his students and early commentators also report his devotion to Aristotle, however, it is only with the publication in recent years of some of Heidegger's very earliest work – particularly 'Phenomenological Interpretations with Respect to Aristotle (Indication of the Hermeneutical Situation)' – that the details of the specific influence of Aristotle over Heidegger's thought here has become evident.[29] Here it is important to note, therefore, that whereas he first encountered phenomenology through his teacher Husserl, and that he derived his more radical formulation of phenomenology not only from many contemporary philosophical influences – including, for example, Schleiermacher, Dilthey, Lask and Natrop – but also from the way he read the classics, the real master of phenomenology for Heidegger was Aristotle:[30]

> What occurs for the phenomenology of the acts of consciousness as the self-manifestation of phenomena is thought more originally by Aristotle and in all the Greek thinking and existence as *aletheia*, as the unconcealedness of what-is-present, its being revealed, its showing itself. That which phenomenological investigations rediscovered as the supporting attitude of thought proves to be the fundamental trait of Greek thinking, if not indeed of philosophy as such.
>
> The more decisively that insight became clear to me, the more pressing the question became: Whence and how is it determined what must be experienced as 'the things in themselves' in accordance with the principles of phenomenology? Is it consciousness and its objectivity or is it the Being of beings in its unconcealedness and concealment?
>
> Thus I was brought to the question of Being, illumined by the phenomenological attitude.[31]

Hence, whereas the Being question radicalised both his phenomenology and his hermeneutics, his phenomenology not only effected a particular affinity with, and reading of, the Greeks in general, but of Aristotle in particular.

Heidegger thus ontologises both phenomenology and hermeneutics, which hitherto had consequently been neither phenomenological nor hermeneutical enough for him, when enlisting them to deconstruct the philosophical tradition in order to get at what it covered-over; namely the ontological difference between Being and beings, presencing rather than presence, difference as such; the very uncanniness of Being and thus of human being and of Language, in which each is disclosed. Such destructuring – like the later Derridaean version of deconstruction[32] – was not, of course, a radical turn away from or step out of tradition, because tradition is not something which is first given and then decided upon. Tradition is only tradition in the act of taking something up in one way or another, which is to say also saying in the process what that something is. Destructuring was, therefore, a radical new turn towards the history of philosophy, or step back into it. Rather than disowning what has gone before, the tradition here becomes tradition in being re-won and newly owned. If the target of the destructive move of this deconstruction was consequently not the tradition as if it was some reified object but the processes of reception by which the tradition comes to be as tradition, its prize was a more original, thoughtful, and thought-provoking appropriation of that tradition. Heidegger's way of doing this, *Auseinandersetzung*, was deliberately and forcefully agonistic:

> *Auseinandersetzung* brings philosophers into the sharpest focus and it unfolds their meaning in the history of philosophy by taking each thinker seriously as an adversary, as someone who demands that certain decisions be made about essential understandings of the world and of Being. By forcing a confrontation with one's faith, ideas of nature, or ideals of political belonging, such decisions can wound, even kill, before they are complete in this duel – demanding that we defend, give-up or transfigure cherished beliefs and conceptions which order our lives. In confrontation, *what* – or rather *how* – we are is at stake. Without this principle of interpretation, a thinker cannot make out his *own standpoint*, so that he also cannot get at the opposition he wants.[33]

Here it is worth reinforcing the point that the contemporary thinker who has taken Heidegger's method most to heart – and, indeed, practised it most directly and forcefully upon Heidegger himself, precisely because of the vital importance of what he thinks is at stake there – has been Emmanuel Levinas.

While it seeks to rediscover something in the past, rather than of the past, like genealogy, however, a term which Heidegger uses twice, the critique of this deconstructive *Auseinandersetzung* is not 'fault finding or underlining of errors'.[34] Rather, it is an insistence upon formulating and meeting today's challenges by posing more originally those questions the answers to which, having formed the present, threaten to entrap us, unsustainably and unsurvivably, within it if they are not reformulated and re-posed (recovered) in response to our present need to think and live-out our existence futurally. Such thinking is not only forcefully aimed at the present, therefore, it is also aimed at rethinking past questions and ways of posing questions, the answers to which have given rise to the present.[35] For: 'Every answer keeps its force as answer only so long as it is rooted in questioning'.[36] The release of the present into a different future is, then, propelled less by new answers – architectonic principles and systems – or by the reoccupation of positions established by previous questions.[37] Instead, it comes through new ways of formulating old questions or, rather, by the new questions which such re-formulation poses in and to the challenges of a present which becomes a fatal *cul de sac* – deathly enclosure – if it cannot be renewed by such appropriative questioning.

This double ontologising move was related, *inter alia*, therefore, to the way in which Heidegger understood tradition as 'that-which-has-been-preserved-in-being-passed-along';[38] to the tradition as the history of the forgottenness of the ontological difference and thus of Being; and to the inauguration of an attentive responsiveness to Being by paying attention to what can be heard about what concerns us, namely what is it to be and how to be, but has so far not been specified as such within that process of the reception, posing and answering of questions which constitutes the tradition itself.[39] This is tradition understood not in terms of 'reification', therefore, but in terms of its necessarily contested 'relation'.[40] All this, in turn, was related, in addition, of course, to the existential analytic of *Dasein* in which comprehensive emphasis was placed upon understanding human being as itself a radically situated – in time and place – interrogatory understanding of Being.

Acting brings new things to presence, just as making does. And making entails artistry, just as acting does. But, it is the process of things coming to presence, to which the Greeks gave the terms *phainesthai* (to show itself) and *Logos* (to make manifest – hence phenomenology), which therefore preoccupied Heidegger. 'Truth' here, then, becomes a heterogeneous process of revealing in which there is nonetheless also, simultaneously and necessarily, a concealment; a dual process to which, he initially argued, the Greeks gave the term *aletheia*. What is concealed is the surplus of Being as such.

In telling the history of truth, that is to say truth as correspondence – propositional truth, or the truth of assertions which conform to the state of affairs about which they speak – Heidegger noted that before an assertion can be made the entity which is being spoken about must already be manifest. That is to say, it must always already be out in the Open to be spoken about. Consequently, the assertion must presuppose the manifestness, or opening, of entities and the manifesting that allows them to be there.

Heidegger's later conclusion, however, as John Caputo put it, is that the Greeks 'got to phenomenality but they never named the clearing itself', and that *aletheia* does not name truth but the opening of presence. Thus Heidegger argues:

> Insofar as truth is thought in the traditional 'natural' sense as the correspondence of knowledge with beings demonstrated in beings, but also insofar as truth is interpreted as the certainty of the knowledge of Being, *aletheia*, unconcealed in the sense of the opening may not be equated with truth, rather, *aletheia*, unconcealment thought as opening, first grants the possibility of truth. For truth itself, just as Being and thinking, can only be what it is in the element of the opening.[41]

He, therefore, abandoned the word *aletheia* as a way of both naming and thinking about this presencing and used the German term *Ereignis* instead.

Ereignis, like all of Heidegger's key words, and indeed like the way he thinks of Language itself, does not simply mean one thing. Indeed, it is not clear that it is meant to mean as such, so much as to disclose, or perhaps in a way even to mimic or pun, disclosure itself. Translated as 'Event' or 'Happening', that is to say an occurrence, Heidegger, who exploits other connotations of owning and appropriating which can also be derived from it in German, also finally abandons Being with the introduction of this word, because a shift of word for Heidegger is no mere substitution of one term for another but a means of reflecting ever more deeply upon that which concerns him. Moving from one word to another is, therefore, also a movement of thought for him. Consequently *Ereignis* is not, as might be supposed, the event of Being but of what is usually translated as the event of 'Appropriation'. It would take a long exegesis to try to figure out what is happening here and do justice to it. All I can do at this juncture is offer some clues.[42]

Appropriation usually means to take into one's possession. In Heidegger it has the additional senses of being taken over, or caught-up by, as well as of entering into and making one's own, and it occurs as he tries to think more about the presencing of things and the intimate way human being belongs to that presencing. Human beings, therefore, exist in the sense that they are 'given-to', simultaneously in receipt of and captured by, existence (in the way that some are given-to drink). Hence, *Ereignis* is the event of that play of existing in which there is an ineradicable belonging together of Being and the 'there' of Being, namely human being (hence the term *Dasein*), in which human beings find themselves 'given-to' existence, and wherein their own existence is at play as they find themselves challenged to make it their own in accordance with it as a possibility which has continuously to be assumed. The play, of course, is deadly serious; although it has its funny side – funny peculiar, as well as funny 'ha! ha!'.

Truth, then, is no longer a property of thought or discourse. Neither is it any longer a product of representative–calculative technique. Rather, it is a heterogeneous event of disclosure with which untruth is integrally involved as well; hence the originary and radical uncanniness of the opening whose lighting (revealing presencing) is always also traversed by darkness (the concealment of the superabundance of what is not).[43]

In other words, for beings to be there has to be a space or clearing for them to be in. For there to be the presence of things there has not only to be presencing as such but also, integral to that presencing, concealment; because to be manifest means not to be concealed, or to have been brought out of concealment, where concealment is the plenitude of what is not. Because Heidegger does not give-up on this crucial point, however, you cannot give-up on it either if you are to respond seriously to his thinking. But that does not mean that you must rest with Heidegger's account of, or rather with what seems most to preoccupy him about, the clearing; namely, what many charge him with, his privileging of Being, his essentialising of Being and his particular brand of mythologising. Caputo, for example, taking his cue from Emmanuel Levinas, radicalises this declension of truth as disclosure into the event of manifestation by lifting it out of Heidegger's history of Being, wherein he suspects it of a mythologising privileging of a certain historical epoch (that of the Greeks), and gives it a new critical function on behalf of Justice by insisting that every time is a manifestation of manifesting. Thus 'possessed of its own grace and its own malice', each time, including of course our own, is a time of presencing, argues Caputo, in which the event of the obligatory freedom of human being has to be responsibly assumed and Justice is called for.[44] Even with Heidegger, however, it is nonetheless powerfully evident that this clearing is a site of ethical encounter. For, in calling the entire epistemological background and ambitions of contemporary philosophy into question, Heidegger was attempting to provide a radical – 'that meant a more ethical'[45] – understanding of human being-in-the-world.

It must be emphasised that 'ethical', here, does not mean a system of ethics in the form of a regional ontology of metaphysical thought. Nor is it a command ethic specified and handed down by some sovereign unappealable authority exegetically elaborated through theology. Just as Heidegger was attacking the epistemological hubris of contemporary philosophy by insisting that his herm-eneutical phenomenology was a way of *indicating* the general structures of being-in-the-world for a being that had nonetheless to take-up its being in its own ways – and that he was therefore not attempting to offer a secure, or securing, epistemological account of such a being – so also the very ethicality of that being equally derives from being thrown into the world in a way that obliges it to take-up its being there. In each instance, Heidegger is showing something not claiming, or aspiring to, adequation between his concepts and the thing itself, simply because the thing itself here, namely human being, necessarily exceeds the concept.

It does so, first, because for Heidegger, as a 'phenomenologist', the brute fact of factical life is that we exist. But this existing is not the brute factical life of being a prey to so-called mere sense data, it is existing always already in a domain of meaning and value whatever we may yet come to think about it. In a cognitive sense he thinks we only come to think about it formally when it breaks down. Hence, we first live. Therefore we know how to live. Thus we live before we 'know'. Consequently there is a fore-knowing in living. Seeing this is not merely phenomenological seeing whose task is to point out the fore-knowing and retrieve it for us again. It is precisely hermeneutical phenomenology because it is concerned to bring this fore-knowing, or pre-hension of existing which life itself has, forward through an interpretive act. This is not an epistemology of cognitive conceptualisation but the how of human being as such. Thus 'The primary relation to Dasein is not that of contemplation, but *being* it'.[46] Secondly, in having its being to be human being is both responding to the Otherness which, in harbouring it, human being is nonetheless also exceeded by, and to the call to take-up its being in a project the specific realisation of which happens to take place in particular historical circumstances. Thus:

> As uttered sentences, all expressions about the being of *Dasein* ... have the character of indication: they only indicate *Dasein*, though, as uttered sentences, they at first mean something present-at-hand ... but they indicate the possible understanding of the structures of *Dasein* and the possible conceptualising of them that is accessible in such an understanding. (As sentences indicating such a *hermeneuein*, they have the character of herm-eneutical indication.)[47]

In this hermeneutical phenomenology of manifest being, existence is, therefore, nothing but being possible: '*Dasein* as human life *is primarily being possible*'.[48] The singular and the possible thus comprise human being-in-the-world and are consequently always already higher than the general and the actual which derive from a certain kind of cognitive reflection (that, now, of representative–calculative thought) upon it. This is why the concept can never be adequate to existence.

Directed at the whole of existence – philosophy's domain of reflection – Heidegger's philosophy is consequently ethical from the 'ground' up. 'What is at issue in its situated behaving', he observes 'is the way *Dasein* can be'.[49] This being we call human being, Heidegger is saying, does not merely ask the question what is it to be and how is it to be itself – asking in effect, what is its *ethos* and how is to be assumed in these the current circumstances in which it finds itself – it simply is that question answering to itself. Its being is being manifest (phenomenal) hermeneutically. Here it is also appropriate to note that after his so-called 'turn', Heidegger's later work does not so much abandon, although it does give-up the 'scientific' aspirations towards a fundamental ontology *via* hermeneutical phenomenology of, his earlier work because this 'had run the risk of reinforcing subjectivity'.[50] Rather, while disparaging his 'juvenalia', he returns to thinking the project in other 'more original' terms.[51] Fortified by Gadamer's observation on Heidegger's early essay on the phenomenological interpretations of Aristotle that 'even a great man himself can underestimate his own brilliance and, above all, the rich promise of his beginings',[52] I nonetheless continue, therefore, to talk in terms of hermeneutical phenomenology; albeit developing it by reference to tragedy and the tragic. For hermeneutical phenomenology is not a mere method of analysis, nor simply a framework of interpretation. This radical hermeneutical phenomenology is 'the primordial project of the possibilities of *Dasein*, insofar as *Dasein* can relate itself to being from within the midst of being'.[53] It is constitutive of the is-ness of human being as a way of being.

Despite the sometimes well-aimed charges against Heidegger, therefore, that sometimes he arrests and elides the ethical in a variety of ways and for a variety of reasons, that other times he expresses it in the 'wrong' mythopoeic way, Heidegger's hermeneutical phenomenology of facticity is itself fundamentally an ethical warrant.[54] It is equally clear, however, that it takes the philosophical violence of Emmanuel Levinas' own *Auseinandersetzung* against Heidegger to advance that ethical warrant to the point of making Ethics, rather than Ontology, First Philosophy. It is that warrant, wrested from Heidegger by Levinas through the radical amplification and enunciation by which he advances it to the fore of thinking, but nonetheless firmly related somewhat against Levinas to human freedom, which I seek to ally here to the recovery of the question of the political. The issue is, therefore, not whether Heidegger was concerned with the ethical.[55] His entire corpus of thinking forces us to confront how a being whose way of being is a project for itself is to take its being, which is always already a being-with-others, into its care. The issue is, instead, this: *What* does the fundamental ethicality to which Heidegger's thought is devoted, in its account of the obligatory freedom of human being, consist in? and, *How* is it to be assumed and related to the question of the political? Herein, precisely, is the site of that ethico-political

Auseinandersetzung with Heidegger which his questioning of the metaphysics of traditional ethical and political thought opens up.

Heidegger is, then, neither a traditionalist nor a radical, neither realist nor idealist, in the (metaphysically determined) ways in which (modern) traditionalists and idealists, radicals and realists, interpret these categories. In consequence, he is a much more deeply disturbing thinker than contemporary thinking can give credit for in its habitual ways of measuring thinkers. That is why he is, at different turns, such an uncomfortable, troubling, untrustworthy and frustrating figure for all such thinkers.

With Heidegger, therefore, politics – in the sense of the essence of the political – can neither be the making nor the acting of metaphysics. Neither, of course, can it be the making and the acting of the metaphysically conceived human being. For, in Heidegger, human being (being-there, *Dasein*) is also profoundly complicated beyond the idea of human subjectivity which corresponds with such metaphysically conceived making and acting. Consequently, the complication of human being – which being, freed to have its own being to be, must henceforth be understood as differentially constituted by the play of differing of the disclosure in which its being stands-out as the being that it is, and to which it is freed to comport itself – necessarily also gives rise to the complication of the political. Politics, or rather the whole question of the political, is necessarily, therefore, re-staged and re-posed by these movements of thought because they so profoundly challenge our understanding of human being as such.

Politics, too, then, also becomes problematic. Or, rather, the inner problematic of the political becomes a matter for thought once more. Hence, what the political is, and what politics might then be, become that which the end of metaphysics, and hence the end of metaphysical politics (in terms of the classical ideas of both acting and making), forces us to re-cover – go back over, re-collect, re-think – in as much a material as a philosophical way. It does so both because of this different understanding of what human-ness is – for Heidegger, in effect and literally, an obligatory freed in-finite possibility – and because also of what has been happening to human-ness; mounting, systematic, and threateningly total, reduction (especially through those logics of self-immolation which are systematically at work in all the automated forces of our (inter)national politics of security[56]) to the mere stuff required of calculability. We are therefore provoked, in addition, to ask what kind of phenomenon – that which shows itself from itself (*phainesthai*) – is being encountered in the global technicity of the (inter)national politics of late modernity. How have we become so committed to making it? In the process, what is it making of 'us', the human, as the very idea of politics becomes suborned by the technicity demanded by the practices, institutions and concepts of representative–calculative (political) thought? Practices which I see as exemplified in our (inter)national politics of security; by which I mean both the 'West's' principially-based understanding of politics in security and the manifold globalised practices of the (inter)national security politics of States.

THE RECOVERY OF THE POLITICAL

Heidegger consequently not only challenges us to confront a way of thinking which refigures the claims which have allowed us to think in the ways that we habitually do think, he also senses, and seeks to make a sense of, a certain sensibility. That sensibility is the one which makes us think that these traditionalistic ways of thinking, together with the (inter)national politics derived from, and deeply implicated in, them have become dangerously out of touch with what it is to be human. There, the human appears in opposition to itself, as a self in denial of its freedom cut off from itself and from the renewing sources of the self, possessed of an epistemological hubris whose object is to confine it in, by securing it from, that obligatory freedom, and the profoundly ethico-political questioning continuously posed by it, precisely through a radical subjectification of it. Technology, one might therefore say, makes human being flat-footed in respect to its ethical comportment towards itself as the uncanny – both native and stranger to itself – being with others in the face of the Otherness that it is. The *krisis* of metaphysics – detailed in Heidegger's thought through the way in which he asks the very question, the question of Being, which provoked it and drew it together as a tradition; and now more generally explored in what has come to be called the philosophy of the limit[57] – necessarily thereby calls for a recovery of the question of the political itself.

This is a recovery which means going back over the tradition of metaphysical politics – including its putative inception in the Greek world – not because any definitive answer to the 'inner problematic' of the political lies there (what Heidegger says about the 'inner problematic' of philosophy may be adapted to that of the political; 'Plato's question', he says 'must be retrieved. This cannot mean that we retreat to the Greek's answer'[58]), but to recover it; not only from (metaphysical) political philosophy but also from the area studies, regions and disciplines through which the study of politics in general, and that of International Relations in particular, now dissipates the concern with the political and substitutes, instead, a fascination with the manifold globalised and globalising technologies of order that have emerged to administer human being. For much of the project of contemporary political analysis itself displays technology's own aspiration to technical virtuosity, preoccupation with concepts of method, system, rule and function, and obsession with the ideal schema through which every formal and thematic property (of politics) might be accounted for. Devoted to making politics intelligible according to the norms of representative–calculative thinking, it judges itself (and is judged) by whether it gives us back an image of 'political man' which is said to correspond with universal and determinable (hence closed) human nature, or has disclosed in its systematic workings the technical mastercode of politics as such.

One is, therefore, inevitably brought to encounter the limits of 'the school', or 'the discipline', under the extra-curricular, or even non-curricular, impulse of Heidegger's thought. Through it one can recognise, for example, the extent to which an understanding of politics is increasingly neither pursued nor taught in the 'schools' of politics. Rather, we introduce each other and our students to various spheres of (inter)national life in which the technology of calculative order operates, and insist upon the need for it while moralising in realistic and idealistic tones about the variously conceived necessities of it.

The object of the recovery of the political within and from the putative and problematic tradition of the 'West' is, rather, the renewal of obligatory freedom itself. For, if it is possible to recall how things originate, specifically through recalling how they have originated within that tradition, because it is that tradition which has had – and is continuing to wreak – such dramatic global consequences, two important points follow. First, it becomes possible to recall how, downstream from those beginnings, we have ended up where we are; and how we are. Second, it becomes possible to explore the possibility of renewal in our own times from out of the very resources – dangers and circumstances – which that tradition (and for Heidegger, remember, human being is always already situated relationally in such a world of meaning and relevance) itself makes available, because it continuously bears the trace of renewal within itself. Third, without recalling ourselves to ourselves, and the Otherness which we harbour, in this way, 'we' cannot respect nor find respectful ways of relating to others.

Heidegger is a thinker who in every sense, then, forces us to ask first and foremost, not 'Where do we go?' but, 'How are we?' How are 'we' situated? And, what possibilities of renewing our possibilities as human beings – so remembering and celebrating that we are and how we are human – lie exposed to thoughtful recovery within the very situation in which we find ourselves? Hence, contest over where to go is always a disguised contest over where we are at. For it is only when we understand where we are at that we can say in which way we need to be moved.

Heidegger did not, therefore, step outside contemporary politics but sought, instead, and through these means, to step back into it, re-engaging post-Socratic understandings of the political theorised through philosophy by re-thinking philosophy itself. And what that meant, above all, was rethinking truth. That way, too, he sought to remember things about the political which metaphysical thematisation and current practice elide or conceal. In consequence, his thinking was, and remains, deeply at odds both with the conventional understandings of our tradition of political thought and with our contemporary political ideologies and forms of rule. Combine this with his devastatingly destitute commitment to the Nazi Party and it is no surprise that the relationship between Heidegger and 'politics' should have become such a confounded one; a prey both to the unthought political and philosophical baggage of many of those who have debated it, and the ancient project of preserving the love of wisdom (*philosophia*) free from political life (*politeia*).

To clarify the distinction between the political and politics very crudely for the purposes of an introduction (while drawing also upon the distinction between *le politique*[59] and *la politique*[60]), if we look to the 'beginning' and to the history of politics we are confronted with two basic options for understanding the political (le politique), the inner problematic or essence of politics.[61] Politics can be understood as a form of making or *techne*. As *techne* it is essentially conceived in Platonic terms as something that must be constructed, instituted or founded; the product of craftsmanship. Alternatively, politics may be understood as action – *praxis*. As *praxis* it is essentially conceived in Aristotelian terms to be a mode of action which takes place in a public world or public space – classically, the *polis* – concerned not simply with all the questions that arise in respect of living together, but with enacting who we are both individually and collectively. In this sense politics is neither making, nor mere problem solving, though such happens in and through it. Politics is the continuous opening of the space which allows human beings to appear – agonally to disclose themselves – in the fullness of what it is to be human.[62] But, even as it came to be enunciated by Aristotle, the sense of this understanding of politics, first articulated in tragedy rather than philosophy (and favoured by Heidegger, especially considering also the extensive influence of Aristotle on his early work), lost something in its thematisation because that thematisation subjected it to the grammar, and ultimately the logic, of thought required by metaphysics.

Now, Heidegger complicates matters. He always does. For him this is a virtue. That was part of the way in which he understood the task of thinking and his vocation as a thinker. 'The basic direction of philosophical questioning', he wrote in one of his earliest essays 'is not added on and attached to the questioned object, factical life, externally'. Rather 'it is to be understood as the explicit grasping of a basic movement of factical life'. In as much as human being for him is a way of being that has to undertake its being – is concerned about its being even when it is trying to avoid that concern and make it easy on itself – it necessarily finds its being difficult to bear. It has to question, and answer to, itself in respect of its being because that is its own way of being. Life, then, is intrinsically troublesome because, comprising a question, it is an interrogative existence charged with questionability that must continuously answer for itself. It necessarily, therefore, does not merely encounter but also generates states of affairs which it confronts as problems. It's tough, but that's the way it is. Hence the purpose of thinking is not to proffer easy ways out – the business of snake-oil salesmen – but to elucidate, explicate and deepen, instead, one's understanding of that toughness by questioning the more insistently and originally. Indeed, by continuously keeping open questioning itself, and not by trying to close it down for future generations, thought is the repetitive generation of questioning (all repetition is inventive), rather than the resolution of problems. Hence 'the genuinely appropriate way of access' to this difficult freedom, and of keeping faith with the truthfulness of it 'can only consist in making it difficult'. 'Philosophical research', he says 'must fulfill this duty, if it does not want to miss this object completely'.[63] Making difficult is not obscuring things, however, but continuously retrieving the translucent liveliness of life in, and on, its questioning way through questioning itself; a retrieval of life now from the technologising of it with which the (inter)national politics of political Modernity has become so deeply complicit.

He complicates things here, first, therefore, because although often exhibiting a deep preoccupation with beginnings (especially with the poetic re-founding of a 'world', a 'people' or a 'State') that preoccupation is never expressed outside his concern with what he calls 'the tradition' of Western thought. He is equally preoccupied, therefore, with the character of a tradition, and especially with the prospect, which the very nature of tradition offers, for beginning again in virtue of the resources contained within the tradition itself. It is tempting to resolve the difficulty of classification which he poses to our established ways of thinking, therefore, and to return to terms which I discussed earlier, by labelling Heidegger either a radical – committed to providing the grounding practices which will found a new order – or a deeply conservative traditionalist – concerned only with working out what is feasible, necessary or good in the concrete circumstances of what is given. Many commentaries on Heidegger and politics rebound between these poles. But this does not work because, rather than aligning himself with either of these two things, Heidegger problematises the very interpretative schema within which radical and conservative arose as classificatory categories, and through which they are distinguished as such in contemporary thought and politics.

Heidegger complicates matters, secondly, therefore, because his own thought is deeply hostile to this very binary form of thinking and choosing. Consequently, there is no facile way out of having to confront what he does say by classifying him in categories which already appear to make sense to us, for Heidegger subverts their very sense and forces us to think about them anew. Specifically, he forces us to think and talk in terms of the very duality of this riven existence of human being. You need bi-focals, then, to read and think along with Heidegger, for his hostility to a unifocal view of Being and being is as profound and pervasive as is his commitment to thinking the radical duality of their mutually disclosive interdependence.

Specifically, and thirdly, Heidegger makes things more complicated precisely because, though concerned for both making and acting, he challenges the understanding we currently have of each of these categories as well, and so also of the way in which they might be used to classify him politically. For Heidegger, it is neither making, revealing as *techne*, nor even action, understood in the traditional sense as the exercise of the will of a subject, which excites his thought. They do excite his concern, of course, because he sees them, especially in the modern cult of the subject and of subject/object thinking – or representative–calculative thought – as well as in the development of technology (what might better be called *technicity* or *technics*: which, as the positing, ordering and placing of all beings, including human being, at the disposal of an enframing mode of representative–calculative knowing and making, is itself a mode of being that increasingly cuts human being off from its free mode of being), as fundamentally impoverishing of what it is to be human. It might even be possible to say that making politics a world of responsible action in an age of technicity – where responsible action is a resolute openness to the obligatory freedom which is the truth of disclosure, or what Derrida has called 'the non-passive endurance of the aporia ... [of] the condition of responsibility and decision'[64] – is the most radical project of all.[65] For such a responsible politics, in contradistinction to those which are derivable from a command ethic, becomes radical in a world where, because technology now allows us to make everything impossible possible, submission to a command ethic – any command ethic[66] – as Arendt noted in her analysis of Totalitarianism,[67] can and has summoned unimaginable evil into the world. Practically, it now also entails the real possibility of human extinction.

However that may be, Heidegger struggles to speak a language which comprehends the integral duality of Being and beings (dis-closure, the play of revealing and concealing) and therefore also of human being. Insisting, first, upon the critical importance of the ontological difference between Being and beings, he proceeded eventually to stress the fundamental significance of difference, and of the event of differing, as such. That, as we shall see, is why he is also drawn, ineluctably, to the tragic.[68] Hence, just as all of Heidegger's thinking might be characterised as an attempt to read Being and Time into one another,[69] in order to recover and re-pose the inner problematic of philosophy, the question of Being, so this book might be read as an attempt to read security and insecurity into one another, in order to re-raise and re-pose the inner problematic of the political – the question of human being's obligatory freedom. Security and insecurity thus become convertible terms for me, too, as I seek to beat a path to re-raising the question of the political.

THE RIFT BETWEEN POETRY AND THINKING

'The tragedies of Sophocles', Heidegger once noted, 'preserve the *ethos* in their sagas more primordially than Aristotle's lectures on "ethics".'[70] If the political tradition of the 'West' is a tradition within a tradition, therefore, then that tradition – as indicated by the ancient conflict between poets and philosophers – goes back to Sophocles (and the rest of the poets) as much as it does to Plato and to Aristotle.[71] Heidegger consequently also raises the question of the political and its integral relation to the ethical in a second fundamental way. Not only does he challenge the metaphysics of thought within which the political and the ethical have hitherto been thought, he also re-opens 'the rift between poetry and thinking', and necessarily thereby not only re-opens the site where that rift originally took place – namely the *polis* – but simultaneously also raises again the issue of what was at stake in that conflict; namely the *ethos* and the future of *politeia* (political life). It, therefore, follows also that if Heidegger's thought calls for a recovery of the very question of the political in a way that challenges us to recover – which means to rethink – its 'origins', that hybrid 'beginning' must begin with the tragedies themselves, including their reflections upon 'origin' as such.

Recovering the political consequently entails recovering some sense of the tragic as well, and of what tragedy tries to achieve as, inhabiting the rift between poetry and thought, it seeks to depict, celebrate and preserve the open space and the agonal character of the *polis*. Rift [*der Riss*], Heidegger elaborates:

is not rift as a mere cleft is ripped open; rather, it is the intimacy with which opponents belong to each other. . . . This rift does not let opponents break apart; it brings the opposition of measure and boundary into their common outline.[72]

This rift, then, is another way of speaking about the event of differing. Rift refers to the cleaving through which human beings are not only projected into their obligatory freedom but also cleave to each other (more often than not, I agree, with cleavers) in the differencing which presents them as the singular, specifically differentiated, things that they are. Rift is not only the wherein wherein which tragedy itself operates, therefore, it is fundamentally also what tragedy itself phenomenologically allows to manifest itself as the existence of human beings who, given-to it, share it as well as endure it while they struggle to assume it as their own.

Tragedy, I suggest, overcomes more readily phenomenology's enormously difficult category problem of finding the right words for that pre-theoretical description of the fore-knowing of life to which phenomenology aspires and that 'non-phenomenologicalisable' uncanniness of existence in which what is hidden appears as hidden. Given that the phenomenon of human being is itself radically hermeneutical in the way that I explained earlier, tragedy does this because of the way it depicts the hermeneutical situation of the phenomenon of the hermeneut that is human being. And, here, also as a non-philosopher, I concur again with Gerald Bruns, who notes that,

> for non-philosophers like myself it has never made sense to think of hermeneutics as a philosophical program, and, much to the same point, the first thing a critic learns from hermeneutics is that it can't be converted into a technique of criticism either. You won't find it in the shopping mall of projects, methods, and schools. So in a way neither should you go looking for hermeneutics along the road that runs up or down from the end of philosophy. Hermeneutics is just elsewhere, perhaps not so much behind or beyond philosophy and its projects as prior to them, or say 'older than philosophy'.[73]

Older than philosophy is precisely not only what the tragedies are but also where radical hermeneutics – that is to say hermeneutical phenomenology – takes place in an exemplary manner. For tragedy is not only made up of a family of questions about what happens as human beings enact their understanding of how things are. Much less, of course, was it a 'scientific' exercise aspiring to produce 'objective' knowledge, or a project committed to grasping once and for all the phenomenon of manifestness. Albeit a radical hermeneutical phenomenology, tragedy is radical perhaps only in the ways in which Martin Heidegger radicalised hermeneutics and phenomenology. Tragedy is a radical hermeneutical phenomenology also, and decisively, because tragedy, itself, is not simply an interpretation. It is a show which allows an understanding to happen.[74] Indeed, it was integral to *making* the understanding of the *polis* itself happen. That understanding was also an understanding of the appearance of the inapparent.

Tragedy was therefore an event, not a supposedly dis-interested critical project, which staged the event. That staging also produced meaning where meaning was missing, while not claiming to exhaust meaning, because its very own phenomenal character, recalling the enigma of phenomenality as such, sought to allow the mystery of existence its play as well. The consequently manifold meaning it brought forth was this: exposing human being to the exposure of its ungrounded existence, tragedy nonetheless celebrated and preserved, as it rigorously explored the *aporias* of, the political life which such existence made possible, and of the limits beyond which such a life was also impossible. It brought these *aporias* before the *polis* in order to bring the *polis* itself out into the Open before them. That limit was the limit of hermeneutical self-knowledge itself; because, *pace* the Oracle (if its motto was not intended to be ironical), and as *Oedipus Rex* in particular emphasises, self-knowledge is not the problem. Rather, self-knowledge is never enough. Never enough for that way of being which comprises and is traversed by Otherness and is consequently always already, in its being, divided within itself and estranged from itself as it undertakes the project of itself. The meaning which tragedy presents us with, therefore, is that in encountering existence, and most when encountering itself, human being cannot escape its encounter with that ineradicable Otherness – in, of and beyond itself; hence of which it essentially comprises – which never concedes to the power of human being's own self-knowledge. In experiencing that hermeneutically phenomeno-logical project of self-understanding, which is the human way of being, human beings ultimately always also 'experience the refusal of the other to be contained in the conceptual apparatus' which they have prepared for it; or, rather, which their 'own time and place have prepared for it'.[75] This necessarily, therefore, not only alters their relation to their understanding, it alters their entire self-standing within existence itself. Hence, neither scientific ideology critique nor post-modern comedy offer an escape from human being's continuous encounter with its own constituent historicality. Rather, each will encounter Otherness through its own project in its own un-Just way.

The missing meaning that the tragedy brings before us is, however, not only that we are fated always to discover this limit to our hermeneutical selves, even when we are most hermeneutically adept and devoted to ourselves as *Oedipus* was – in short, that ultimate meaning for us is missing, or unavailable to us, and that the very pursuit of it is a fatal one – but also that respecting this limit is integral to the preservation of the freedom of the human way of being to which the political life of the *polis* is dedicated. If in practice the *polis* confined such a freedom to men, and built it on the backs of women and slaves, the meaning which the tragedies presented to, and on behalf of, the *polis* was nonetheless one which, even at that time, exceeded, because it also problematised and debated, these specific and for us now deplorable circumstances of the *polis*.

Through the tragic, in general, and through *Oedipus Rex*, in particular, I, therefore, find an elucidation of that dual sense of crisis to which I referred earlier. That is to say, of a time in extremity and of the complex moment of resolute 'judgement' (of how we may justly come to stand) for which such a time calls. My conclusion is, however, that all times are at their limit in as much as limit is necessary to circumscribe and so make any thing of anything at all, including the further dispersion of it. And that all time and all life, in virtue of the fact that without limit (specifically that of death itself) it is nothing, mundanely requires, amongst other things, such critical resoluteness. The heroic temper of this moment is not, therefore, one for which only special people, or a special 'people', are equipped – *Oedipus* is the figure of all mortal beings. Neither is it one that only arises at particular times. *Oedipus Rex*, part of a trilogy, is also part of a genre in which this moment of resoluteness or decision is continuously explored because it continuously recurs. Nor, finally, is it heroism alone that may be provoked by thus being of the limit. The very excess of human freedom gives rise to all manner of other ways in which its difficulty may be assumed without diminishing that freedom itself, including in addition to different forms of heroism: serenity; grace; forgiveness; releasing love; mercy; humour; generosity; hospitality; invention; and surprise. All of these may arise at any time, but always in the particular ways peculiar to those times. Mortal being, anywhere, at any time, displays a certain kind of heroism, however, when it stands-up in the everyday circumstances in which it finds itself, and seeks to recover for its time its very own free potentiality-for-being. And this I take to be the political moment *par excellence*; resolute determination, in the face and on behalf of obligatory human freedom, continuously to discover appropriate ways of remaining responsible or open to (quite literally of continuously discharging our response-ability for) that freedom. This rare thing nonetheless arises daily in the manifold doings of human beings in all parts of their worlds.

I do not think that this moment of resoluteness is, however, all that there is to say about the political. Nor, indeed, is this all that tragedy has to say about the political. Sophocles' *Antigone*, and Aeschylus' *Oresteia* trilogy, explore the theme of Justice more intensely: of how human beings always already find themselves in the situation in which they are challenged to give things their due; of how, in and through the *polis*, they come to give law to themselves; and, finally, of how they acknowledge that as the call for Justice arising through it nonetheless always collides with, while also escaping from, any system of law. Here, then, the fundamentally agonistic relationship between the law and the 'Law-of-the-law' which is what the political discloses and mediates is explored in its full force.[76] Yet, I came to concentrate upon *Oedipus Rex* because, and decisively, it illuminates that very disposition which Heidegger made the apex of his *magnum opus, Being and Time*, and with which he arguably remained most concerned, namely standing or comportment itself, but in the trial of which he seems to have effected his very own 'down-fall' as a thinking person.

Heidegger's understanding of the human condition is fundamentally that of a being-toward-death which precisely because it is a being-toward-death is possibility. As possibility it is ordinarily sunk in the world, however, and forgets itself. But precisely because it is as possibility it nonetheless therefore also has the possibility of assuming its potential in an 'authentic' way. According to Heidegger it does this by relating to its death; i.e. by assuming rather than fleeing from its very finiteness, its mortality. Thus:

> The end of my *Dasein*, my death, is not some point at which a sequence of events suddenly breaks off, but a possibility which *Dasein* knows of in this or that way: the most extreme possibility of itself which it can seize and appropriate as standing before it. *Dasein* has in itself the possibility of meeting with its death as the most extreme possibility of itself.... The self-interpretation of *Dasein* which towers over every other statement of certainty and authenticity is its interpretation with respect to its death, the *indeterminate certainty of its ownmost possibility of being at an end.*[77]

That is to say, in having its being to be, individual human being, for Heidegger, is ordinarily taken-up with day-to-day affairs (fallen-ness), and only rarely in confronting the awesomeness of its being-towards death in this way does it authentically assume that being in a resolute way. If fallen-ness is the ordinary condition of human being, then, resoluteness anchors it at one extremity in the possibility of authenticity: 'The *authenticity of Dasein* is what constitutes its *most extreme possibility of Being*'.[78] At the other extremity it appears as if there is only what Heidegger calls the 'they' or the one. The radically fallen and forgetful unthinking mass; from out of which authenticity has continuously to be won. There is, however, in addition, the extreme posssibility of suicide, the ultimate betrayal of the very possibility which human being consists in: 'Through suicide . . . I precisely relinquish the possibility as possibility'.[79]

There has been considerable discussion and criticism both of authenticity, which detractors say smacks of elitism, and of Heidegger's notion of the they, which smacks of the denigration of everyday life and of ordinary people. My point, however, is that there is still a point in the point of resoluteness despite the fact, and also in virtue of the fact, that Heidegger's own actions, together with the *ersatz* resoluteness of National Socialism,[80] did so much radically to discredit the resolute moment of decision for which human freedom and responsibility I think *routinely* calls, and upon which it necessarily always depends.[81] If you like, I want in this book, therefore, not merely to argue for a recovery of the question of the political by drawing upon Heidegger; I try, in addition, to recover the resoluteness integral to human freedom from the fallen example of it with which Heidegger himself presents us. The mystery as well as the profound political significance of this moment of resoluteness – of all that it entails for, and of all that it may exact from, human beings – are explored and displayed with a still unmatched subtlety and brilliance in Sophocles' thought-provoking masterpiece.

There is, finally, one additional reason for recovering *Oedipus Rex*. Much of what follows necessarily comes in a form – that of assertions and propositions – inappropriate to the matter at issue. Such is what might also be called the phenomenological problem after Heidegger and, of course, he continuously returned to this difficulty. 'The lecture's risk', he noted in a seminar on his lecture *Time and Being*, 'lies in the fact that it speaks in propositional statements about something essentially incommensurable with this kind of saying'.[82] The poetry of the tragedy, however, does not. No doubt that is why it has been able to remain true for so long to the matter for thought which originally claimed it, and which has now claimed me; the *aporia* of obligatory freedom which is the *aporia* of the political itself.

FREE BEING AS ETHICAL ENCOUNTER

Because it is concerned with a being, namely human being, whose very essence according to Heidegger is that it is a continuously interrogatory being which is simultaneously also a being-with other beings, the free being of human being-with-others is construed through this thinking as an ethical encounter. That is so because it is fundamentally concerned with how that being is to dwell in the world in respect of its obligations to its very own possibility of being; which being, one must not forget, is not only always already a being-with-others but also a being with Otherness itself. Constituted as openness to Being it is traversed by the Otherness of Being in its own being, namely the ontological difference. Hence, exteriority and transcendence are not contrived additions but integral and constitutive features of it, and the obligation it finds itself compelled to undertake in having its being to be is consequently, therefore, an obligation in Otherness to the other. Thus, and to quote him at some length as he takes issue with Kant's account of freedom:

> We can characterise the essence of freedom more originally by explaining it in terms of transcendence than by defining it as spontaneity, i.e., as a type of causality. To say that a free act is one that is 'initiated by itself' or 'begins with itself' is merely to offer a negative way of characterising freedom. It is merely to say that no determining cause can be said to lie behind the free act. Above all, it is to err on an ontological level in making no distinction between 'initiating' and 'happening' and in failing to characterise what it means to be 'a cause' in terms of the peculiar mode of Being of the being which *exists* as cause, namely *Dasein*. Spontaneity ('being initiated by itself') can serve as an essential feature of the 'subject' only on two conditions: 1. Selfhood must be ontologically clarified in order to provide an appropriate manner of reading the phrase 'by itself'. 2. The same clarification of selfhood, if it is to be able to define the sort of 'move' involved in 'initiating', must somehow explain the 'eventful' character of the self. *But the selfhood of the self, which lies at the basis of all spontaneity, itself lies in transcendence*. . . . Only because freedom constitutes transcendence can it announce itself in existing *Dasein* as a distinctive kind of causality. In interpreting freedom as 'causality', however, we work on a peculiar understanding of reasons that precedes and suggests the

interpretation. As transcendence, freedom is not merely a particular 'kind' of reason but the *origin of reasons* [grounds] *in general. Freedom is freedom for grounds* [reasons].[83]

What is crucial about this understanding of being as a way of being, and of the very event of Being as such disclosed through it, is that freedom and the ethical are necessarily and intimately tied together. The ethical here does not arise as a command ethic issuing from an original causative source. Rather it is the event of freedom itself. For the question, 'What is it to be?' is the question that distinguishes the human way of being. Indeed, it arises in and as the very interrogatory freedom of that being, a being distinguished as such by the fact that it *has* to ask this question of itself in the circumstances – always historical, not deterministically socialised – in which it necessarily always already finds itself, simply because that is its way of being. 'What is it to be?' is also, of course, fundamentally an ethical question.

Given the account of this freed self as not only bearing difference within itself but also as a manifestation of difference and consequently, therefore, in addition, an unavoidable encounter with Otherness, the care of this self, it-self, necessarily entails having a care for Otherness; although the self is necessarily also free, of course, to refuse or renounce this obligation, and ordinarily falls short of its demands (something Heidegger, in the form of fallenness or inauthenticity, thinks of as the everyday condition of human being from which a more authentic relationship to its freedom has to be won back).

The recovery of the political is, therefore, inescapably bound-up with the recovery of the ethical as well. For, to concur, and at some length, with Caputo's Levinasian forcing of this thought in directions which Heidegger would no doubt have resisted:

> On the view I am defending ethics is always already in place, is factically there as soon as there is *Dasein*, as soon as there is world. Ethics is not something fitted into a world that is somehow constituted prior to it. Ethics constitutes the world in the first place. . . . If you want to think what truly 'is' you have to *start* with ethics and obligation, not add it on later. To put it in terms that I would prefer, the space of obligation is opened up by factical life, by the plurality of living bodies, by the commerce and intercourse of bodies with bodies, and above all, in these times, in the times of holocausts and of killing fields, by bodies in pain – but no less by thriving and flourishing bodies, by bodies at play.[84]

Later, albeit only in a sketch, I will therefore argue that the political is precisely this: the continuous challenge to put human freedom as an ethical encounter with others, and within the Otherness that is integral to its own constitution as a way of being, into work in the world.

To put to work, even indeed to put into a work, is not to aestheticise politics. Rather, it is to construe politics as being concerned with responding to the call of the obligatory freedom of human being which is a kind of irrepressible ethical insurgency always already at work in the being of human being that operates against all architectonic impulses; not least those of State builders as well as those which comprise traditional political philosophy itself. The political, here, I argue Heidegger-like, is thus disclosed in a mood, but the mood is that of outrage at the injustice of the world in the obligatory freedom which calls us incessantly to give things their due as the things that they are and not as mere raw material at the disposal specifically, now, of the politico-economic structures and practices of the (inter)national politics of political Modernity.

Just as the political has always to be put to work because it is a possibility, and not the subsistent object of a regional ontology, so also Justice has to be continuously reinvented, for it does not exist as a subsistent object either. It is not a code transparent to revelation. Neither is it already encrypted in the timeless wisdom of a tradition, decodable through the arcane hermeneutical arts of a specialist caste of traditionalists. Similarly, it is not an object discernible and specifiable through the operation of communicative rationality. It is, instead, the obligatory commission of the event of freedom itself. And nowhere is it more called-for, or called forth, than in the (inter)national politics of political Modernity.

Human freedom is obligatory because it cannot be escaped. As Heidegger says, *Dasein* is thrown. There is no choice about whether or not to be here; if you are, why then you *are*. It is obligatory also, however, because there is always already also an obligation to choose the ways in which that freedom is to be taken-up. Differentially constituted, each human being is a being which is not only manifested in the manifesting to which the ontological difference testifies, it is a being face to face with others in Otherness; to combine both the Heideggerian and the Levinasian prefixes in a way that does some violence to each.[85] To be is to be obligated to respond freely to this belonging together which is constitutive of the way of being of human being. Because there is this obligation to respond freely, human being is called before Justice to do Justice to this way of being. Here I use Justice to function somewhat in the way that Levinas uses Law. I prefer to use Justice, however, because I am suspicious of the way in which Levinas, seeking to reintroduce an albeit re-tooled command ethic, places freedom at odds with Law in a way that threatens to return the question of freedom and politics back to those who have always been disposed to think it in terms of rule and violence rather than response-ability to the call of Justice.

Justice, then, is called for in the opening within which this open way of being exists or stands out. Hence, Justice is precisely the question of the comportment – how it stands and comes to a stand in respect of its belonging together with others and with Otherness – of human being. Like the political, in which it arises as a public question, Justice is a possibility; the higher unrealisable possibility which always haunts the existing legal and political actuality of human worlds. Obliged to be free, human being is obligated to care for the others and for the Otherness with whom, and within which, it always already finds itself existing as the way of being that it is, because that is its uncanny estranged way of being. As human freedom is an in-finite freedom which has to be borne, so also is the call for Justice which echoes throughout it. For, if existence is nothing but being-possible, this being-possible as the opening up of a world is a being-possible be-fore Justice. World is, therefore, the possibility of Justice; which necessarily also means, of course, the possibility of injustice and thus the impossibility of Justice – in the sense of any finished realisation of it – as well.

Heidegger is a thinker convinced that our ways of making sense of the ways that we make sense now – and, for me, our ways of making sense of the (inter)national political sense we claim to make – just do not make sustainable and survival sense any more. It was no mere coincidence to him that the global civilisation which has arisen out of the crucible of that undefinable thing, the 'West', experiences this crisis directly less as an exposure to, and an adventure in, obligatory freedom than as an immediate and everyday political emergency. For its distinguishing political achievement, the State, is a State of emergency – a formation of technologised and technologising practices – which simultaneously induces as it claims to ameliorate this very condition of emergency in the name of security itself.[86]

In his reflections on this crisis of sense, Heidegger takes as his 'beginning' the beginning he claims to perceive in the very beginning of the 'West' in Greek thought. That beginning was precisely not the mood of radical insecurity which seeks security through its many cognates: salvation; certainty; or the right to be. Neither was it the mood of outrage at injustice. Rather the mood to which Heidegger still appealed arose from the one which effected the inception of philosophy itself, namely the wonder (or *thauma*) at the overwhelming manifestness of beings as the occurrence of *physis*, of the beginning of Greek thinking. In his reflection upon that wonder, Heidegger finds that being human is not only a way of being rather than a substance, but is a way of being which, because its very being at all is always an issue for it, is distinguished by being-able-to-be. And in that ability-to-be, of course, lies its very capacity to begin, and begin again. Begin not *de novo*, of course, for human being is always already situated. Indeed, Heidegger's entire philosophical corpus continuously insists upon our being within something, in the midst of things, and upon our always having to find ourselves within the world in which we arise as such. 'Begin' then must always be understood in the sense of beginning again in the particular historical circumstances in which we find ourselves and in the location of which, none-theless, the familiar world appears startling and unfamiliar to us. Thus seen, as if for the first time, that world holds-out possibilities into which human being may enter and so begin afresh, refreshed.

But *wonder* – which he is careful to distinguish from the *amazement* that merely exoticises difference; the *admiration* which esteems difference only to advance its own judgements; and the *astonishment* at the unusual which suspends position-taking, precisely because they all focus upon the unusual as opposed to the strangeness of the mundane which so decisively distinguishes wonder – was the inception of Greek philosophy.[87] It cannot, therefore, be the basis of the new beginning which he anticipates is possible in the current condition of the end of that philosophy. The power of that inception has run its course. A new one, if there is to be a new course, would have to be empowered by some other inception. Heidegger reflects, therefore, not only on the initiatory capacity of wonder, for it is lacking in our current technological era, but also on that of its very absence. And it is by that very lack that he introduces us into reflecting on the possibility of a new beginning. I pursue that reflection less driven by wonder, however, and more by the insatiable call of Justice which arises for a being which while it is free either to respond to or reject that call will never finally answer it. That being, and the aporetic circumstances in which it finds itself, was first, and most thoroughly and convincingly, explored as tragic being.

FREE BEING AS TRAGIC BEING

By tragic I mean nothing to do with tragedy as it is now popularly understood. That is to say, it is neither passivity nor determination. Neither is it the condition of despair, nor is it transgression of the will for the strengthening of the will conceived as the embodied desire for sensational gratification. All of these are derelict ways of understanding the tragic brought about, not exclusively but in particular, by the tradition's development of subject–object thinking. Rather, tragic describes that temporal mode of being which is free but is incapable of mastering that freedom (and hence itself), because, in the bearing of its freedom, it is always fated to encounter the unassimilable Otherness to which that freedom is irreducibly indebted. Tragic is the word which best describes Heidegger's understanding of the 'essence' of human being.

First, of course, human being (or what he calls *Dasein*) is a verb for Heidegger, not a noun. In other words, it does not refer to a *what*, an object or an entity in the traditional sense, but to a *how*, a distinctive manner or way of being: 'the fundamental category of this entity is its "how"'.[88] Indeed, it is precisely because the tradition is reduced to thinking human being in terms of an entity which it is not – the *res* or animal – that something has then to be added to the human – for example, reason or the soul – in order to distinguish it from other entities.[89]

Its how is a questioning and a relating which makes of human being a hermeneutical way of being – a hermeneutical phenomenon – concerned with, and continuously undertaking projects in respect of its being-in-the-world in which it always already finds itself thrown. Second, however, as a mode of being, it is actually constituted by, and continuously, therefore, exhibits, a complex and fundamental lack or absence. Third, this lack, this absence which is other than itself, is something that it nonetheless and necessarily bears within itself so that human being is, therefore, also traversed by Otherness because it is in fact differentially constituted. Human being, in other words, is not one, self-susbsistent, uniform, stable or contained. Rather, it is plural, needful, hybrid, mobile and open. Differentially constituted as a lack by a lack, human being is, then, for Heidegger, not simply different from other ways of being, difference is integral to the composition of every singular human being. Neither, therefore, is one human being merely differentiated from another. Each bears difference within itself and not merely in relation to others. That is why, in virtue of the ontological difference, human being always already finds itself within (this) difference because it arises as a manifestation of it.

In the first instance, this lack arises because human being does not give itself the time in which it exists as a temporal mode of being. As Conrad says of Mistah Kurtz:

> Everything belonged to him – but that was a trifle. The thing was to know what he belonged to . . .[90]

Human being discovers itself already thrown into this original temporality which is the enigma of the manifestation of differing itself. Human existence owes its being, then, to this temporality in a fundamental and original way – 'that origin without origin or beginning', to quote Foucault's critical examination of Heidegger's thesis 'on the basis of which everything is able to come into being'[91] – and cannot escape it because it is always already, that is to say simply by virtue of being, indebted to it. A temporal mode of being, it can never master temporality and is in a sense, therefore, dispossessed of that very thing of which it is a manifestation; namely, the power of temporalising itself. It is. But it is not Being. There is a difference. That difference is what Heidegger calls the ontological difference. 'What is conveyed in the immediacy' of this account of 'origin', Foucault elaborates, 'is, therefore, that man is cut off from the origin that would make him contemporaneous with his own existence'. Human being is thus and necessarily a stranger to itself in its existentiality: 'amid all the things that are born in time and no doubt die in time, he [the representation of human being as man], cut off from all origin, is already there'. Moreover:

> rather than a cut, made at some given moment in duration, he is the opening from which time in general can be reconstituted, duration can flow, and things, at the appropriate moment, can make their appearance.[92]

Thus disposed, this temporal existence is the ability to respond to the very possibility of being made available by temporality itself, as human being manifests temporality in and through its own finitude; and is challenged to compose itself in, to and as that way of being. To be, then, is to be indebted in virtue and as a manifestation of the ontological difference; and, therefore, already to be in debt to the possibility of existing which it discloses. This difference is not merely something which human being takes-on as if in being at all it had any choice in the matter. Neither is it inscribed upon or within human being by some supreme scribe. Human being arises in this difference as a manifestation of it. Indeed, for Heidegger, Being arises in beings but is disclosed in the human mode of being as a questioning about its own being which revolves around *the* question; that of the Being of Being as such.

Such a debt is not, of course, a payment owed to some subsisting entity. (Specifically, Being is not an entity. It is no-thing. Thinking of it as an entity is precisely the oblivion of Being which characterises the tradition of onto-theology.) It does not consist in some determinate situation or occasion of mortgaged deferment, or of some failure or refusal in our being. Neither is it a 'negative' thing which has to be eliminated or redeemed. Rather, it is a plenitude. 'It never enters the field of view of our calculating reason', Heidegger notes,

> that a no and a not may arise out of a surplus or abundance, may be the highest gift, and as this not and no may infinitely, i.e. essentially, surpass every ordinary yes.[93]

In short, this indebtedness is not original sin, and it entails no 'moral' judgement. Rather, it is simply the factical ontological condition of this the human mode of being. For '[f]acticity', as Michel Haar succinctly put it, 'entails *not knowing* our most ancient provenance'.[94] This lack, or absence, is precisely *not* the absence or lack of a presence. Rather, it is the irreducible absence which a presence, paradoxically, signifies. That is why this absence, which is not that of an absent presence, is no deficiency but an abundance or excess. As superfluity, it is the completely other which transient presence announces despite itself, and, ironically, announces most when it most insists upon its own completion and permanence.

Herein also lies Heidegger's understanding of human being as free being. For the temporality which human being enjoys is, as a domain of possibility, a domain of freedom. Heidegger frequently calls it the Open. Hence, human being lives life in the Open, exists or stands out in it by virtue of it. This freedom, therefore, antecedes the freedom of subjectivisation in that it is the thrownness of human being into existence. As thrown existence, human being is traversed by the power of possibility that arises within the temporality it enjoys. It asks the question, 'What is it to be?' simply because it has its own being to be as an enterprise or project that it must continuously undertake. It is that kind of being, therefore, for whom its being is an issue at issue for it. That, for Heidegger, is the essence of its freedom. I call it an obligatory freedom for three reasons. First, because there is no choice in the matter. Second, because it obliges each human being to assume – take-up and take-on – that freedom one way or another. Third, because, as a being-with-others in Otherness, human being in assuming its freedom is necessarily, therefore, also obliged one way or another to have a 'care' for others and Otherness within the structure of care which is *the* fundamental part of its ontological constitution.

Human being is not, however, thrown in some general, abstract or limitless way. Precisely to the contrary, it is thrown in the very specific and practical sense of having its own being to be, a being which it must struggle to make its own. That is to say, one way or another, it is in the position of having to assume its being, to take over the responsibility for it or give grounds for it; while, nonetheless, not being able to master that very freedom to be – granted by manifestation as such – which is its 'ground'. As Heidegger says:

The Self which as such has to lay the basis for itself, can *never* get that basis into its power; and yet, as existing, it must take over Being-a-basis.[95]

This freedom is, as he says in *The Essence of Reasons*, quite simply a 'freedom for grounds', or a 'freedom for reasons'.[96] It is, in my rendition of it, a freedom to be obliged to give reasons in respect of itself and other beings before the Otherness in which they arise, because:

> *Dasein* happens in man, so that he can understand obligation to himself in the essence of his existence, i.e., he can be a free self. Thus freedom reveals itself as that which makes bonds and obligations possible in the first place.

And in as much as this *Dasein* of Heidegger's, according to his own account of it, is differentially constituted in difference as a manifestation of the differing of manifestation as such, and is thus *in itself* an encounter not simply with others but with the very Otherness of this uncanny event, this obligation to itself cannot be dissociated from, and therefore cannot be thought without simultaneously also thinking the character and implications of, the constitutive, free and obligatory relationship of which it is actually comprised as a way of being with others within Otherness. The question of its being, and of its obligation to its being, can never be divorced, therefore, from its being with others and from the question of what this constitutive Otherness demands of it. For that demand does not arise as it were from outside the self. Rather, it arises with – or more precisely *as* – the advent of the self it-self, even as it necessarily always already exceeds the self. Thus in itself the self is neither an inside to be commanded by, nor prised open to, an outside. Rather, the self simply is as exteriority; an openness.

Moreover, human being also finds itself always already inserted into some specific and determinate historical possibilities as it takes-up the issue of its being. Here, too, the compound lack at the heart of human being manifests itself again. First, because it never chooses the determinate situation in which it finds itself, but always inherits it. Second, because, as it decides, something must also always escape human being and remain hidden from it in the very act of its choosing; such that:

> . . . in having a potentiality-for-Being it always stands in one possibility or another: it constantly is *not* other possibilities, and it has waived these in its existential projection.[97]

All decision, in short, necessarily entails a no which is indissoluble from its yes. Because every yes contains a no, human being consequently also has to bear the absence of the possibilities forgone in the determinate possibility that it is, in the particular historical moment in which it finds itself thrown. Somehow human being has to find the resources to bear this existence and give it its due, for this gift 'is more difficult to bear than any loss'.[98]

The echo of the Greek understanding of the tragic is very powerful here. For there, human being was explored in terms of the inherently 'monstrous', order-violating as well as order-constituting, character of the human way of being. Monstrous, because such a way of being continuously exceeds stable categorisation and identification even as it categorises and identifies. Monstrous, in that it is inherently dualistic – creating yet created; neither beast nor god but possessing something of the supposedly determinate nature of each. Terrible in its liminal marginality – that of its very mortality – it is a being that is freed to exist in the margin between its coming and its going. Unnatural in its very duality, this is the condition of the tragic way of being as the Greeks understood it. In tragedy this being is not, however, rejected for the very finiteness which distinguishes it, nor for its loathsomeness as that which is both more and less than one, hybrid and excessive. Neither is it subjected to the disciplinary practices whose objective is to make it a calculable object transparent to the light of cognition; which, then, safely defuses it because it has transformed it into a uniform domain of commensurability amenable to certain, certifiable and calculative knowing. Instead, it is affirmed as a way of being that contains within itself a capacity for transfiguration in which it can give itself back to itself – that is to say, in reclaiming, renew itself – in that it is itself a process of being rather than a substantive entity; and hence a continuous, and continuously open, transformative possibility-for-being so long as it preserves its openness to the liminality of the limits which drawing it together also disseminate it in time.

Challenged by the power of Being to be, Greek tragic being understands human being, responding through its own power to be, as continuously confronting the enigmatic limits of presence granted by the power of Being. Astonished at Being, and fearful of its own power to be in this fearful encounter with Being, Greek tragic being thereby also understands human being as acquiring a tragic awareness not merely of its own limits but of the liminality of those limits; that is to say, of the specifically determinate, rather than limitless, creative possibilities entailed by them. Herein also, in respect of limits, lies its understanding of responsibility.

Precisely because there is a kinship between the no longer metaphysical thinking, to which Heidegger is trying to beat a path, and the not yet metaphysical which is expressed in Greek tragedy, Heidegger's later thought, especially, is devoted to exploring what is said and unsaid in pre-Socratic poetry and sayings. It is, therefore, deeply influenced by the thought of Being and the thought of mortal beings which he finds expressed there. Hence, the approach to the political which begins to emerge from Heidegger's thought is very closely attuned to pre-Socratic understanding of the political expressed in and through the tragic.[99] This he also tries to develop further by reflecting upon the essence of art in general (specifically not aesthetics), and the dialogue between the poet and the thinker in particular (intimately related ways through which, in conjunction with that of the *polis*, Greek tragic being responded to the challenge of the overwhelming power of Being as such).[100] Poetry for Heidegger was possessed not only of an Orphic quality which was able to bring things to presence by naming them but also, and increasingly, especially in his later work, of an Hermetic quality in that it exposes us to this the very uncanniness of existence as human being manifests it in and through the uncanniness of Language itself.[101] Hence, he identifies this lack integral to human being in his later thinking as deeper still than a mere lack within human being alone. There it becomes 'a character of Being and not of man', although it continues to determine human being 'through and through'.[102] This move from, although still entirely related to, *Being and Time*, also begins to mark how and where Heidegger's thought, as it develops, perhaps also diverges from the Greek sense of the tragic.[103]

COGNITION TO COMPORTMENT

There is also, however, a distinctly corporeal tone to the movements of Heidegger's thought, and to those subsequently influenced by it. I want to extend and capitalise upon that tone here. Listening, attending, saying and questioning, for Heidegger, supplemented the tradition's preoccupation with the sight of cognition and the discourse of the *logos*, and so ears were added to the eye and to the 'tongue' (speech) in a radical reinterpretation of Language itself through a significant extension of philosophy's register of corporeal sensibility. These moves were integral also, of course, to how Heidegger subverted the modern cult of the radically abstracted universal, sovereign, conscious, rational subject of cognition. Thrown, we are let go as bodies. Bodied we are always already turning not only into someone, but also into something, else. Hence the body – our finitude, or being mortal, which means to say also our being other in the Otherness of Being – as Gerald Bruns observed in a stunning phrase, 'is a satire upon rationality'.[104] Thus, for Heidegger:

> speaking is at the same time also listening. It is the custom to put speaking and listening in opposition; one speaks the other listens. But listening accompanies and surrounds not only speaking such as takes place in conversation. The simultaneousness of speaking and listening has a larger meaning. Speaking is itself a listening. Speaking is listening to the language which we speak. Thus, it is a listening not *while* but *before* we are speaking. This listening to language also comes before all other kinds of listening that we know, in a most inconspicuous manner. We do not merely speak the language – we speak by way of it. We can do so because we always have already listened to the language.[105]

Heidegger's hermeneutics is then best understood as a sounding, in which the hermeneut itself (human being) continuously sounds itself out amidst the abundantly telling dis-closive silence which contours Language; wherein which, and to which, it always already finds itself bodily given.

Later, with my account of the tragic in general, and of *Oedipus Rex* in particular, I want to push that extension one step further – progressing from eyes through ears to feet, or, if you will, effecting a radical shift from cognition towards comportment – by amplifying and appropriating another tone which is powerfully at work in Heidegger's thought. Hence, in re-raising the question of the political and allying it to that of the ethical, I try to depict that complex interplay between standing straight and seeing straight which necessarily afflicts the being, namely human being, which is always already moved (thrown) and moving (understanding, interpreting and projecting) because it always already finds itself on the move (i.e. temporal). It is on the move by virtue of the fact that it is a finite being which, manifestingly standing-out in the manifold movement of time itself (the ecstases of temporality, past, present and future; in which, while each ecstasis temporalises with the other two, that of the future has priority[106]), is always already on the way from birth to death the instant it is conceived.[107] Hence, just as '*Dasein*, conceived in its most extreme possibility of Being, *is time itself*, not *in* time',[108] so human being is motility rather than simply in motion. Furthermore, not only is motility therefore integral to the ontological constitution of *Dasein*, such an inherently mobile way of being – in that it *is* as motivation – must also be essentially oriented not only towards other beings but also towards the future rather than, as the tradition would have it, towards the idea of permanent presence. For, if it is *as motivation*, its orientation, however much drawn on interpretations of the past and the depiction of present necessities, is ineluctably futural towards the continuous projection and assumption of this very motivatedness. The challenge it necessarily confronts in any particular present, therefore, is how to be futural. 'This is the first principle of all hermeneutics.'[109] Hence the phenomenon of the human as hermeneut is fundamental once again here, while being elaborated in terms of its mobility and futurality rather than in terms of stability and permanent presence.

Thus essentially motivated in its motility, human being not only comprises directionality towards that which concerns it, its future in Otherness with other beings, this directionality is also a bearing. (I would also play on 'bearing' to invoke 'baring' here in order to recall, simultaneously, the openness of this way of being). Albeit that for Heidegger *Dasein* is a being-towards-death, it must also experience birth if it is to die. Its bearing is therefore also a being pregnant with possibility. Furthermore, bearing itself comprises also posture. In its way of being, human being is not only, therefore, orientated, it is also disposed and composed; that is to say, bears a composure which entails a stance.

Such a stance necessarily also comprises simultaneously both distance and proximity, nearness and apartness. For how else would a human being be that singular thing which it is if it were not set apart. And yet how else, also, could it be a being-with-others – which it must necessarily be in being set apart; for in being set apart, it must be set apart from others – if it were not also a being in proximity to others. (And, indeed, to that unassimilable Otherness which human being harbours within itself – this setting-apartedness itself – because it is constitutive of itself.) Such a stance is not, however, static. How could it be in the fundamental motility of temporality as human beings manifest time? As with dancing, therefore, the knack of composing oneself continuously entails contriving the distance appropriate to the nearness that allows oneself and others their due. In as much as each participant here intimately belongs to movement, because it is constitutive of their way of being, however, each necessarily also, therefore, belongs to each other. They belong to each other even as motile temporality spaces them out as the specific individual beings that they are. Sharing-in they are also, in other words, shared-out through the motile temporality which they share. Sharing in movement as movement nonetheless does not make human beings identical. To the contrary, it is precisely what differentiates them. But they are joined – one might even say bonded – in this agonal or polemical relating by which they continuously struggle with the struggle of the assumption of identity in difference afforded by the motile temporality granted to and manifested by them. It is this which makes them, in the Heideggerian sense of the term as fundamentally distinct yet fundamentally also related in their difference, the same. In such liminal hermeneutical intercourse with the phenomenon of the Being of their being – a being with others in an unassimilable Otherness which they harbour in themselves – they dream, conceive and give birth to possibilities; through the operation of limits, specific conjunctions at which gathering and disseminating simultaneously takes place, which realise possibility as determinate actuality.

Thus *mobile* in its bearing, human being must nonetheless also be *labile* as well; prone to slip, fall, or lapse. For there can be no possibility of standing without falling. No bearing without the prospect also of a loss of orientation or the dissolution of composure. No dancing without the danger of making a false step. No birth without death, and no death without birth. Hence not only the open mobility but also, of course, the fragility and fallibility of this b(e)aring-being, whose mortal natality which is also a natal mortality makes of it a continuous birthing-towards-death.

If listening and attending are the characteristic features of Heidegger's hermeneutical phenomenology, ears are its motif.[110] Standing and disposition are, however, the characteristic features of what might be called the hermeneutical phenomenology of ethico-political facticity which I seek to draw-out of Heidegger's thought in order to emphasise the inescapable, and inescapably difficult, comportment of obligatory freedom which characterises a being that simply *is* in the state of *being moved*. Feet, then, exemplified in the form of *Oedipus'* bad foot, become its motif. That in turn makes the International Relations of political Modernity a site of extraordinary importance. For in the (inter)national politics of political Modernity not only our relation to others but also to the very Otherness which human beings inhabit, because it inhabits them, is fundamentally at issue and continuously exposed to fatal steps.

Facticity, here, it should be stressed, is not the object of hermeneutics. Rather, it is the very way of being pertaining to the ethico-political facticity of human being in which the (political) empiricism of (inter)national politics is seen to be not 'empirical' enough, while its (political) realism is never nearly 'real' enough, as an account of the experience of the politicality of human existence. Each is an artificial, specially contrived and limited comportment towards the excess of that existence.[111] Radically confined by the host of unexamined theoretical assumptions which both comprise, neither can deliver what each necessarily presupposes, namely the ideal of and for thinking the norms of absolute validity and referential truth. Moreover, in their failed attempts to do so, each offers a radically impoverished account of the hermeneutical phenomenon of the ethico-political facticity of human being, and exhibits a special (inter)national violence in respect of it.[112]

SECURITY TO TRAGEDY

I try to follow the movement of Heidegger's thought, therefore, in terms of how it relates to the question of the political. This does not take the form of a detailed account of what he had to say about politics in his writings. In a conventional sense he did not have very much directly to say. But it is now perfectly clear that almost everything he did say had, and was in a sense intended to have, a direct and disturbing purchase on the entire question of the political.[113] 'For Heidegger', Emmanuel Levinas wrote,

life isn't simply a game which is played in the last analysis for thought. He is dominated by history, by his origin in which he had nothing to do, since he is thrown into the world.[114]

In as much as he questions the foundation of modern thought, I have noted, Heidegger problematises traditional political thought. In as much as he also and simultaneously questions the alliance between modern science, technology and the modern State, which he does quite explicitly in his Nietzsche volumes in particular, he problematises the foundation of modern (inter)national politics.[115] With Heidegger the entire domain of politics – from the essence of the political, through the regimes and institutions of politics, down to the moment of political decision – is consequently at issue once more. And at issue less in terms of ideology than in terms of the globalisation of technology – the very being of representative–calculative thought. For the world into which Heidegger was thrown was, and remains for us, one dominated by technology. The recovery of the obligatory freedom of political life is to be recovered now, therefore, from and within our current global technological mode of existence, which incorporates but also goes beyond our dominant modes of production in the way that it determines our (inter)national politics globally.

World, temporality and human being (*Dasein*) are, therefore, at the centre of that destructuring of metaphysics through constant engagement with many of its canonical thinkers – such as Aristotle, Plato, Augustine, Descartes, Kant, Hegel, Nietzsche, Kierkegaard and Husserl – which, together with a return to early Greek thinking, constituted Heidegger's single-minded pursuit of the question of Being. In following the movement of Heidegger's thought, I therefore also try to engage in a certain kind of repetition, rather than detailed exposition, of it.

That repetition is often a conscious mimicry. Mimicry that disrupts the very idea of an authentic Heidegger by continuously dilating the ethical and the political character of the obligatory freedom of human being. Neither is the voice which I adopt properly mine. For it is that of the tragic which I already find in Heidegger as well. As I mimic it, so I throw and project it, continuously trying to amplify, intensify and focus that voice in the direction of the ethical and the political. There is a violence – a certain caricaturing and aping as well as a necessary mis-representation – in all of this. It relies, in addition, upon a measure of English word play that struggles to intimate something of what goes-on in Heidegger's German. My mimicry ends with a reading of *Oedipus Rex*, which, in continuing the mime, also offers the tragedy as an allegory for the (inter)national politics of late modern times.

What licences this strategy? My reply is that it emerges from out of Heidegger's thought of Being and the there-being of human being itself. Obligatory freedom (and the call for Justice which resounds throughout it), he teaches, is not a command but a commission to be taken-up . . . repeatedly. Assuming that commission is what licenses my mimicry.[116] It is licensed, also, by the 'method' of creatively exaggerating what the work itself proclaims, which Heidegger shares with Levinas.

My point of entry for all this, I have already noted, is a word. That word is 'Security'. More specifically, such a repetition enables me to offer an interpreta-tion of the Western tradition of political thought which foregrounds its pre-occupation with security, and to call that preoccupation into question in ways stimulated by Heidegger's thinking without having to be 'true' to that thinking. That is to say, without having to make my interpretation correspond exactly to Heidegger's; whatever that might be. In engaging in that repetition I enlist the support of, and tensions afforded by, those thinkers – particularly Arendt, Derrida, Foucault, Levinas, and Nancy – who themselves not only think with, but also powerfully against, the limits of Heidegger's thinking. And, finally, I try to do this through drawing-out the tragic sensibility at issue there.

This tragic sensibility is one which I deliberately explicate in my own way, and deploy for my own purposes, in order to fashion a comportment for myself through which I might get a more powerful purchase not only on Heidegger but also upon the character of the (inter)national politics of political Modernity. I do this in order to amplify, and explore the register, of the tone of freedom, responsibility and obligation that exists not simply in Heidegger but in the tragic and in all the thinking which Heidegger did so much to release. Such a sensibility is one which, even as I draw upon him, I have come to understand better through the violent way in which Emmanuel Levinas contests it. 'All civilisations which accept being, the tragic despair of which it consists and the crimes which it justifies', he says, 'merit the name barbarian'.[117] I, in turn, contest Levinas' association of the tragic with despair, however, especially in my reading of *Oedipus Rex*, which is often taken to be the most despairing of tragedies. Instead, I explore the way in which the tragic explores the ineradicable belonging together, and aporetic difficulty, of the insatiable call of Justice which as it resounds throughout necessarily also sounds-out – plumbs the depths of – human being's obligatory freedom.

I try not to draw on these thinkers, however, simply for their authori-tative/citational support. Neither am I committed merely to explicating their own positions and the important differences which obtain between them; although I try not to elide them either. I draw on them, instead, to contrive from their thinking a depiction of that free, creative, agonal and ethical tension which comprises the very space of the political.

I recognise the danger that this movement of mine could be taken to excuse paying insufficiently close attention to Heidegger's texts, or of failing to understand enough about what Heidegger has tried to say, and of similarly failing to do justice to these other complex and important thinkers. Such a danger will always exist, of course, especially when dealing with a thinker who is not only as difficult and subtle, not to say obscure, as Heidegger, but whose thought also evolved in important ways, exciting powerful responses from other eminent philosophers. Although I may very well fail on all these counts I do not intend, however, to take any liberties either with Heidegger or with the others. Rather, I am mindful, here, of Robert Bernasconi's wise observation. Issued specifically in respect of Heidegger, it has a certain relevance to these other thinkers as well. 'One cannot readily say *what* Heidegger says', Robert Bernasconi notes,

> for the simple reason that Heidegger overcomes the 'what' of *essentia* by transforming the way of saying. Hence all writing about Heidegger should begin and end with a disclaimer. The disclaimer, in attempting to be faithful to *what claimed* [my emphasis] Heidegger, must at the same time disregard his warnings and lift the silence about silence.[118]

My object, then, is not to provide myself with excuses in advance but to explain instead both how I have tried to go about this work, and that – as I pursued what claimed my attention; specifically the *aporia* of obligatory freedom as it is simultaneously both disclosed and endangered through the preoccupation with security – the very path of my own thinking, as well as the content of it, began to change.

'What happens', Gerald Bruns asks, 'when you try to follow Heidegger up or down one of his paths of thinking, studying him, trying out his moves, finding yourself caught up in him?' His response seems to me to be an exemplary one. One of the things that happens, he says, 'is that you begin to appreciate why people are careful to confine themselves to forms of mental activity that have no history'. By that he meant:

> purely analytical programs like formal logic, philosophy of language, linguistics, semiotics, most forms of literary criticism, perhaps most of what gets taught in school: programs you can get in and out of quickly and cleanly without the burden of having done anything more blameworthy than test, or apply, a certain method, skill, technique, or training.[119]

Precisely because it is so dangerous – and dangerous precisely because it is so intimately connected with history – there is often an almost desperate, and even violent, insistence that politics, too, both as a practice and as an object of study, be reduced in this way. In short, technologised. So-called political 'realists' and 'idealists' alike, for example, and for similar reasons, would reduce the political to the formulaic so as to settle its hash once and for all. I take their responses, however, to be symptomatic of a persistent and ancient desire to escape the sheer difficulty as well as the historicality and singularity of the political.

One cannot take up the question of the political, then, without taking up the question of history. That means that the 'scientific', purely analytic programmatic, approach to politics is not only out, however, it also means that it is construed as another expression of the technologising of the thought and life of politics, of which politics itself threatens to become the instrument. Just as the political, I will argue, arises neither from an Augustinian nor a Hobbesian lack (the original fall from God's grace, or the radical insecurity of the state of nature) but from the ebullient free excess of existence itself, so the hermeneutical phenomenological study of politics that I would advocate would similarly not be a science out of a lack either, since it also springs from the superabundance of the very event of (a potentially political) existence as well.

Similarly, in response to many of the same instincts and for many of the same reasons, precisely because it is so dangerous – and dangerous precisely because, again, it is so intimately connected with history – there has been an almost equally desperate concern by some to sanitise Heidegger, or, conversely, a violent insistence by others that his work be avoided altogether as political anathema.

I detect an important symmetry here, however, between the question of the political and the question of Heidegger. Heidegger, I would argue, like philosophy itself, simply is a political question because he (like philosophy) raises the question of the political in all its violent and challenging form. Hence, I suspect that the desire to escape Heidegger is the desire to escape the political as well; and that each displays a similar, if not the same, comportment towards existence. Worse, the desire to escape the political Heidegger is sometimes the donnish posturing of those who pretend that they have resolved the question of the political sanitarily and satisfactorily for themselves already (or had it solved for them), or the monkish reticence of those for whom the question of the political is too difficult because it is too dirty.[120]

Neither Heidegger nor the political can be avoided, however, because one cannot take up the study of Heidegger without also taking up what Fred Dallmayr called his 'heavy political mortgage'.[121] Heidegger's heavy political mortgage is not, however, Heidegger's alone. It is also ours, because it is the (inter)national political mortgage of the twentieth century as a whole. This therefore means that if you want to think about the political at the end of this century you cannot avoid taking up the political at the extremity of thought and action to which the (inter)national politics of this century has given rise. That means taking-up the figures both of Heidegger and the Holocaust; by which I mean the way in which the Nazi-inspired destruction of European Jewry signalled human being's capacity not only systematically to destroy sections of itself – something it has been doing for millennia[122] – but also, now, its rational political potentiality to deny the freedom of the human way of being as such and destroy the species as a whole.

In short, it is not simply Heidegger's work, nor also one's own study of it, as Gerald Bruns has persuasively argued, that is politically mortgaged in a note that is unpayable. Since the political and technological developments of the twentieth century, the very study of (inter)national politics itself has become mortgaged in exactly the same way as well. It is thus not only a matter of asking the question 'how can one think after Auschwitz?' It is a matter of asking how one can think politically after Auschwitz. To be political now in one's political thinking, therefore, means to remain as unreconciled to Heidegger's texts as one remains unreconciled to the (inter)national political developments of the twentieth century, as one continues to encounter both Heidegger and the political at the end of this century. In following the movement of Heidegger's thinking in relation to the question of the political I am consequently also trying to move along certain intersecting limits – that of our times and that of his thought – and to do so where those limits gesture, sometimes implicitly, sometimes explicitly, but always insistently, to the excess in which each shares; specifically to that dangerous excess of the ethical and the political within both Heidegger and our times, and to how we might, then, think about each of these intimately related constituent elements of obligatory human freedom again.

My previous chapter explored the relationship between politics and philosophy, and the significance which that relationship has in this time of extremity and limit. Its conclusion was that the politics of the 'West' is a politics of security precisely because metaphysics itself is a preoccupation with security, and that this is the well-spring of the technologising which distinguishes both. In calling attention to the philosophy of the limit it also recalls that security and danger are concerned with the *terminality* of a limit situation from which the political, it is said in our tradition, is derived. My next chapter will explore the question of the political as it might arise out of Heidegger's thought by concentrating upon those aspects of it which I think most directly call into question the way in which we think about the political, namely: difference; truth; Justice; the obligatory freedom of human being; the mutations of metaphysics; the art of *politeia*; and the advent of technology. It does so by suggesting that political thought has yet to be thought again, and that the way to begin to think the political is through a radical hermeneutical phenomenology. But the chapter does not neglect to reflect upon how Heidegger's own thinking offers a discourse of danger from which he, too, seeks to derive an understanding of human conduct and what is required of it in the perilous closure of metaphysics.[123]

Chapter 4 turns back directly once again to security. It provides an 'etymology' rather than a genealogy of security, specifically introducing and deliberating upon *asphaleia* – the privative of *sphallo*, to fall/fail or trip-up – which is the Greek word for security. Etymology is, however, embraced as a specific philosophical move – a radical hermeneutical move which, guided by our current needs, seeks to hear the unsaid long said in the word itself – and I try to explain why and how. For although the word is only a fragment its very fragment-ness is its value. As mortal creatures inserted between birth and death into time with others, we too are fragments since a fragment 'is a work interfered with by death;'[124] and human being, fragmented fragments of being, are born to die. It is this shared fragmentedness which, therefore, alerts us to the bond between ourselves and words; and so, because of the way, as Language discloses, it simultaneously brings things together and sends them on their disseminating way again, to the disclosing and bonding of human being with itself through the bond which it has with Language itself.

Addressing the word, then, transports us into what Heidegger would call 'the essential nexus that engages our thinking down to its very foundations',[125] which lies hidden there, and into 'the inner multiplicity of the disposition',[126] to which it gives rise. Security does not disclose a stable ground, for there is none, but betrays instead its own essence as an insistent demand for such a foundation. By asking what the word says I pursue both what it allows us to think as well as how we are disposed to think through it. This not only discloses that the preoccupation with security is concerned with grounds – with questions of grounding, standing and falling, which, under the modern Cartesian dispensation, is expressed and pursued as the certitude of the subject, so that the subject itself has to be secured not only if thought itself is henceforth to be secured but also if the subject of politics, the political subject itself, is to be secured; by first being rendered calculable so that it can be securely represented[127] – but also that the conflict at the heart of security is the very impossibility of the ground which it seeks. The word itself, then, discloses that insecurity is always already folded into security, that it is impossible to have one without the other, and that this duality of (in)security is another way of referring to the abyssal ground of foundation-less freedom of the human condition, in which having to be happens to human beings in a way that obliges them to respond to others and to the Otherness which is integral to their very freedom.

The etymology is necessary, in addition, to provide further illustration of how and why this condition is interpreted as tragic. *Asphaleia* thus directs me to a political reinterpretation of *Oedipus Rex*. Here, concentrating as much upon *Oedipus'* crippled foot as his clear-sighted cognition, I explore how tragedy always already understood the belonging together of security and insecurity – the *aporia* posed by their absolute indissociability – and directly addressed the manifold problems and dilemmas which arise in the living of it; specifically, in this play, with the resoluteness required in having such a being to be, and the madness of decision – to use Derrida's Kierkegaardian expression – entailed by that obligatory freedom.

Chapter 3

The *topos* of encounter

Entering into being-there, its instant and its place: how does this occur in Greek Tragedy?
(Martin Heidegger, *Gesamtausgabe 65*)

Reiner Schurmann notes that even after his so-called turning, Being as time remains 'in a way' the ultimate condition of phenomenal presencing for Heidegger.[1] But if Being is to be thought as time, time cannot be listed in the archive of names given to the first thing, more originary than which nothing can be thought, which provides that simple and determining principial referent (*arche*) back to which everything that is can be securely referred or gathered. Time, as Heidegger thinks it, is not like that. His time is an originally discordant time of the rivenness of the 'there' and the 'not-there' whose very disjection effects a jointure without which one could not even talk of the ontological difference. Manifesting time is always already, therefore, 'out of joint'. For human beings (the there of Being), the experience of this condition is the experience of ek-sistence (standing-out) as *their* existence; one which they are warranted by their mortal share of time continuously to assume for themselves. That existence is one, also, in which this condition and its uncanniness is encountered as a demitted call of Justice to give things their due, the 'overdose' of which commits us to continual discord about the law.[2] ('The time is out of joint. O! cursed spite that ever I was born to set it right'.) 'The experience of beings in their Being which here comes to language', Heidegger says, 'is neither pessimistic nor nihilistic, nor is it optimistic. It is tragic.' And, more particularly,

> we discover a trace of the essence of tragedy, not when we explain it psycho-logically or aesthetically, but rather only when we consider its essential form, the Being of beings, by thinking the *didonai diken . . . tes adikias*.[3]

That is to say, when thinking the giving of Justice.

I want to leave the question of Justice open at this point because its very openness is the point. Nonetheless, in his reading of the Greek word which is usually translated as 'justice' or 'order' (*dike*) in 'The Anaximander Fragment' and through a further discussion of it in his Parmenides lectures, convoluted and difficult as these readings are, Heidegger is clearly also arguing that there is an 'order' to the demission of time, and that it is possible to transgress that order just as it is possible to comport oneself properly in respect of it. What he does not do in either case is very much elucidate how; albeit clearly accepting the movement of time and the finitude of existence is fundamental. Beyond that I find his path of thought still rough and overgrown. More of this shortly.

This call of Justice recalls that of Levinas. There is a similarity and there is, of course, a significant difference. The similarity is that each issues from the excess or superfluity of Being, and each sees it as a demission from out of which a commission arises which may or may not be assumed. Even when assumed it remains an endless project rather than a discrete enterprise.[4] The difference lies in the way in which Levinas conducts his *Auseinandersetzung* against Heidegger's account of metaphysics by continuously dilating the question of what I call Justice (and he calls Law) and the Other, as well as subverting the question of Being (as it arises largely in *Being and Time*) in order to displace it in favour of that of the Ethical.

This is not a legislated nor a legislating time, therefore, but a time whose very demission issues in a commission to legislate. The law is thus not given but has to be engendered. Law, continuously called for and called forth, is destined continuously also to be transgressed, precisely because there is no resolution of the demission of fracturing time whose simultaneous there and not-there of Being is the open domain in which human being stands out in its obligatory freedom, and must continuously take a stand. For, once effected, the law is immediately transgressed and called forth anew in the futural projecting which simply is human being. There is therefore no end to the law, for human being is the articulated articulating juncture – encounter as instant and place; place as instant and encounter; instant as place and encounter – with a demission whose very *for(e)going* effects both the futurality and the freedom, as well as the insatiability, of the commission to give things their due. Always already exceeded by the commission of the call of the very demission of Justice, the law is destined continuously to be exceeded in picking-up the tab of that demission (its remit) as commission; a commission which entails adopting a certain fundamental composure within and towards the Being of beings.[5]

Consequently, with the turn, Heidegger pursues the retrieval of the question of Being under the aegis of an invocation – that which heads this chapter – somewhat different from the Platonic one with which he launched *Being and Time*. This epigraph invokes the tragic – 'its instant and its place' – and the pursuit of *the* question is opened-up further to the insight which Attic tragedy had into the ways in which human being suffers 'a condition that is originary without being simple'.[6] Mortal natality's natal mortality warranted to live the difference of tragic differing is not mandated to resolve it, nor merely to bear it, but ever more fully to disclose it in the preservation and cultivation of itself as the possibility in the actuality, of itself and the world, into which it always already finds itself thrown. Towards the end of his Parmenides lectures, Heidegger speaks of this in terms of a 'security' project, radically unlike those of metaphysics, committed to preserving the freedom of human being in which it and other beings stand-out.

Within the tradition of the 'West', Being as the simple 'one' results in a politics which finds its ultimate determination as a time, a project, a subject and a law which is continuously driven to command – or at least to hold-out the promise of the guarantee of – the securing of the succession of permanent presence, if it is to be true both to the truth and to the subject which it conceives to be true in its conception of the truth. Being as discordant time obliges us to think the political in a different way with a canny eye to the uncanny character of the obligatory freedom which gives rise to it. In what way, is the problematic of this chapter. But that way is already indicated by the shift towards the tragic, towards the instant and towards the place. Indeed, towards the instant and the place (of being-there) as the occasion or *encounter* of obligatory freedom whose essentially tragic *topos* is what the chapter explores as the site of the political itself. Which 'origin', in turn, requires us to find our feet and compose ourselves within the topos of encounter through an agonal politics that is continuously taking the measure of it; and, more often than not, it measures its length in trying to do so. That political topos of encounter is later explored in terms of its defining agonal, pivotal, and public and chiasmic, features.

Levinas, too, recognises the tragic in his contest with Heidegger:

Who or what is does not come into communication with its existence by virtue of a decision taken prior to the drama, before the curtain rises: it takes up this existence by existing already.[7]

And notes its place:

The fear of Nothingness is but the measure of our involvement in Being. Existence of itself harbours something tragic which is not only there because of its finitude. Something that death cannot resolve.[8]

How one is, may reveal the nature of the tragedy for Levinas, because certain conditions (moods?) disclose not limits but limitlessness. 'We can', he says 'be more or less close to this limit situation'.[9] So it is, for example, with indolence: 'The tragedy of being it reveals is then the more profound. It is a being fatigued by the future'.[10] 'In the tension and fatigue of beginning', he elaborates 'one feels the cold sweat of the irremissibility of existence. The being that is taken up as a burden.'[11] Consequently:

here what is called the tragic in being is grasped in its very origin. It is not simply the sum of misfortunes and deceptions which await us and occur to us in the course of our existence because it is finite. It is, on the contrary, the infinity of existence that is consumed in an instant, the fatality in which its freedom is congealed as in a winter landscape where frozen beings are captives of themselves.[12]

This tragedy is intimately bound-up also with the paradox of obligatory freedom:

The freedom of the present finds a limit in the responsibility for which it is the condition. This is the most profound paradox in the concept of freedom; its synthetic bond with its own negation. A free being alone is responsible, that is already not free. A being capable of beginning in the present is alone encumbered with itself. . . .

The tragic does not come from a conflict between freedom and destiny, but from the turning of freedom into destiny, from responsibility.[13]

For Levinas, however, what is tragic is simply *that* one is. For simply that one is means that one necessarily limits the limitlessness of the responsibility which is incumbent upon one's being at all, because one is necessarily singularised by being and to that extent cannot ever totally substitute for the other in the way in which he thinks Justice requires, so he is driven to deny us any of tragedy's undeniably hard – and political – comforts. Only a radical passivity can possibly begin justly to expose us to the limitlessness of responsibility which being at all demits to us.

Here, alternatively, the tragic is not simply located in the terrible radically unjust fact of human facticity, egoism and singularity, but in the equivocal liminality and (in)finiteness of it, where the call of Justice allows injustice and justice their political possibility to be. Whereas, then, I will argue, attuned to its freedom tragedy affirms and defends the tragic condition by disclosing the necessity and liminality of limits, Levinas concedes limits only in order to extol the limitlessness (of responsibility) rather than explore the (politically burdensome) continuous unfolding of limits, without which there could in any event be no sense of the limitless, with which tragedy engages. *Job* rather than *Oedipus* therefore becomes Levinas' anti-tragic tragic anti-hero, as he elevates the command of Law above the aporetic political challenge of freedom. The tragic says take-on the liminality of limits, Levinas says accept the dissolution of all limits. The one is a political, the other is a prophetic voice. Siding with the ethical insurrection that pervades Being, Levinas, in the way that he chooses to become its voice, however, amplifies and intensifies its call by denying the ethical valency and purchase which is integral to the political project of the tragic.

This disjected discordant time of Being and being through which human being is freed by birth into no escape from death is an (un)bounded time comprised simultaneously of the centripetal and centrifugal forces of gathering and dissemination, of being thrown into the world and yet also of projecting in, upon and through the gathering of a world to effect order and form. A tragic denial, of monumental violence, is therefore required if the univocal law and unilinear politics of a unifocal sense of Being are to be instituted to effect their *telos* of mastery through an end to the conflict, with which they are endowed by the demission of the discordant time in which they arise, that the law and the political necessarily harbour within themselves.

Whereas tragic denial is wilful blindness to this conflict, 'to go through life with one's eyes open' means 'to see tragic denial shape the entire morphological scope of the law'.[14] To go through life with one's eyes open requires a commitment, also, however, to explore the tragic topos of the encounter that human being has in its own being of obligatory freedom with the uncanniness of Being as such, and the demitted call of Justice which resounds throughout it. Such is the special place of the political that political thought has to think: 'it is more salutary for thinking to wander in estrangement than to establish itself in the comprehensible'.[15] It is a matter for it, then, of remaining faithful to phenomena as they constantly and continuously display this occulting phenomenalising manifested through a temporal being freed by birth into no escape from death, continuously challenged to accord Justice to that condition in the living of it, distinguished by always already knowing beforehand the not-there in the there of its very own there-being. It is precisely here also that the uncanny question of Otherness arises, because:

> From the singularity of being follows the singularity of Not belonging to it, and consequently the singularity of the other. The one *and* the other are binding.[16]

Yes and No, in short, are equi-primordial, co-originary. Yes, there is manifestation and, No, there is . . . what? Something absolutely crucial arises now because the 'No' here is no simple no, no mere symmetrical dialectical negation of the – 'No, there is no manifestation' – capable of realising some final synthesis. Rather, it is the 'No' of – *'No there is no manifestation of manifestation'* – in which the superfluity of the very absence of manifestation, its retraction or withdrawal as Heidegger calls it, is what makes way for beings to have their very possibility to be at all. Withdrawal it has to be, then, if the overdose of manifesting is to be liminal rather than terminal. For if we were always already in receipt of the full dose, let alone overdosed, what would there be left for us to have and to be, to do and to see? If our standing was already commanded or guaranteed – rather than given to be assumed – why should we have to stand at all? Underway through time's making way – the taking place of Being – human being has to find its own way of way-making consonant with the uncanny challenge to be of its specific and concrete, historical passage in truth.

Born to die we always already pre-hend this No in every Yes – this Not-being in anything and everything – by virtue of our very own mortal existing. For we die. Just as visibility never becomes visible, manifestation never becomes manifest. And yet we are manifest because we dwell in manifestation. There has, therefore, to be visibility for things to appear, manifesting for things to stand-out, which is not itself a thing. This is what Heidegger means when he says that Being is No-thing. This is what he means when he talks of the withdrawal or the retraction of Being. There has similarly to be Being for beings to be, but Being is never manifested as such, for that would be the final trip.

Co-originary, the No and the Yes of the Being of being which we experience in and as our existence – our own standing-out in Being, in which the hiddenness of Being takes place, stands-out, in its hiddenness through its questioning by us – are not, however, co-equal. Equiprimordial but without equipoise, there is a radical asymmetry in which the No outweighs the Yes. For, remember, the No – or to be precise, the Not – is no simple negation. Recall how Heidegger insists upon it as superfluity, as the possible that always already stands higher than the actual, as that the essence of which is 'to come'; which, like death is for us, dis-locates, dispossesses, individualises and singularises. For born free there is no way out, either, of our mortality and no one can suffer anyone else's death. Only I can die my death. Knowing that singularises me, removes me from the world and deprives me of any certain meaning other than that of the opaque mystery of not being. And whereas this has often been taken to be either a mystical and mystifying anthropology or, worse still, another account of atomistic individuality, it is of course neither. For this singular being singularised by its birthing-towards-death (its mortal natality and natal mortality) is nonetheless also, it has to be recalled, a being-in-the-world and a being-with-others in unassimilable Otherness. However much the paths of Heidegger's thought may wind through singularisation, world, the other, the four-fold and the very uncanniness which being there at all brings to light, there is no remit for forgetting that it is this composite uncanny phenomenolising – in which human beings share an integral and, as far as we know distinctively responsible, share – which is at issue.

Here, then, in this obligatory freedom we have the opportunity not only to give things their due, but also to give manifesting itself its due. There would be no Justice, however, in granting these only what their manifest actuality appears to need. Hence the excess of the appearance of inapparent Justice once more. For, in as much as possibility is always already manifest in and higher than that actuality, Justice requires giving more to the Being of beings than their mere actuality requires, because the Being of beings – most especially our own – is not simply encountered in its actuality but more fully in the possibility which that actuality continuously, and inevitably, discloses. Hear Lear's primordial cry: ' O! reason not the need'. The (d)emitted call of Justice is generous without measure because it issues from, and continuously turns us towards, the excess of possibility to which our being attests consequent upon the possibility of not being. One cannot begin to give things their due, therefore, without first extending this original grant of generosity to them; which is to say, without granting the very measure that they are owed what is due to them. And in as much as the possibility in and of their actuality is higher than their actuality, that measure is addressed to their possibility rather than their actuality. Hence, one might say, the first 'law', or precept, of this Justice is the inviolable law of the possible. One might even add that one cannot begin to be without the extension of that generous 'law' to oneself.

One has consequently always to give things more than their due if one is to do Justice to them.[17] Freed into no escape from death we are nonetheless also free, however, to deny demission's commission and are prone ordinarily to do so. Such is the common anti-political fallenness which technology has made its own, in its own specific enterprisingly narcotic way, from which the political has to be recovered in our age.

The radical hermeneutical phenomenology which issues from Heidegger's thinking and questioning shows how we understand as we do because we exist as we do. Understanding as we do in the way that we exist, we came, in the tradition of the 'West', to think metaphysically. Metaphysics asked about the truth of Being, of what is, but answered with an account of the truth of the Being of beings, that is to say of things we find present to hand. Truth was therefore thought to be lodged in the truthfulness of the assertion about the Being of beings. In the absence of God it came to be founded in the subject making the assertion. The result was the dominance of the representative–calculative thought of modern subjectivity in which truth is a measure of the adequation of the correspondence between the thinking subject's assertions and entities themselves. (Such that: 'For representational thinking everything comes to be a being'.[18] Even Being.) Hence, the absolute centrality of the subject in the modern age. For a flakey subject – riven with Otherness and bearing difference within itself – becomes an absolute abhorrence to truth itself when truth and knowledge demand a secure and reliable subject for their certain foundation: 'But not every way of being a self is subjectivity'.[19]

Heidegger's entire corpus of thinking is tenaciously devoted to uncovering metaphysics' missed ontology not only in the various projects ('ontology', epistemology, phenomenology) – and the core concept (correctness), method (logic) and epistemological ambition (theory, or the report of the sight of the truth) – of Western thought, but also in the very life of the 'West' itself (technicity). Show Heidegger a thinker, a thought, a practice or a way of life and he will go after the ontology – ontic (metaphysical) as well as fundamental – sequestered there. In this respect, his lecture course, *Basic Questions of Philosophy. Selected 'Problems' of 'Logic'*, is a virtual text book on the way he habitually proceeds.[20] In every epistemology, too, there is an ontology. Because we are as we understand and think, in our modern political practices as well as in our 'political science' – or knowledge of politics where a well-founded modesty about scientific pretensions is expressed – there therefore lurks the ontology of metaphysics. Heidegger's deconstruction of metaphysics consequently leads to the following chain of thought, in which we must also never lose sight of the mutually disclosive two-fold duality of Being and beings.

Thrown, we exist. Existing, we project and understand. Existing, understanding and projecting as thrown we are obliged to think.[21] Thinking we think Being. Thinking Being, we have not only come to think ('ontologically') the Being of beings, but also the Being of Being as an, albeit Supreme, being ('onto-theology'). Thrown into existing as understanding and thinking we inhabit worlds. The world we inhabit expresses the ways in which we have come to understand and think. The end of the way that we think – metaphysics – is technology. Technology is the mounting oblivion of the aletheic truth of the Being of human being, and the radical impoverishment of human being's capacity to create and live in a world, a condition globalised by the ballistic power of technology's trajectory. *We, therefore, think the political in the way that we do because of the way that we think*. Thinking the political in the way that we do because of the way that we think, the political too has become technologised such that politics threatens to become identical with technicity. The political problematic of the modern age, as

Heidegger might have expressed it, is the globalisation of technology as politics and the globalisation of politics as technology.

Thinking differently, Heidegger necessarily, therefore, came to think the political differently as well. Specifically, when he came to think differently about the political he inevitably did so through the different thought of the truth of Being, and the Being of truth, to which his entire deconstructive mode of thought was devoted. That different thought of truth was primarily expressed and explored through his rethinking of the Greek word for truth, *aletheia*, where truth is the truth of disclosure in which revealing and concealing are simultaneously involved. We cannot think with and against Heidegger's thought of the political therefore without appreciating how the political arises for him through the aletheic character of truth. Truth and politics are as intimately related for Heidegger, therefore, as ever they are in modern thought.

Thinking truth differently, Heidegger necessarily thought 'origins' differently because of the belonging together of truth and origins. Thinking truth and origins differently – as 'the free', or 'the open', of aletheic truth: 'the freedom that first releases even space–time as an "open" extension and spread'[22] – he also thought the way of being human differently or, rather, the human way of being as such differently. Truth, origins and ways thought differently meant the existence and practices of those born into this freedom thought differently as well. 'The "free of" and the "free for",' he notes of traditional accounts of freedom based upon the will, 'already require a clearing in which a detachment and a donation constitute a more original freedom that cannot be grounded on the freedom of human comportment'.[23] Given the sum of these things, he necessarily thought the origins, truth, existence and practices of politics differently also. In sum, in as much as Heidegger's truth is such a radically different, antecedent, truth, so also the relationship between truth and the political – hence the truth of the political as such – arises differently for Heidegger. Human being is political, then, not because it has politics, much less power politics. *Human being has politics because it simply is political in the freedom of aletheic truth*: that is, it is the bearer of an uncanny, agonal and obligatory freedom, where the struggle to be is a continuous questioning of the questionability of what it is to be human that takes the form of a challenge to grant this existence its due in the worlds in which it realises its integral being-with. Much of its politics, especially its modern politics, is in fact designed to displace the essence of the political and the political essence of human being.[24] The possibility of politics is, therefore, conditional on the existence of an entity for which not only its own being, but also Being as such, is an issue. This entity is the site of an absence or lack which is privative in that there is no determination, and yet also abundant in that there is the uncanniness of a radical excess. Such an entity has to be a site of, or, better to say – because of its temporal character – an encounter with, freedom. Should it seek to end questioning and the inescapably conditional character of its freedom by refusing its responsibility for it, it not only fails to be political, it threatens its own destruction.

Neither can we appreciate how Heidegger thinks the political – follow the trajectory of that thought, or seek to affect its trajectory by entering disruptively into the thought of truth, origins, freedom, Justice, existence and practices from which it derived its motive force – however, without equally appreciating the way in which he thinks how aletheic truth comes to pass. For, if the political is intimately related to the truth of Being – which he first tried to think through *aletheia* – we have to understand how he thinks the disclosive truth of Being is most disclosed. The answer he gave to this puzzle was simple. It was the 'simple' compound of Language itself. Not Language thought in the technologised and instrumentalised ways of modern thought, of course, but in the very disclosive, Orphic and Hermetic, character of Language itself as the giving of the word as such, the *highest* expression of which was art – because art seeks to disclose the disclosing – and poetry in particular.

Here, Heidegger is often charged with contributing to the aestheticising of politics. The charge misses the point on a number of counts. First, art, as he understands it, is not that regional ontology of metaphysical thought, called aesthetics, concerned with the beautiful.[25] It is, instead, the practice whereby the disclosive truth of Being – that making way whose wake allows other ways to be – does not simply find some private or individual expression but is capable of giving form to the belonging together of human beings – their being-with, about which more later – by drawing them together as a 'people'. A 'people' for Heidegger would not – could not – exist antecedent to the practices which constituted it. It would be a 'people' – rather, I suppose Foucault might say, than a population – in virtue of the practice of disclosure around which it revolved. This is what he meant when he said that great art, or poetry, is capable of opening-up an 'historical' world and of founding a 'people'. 'We know from Heraclitus and Parmenides', he observed in *An Introduction To Metaphysics*, 'that the unconcealment of being is not simply given'. He continued:

> Unconcealment occurs only when it is achieved by work: the work of the word in poetry, the work of stone in temple and statue, the work of the word in thought, the work of the *polis* as the historical place in which all this is grounded and preserved. . . . work is to be taken here in the *Greek* sense of *ergon*, the creation that discloses the truth of something that is present. The struggle for the unconcealment of the essent and hence for [B]eing itself in the work, this struggle for unconcealment, which even in itself is continuous conflict, is at the same time a combat against concealment, disguise, false appearance.[26]

Art, as the disclosing of disclosure, tragic art was once the political art which became the pivot around which, drawn together by it, the life of a certain 'people' – the ancient 'Greeks' – revolved.

In being gathered together a 'people' is not fixed. Neither is the fixing itself. The ensemble, of pivot/people, is simultaneously also disseminated, committed to composingly recomposing itself, within and to the aletheic truth of time. Hence, its historicality. For a pivot, the mobile fulcrum of motility – that space which is the real and empty place of politics and power – is the focal point of centripetal and centrifugal forces.[27] A tie, it also effects turning, torsioning and recoil on and through the pivot itself, as pivot and people describe their historical passage in the disclosure of (aletheic) truth.

Here, of course, in seeking not just to elaborate this thought but in making a political intervention in order to help to realise it, Heidegger effected his own downfall. Perhaps – an audacious thought but one that is nonetheless possible – he did not understand this thought well enough. Making his intervention through terms which were deliberately designed to resonate with those of the Fascists in order to get some purchase in and on the Movement, and thereby betraying his own thought, he also betrayed a personal comportment which seems to have been deficient in precisely those areas which Levinas' philosophy was counter-designed to amplify and extol: namely a defining mood of in-justice and responsibility for the other. In political terms, too, I would argue, it was deficient in respect of that which his own philosophy had dramatically staged and celebrated, namely the resolute responsibility of composure required of the struggle of obligatory human freedom itself.

Second, tragic art is not that thing which Walter Benjamin called, and devastatingly explored as, *Trauerspiele*.[28] *Trauerspiele*, I suggest, is what became of the tragic sensibility in the destitution of the 'West' and its intensifyingly baroque politics of political realism. Third, the poetry Heidegger extols, for example that of Hölderlin, is not tragic art either. He values it precisely because in the age of modern technicity – where all beings including human being are calculatively assembled as mere raw material for ordering consumption and consumptive ordering – such belonging together is barely thinkable let alone possible. That poetry is the poetry, therefore, of destitute times, valued because he thinks that it is there that the light of disclosure is reticently tended and barely kept winking; there, also, that the prospect of another epiphany (of ethos) is kept open.

Being, that making way whose wake allows other ways to be, in the wake of its way opens-up the tragic temporal space of beings. Or, rather, the wake of Being opens-up the tragic temporal space only if there is simultaneously always already an occasion through and at which its wake is actually encountered. In short, it is only ever manifest as a specific taking place. No wake without the watch that bears witness. That occasion or location, that located occasion, the temporal space of this encounter, is the there of Being. And the there of Being is Heidegger's rigorously non-subjectivised way of talking about human being: 'Man is the sight of openness, the there'.[29]

Hence, despite the way Heidegger's ways deferred to Being, especially in his later thought, the insistence on the mutually disclosive need of *Sein* and *Dasein*. As Levinas also noted: 'The relation between beings and Being does not link up two independent terms'.[30] 'Being, the "it is" of a being', Heidegger emphasises 'is never autochthonous in beings, as if Being could be extracted from beings and then stood upon them as on its ground'.

It is only beings in relation to beings that are autochthonous. Being, the never autochthonous, is the groundless. This seems to be a lack, though only if calculated in terms of beings, and it appears as an abyss in which we founder without support in our relentless pursuit of beings. In fact we surely fall into the abyss, we find no ground, as long as we know and seek a ground only in the form of a being and hence never carry out the leap into Being or leave the familiar landscape of the oblivion of Being.[31]

In short, the encounter with the wake of Being is human being. In short, too, if Being is to make way differently, as Heidegger in his soteriological moment thinks it must and may, nonetheless only in human being's looking-out for its wake would that different way-making also materialise. The saving turn that Heidegger speaks of, if we are to remain consistent with the way in which he thinks the ineradicable, indissociable, mutually disclosive belonging together of *Sein* and *Dasein*, could not be a simple grant of Being as if (the metaphysical error) Being was an entity – a *deus ex machina*.[32] It would have to be a new epoch of disclosure in which this mutually disclosive play is to be played-out differently somehow (*the* political problem of the modern age if human being is to out-live the modern), through the way in which human being itself, perforce questioning its questionability, aligns itself differently with the Being of its being. Hence, Heidegger thought thinking and poetry had a special role to play in listening-out for such a turn.[33]

The political, like anything else therefore, arises out of the aletheic truth of Being for Heidegger. The very occasion or encounter of this disclosive truth is human being. The everyday condition of human being is, however, one which has ordinarily fallen-in with a preoccupation with all those things which, being ready to hand for its projects and its projecting, comprise the referential matrix of its world. This fallenness elides the uncanny truth of its being. It is in a sense also a relief from it. Nonetheless, in facing its death, human being can recover a proper sense of its way of being as a being-with – its obligatory freedom as a responsive possibility with other beings in the unassimilable superfluity of the uncanny Otherness of the truth of Being – and seek in turn to give this giving, of which the essence of its own being is such an integral responsive and responsible part, its due. Art, for Heidegger, has such a special place because – in seeking to disclose this disclosing or, rather, being that 'technique' capable of disclosing this special (empty) place by contriving an ethos, and even part of an institutional order, for it – art attunes human being more essentially to the (aletheic) truth of its being. It may even become the pivot for that being-with of human belonging together which constitutes the tragic temporal space of disclosure; pivotal to its more essential disclosedness. It follows, therefore, that the political for Heidegger must come to pass in this way also, so that the art of political life – the *polos* of the *polis*, as he would explore it further in his Parmenides lectures – is the attunement of the being-with of human beings to the aletheic truth of the Being of their being. Thus it is that there is an intimate relation between art and politics for Heidegger.

Further substantial reflections on that relationship came, after *An Introduction To Metaphysics*, in the lecture courses Heidegger gave in the 1940s on Hölderlin. In the immediately following lectures on Parmenides he also addressed himself in similar vein, but more intensely and directly, to Plato's *mythos* of the *polis* via an extended account of the character of truth and untruth and its transformation from the Greek via the Roman and Medieval worlds to the Modern.

These lectures are critical to understanding both how, through Heidegger, we can think of the ways in which the question of the political in the modern age has come to be posed in the ways that it has, and how, posed and understood differently by the Greeks, it might be understood differently again. The point has to be made, once more, that what is entailed here is no nostalgia for the Greeks and no spurious desire to return to the Greek *polis*. That would be plain silly. And whatever else Heidegger was, he was not stupid. What is at issue is a profound interrogation of the tradition out of which politics has come to be understood, in order to fuel fundamental reinterpretation of it to meet the necessities of an age threatened by the very character of its politics. That project may, in turn, release what Peg Birmingham goes so far as to call 'an emancipatory notion of political action'.[34] What emerges from this interrogation, amongst other things, is the indissociable and determining relationship that obtains between truth and politics. So that is where we must focus our attention.

THE TRANSFORMATION OF THE ESSENCE OF TRUTH AND THE TRANSFORMATION OF THE ESSENCE OF THE POLITICAL

If we think the political in the way that we do because of the way that we think, the way that we think truth is most decisive for the way in which we think the political because the way that we think truth, for Heidegger, determines our being. More than that. Because we are not dealing with a unifocal concept of truth, here, but with a complex bi-focal belonging together of both truth and untruth, in which the issues of freedom and Justice also arise, it is the way in which we think that complex which matters most. For the way in which we think truth and untruth stages the entire problematic not only of politics but also of law and freedom.

Heidegger's entire life's work was devoted to exploring what he thought of as a transformation in the essence of truth in the tradition of the 'West'. Indeed, the extent to which one can talk about 'the tradition' or 'the West' depends upon this story about truth, its emergence in the Greek world and its transformation through the Roman and Medieval worlds into the Modern. The point about the transformation of the essence of truth is that it is a story about the transformation of the essence of politics, law and freedom as well, because of the ways in which these all depend upon how truth is disclosed, what truth is understood to be and how such a disclosive understanding pervades and grounds a way of life or a world. A transformation in the essence of truth necessarily, therefore, also entails a transformation in the essence of politics, and it is this story which Heidegger recounts in an extraordinarily dense fashion in the Parmenides lectures. That is the only place in which he connects-up the transformation in the essence of truth to the transformation in the essence of politics in any extended way. Even then, the argument is cryptic and undeveloped. But the conclusion to which it points is, nonetheless, very clear. Whereas the Greek *polis* is founded on, or grounded in the understanding of truth as *aletheia*, the transformation in the essence of truth means that politics is no longer determined upon the basis of *aletheia* but on the understanding of truth as certainty and correctness. It is there also, therefore, that he demonstrates how the transformation in the essence of truth is intimately connected with security. For, in addition to arguing that the essence of truth as disclosure first becomes lost, and then transformed through its Latinisation, so also he argues further that:

> The inception of the metaphysics of the modern age rests on the transformation of the essence of *veritas* into *certitudo*. The question of truth becomes the question of the secure, assured and self-assuring use of *ratio*.[35]

This story needs briefly to be repeated because it prepares the way for further advancing the sketch of how politics, law and freedom might be thought differently; less as a security project and more as, in terms I used earlier, a tragic topos of encounter.

As I repeat the story, however, my sympathies are with those, like Derrida, Caputo and Bernasconi amongst others, who would treat it as an account of the structure of the demission of time, and of the uncanniness of the ontological difference of Being and beings, rather than a *mythos* of the 'West'; a *mythos*, too, in which, to nail the supposed nostalgia for the Greeks once and for all,

> 'Greek' does not designate a particular people or nation, nor a cultural or anthropological group. What is Greek is the dawn of that destiny in which Being illuminates itself in beings and so propounds a certain essence of man.[36]

It is as if, in this his recounting of the tale of the history of Being, Heidegger was a kind of philosophical dramatist who came to believe in the tragedy he had written; forgetting that the story line is merely a vehicle for disclosing something about the very topos of tragic life itself. As I will repeat later, following his own argument about the political, there is tragedy only because there is the tragic. Ultimately, it is not the story that counts but the tragic way of being which transcends the story and gives rise to it. To put it another way, just as one does not have to believe in the story of *Oedipus Rex* in order to appreciate the point it is making about the tragic topos of encounter of a being that knows not from whence it came or where it is headed, one does not have to believe in Heidegger's tragedy of the history of Being in order to appreciate aletheic truth and understand how, standing-out in aletheic truth, existence is a tragic topos of encounter. Similarly, one does not have to believe all he has to say about the historical transformation of truth in order to appreciate the profound political and ethical differences which obtain between truth understood as equivocal disclosure and truth understood as command.

'The political, which as *politikon* arose formerly out of the essence of the Greek *polis*', Heidegger observes, 'has come to be understood in the Roman way'. Consequently:

> Since the time of the Imperium, the Greek word 'political' has meant something Roman. What is Greek about it is now only its sound.[37]

Whereas the Latinisation of truth transformed the essence of truth into certainty and security, the Latinisation of the political correspondingly transformed the essence of the political from – in my terms – obligatory freedom's tragic topos of encounter, into – his terms – an imperial project of dominion and domination.

'The imperial', he elaborates in a way which anticipates and, therefore, irresistibly and powerfully recalls Foucault's notion of the disciplinary power–knowledge of modern reason, 'springs forth from the essence of truth as correctness in the sense of the directive self-adjusting guarantee of the security of domination'.[38] Thus, and in a way that further and equally powerfully recalls the politics of Hobbes' *Leviathan*:

> The 'taking as true' of *ratio*, of *reor*, becomes a far reaching and anticipatory security. *Ratio* becomes counting, calculating, calculus. *Ratio* is the self-adjustment to what is correct.[39]

It is that, too, which subsequently becomes technology or the essence of technicity which he believes dominates the politics of the modern age as much as its understanding of truth. Because of their fundamental importance, a little further elaboration of these points is required.

What happens, according to Heidegger, is that just as politics is imperialised as rule and dominion – in effect translating the *ethos* of the political which is obligatory freedom into the *ethos* of command which is rule – so also the 'Justice', or what he later in the Parmenides lectures calls the 'ordering', of the Greek *dike* is similarly imperialised by being translated into the justice of the Roman *iustitia*, the 'to-be-in-the-right' and 'to have a right' bestowed by the imperial ordering effected by command: 'Accordingly, *iustitia* has a wholly different ground of essence than that of *dike* which arises from that of *aletheia*'.[40]

'*Imperium*', he says, 'is the command in the sense of commandment'.[41] Furthermore:

> *Imperium* says *im-parare*, to establish, to make arrangements: *prae-cipere*, to occupy something in advance, and by this occupation to hold command over it, and so to have the occupied as territory. . . . The Roman law, *ius – iubeo* – is rooted in the same essential domain of the imperial command, and obedience. Command is the ground of the essence of domination: which is why a clearer and more proper translation of *imperium* is 'high command'.[42]

It is also the territory founded and occupied in advance on the basis of this command. Command and dominion founds a certain kind of order of rule such that:

the dominated are not kept down, nor simply despised, but, rather, . . . they themselves are permitted, within the territory of the command, to offer their services for the continuation of the domination.[43]

The operating force in the establishment of this *imperium* is not simply that of the *imperium* of the Roman State but also that of the Church, the *sacerdotium*. And the reason for this is that the imperial is not the basis for the transformation of the essence of truth from *aletheia* into the Latin *veritas* – the propagation and teaching of whose essence was the domain of the Church. Rather, the imperial is a consequence of the transformation of the essence of truth from that which issues as equivocal dis-closure into that which is issued as irrefragable command.[44] One outcome, others have noted, was the early politics of security of the redeeming politics of the Christian world's *ecumene* of belief in such a truth.[45]

'The not-false, said in Roman fashion', Heidegger goes on, 'is *verum*', and Christian faith is proclaimed in its totality as 'the' *veritas*, 'the' *verum*, 'the true'. It is in this transformation in the essence of the true that takes place with its translation into *veritas* that the idea of command or *imperium* originally resides. For the stem *ver* means 'to remain above, to maintain oneself, to keep one's head up, to be the head, to command'. In sum:

> *Verum* is the remaining constant, the upright, that which is directed to what is superior because it is directing from above. *Verum* is *rectum* (*regere*, 'the regime'), the right, *iustum*. . . . 'being-above', directive for what is right: *veritas* is then *rectitudo*, 'correctness' we would say.[46]

Correctness is to take the irrefragable as irrefragable, accept it as such and adjust oneself to it. To take something as something is in Latin *reor*, the corresponding noun of which is *ratio*. Consequently: 'The essence of truth as *veritas* and *rectitudo* passes over into the *ratio* of man'. Disclosure, then:

> is transformed into the calculating self-adjustment of *ratio*. This determines for the future, as a consequence of a new transformation in the essence of truth, the technological character of modern . . . technology.[47]

He ends this condensed account of the declension of truth in the following way:

> In order to attain the true as what is right and correct, man must be assured and be certain of the correct use of his basic power. The essence of truth is determined on the basis of this assurance and certitude. The true becomes the assured and certain. The *verum* becomes the *certum*. The question of truth becomes whether and how man can be assured about the being he himself is as well as about the beings he himself is not. . . .
>
> The question of 'the correct use' treats of the will to secure the certainty which man, on his own, standing amidst beings, must attain and wishes to attain. . . . The true, *verum*, is what is right, what vouches for certainty, and in that sense it is the righteous, the just.[48]

'Correct use', powerfully recalls the way in which Language thus becomes presented in early modern political theory as, to quote Hobbes, the means of right reckoning, and why Locke amongst very many others evinces such a violent drive to strip Language of all metaphor and excess so that it is fit to act as the unambiguous calculus of reason. Freedom here is not the antecedent obligatory freedom of human being to be, but freedom within that order of command – to 'have a right' – in order to adjust oneself to its justice – 'to-be-in-the-right'. Peace is the order of that order. A further defining feature of modern politics also emerges now, however. For, if the true is that which, on various grounds self-asserting, is derived from above, a need to identify that highest point is necessarily inspired. As Heidegger notes, 'the "above", the "highest", and the "lord" of lordship may appear in different forms'.[49] That lord may be 'God', 'Reason', 'World-Spirit', or 'Will to Power'; or, one might add, the State. The point simply is that there has to be a sovereign. No *imperium*, or *veritas/rectitudo* and *certum*, without a sovereign. No sovereign either, therefore, without the imperial world of *veritas/ rectitudo* and *certitudo*.[50] You cannot have one without the other. Better to say, in fact, that you would not have the one without the other. Hence, the defining problematic of the political becomes the need to secure the secure location of sovereignty, whatsoever sovereignty is associated with, and legitimise its claim to command truth; a command that is finally secured in the modern age via the security of calculability as such. Indeed, of course, there can then be no (imperial political) order without sovereignty. For every idea of order first requires this first principle or *arche* which issues or effects the command. Hence, *pace* the theorists of international society, modern subjectivised politics remains a domain of competing imperialisms, or sovereignties, which seems incapable of finding a way out of the fatal *cul de sac* effected by its very principle of formation. The strategic language of political realism, of *raison d'état*, balance of power and so on is simply modern political order thrashing about in ever more violent ways on the point of its own spear, consoling itself with the *hubris* of its belief in the saving power of the calculative competence which impaled it there in the first place.

Sovereignty's association with territory is an equally well-established one. Whereas, Heidegger maintains, earth was understood by the Greeks to be 'the in-between, namely between the concealment . . . and the luminosity, the disclosiveness',

> For the Romans, on the contrary, the earth, *tellus, terra* is . . . that upon which construction, settlement, and installation are possible . . . *Terra* becomes *territorium*, land of settlement as realm of command.[51]

But, association with territory is not a necessary condition of sovereignty. Ultimately, it relies on the necessity of having a point from which certitude can be derived.

What is also important in this story is that the nature of untruth changes *pari passu* with that of truth, such that what is to be warred against as untruth also changes:

In the transformation of the essence of truth from *aletheia*, by way of the Roman *veritas*, to the medieval *adequatio, rectitudo*, and *iustitia*, and from there to the modern *certitudo*, to truth as certainty, validity, and assurance, the essence and the character of the opposition between truth and untruth are also altered.[52]

The political significance of this is, first, that truth is thought to be stripped of all relation to the untruth and, second, that untruth is thought as the simple opposite of truth; namely, the false, where false is taken to be 'error in the sense of the incorrect use of the human power of affirmation and denial'.[53] Judgement therefore becomes 'determined in reference to what assures man's self-certainty'. The outcome is that:

> The intention toward certainty now determines for its part the direction, the kind of sight, and the selection of what is represented as that to which the judgements of affirmation and denial are imparted.[54]

There could be no more concise or telling summary of the prevailing modern view of the epistemological ambition, object, or purpose of political thought and analysis. Modern political thought is predominantly the politics of security of the politics of security. Thus its fatal complicity with the politics (of truth) of its times, and its consistent susceptibility to being trumped by the baroque politics of political realism.

THE CONFLICTUAL ESSENCE OF THE POLITICAL

The essence of the political – where essence for Heidegger it has to be remembered is not a substantive but a questionable way of being – arises out of the aletheic character of truth. I have already noted, therefore, that it cannot be understood without understanding both how Heidegger characterises aletheic truth and how he thinks that truth comes to presence, or comes to pass. Aletheic truth is the truth of dis-closure, the appearance of things from out of unconcealment in which nonetheless concealment itself, the Not-being of their being at all, is also evident and capable of being thought by thought and disclosed also by art.[55]

Because, traditionally, truth has been that which has been taken to be beyond all conflict, 'we do not understand to what extent the essence of truth itself is, in itself, a conflict'.[56] The essential character of this aletheic truth, for Heidegger, is therefore conflictual. That is to say, there is not simply conflict over truth, about truth or even for truth. Conflict is indigenous to the very essence of truth itself: 'The primordial essence of truth is conflictual'.[57]

In addition to that: 'What conflict means here remains a question'.[58] It means 'something other than mere quarrel and fight, other than blind discord, other than "war", and other than competition'.[59] The very agonal *polemos* of Being itself, this conflict is not neatly defined by being identified in this way. Rather, an ancient sense of primordial conflict associated with the struggle to be itself is invoked. That struggle is the very struggle of wresting something unconcealed – disclosed

– from the concealment – Not-being – that surrounds it and continues to permeate its being at all. Hence, for Heidegger:

> 'Truth' is never 'in itself' available by itself, but instead must be gained by struggle.[60]

It is 'in its very essence a conflict', something to be won through a kind of work, in a work worked into existence itself.

Remember also this truth is a tragic truth and as a tragic truth, it has also to be thought in conjunction with the demitted giving of Justice which bequeaths us a conflict over justice and injustice. If the aletheic truth of disclosure has to be won by being worked into the world of human beings, so also must the commission to be Just which arises from the demitted call of Justice of that truth. If truth in its essence is agonal, so also must the Justice which silently calls throughout it. If concealment continuously haunts the unconcealed in its very unconcealedness, so must Justice haunt the law in its very legality. If there is a struggle to bring disclosure to presence, so also must there be a struggle to bring Justice to presence. If the work of art is capable of disclosing the disclosure of truth in its essentially conflictual duality, so also the art of giving the law (politics) might be said to be capable of disclosing the call of Justice in its conflictual duality – apparent inappearence – as well. Which Justice is granting things their due by allowing beings their being to be as they are, in the possibility of their actuality and not just in their actuality. I might then usefully repeat myself and say, like truth, in its very essence a conflict, Justice is something to be won through a kind of work, in a work continuously being worked into existence itself. Moreover, its fugitive character persists because 'worked-in' means only that it is there to be worked at and in again. For remember that this is the hidden coming to presence as hidden. The work of art does not enclose the truth, it discloses the disclosing of the truth; does not freeze-frame it but lets it lie before us in its continuously creative – liminal – way. So also, I suggest, may the liminal art of giving things their due.

Now, it follows that if the political for Heidegger derives from and is intimately associated with the aletheic character of truth, the essence of the political will also display the fundamental agonism of truth.

> If now, however, as the word indicates, *aletheia* possesses a conflictual essence, which appears also in the oppositional forms of distortion and oblivion, then in the *polis* as the essential abode of man there has to hold sway all the most extreme counter-essences, and therein all excesses, to the unconcealed and to beings, i.e. counter-beings in the multiplicity of their counter-essences.[61]

Hence:

> the frightfulness, the horribleness, the atrociousness of the Greek *polis*. Such is the rise and the fall of man in his historical abode of essence – *upsipolis-apolis* – far exceeding abodes, homeless as Sophocles (*Antigone*) calls man. It is not by chance that man is spoken of in this way in Greek tragedy. For the possibility,

and the necessity, of 'tragedy' itself has its single source in the conflictual essence of *aletheia*.[62]

Here others and Otherness is always already on the inside, integral to political life, and not something which is thought to exist only on the outside against which the inside must be secured by extirpating the enemy – the radically other – within and without. No greater contrast could be found than, for example, with the Schmittian definition of the political. For Heidegger the political problematic arises out of the ineradicable constitutiveness of the other and of Otherness to politics *within* the *polis*. For Schmitt:

> The specific political distinction to which political actions and motives can be reduced is that between friend and enemy.[63]

The political enemy he elaborates,

> need not be morally evil or aesthetically ugly; he need not appear as an economic competitor, and it may even be advantageous to engage with him in business transactions. But he is, nevertheless, the other, the stranger; and it is sufficient for his nature that he is, in a specially intense way, existentially something different and alien, so that in the extreme case conflicts with him are possible.[64]

It is evident with Schmitt that it is not so much the scale of the threat of the other but its existential possibility that is so threatening; and precisely because of the way political community itself is conceived as an 'organised political entity, internally peaceful, territorially enclosed *and impenetrable to aliens*'[65] (my emphasis). In consequence the defining need of the political for Schmitt sets up a requirement to eliminate all 'unwanted perturbations or unwanted needs'.[66]

Similarly, whereas the traditional idea of truth has been taken to be that which is beyond all conflict, so the truth of politics has traditionally been to align politics with the secure and certain core of that truth; if not to achieve perpetual peace (perhaps Kantian as well as Christian), or an (Hegelian) end to history, then at least to secure a measure of tranquillity at home and a winning streak abroad against the egoistic war of all against all. Projects which, one way or another, must seek to move the ineradicable other and Otherness to the outside and keep it there; in order to secure the lasting order and certain truth they seek to install in their practices because, in fact, they assume it as their foundation; which is why so much of their practice, necessarily repeating the inaugural moment which they take to be their foundation, exposes the violence of it.

Such a war, incidentally, differs from the agonism of truth, Justice and politics I am talking about here, in as much as these refer to the struggle entailed in bringing things to presence whereas the war of all against all presupposes the very egos which, as it turns out, installing such a war as the inaugural moment of the State itself does bring to presence in the classic radically technologised form of modern subjectivised politics.[67] Remember also, the agonism of truth, Justice and the political is not a dialectical conflict either. For the Not is not the no but rather, as excess itself, exceeds the no of a dialectical relationship.

Consequently there is not simply conflict over politics, about politics or even for politics. The essence of the political is itself also conflictual. And conflictual in the polemical agonal way that distinguishes the conflict of aletheic truth. The *agon* in the agonal character of politics, therefore, derives from the *agon* in the agonism of aletheic truth itself. The political too has to be wrested from concealment in as much as it is also a disclosure, a way of being, which displays all the characteristic features of a work in the sense in which Heidegger referred to a work when talking about truth. That is why the political does not refer to the template of a political order waiting to be applied or, once implemented, finished and complete. Neither, then, is it that problematic/project of dominion which finds its most condensed expression in the word 'sovereignty'. It is itself, like human being itself, an obligatory free agonal project continuously projecting and challenged by Justice's inviolable law of the possible to give things their due. To repeat my repetition once more, the political is also something to be won through a kind of work, in a work continuously being worked into existence itself: at *one* time, in the art work of political life, which the Greeks called the *politeia* of the *polis*, disclosed by tragedy. Always already thrown and with a propensity to fall, this aletheic politics is always also a struggle towards the freeing of this freedom – towards continuously finding its feet. The political, in short a tragic project, was first disclosed as such to the tradition of the 'West' through the tragedy of the *polis*.

THE PIVOTAL ESSENCE OF THE POLITICAL

The truth that Heidegger is concerned with is the agonal truth of disclosure. The essence of the political is grounded in the essence of truth as agonal disclosure – even though the Greeks, he says, especially Aristotle and Plato, did not explicitly think through, as such, the understanding of truth as *aletheia* in which they lived and thought – and therefore the essence of the political, as the Greeks thought it, is grounded in this understanding of truth as well.[68] Thus 'the essence of the Greek *polis* is grounded in the essence of *aletheia*'. Further:

> the difference between the modern republic, the Roman *res publica*, and the Greek *polis* is as essential as that between the modern essence of truth, the Roman *rectitudo*, and the Greek *aletheia*.[69]

If politics is to do with *res publica* or *res populi*, the public things which concern an organised population or 'people', there is however the antecedent question of a how a 'people' came to be a 'people'. How they came to be a 'people' is necessarily what is in a sense most public to them – because it brings their sharedness to presence – but also something which is often most hidden from them because so taken for granted by, or systematically indoctrinated into, them.

Now, there is a lot of talk about a 'people' in Heidegger, and talk too about a

German 'people', which talk was dangerous, and perhaps deliberately dangerous, as well as unforgivably *care-less* talk, at a time when the notion of a 'people' was being invoked to perpetrate and justify the most apalling evil; specifically, but not exclusively (because the politically powerful appropriation of the idea of a 'people' and of 'the people' is not a German but a modern invention), in the name of a so-called German 'people'. The fundamental question concerning a 'people' which Heidegger raises, however, is precisely this. How does a 'people' become a 'people' and, particularly, how is such a thing as an 'historical people' formed?

The answer he gave was also specific, and had nothing to do with modern political and subjectivised notions of race, ethnicity, culture or nationalism and their self-serving historiologies; all of which might also be thought as simply further violent attempts to locate the fugitive location of that 'lordship' or sovereignty which the imperial idea of politics requires.[70] Indeed, just at that point when the tide of war began to turn decisively against Germany in the winter of 1942–3, Heidegger says the following:

> The concepts of 'people' and 'folk' are founded on the essence of subjectivity and Ego. Only when metaphysics, i.e., the truth of beings as a whole, has been founded on subjectivity and the Ego do the concepts of 'nation' and 'people' obtain *that metaphysical foundation from which they might possibly have historical relevance*. Without Descartes, i.e., without the metaphysical foundation of subjectivity, Herder, i.e., the foundation of the concept of a 'people', cannot be thought.[71]

> (my emphasis)

Might possibly have historical relevance? What could that mean for Heidegger? The history of Being as metaphysics is the oblivion of Being which culminates in the age of technology. If they are to have historical significance in his mode of thought, therefore, it could only be as derelicted modes of human there-being in which the political has become radically technologised as well. Contrariwise, a 'people' is a 'people', specifically, an 'historical people', for Heidegger, by the way, and no other way than this way, in which it is brought together in virtue somehow of its recognition of, and subscription to, *aletheia*; the truth of disclosure. That is also why it is crucial to understand how it is that the truth of disclosure comes to pass. By this route also the pivotal importance of the tragic and of the tragedies, not only to the Greek *polis* but also to any Heideggerian understanding of how the political may come to presence in the form of a mode of belonging together that would constitute what he would recognise as a 'people', may be fully appreciated.

This move now introduces us directly into Heidegger's understanding of Language and the word, because, for him, disclosure comes to pass through Language understood essentially not as a 'tongue' but as the giving of the word as such. Here, too, the difference between 'the imperial' idea of politics as command and 'the political' idea of politics as the tragic topos of obligatory freedom becomes more apparent as well.

Before I proceed, however, I have also to note that how a people is a people nonetheless also raises the allied and equally primordial question of how a people is a people in terms of how it simultaneously also relates to other 'people'. There simply cannot be a people without the strangers that the formation of a people, even in this aletheic way, perhaps mostly in this aletheic way, simultaneously also bring to presence. Such strangers are as much on the 'inside' as they are on the 'outside'; as slaves and women as well as barbarians might have attested in the Greek *polis*. In the question how a people is a people, to mimic Heidegger, the questions of native and stranger are, therefore, co-originary and equi-primordial. There simply are no people without strangers; indeed no *Dasein* without the uncanny Otherness of *Sein*. And what strangers do, as Maurice Blanchot observed, is disclose the very uncanniness or strangeness, to which Heidegger continuously refers here in the Parmenides lectures and elsewhere, that pervades human being.[72]

How the ineradicable strangeness of human being – its homelessness – is politically accommodated is another way of speaking about the essence of politics as he himself broaches the issue of that essence. But, here, there is an enormous lacuna in Heidegger's thought, which no doubt also contributed to his own gross flat-footedness in supporting the Nazis. The best that can be said about it is that Heidegger broaches but does not pursue the question. He remained extraordinarily reticent about it. Rather, to the extent that he approached it at all it was only by opening-up the question of how a people is a people as such. In doing that, he nonetheless remained more preoccupied with the gathering than with the dissemination effected by the formation of political community via the *polis*.[73] In particular, he did so in thinking of the place or topos of encounter (*topos*, he tells us, being the Greek word for place), while allying it with the German *Ort*, only as a place of holding or gathering, thus momentarily abandoning his otherwise persistent attempts to articulate the duality of his own bi-focal observation of the Being of beings.[74] For an absolutely crucial moment we, or rather he, loses his bearings here. And by that I mean everything to do with the way I used bearings in Chapter 2. He seems to lose his composure and does not think the ways in which this topos of encounter – this bare exposed place – is precisely the place where bearings are continuously taken and given, and the burdens of a particular (political) bearing undertaken, in the continuous gathering and dissemination which goes on through it – indeed, could not be contrived without it – in the constant passage of an embodied life that is the very place of difference. In which, of course, because it is as motility, 'orientation is always already given in the activity of involvement whose basis is the deseverance and directionality of embodiment', itself.[75]

The essential word of Language, Heidegger says, 'is not the command, order, proclamation, promise or "doctrine". *A fortiori*, the word is never the merely adventitious "expression" of "representations"'.[76] So much for the suggestion that Heidegger engages in mere word-play. Language, as 'the house of Being', its place of disclosure, could not be given a higher priority.[77] Rather, the charge might be that he gives it too high a priority. But, then, the detractors have to *say* what the limits of Language are and *say* how things may then be. The issue is falsely posed as that of the reality of things outside of Language. The issue is the mystery of Language itself, and of how entering into Language the beyond of Language simultaneously also comes to presence in its absence. To quote a different joker for a change:

> There is no question that there is an unseen world. The problem is how far is it from midtown and how late is it open.
>
> (Woody Allen)[78]

Heidegger thought that it was getting close to closing time. In any event, for Heidegger, through the Latinisation of *logos* into *ratio*, Language becomes one faculty amongst others and, in the subsequent philosophy of this faculty (the philosophy of Language):

> The word is explained on the basis of vocalisation, and the latter is explained on the basis of language as a phenomenon of expression which happens to be at our disposal. Language and the word serve to assume 'the true' and 'truth' into the expressive form of the articulation of speech, and in this way they serve to announce them. Taken for itself, however, 'truth' as 'correctness' is a matter of the representation of objects. The representing takes place in the 'interior' and language is the 'exteriorisation' of this 'interior'.[79]

Conversely, for Heidegger:

> The word is a way of the disclosive preservation of the unconcealment and concealment of beings.[80]

Unlike modern understandings of Language and of the word – particularly it might be said of those which characterise early modern political theory – the word, for Heidegger, is the focal point – the pivot – of that gathering and disseminating, of the centripetal and centrifugal forces, of *aletheia*, or the disclosive truth of Being, in which not only does human being stand-out, but simultaneously also what is absent comes to presence in its absence:

> In the word the being we call man comports himself *to beings as a whole*, in the midst of which man himself is.[81]
>
> (my emphasis)

And, remembering my stretching of Heidegger, what comes to presence in its absence in this occulting dis-closure is the resoundingly telling silence of the demitted call of Justice as well.[82] The word is the pivot of disclosure, and human being is the being which has the word.

In fact, Heidegger insists that only Greek being had the word. But, just as Caputo has persuasively argued that *aletheia* may be regarded not as a story about the Greeks but 'a structure', – that is to say 'not a moment *in* time but a structure constitutive *of* time',[83] – there is no reason to accept Heidegger's argument that only these ancient Greeks could have had 'word' of it. Word, too, is not a story but a structure – as his own word-play, together with Derrida's persistent disruption of the mythologising Heidegger, makes evident – of the continuous de-limited dissemination of meaning.

That is why Heidegger pays so much attention to words, and refuses to treat them as terms with precisely calculable use value. That, too, is why he finds so much space in a word – a play of gathering and dissemination – and not a closed point. But the word can be pivotal, in the sense in which I am using pivotal here, only when, its spaciousness opened-up, it is kept open for a de-limited play of meaning. The same, I want to say, applies to the political itself and to the art of politics.

How then might human being as the being which has the word, speak the word in a way which brings it together as a 'people' in the truth of disclosure? How does the possession of the word in this way become the possession of a belonging together in the disclosive truth of the word such that the pivot is a pivot – space that is an empty place which, in a sense, is nothing spatial but the taking place (event) of the liminal occasion of a way of being that is localised, specific and de-limited[84] – for a 'people' and not just for a person?[85] Such that, one might say, the pivot operates as a public and not a private thing, and discloses the publicness of human beings – that is to say, that in which, as beings-in-common, they share – as such. This, for Heidegger, is the *mythos* of the *polis*.

The pivot, I would argue, was actually tragedy. The very publicness of the publicness of the *polis*, that which brought it together by disclosing its sharedness as a 'public' or a 'people', was spoken – disseminated, explored, and developed – by word of tragedy. The 'essence' of the *polis* as a questionable way of being came to presence in tragedy. It was tragedy which spoke the very *word* of the disclosive *ethos* of the *polis*. And there, the inapparent was also allowed to appear as inapparent and preserve its power as such; which absent presence, I repeat again, issuing in the tellingly demitted call of Justice, was one of the single most important preoccupations of tragedy.

Heidegger approaches this insight into the essence of the *polis* as pivot, and into the notion of pivot as the essence of the *polis*, in a typical fashion. He asked about the word itself, and noted how:

> *polis* is the *polos*, the pole around which everything appearing to the Greeks as a being turns in a peculiar way. The pole is the place around which all beings turn and precisely in such a way that in the domain of this place beings show their turning and their condition.[86]

(In fact the *polos* was also the pivot inserted into the sections of the columns of Greek temples in order both to allow them a certain movement, tolerance or latitude, as well as to provide that tie which bound them together.) The pivot around which this 'people' turned, the *polos* of the *polis* was how they and other beings were – agonistically – turned-out of concealment yet gathered together, and so allowed their free space to be. The character of this pivot as occasion or place – what I was referring to earlier as place of encounter – as well as the disclosive character of this pivot is emphasised:

> The pole, as this place, lets beings appear in their Being and show the totality of their condition. The pole does not produce and does not create beings in their Being, but as pole is the abode of the unconcealedness of beings as a whole.[87]

Although Heidegger does not make this point, the objection that only some – privileged – beings were allowed their beings to be through the operation of the *polos* of the *polis* is obvious; one other good reason why a return to the Greek *polis* is not only impossible but also undesirable. But the other and more enduring political point concerning human freedom nonetheless, I think, follows irresistibly, that the operation of the *polos* of the *polis* – hence the essence of the political as such – is announced as the disclosing of the disclosive power of the truth in which human being is freed into the Being of its obligatory freedom to be and to give things their due. The insurgency of freedom and ethicality which that lets loose is not one that can be contained by the historical limitation of the privilege of being of the *polis* to certain categories of men, as many tragedies themselves attested. Its extension to human being as a whole – to the *demos*, or human being as 'the people' – ineluctably follows. And so the very agonal, aletheic character of the political itself incites the question, and ignites the fugitive project, of how to give this human being in the midst of beings as a whole, and the uncanny Otherness of which the domain of beings is integrally comprised, its due as a political project of beings-in-common.

THE ESSENCE OF THE PIVOT OF THE POLITICAL

It is clear, to some extent I hope, that the pivot of the political is aletheic truth and that tragedy was pivotal to this in that it was the work of art, which disclosing the disclosing of aletheic truth, was pivotal to the political life of the *polis*. Tragedy did not constitute all that there was, however, to the political life of the *polis* because it was only pivotal to what was pivotal about it; namely aletheic truth. If we are also to be clear, therefore, about what the political is about, here, we have to have a fuller idea of what is demanded of human beings by the essence of the pivot; namely, aletheic truth.

I have been doing my own dilating of Heidegger in order to do this: by continuously insisting upon, and working-in to my account, the obligatory freedom which he says aletheic truth devolves upon human being; by insisting upon, and working-in, the telling silence of the demitted call of Justice which he also says devolves upon human beings a responsibility, integral to the way of being of human being as responsiveness, to give things their due and to comport themselves appropriately in the motility of the ecstases of time; and by continuously insisting, finally, upon the gathering *and* dissemination of the centripetal and centrifugal forces at work here without privileging the one over the other. This is dangerous stuff because Heidegger is nothing if not obtuse and cryptic when it comes to these questions of Justice and of freedom. And no wonder, given the way in which he completely botched them when he tried to fashion a political intervention out of the understanding of Being and beings he had attained by the early 1930s. It is tricky also because, whereas my preoccupation remains with the tragic topos of the obligatory freedom which I think is the origin of the political and which has continuously to be won in the conduct of human affairs, he remained a thinker who was not only concerned ultimately with the event of Being as such, but also one overly devoted to his own tragic storytelling at this point. I cannot ignore what he has to say about that event, of course, because it is integral to how one understands human being and consequently the entire question of the political. On the other hand, I am most preoccupied with that region of his thought which – ostensibly – preoccupied Heidegger least. What he gives me to think here is less than what he has given others to think elsewhere. I think that what he gave himself to think here was also perhaps less than what he gave himself to think elsewhere. This, too, may have something to do, also, with why his political intervention was so disastrously misjudged.

It is, then, this originary politicality derived from the very aletheic truth of Being in the midst of which human being always already finds itself gathered and thrown, which opens-up the possibility of political life; specifically, here, the *polis*. The political is not, therefore, determined 'politically'. Rather, it is the political which offers the possibility of a political life. Such a political life has nonetheless to be continuously worked, put to work in a kind of work and worked into existence. Tragedies, once written, for example, have continuously to be worked and re-worked to work their effect; which is to recall the political responsibilities and aporetic difficulties of the freedom of tragic being, within which an artful way has continuously to be found of granting Justice its inexhaustible (s)way.

Obligatory freedom's tragic topos of encounter, where human being, as much possessed by as in possession of the gathering *and* disseminating word (*Logos*),[88] is therefore the locus of the encounter with the tellingly silent demitted call of Justice whose absent presence uncannily resounds throughout the aletheic truth of the Being of beings. This obligatory freedom, the articulated pivot of disclosure itself, is mine yet shared, mine yet shared through the phenomenon of the word itself. For: 'In discourse Being-with [*Mitsein*] becomes explicitly shared'.[89]

But, what is pivotal about this point is that obligatory freedom always comes over as a possibility. It is not handed over on a plate. Hence the existence of human being as a continuous questioning of its questionability, having its being to be and continuously assuming its being as a (political) project. That is why this freedom is a freedom to be worked, continuously put into work and worked into human existence. The pivot of disclosure itself needs pivoting. The encounter, that is to say, needs encountering, has to be institutionalised and earthed, because it is no ethereal but the real and material ethico-political experience of human existence not as a mere private thing but as simultaneously both public and private, both mine yet shared.

A pivot gathers, it ties. But a pivot is also a fulcrum of movement around which things turn. There is no pivot, therefore, without a spin-off. In other words, despite the emphasis of gathering which Heidegger consistently gives it in the Parmenides lectures and elsewhere, I want to emphasise that it simultaneously also gathers *and* disseminates. In order to do that I have also emphasised, however, that what is pivotal here is a certain understanding of space which is more than merely geographical, territorial, institutional or even 'historical', in the sense of an historiographical succession of 'nows'; including that of the Greek *polis*. That is to say, of a space which is not already fully occupied by a determination – geographical, territorial, institutional or historical – as if it were therefore always already a point, complete and closed in upon itself. Rather, it is an empty place in which determinations themselves can be arrived at. For if the space were already pre-occupied and pre-determined – particularly, for example, being pre-occupied by some prior determination or with a rage to determine – there would, of course, be no determinations to come – no decisions to make, no decidedness to commit oneself to, no burden of judgement to carry – only submission to a technical implementation of the already determined.

I have compounded this sense of pivot by suggesting: first, that according to the radical hermeneutical phenomenology of the existential analytic of human being as there-being (*Dasein*), human being is effectively the pivot, place of encounter or occasion of encounter, of the ontological difference of Being and beings. It is this, according to Heidegger, because it has Language; more specifically the word as that which in itself revealing and concealing bears the same structure as, and, therefore, repeats the disclosure of, aletheic truth. It is this, too, which constitutes its obligatory freedom. Hence human beings have politics because they are free, they are not free because they have politics. Rather the political – the essence of politics which is this freedom – continuously stalks and haunts everyday politics. It bears the same fugitive relation to politics as Justice does to the law. Just as the demitted call of Justice invokes law-giving, so also the demitted call of the political invokes the constitution (think also composure as well as institution with this word) of political order.[90] But, in as much as no law can comprehend all Justice, no political order entirely comprehends the freedom of human being. Justice and the political effect a continuous insurgency against all limits even as the operation of limits is the very means by which we encounter their absent presence. And, since politics is concerned with the giving of the law, hence the integral relationship between Justice and the political. Justice, then, is not determined by the *polis*, or by politics, or on the basis of a relation to the *polis*. It is what the *polis* – or politics by virtue of being political – is given to be concerned with and must continuously comport itself towards.

In the Parmenides lectures, Heidegger continuously translates *dike* as order and ordering, deliberately avoiding the translation of it as 'justice' or 'right', in order to give himself distance from traditional thinking about justice and right in respect of command, and so contrive some space for thinking about the presencing of presencing characteristic of the aletheic truth of the demission of time. By thinking *dike* as order and ordering, Heidegger is trying to give some substance to what must be demanded of a being whose way of being is lived in aletheic truth. Naturally, it cannot be ordained by a set of commandments; however they are thought to be issued. He therefore thinks of it as a challenge to compose oneself in a way that is consonant with the presencing of aletheic truth.

The presencing of aletheic truth, for him, takes its character from *phusis* which is the Greek sense of the self-disclosure of beings. *Phusis*, the power of that which while showing itself from itself as itself, nonetheless, simultaneously also bears the trace of the absent presence of concealment; which is to say, its not-being. Hence, once more, possibility is higher than actuality. Thus, comporting oneself to and within aletheic truth is not just a matter of attuning oneself appropriately to the very motility of time, and one's finitude within it. Nor is it simply also attuning oneself to this process of self-revealing in which things come to presence as they are. But, it also entails having the process of things coming to presence as such handed-over into one's safe-keeping.[91] Human responsive responsibility is not only to be discharged in respect of itself and other beings but also in respect of the mystery (concealment) of presencing as such. This sounds like a rather large commission. And it is. But, it can be no other way, since Being and being are not thought of as two independent terms, and human being is correspondingly also thought of as the there – here, the taking place – of Being.

I have deliberately chosen to refer to *dike*, however, as the capitalised Justice to effect a certain disruptive connection with Levinas. For, thinking this Justice is what Heidegger does least well, and what Levinas, by contesting Heidegger's fundamental ontology from within, insisting upon the radical alterity of the inassimilability of the other, to a degree does better because he corporealises the responsibility of the commission of the demitted call of Justice as an everyday, immediate and physical encounter. Levinas proceeds by realigning self and other out of the Heideggerian being-with and into the Levinasian face to face relationship. In that way he emphasises the fundamental divide between self and other, thus preserving its radical alterity from the self. In that way, too, he is able to insist that in thus meeting the other face to face as something which the self cannot absorb, the self undergoes an ethical encounter with the other's alterity. Secondly, whereas, for Heidegger, *Dasein* is hailed by the call of conscience, the self, for Levinas, is hailed by the call of the other.[92] Levinas achieves this amplification of the question of the ethical, and in his terms of the Law, however, by reintroducing an, albeit somewhat rethought, notion of command; that which issues through the face to face relationship in which I am commanded to substitute for the other. He achieves it also at the cost of making the ethical encounter a private affair, not a public question. And what that means is that he achieves it at the cost of conceding a politics which in practice can only command the other's submission to the law or its expulsion from the law; in which latter condition it is therefore in danger of becoming either a menace to be eliminated, or a an object to be preyed upon. Perhaps this is why, when it came to his own limited political interventions – notably when asked about the case of Israel and the Palestinians –

he proved to be as imperialistic as the modern imperium of politics itself.[93] Justice, then, is the challenge to allow 'the always embodied other to appear as who he or she is'.[94]

The obvious question then arises as to whether some forms of law-giving and of constitutionality are superior to others. And the answer 'yes' begins to arise not merely in the form of technical arrangements but also in respect of a more encompassing ethos, or comportment, of freedom. For human being, in its way of being, has to work the word, in order to work into its own works what the word is capable of disclosing by virtue of its own structure; namely the aletheic truth in which human being exists in its freedom with others in Otherness. Tragedy, I suggest, performed this function for the *polis*; a constitution (think composure again as well as institution) whose ethos was informed by an appreciation of the tragic truth of human being and whose practices sought responsibly to undertake it, at least for some. I also implied, earlier, that the the question of democracy poses the question of the extension of this ethos and of its practices from the publicness of a few to the publicness of human beings as such, which is why that ethos of freedom must be a democratic ethos.

Now, what comes to presence in its absence here, the points I am amplifying in Heidegger against the 'spirit' of many of the things he says, but I think in the spirit of others,[95] is the (political) freedom to give Justice by responding to the demitted call of Justice. This requires limitation – some time and some place, some composure and some institutional arrangements. That is why *the space of* the political is *the taking place of* the demitted call of Justice, and the assumption of responsible solicitude is the rejoinder we make to it, when, being put on the spot, deciding we are decided. But the point is that specific political arrangements can never satisfy this call and that they always have to be judged against the excess of its measureless standards; those of the ethicality of politicality. That is the source of the radical questionability of all politics which the political itself – that obligatory condition of freedom to give things their due – insistently introduces into the practice of politics.

Dike and the *polis* have just as essential a relationship for Heidegger, therefore, as *aletheia* and the *polis* because the call of *dike* resounds throughout *aletheia*:

> Just as impossible as is an interpretation of the *polis* on the basis of the modern state or the Roman *res publica*, so is an interpretation of *dike* on the basis of the modern concept of justice and the Roman *iustitia*. *Dike* understood as the order which ordains, i.e. assigns to humanity its relations and comportments takes its essence from *aletheia*.[96]

The difficulty is, however, that Heidegger's account of *aletheia* is much clearer and much more extensive than is his reading of *dike*, and also easier to detach from a certain mythologising of his own here. But the essentiality of the relationship is nonetheless clear enough, precisely because part of what comes across in the truth of disclosure – part of what human beings come across in their exposed existence in the truth of disclosure – is the demitted call of Justice and the requirement it issues to withstand the manifold motions of the ecstases of time through effecting an appropriate composure towards it, and towards other beings with which we are integrally related.

More than the attunement of a mood, more than the resonances of the tympan or the tonality of the voice, therefore, what is required is the composure of a certain standing. This, for me, is where the philosophical shades into the political and where the art of politics begins to become manifest. For taking a stand is where judgement and commitment, in addition to, albeit allied with, reflection, take place. This is where the risk – the radical (in)security – of human being is decided daily. Here, too, the register of aletheic truth is extended beyond the encounter with the truth of metaphysics into the encounter of the corporeal excess of existence which aletheic truth announces. Here, then, courage and fortitude, love, joy and duplicity, cowardice, hate, lies and deception, equivocation and prevarication, acquisitiveness and ignorance – in short the whole tragic gamut of human experience – intrudes into the sometimes overly refined and anaemic, sometimes mythologised, question of truth. Character, if you like, is allied to plot. The thing becomes flesh and blood, and the prospect of being mortally wrong is encountered as well. Heidegger above all, I think, also knew this.

What is uncanny about the political is precisely that the requirement to give things their due arises at all. What is, therefore, uncanny about human being is that it is the opportunity to do so. This uncanniness is not something which appears only once or occasionally. It shows itself everywhere, all the time, and within the everyday:

> the uncanny, or the extraordinary, shines throughout the familiar ambit of the beings we deal with and know, beings we call ordinary.... its essence is the inconspicuous, the simple, the insignificant, which nevertheless shines in all beings. ... the simple which shines into the ordinary, and which does not stem from the ordinary, but nevertheless appears in advance in all that is ordinary, shining though it and around it.[97]

We ordinarily think of politics only in terms of the representation of subjects, presenting before themselves and others the objects (including other subjects) which they seek to grasp or master, and the 'interests' which they seek to pursue and realise.[98] Here, politics is being thought, instead, even in respect of our sometimes viciously subjectivised politics, as to do with how human beings come to be integrally involved in taking-up their responsibility for their uncanny phenomenality and phenomenolising capacity in order to grant it its due. Not forgetting that this takes place with others in Otherness is what also distinguishes this acceding to Justice from some supposed unbridled exercise of the will. Not forgetting that this is an open way of being in openness, is what similarly distinguishes it from a programmatic prescription for its confinement within the bounds of some security project or other. Not exhausted by representation, consciousness, the merely phenomenal or even the poetic, it is essentially involved with the art required continuously to compose oneself in the freedom (mine yet shared) that one inhabits; which freedom brings inapparent Justice to presence in its absence in respect of the way we treat each other, other beings and Being as such.

Such composing demands resoluteness, and that resoluteness is a public political composure of free being: 'The place of authenticity is the political place of Being-with (*Mitsein*)'.[99] Furthermore:

> *Dasein's* resoluteness towards itself is what first makes it possible to let the Others who are with it 'be' in their ownmost potentiality-for-Being, and to co-disclose this potentiality in the solicitude which leaps forth and liberates.[100]

Hence, the politics of freedom is emancipatory solicitude. The form of that resoluteness has somehow to be attuned to the very necessity of the emptiness of the space which is not already occupied by determination, so that it can allow determination to take place and things to come to presence as they are: specifically, the empty place of the pivot of the political; or, *polos* of the *polis*. Similarly, it has also to come in the form of the word, or what Heidegger would call authentic discourse, whose political character and significance has found few better elucidations, which is why it is worth quoting at length, than that offered by Peg Birmingham.

> Rather than asserting an inner conviction that demands to be recognised and which recognises the other as the same as one's self, Heidegger suggests that the authentic discourse is a response to Others about a common situation of Being-in-the-world. In the discourse of discretion (*Verschwiegenheit*), the emphasis is not on being seen, but instead on the response of the authentic self with Others who share the same world, but who in their ownmost potentiality-for-Being are different. Therefore, the authentic discourse which determines the self is not the silence of the totalitarian regime nor the distracted talk of the everyday. It is the careful, discrete discourse of the differentiated, hetero-geneous space of the political realm.[101]

Listening-out for its call, and listening-in to what has already been said in response to it, our relation to Justice remains radically hermeneutical as well. Consequently, we are not caught-up in the radical heremeneutical dialogue of the phenomenon of Justice by merely being summoned as subjects endowed with linguistic competences. Rather, we are called upon, and put under a claim that we cannot escape even when evading or corrupting it. Justice too has, therefore, to be continuously sounded-out in the radical hermeneutics of such discrete discourse. Such articulate, and articulated, resoluteness is what Heidegger tries to think in terms of letting-be or *Gelassenheit*; a classic account of which I think we find in the tragedy of *Oedipus Rex*.

I have to try to say a little more about how this obligatory freedom, and the fugitive Justice which stalks it, provide – by some art working – the pivot around which the possibility of a political life is continuously excited, pursued and realised. In doing so I have similarly to say more about how the political is itself also the pivot by means of which this obligatory freedom is borne, and by means of which the fugitive Justice that stalks it comes to presence in its absence. I do the former by explaining a little more, in closing this chapter, about the public and chiasmic character of the political. I do the latter, in succeeding chapters, by analysing the tragic in more depth and then recounting the tragedy of *Oedipus Rex*.

THE PUBLIC AND CHIASMIC ESSENCE OF THE POLITICAL

If only a being that is a way of questioning its own questionability possesses the possibility of a political life, similarly only a being whose questionability is not only mine for myself but is simultaneously also shared by myself with others as a being-with can possess that possibility also.

Once more, we are possessed by the possibility of the political not only because we are free in the way that we are free, but also because that obligatorily freed being is necessarily a being-with as well. Here again, too, we have to amplify something that is always already there in Heidegger, but with which he did not concern himself as much as he might have done, and did with other things. For this is the publicness of the being whose way of being grants it the prospect of a political life. The common of this being-in-common arises not because we are identical but because we are 'the same' and because, being shared-out in this condition, we effect its redistribution as well. If it were self-sufficient there would be nothing shared because there would be nothing divided from itself. Dispensed – thrown – we nonetheless share in the share-out. And we can do this only because being always already incomplete and needful, no other – however much complementing me – completes me. Such needfulness is not a debit related to sufficiency, but one related to excess. It is the very rivenness of the being of human being which, therefore, makes it open to others and to Otherness, and not a common identity with the self-same. Neither is that commonness a function of a telos, purpose or end. No more is it a finished or finishable work. Un-worked, it has, instead, to be worked – politically. Being-with does not therefore qualify this way of being, it actually constitutes it. That is why it is inalienably both mine yet shared. Hence the public – 'common' in the sense not of possessed but shared – quality of the tragic topos of encounter of obligatory freedom.[102] But why the chiasmic?

Remember that this way of being that is human being *is* as motility. On the move, it is continuously taking its bearings, and assuming a bearing, in order to give it the headings which its futurality requires. By such means it composes itself in the temporality of its existence. As such, it is the taking place of an interrogation of its own interrogating. Heidegger says simply that orientation or *directionality* is an *existentiale* of *Dasein* – part of its fundamental ontological constitution.[103] The taking place of the intersection of differing through the very interlocution of articulation, the tragic topos of encounter is, therefore, also chiasmic because bearings comprise the meridians of encounter of the very meridian of the tragic topos of existence itself.[104]

Tragedy, in disclosing the shared condition of human being as the place of the encounter with the free responsibilites of being there in existence, is pivotal to that pivoting, which takes place in the place of the *polis*, therefore, because it discloses, that is to say, makes a public performance of and so shares-out, this very sharedness. In disclosing, tragedy does not merely point-out or entertain; neither is it therefore simply consumed. We have to be open to the uncanny phenomenon of disclosing a little more. Tragedy discloses *to* and discloses *for*, and consequently therefore also brings to presence the sharedness *of*, being a public. In its disclosing, tragedy, therefore, pivotally effects that gathering together and disseminating (*polos*) – whose way of life (*politeia*) took place in the place known as the *polis* – in the light of aletheic truth. Tragedy, by way of being the pivot of the pivoting of disclosure, is the pivot of the pivoting of the *polis* whose way of life is determined by its very sensibility to aletheic truth.

Tragedy does not, therefore, make the tragic. There is tragedy only because there is always already the tragic topos of encounter which is human being-in-common. 'All' tragedy does is bring it to presence as it is: singular, yet plural; mine, yet shared; private, yet public; Oedipus', yet Thebes'. Around that, continuously revolves the possibility of a political life which continuously has to be worked into existence.

The essence, or way, of the political here is, then, the very *sharedness*, and consequent capacity for *sharing-in* and *sharing-out*, this obligatory freedom and its demitted call of Justice; (something which differs radically from contemporary subjectivised ideas of community). It is a possibility of the actuality of existence. That is why, for example, in discussing Plato's account of *politeia*, Heidegger is at pains to insist that what Plato was doing was in a certain, but significantly different, way exactly what tragedy was doing; providing 'a recollection of the essential and not a plan for the actual'.[105] That is why, also, he was at equal pains to point out that the essence of this place was neither the *urban* of the city nor the *status* of the state, much less the *doggerel* of 'city-state', but the disclosure of aletheic truth.

Now, aletheic truth is disclosure. But that is not the end of it. Aletheic truth, the revealing concealing in which human beings enjoy their obligatory freedom and are enjoined by it to assume that freedom in the questioning of the questionability of their own mortal being as a continuous project for themselves, is disclosure in which they are challenged to give things their due. This commission arises not as a command – of the word of 'God', 'Reason', 'World Spirit', 'Will to Power', 'Emperor', 'the State' or, even, 'the People' – it arises out of the very disjection of time itself as a demission of time; and that is the truth of it. Justice is not given, it is called for. Precisely because it is called for in the time of a mortal being that is as a mobile possibility, futural and continuously projecting, it is not only a call which may be heeded though never satisfied. It is also one which continuously demands a composure, and not just a saying or a said; the continuous crafting of a public stance which stands-up for, as it stands-up in, the saying and the said. Here, the ethical and the philosophical become the political. Here, too, the political also makes its disruptive intervention into 'politics'. For the disclosure of political composure continuously challenges the uprightness of imperial command which hubristically threatens to substitute (stand-in) for political freedom.

The essence of the pivot of the political, I consequently want to say, is simply this: human being, with its peculiar share of existence, is the occasion of picking-up the tab of Justice. What human being therefore shares is that which it does not have, that which it does not securely possess but must continuously struggle to assume and work. *That*, is its being-in-common; an absence, an excess, the demission of aletheic truth whose obligatory freedom offers a commission whose assumption demands a certain composure which in turn has continuously to be fashioned in the motility of the openness of the discordant time in which it has that freedom to be; which being, as a continuous being-with, shared yet also 'mine', must simultaneously therefore be both 'public' and 'private'. Hence, not only the critical importance, but also the uncanny – emptied of determination so that determination may be continuously arrived at and revised, which is what also makes it chiasmic – space of the public space to which champions of freedom from Aristotle to Arendt continuously attested. This espousal of the taking place of the alien and unhomelike is not done, however, for the sake of becoming at-home, rather it is done for the sake of the dissemination of Justice.[106]

Chapter 4

Interlude

(In)security

The word becomes a name for something indeterminate.

(Martin Heidegger)

The word, any word, is a fragment. Any fragment deprives the present of its peace (and piece) of mind. It breaks the assumed chain of natural continuity, or the presumption that we are in charge of Language and can make it obey our will. For every fragment, of whatever sort, not only indicates that we are always already in the midst of things, but also that we are always already in the midst of incompleteness; that untimely incompleteness of the duration between past and future where the *krisis* that summons us forward to Justice occurs. In what Arendt calls Walter Benjamin's fascination with phenomena rather than with ideas, there was an associated preoccupation with the smallest of things because of the way – as phenomena – they seemed peculiarly well equipped to disclose the uncanny nature of appearance itself. And so it is with words. For words are bits of things, literally incomplete and out of place. Where something is broken-off a breach occurs and so a word is also a space and a spacing; a gap that does not merely recall a gap but constitutes a gap and operates in the ways that gaps do. A space in which things are brought together, therefore, words are nonetheless also a space through which things are disseminated and dispersed. As such they operate as an intersection, transit points which bear the trafficking of Language itself. But the transit point is not fixed. Words not only have histories, such junctions are also constantly moved about to facilitate the commerce of Language. Motility is as integral to words, then, as it is to human being. For words also travel and constitute a record of journeys made. All the attributes of motility apply to them as well: giving; standing; falling; breaking; coming; going; velocity; attrition; consumption; expenditure; exhaustion. Each – the human and the word – possesses a career, describes a history, traces a measure of existence, does more than is knowingly intended and signifies more than they can know. As transit points, however, each are themselves also a break and things are destined to break-off there with them.

Broken-off, words themselves, by virtue of their very fragmentedness, are therefore also destined to break-off. No word is complete. No word is self-contained. No word is fully possessed of self-possession. In short, no word commands that of which it speaks, or what is spoken through it. Neither, however, can words simply be commanded. They slip and slide, evade our grasp and convey both more and less than we intend. They do this both because they have a history and because when we use them we set them off again on their historical way, in the unpredictable ways in which anything which lives in the way that it is received through time remains intractable to the designs that might be made upon it. Despite the art of the spin-doctor, then, you can never determine the outcome of that reception.

Words show, but the showing is simultaneously also contoured by concealment.[1] More to the point, words are therefore also uncanny in the sense that the inapparent appears there somehow also in the word itself. Words therefore escape us not merely because our mastery of them may be technically insufficient but because they bear within them that which escapes us as such. We are always had by words and deceive ourselves when we think that they are only ever had by us. Technologisers seek to master Language by technologising it, and fool themselves in the process. Poets fool around with Language and become wiser in letting words have their way with them. The one ludically enlarges our mentality, the other securingly confines it. Words, however, as technologisers continuously discover to their chagrin, always seem to have the last laugh. Yet their incorrigible recidivism also continuously fuels the technologising impulse.

If the very fragmentedness of words indicates that we can never securely take over proprietorship of the whole – of Language and of existence – they assure us as well, in the way that they resist closure, that there is on the whole always more speaking and living to be done; and that the whole itself is in excess. For these very reasons, they are one of the means which bring forth the uncanniness of the duplicating and re-duplicating repetition of origination, so recalling again that origination is never purely original and that we have always to get on with it in the living that we do.

That uncanniness is the uncanniness also, of course, of mortal existence, the way of being which lives *and* dies, as words themselves also seem to do. Do we mimic words, or do words mimic us? It seems both, in as much as having our being through Language we exist in mutually disclosive and reciprocal need with it. In the word – especially this word – we therefore always encounter the essential relationship between Language and death which the speaking mortal being of human being undergoes. To experience this limit where word breaks off and silence reigns is also, however, to experience the possibility of our freedom. And to experience that is to be subject to the call of conscience and the voice of the ethical.

Our response can nonetheless, of course, vary as it has within the tradition and through the tradition of Western thought. As Giorgio Agamben has noted, 'by rigorously establishing the limits of that which can be known in what is said, logic takes up this silent Voice [the event of Language as such of which every word silently speaks] and transforms it into the negative foundation of all knowledge'.

'On the other hand', he continues, 'ethics experiences it as that which must necessarily remain unsaid in what is said'.[2]

Agamben's thought carries us further along the path of this thought. In a brilliant series of short essays, he shows how Western logic and ethics share a common foundation in the experience of the occurrence of Language as a negativity; the unsayable and the ungraspable. He also shows how the poetic tradition shares this understanding with that of the philosophic tradition, so that the rift between poetry and thought becomes no simple opposition or dialectic but a belonging together in the 'West's' experience of Language as the advent of negativity:

> It is in this silent *non liquet*, rather than in a positive reconciliation, that we should see according to the profound intuitions of Rosenzweig and Benjamin, the essence of tragic dialogue.[3]

'The mythogeme of the Voice', he concludes, is thus 'the original mythogeme of metaphysics':

> but in as much as the Voice is also the originary place of negativity, negativity is inseparable from metaphysics. (Here the limitation of all critiques of metaphysics [including both Heidegger and Derrida] are made evident; they hope to surpass the horizon of metaphysics by radicalising the problem of negativity and ungroundedness, as if a pure and simple repetition of its *fundamental* problem could lead to a surpassing of metaphysics.)[4]

Nonetheless, it is within the poetic that we are brought tantalisingly to the threshold of a different thought which moves beyond negativity to the ethos of our having being and of the appetite of desire and love which that excites in us:

> With the definitive death of the Voice, even philosophy – the soliloquy of *Oedipus* – must come to an end. Thought, which thinks after the end of philosophy cannot still be thought of the Voice, of the taking place of Language in the Voice; nor can it be thought of the death of the Voice. Only if the human Voice is not simply death, but has never existed, only if Language no longer refers to any Voice (and, thus, not even to *gramma*, that is to a removed Voice), is it possible for man to experience a Language that is not marked by negativity and death.[5]

Later, in my reading of *Oedipus Rex*, I find in the verses of Sophocles the suggestion that that voice is the voice of love for no reason.

To take a word, then, is to hold a fragment of life and its mystery in your hand. To invoke a word is to recall a history. To use a word is to set history on its way again. Whoever thought words were not historical has never written nor spoken. Whoever thought that words were not also material has never lived through Language. Only not having been born would secure such an overcoming of Language.

Words recall us to our own fragmented presence in time itself because we live that motivated being toward the future, toward each other and the excess in which we stand out, through Language. Words present the world to us not from a pure point of origin, therefore, but from out of the middle. They betray the pretence that we can ultimately get to the bottom of things by continuously launching us into the middle of things. Hence a word is not a root, but a route which furnishes our entrance into the midst of things because Language is not simply a tool, no matter how much we seek to instrumentalise it. It is something to which we are handed over, something in which we are caught-up. Something ultimately to which we are subject, we are played-out in Language and may experience existence differently as we come to experience the play of Language differently.

There are three specific reasons for turning to the word security itself. The first concerns the radical ambivalence of the economy of meaning contained within the word. The second concerns the way etymology, in deliberately slowing us up, makes us attend to what words have to say more closely and introduces us to a different way of thinking. The third concerns the reading of *Oedipus Rex* which I want to present in a later chapter.

First, and before I return to it in detail, one obvious indication of the radical ambivalence of security is, of course, brought to mind in the quotations which introduced Chapters 1 and 2. For no age has been as insecure and mortally endangered as this our own insistently secured one. As Foucault pithily pointed out, there has never been as terminal a political prospect as the prospect fashioned by our contemporary politics of security.

Second, etymology stops us in our tracks, and is deliberately designed to do so. This move is not concerned to equip us to tell Princes what to do next. It defies the deeply technologised and anti-political view that advising Princes is the standard which determines what thinking about the political is about.[6] But it also defies with equal force any suggestion that such an approach is utterly removed from what Princes do. Quite the contrary, it is preoccupied with what Princes do, but in a radically different way from that of political science, in general, and of International Relations in particular. For Princes will do what they will do and academics will continue to ape them and think of the study of politics only in terms of servicing them. But those who do that fundamentally misunderstand the question of the political itself. Government and rule are not answers to the riddle of the political, they themselves, in themselves, pose that riddle and force us to think about it in ways which, in going through and beyond government and rule, are not determined by the particular means by which government and rule continuously bring it to our attention. Etymology makes a critical contribution to the process of responding to this riddle by teaching us, as Nietzsche says, 'to read *well*, that is to read slowly, deeply, looking continuously behind and ahead, with reservations, with doors left open, with delicate eyes and fingers'.[7] Doing so helps to impede the impulse to treat the founding of politics in security unthinkingly, as if security provided a secure ground. It is in the word, then, that we first encounter the duality which is entailed in the formulation (in)security.

We are always already dealing with the given, and the given is given to us in words. Given the political salience of security, I need some way of effecting an entry, therefore, into what is always already given in this word, and the entry I choose, the *krisis* which I exploit, is one offered by the word itself. It is there that I find the trace of the shifts which occur in the thought of this given, where translation and suppression have been required and where reiteration, supplementation and re-collection are also necessary. I think we find in the word the absence upon which its present tense relies. This turn to Language, specifically to the word, is, therefore, a certain kind of philosophical move rather than an expression of the pedant's desire for the literal. Consequently, neither does it represent an antiquarian faith in origins: 'In themselves the ancient and antiquarian have no weight'.[8] Nor is it meant to be a way of building 'bridges-of-lies to ancient ideals'.[9] Initiating a kind of radical phenomenology, it also displays a Nietzschean desire to 'reduce to despair every sort of man who is "in a hurry"'. For philology, he reminds us, is a 'venerable art which demands of its votaries one thing above all: to go aside, to take time, to become still, to become slow'.[10]

Etymology is consequently also informed by a certain understanding of Language as a whole. For the world in which we already have our bearings, however we think of them and whatever we may think of the track they place us on, is one disclosed through Language. That is the way we experience and encounter it. This turn to the word is a turn to Language understood as the realm in which all things show up for us; rather than Language conceived in the reified Hobbesian and Lockean ways, still powerfully at work in much modern political theory, as an instrument at the free disposal and exact manipulation of a conscious subject for the transparent representation of its world, the calculation of its purposes and the satisfaction of its wants. In the cult of subjectivity which distinguishes political Modernity, however, the vaunted self-determination of the subject ineluctably becomes the determination of the self precisely because Language is reified; and, through that reification, technologised. If, instead, we dispose ourselves in Language towards Language as Language continuously operates to dis-close our way of being to us, then we may ask what is dis-closed in the word security itself? It makes sense, then, indeed it is the only way to make sense, to ask about the way security shows-up in Language. And the obvious place to start is to ask about the word itself.

Security becomes, therefore, a signal or an alarm which summons forces to that deeply political struggle over the character of Language itself which is so integral to the rethinking of politics as such, for reworking familiar terms is part of the ethical project of politics.[11] Its hidden fulsomeness recalls that we are always already beginning in the middle of things; the middle of time, or in the midst of already having begun. Simultaneously the word also flags a point of departure in that it provides an immediate rich new beginning from out of which fresh connections and linkages can be forged. It is not simply a matter, therefore, of using words – security in particular – so as to prise open the sedimented tradition which would otherwise bury the problematic and contingent character of the meaning of the meaning that words do; and the meaning of politics which this word imposes upon us. Words offer themselves for this task and it is therefore a matter of allowing them to enter the contest for the political. In their history of meaning and of having meant, they may do this themselves. Thus security reawakens and disturbs the sedimentation of its own history and recalls the very intersections and cross-cuttings that have gone not only into the making but also into the utilisation of the meaning of it. Sodden with sensibility, criss-crossed with conflicting definitions, competing interpretations and diametrically opposed meanings, the word itself is a *chiasm*. Through it we may come to understand 'that there is no dialectical reversal from one of these views to the other; we do not have to reassemble them into a synthesis: they are two aspects of the reversibility',[12] which signals the very duality of our mortal condition. There it is that 'the generations precipitate themselves'.[13] Recalling its flux and contingency – pregnant with possible alternative paths, phrasings, framings and alliances, so full of contradiction itself – we re-discover that the word, so long bound to the cult of subject–object thinking which systematically obscures the truthfulness of the word, offers a genre for speaking the duality of mortality. And it is that truthfulness, strivingly at work within the word itself, rather than predeterminately standing outside of it, which calls me on.

It belongs to the essence of words, disclosed in their historicality, that they could always mean otherwise. To understand security, therefore, one has to hear what it says, the integral of all its differentiations. In the process, because we cannot escape from this excessive disclosive truth of words, I think we also begin to understand something else: that there is no way – no word, discourse, genre, or technique – which can resolve the crisis of ethical and political judgement anterior to our engagement in the circumstances in which the demand for such judgement arises. We simply have not been given such a word. The recovery of the political is concerned with recalling just that; with always keeping this recollection open.

Etymology is, therefore, also integrally related to genealogy; and, in particular, to the realisation of the genealogical ambition to operationalise and localise the history of metaphysics by calling attention to the power of certain orders of discourse, and their key words, to recall their forgotten meanings and to assess their economy of use in the present.[14] The turn to Language through etymology is also designed, then, to bring us to the point of intersection between the politicising and historicising concerns of the genealogist and the ethico-philosophical concern with the deconstruction of metaphysics. To bring us to the point, so to speak, where genealogy's deep indebtedness to the account of Western thought as metaphysics becomes evident; precisely because it is this account of metaphysics that enables us to address the question of how security enters into the Language with all of the valency that it does, and of how it comes to discharge all the functions that the genealogist would identify in respect of how it circumscribes our understanding of the question of the political by securing it within the confines of a metaphysical imagination.

But, as I pointed out earlier, because a genealogist also asks how security enters into discourse at all there is that task prior to, but intimately related with, the genealogical one, of accounting for how and why it does so. Challenging the metaphysical imagination by opening a space for the questioning of security, and thereby transforming the way we address the relation between limits and politics, therefore requires something different from, but in addition to, genealogy. Something, of course, that complements genealogy by sharing its sensibility to Language and concurring with its interpretation of the essentially disclosive and constitutive nature of Language. It is by turning to the word itself, therefore, that we can find some of that supplement and begin to effect this conjunction.

The third reason for looking closely at the word security concerns tragedy and, specifically, the play *Oedipus Rex*. I am going to explore this in a subsequent chapter because *Oedipus Rex*'s pre-metaphysical reflection upon the question of the political is a classic example of the way tragedy helps to illuminate the challenge political thought faces at the end of metaphysics. Without first disclosing the radical ambiguity of (in)security, and specifically without drawing attention to the Greek word for security (*asphaleia*), however, it is not possible to expose the intimate philosophical connections between security, ground and truth. Similarly, without introducing and exploring *asphaleia* it is not possible to appreciate, dramatically, how Sophocles plays on all the interplay – between eyes and feet, ground and grounding, raising things up and bringing them down, wrestling and climbing, the need to stand and the (im)possibility of ever standing straight and seeing straight – which the Greek word excites. Without *asphaleia* we cannot appreciate why the riddle of the Sphinx also concerns legs and all the variants of crawling, walking and stooping which arise in respect of standing; bringing things to a stand; and movement. Neither can we fully appreciate the deep irony entailed in the way Sophocles has the Thebans appeal for security to a man whose swollen foot ensures that he can neither stand straight nor see straight unless, with fatal exertion, he is capable of bringing everything to a stand-still.[15] And, finally, we cannot appreciate what Sophocles seems to be saying when he portrays how, in the event failing to secure security, no matter how hard he tries, *Oedipus* loses his sight and standing so that he can regain his feet and thereby renews his contact with the earth, with the holy, and with his mortal companions through a new composure; thus recovering from the hubristic catastrophe of exorbitant humanisation with which his calculative competence had threatened him and his fellow human beings.

Although this brief excursion into security's etymology is principally designed, therefore, to begin to investigate what kind of economy of meaning is already installed (but generally overlooked) within the word itself, it offers, in addition, another reason for the recovery of the tragic. For one of the reasons why great tragedy is great, I maintain, is precisely because it satisfies the concern with both genealogy and reading standards to which Nietzsche alerted moderns. It is the one place where the genealogical and the etymological are woven together. For tragedy deftly combines etymology's sensibility to the multivalent, disclosive and constitutive power of the word with genealogy's preoccupation with the discursive inter-plays that produce, orchestrate and direct the history of the present. It is equally both a demonstration as well as an exploration of the character of Language, and of its capacity to say more than one thing at once. More even than that. The tragic poet is an artist working in the understanding that, always already inserted within Language, we can never escape saying both more and less than we intend.[16] Poets, it seems, are especially well placed to articulate the articulated, acquire their bearings from it and thereby speak the truth about the fundamental duality of the uncanny economy of presencing in which human beings occur.

To pursue these themes we have to listen first, then, to what the word security itself has to say. That way we can detect something about the structure of what is going on in it – namely the disclosive structure of truth, the truth of being-in-common whose very rupturedness constitutes a *plethos*, or plurality, which poses the question of the political itself[17] – and seek to ensure that genealogy's access to the very philosophical resources that have incited it are recalled so that they can continue to nourish it.

In attempting this it is useful also to estrange ourselves from the word – to put some distance between it and ourselves – so that it shows-up for us in a way that commands our attention, and makes us listen to what is invested in it. Such a distance is the distance which

> does not mean without all relation. On the contrary, there is a distance that brings us nearer than the disrespectful intrusiveness that characterises all historiology.[18]

This, in any event, is what happens when we return to the Greek and Latin roots from which security arises for us. It is especially so with *asphaleia*; but, as you will see, the radical ambiguity signalled in that word is carried over into *sine cura*, the Latin root of *securitas* from which we finally receive the English word security.

For all these reasons I want to begin by taking security at its word. Let it speak for itself; and observe it recoil back upon itself.

Security

We stand too uncritically under the prejudice of the opposition between security and insecurity just as we do under that between truth and falsity. As with truth and falsity, so also with security and insecurity:

> taken for granted a long time ago ... we do not take offense at the plurality of names signifying it, which we constantly and without much thought use as formulas to discriminate our judgements and decrees.[19]

Because we can never think security without insecurity, and *vice versa*, there is an essential conflict, which the word itself bears within itself, at the heart of security that is overlooked by the traditional study of security. This conflict is a conflict of unequal opposites which are rooted and routed together. We are dealing here, then, with a unified agonal relationship of mutual definition rather than a dialectical relationship in which one term overcomes the other. It is evident, if we pause to think about security for a moment, that any discourse of security must always already, simultaneously and in a plurality of ways, be a discourse of danger too.[20] For example, because security is engendered by fear (fundamentally aroused by the uncanny, uncertain, different, awesome and uncalculable), it must also teach us what to fear when the secure is being pursued.[21] Any appeal to security must, therefore, also and simultaneously be a specification, no matter how inchoate, of the fear which engenders it. But because security is engendered by fear it also calls for counter-measures to deal with the danger which initiates fear, and for the neutralisation, elimination or constraint of that person, group, object or condition which engenders fear. Hence, while it teaches us what we are threatened by, it also seeks in its turn to proscribe, sanction, punish, overcome – that is to say, in its turn endanger – that which it says threatens us.

The word itself signals all this. Security not only means to be free from (danger) but also to constrain. The *Oxford English Dictionary* offers two broad categories of meaning for security. The first is the condition of being secure, for which it offers four sets of usage:

1 The condition of being protected from or not exposed to danger; safety.
2 Freedom from doubt; confidence, assurance. Now chiefly well-founded confidence, certainty.
3 Freedom from care, anxiety or apprehension; a feeling of safety or freedom from or absence of danger. *arch.* Formerly often *spec.* (now only *contextually*) culpable absence of anxiety, carelessness.
4 The quality of being securely fixed or attached, stability, fixity.

The second meaning is a means of being secure, for which the dictionary offers six different uses:

5 Something which secures or makes safe; a protection, guard, defence.
6 A means of securing or fixing in position.
7 Ground for securing something as secure, safe or certain; an assurance, guarantee.
8 Property deposited or made over, or bonds, recognizances, or the like entered into, by or on behalf of a person in order to secure his fulfilment of an obligation, and forfeitable in the event of non-fulfilment; a pledge, caution.
9 One who pledges himself (or is pledged) for another, a surety.
10 A document held by a creditor as guarantee of his right to payment. Hence any particular kind of stock, shares, or other form of investment guaranteed by such documents.

There are, then, a plethora of themes compacted within security. While they immediately establish the fundamental connection between security, economy, truth and certainty, these definitions also betray through the 'sin of security' (the unwarranted absence of anxiety), the connection between security and insecurity.

Security refers, in the first category of definitions, to a state, a thing, something that is already stabilised and fixed, certain. It is a substantive; in short, something substantivised by being secured. Security presupposes, having been secured. When talking about security we must never forget, however much the dead substantive security threatens to make us do so, that because security is also a verb some heavy securing is already going on in order to produce the condition of security. The act of making secure is not the thing security itself, or any thing so achieved. To secure is not a state but a process, a doing. But what kind of process, what kind of doing? It is clearly not an unambiguous kind of process because as the word itself indicates it is both a freeing from (danger) and a constraint or limitation imposed upon it. This is why security is not merely involved in a dilemma as strategic theorists see it. There is something else going on here. It concerns something much more than a technical problem concerned with how in trying to make oneself secure one engenders fear in others. It is not confined to some kind of inconvenient or troubling effect of the practices of securing which security specialists will eventually find means of ironing-out when their technologies have become more refined in recognition of this so-called security paradox. It is something to do with a profound, deeply disturbing and radical equivocation whose reverberations reverberate throughought the very word itself. We cannot rest with the idea of a paradox, therefore, because the word will not allow us to do so. It propels us on, or, rather, sucks us further into, a much more challenging vortex of ambiguity.

By being secured something becomes something that it previously was not. The act of securing both invents and changes whatever is so secured. The flower picked is not the flower given. Similarly the state to be secured is not the secured state. Destruction, disfiguration, violence, transformation, and change must not only accompany this process, they must actually constitute it because that is how the thing to be secured is translated into the object susceptible to being secured, such that that then becomes that which is secured; that is to say, the secured whatever it is which now enjoys the substantive security. Yet, clearly, whatever it is, it is certainly no longer whatever it once was. For it is now secured. In short, for something to be secured it must be acted upon and changed, forced to undergo some transformation through the very act of securing itself. Securing something therefore violates the very thing which security claims to have preserved as it is. Securing an object is only possible on the condition that the integrity of the original thing is destroyed.

This active, privative and ambiguous character of security is better appreciated in earlier than in more modern usage, where a conversion of securing into a universal, ubiquitous, unambiguous security always threatens to take place; suppressing the recognition that there is no security without securing. It suppresses the recognition, in other words, that securing is an assault on the integrity of whatever is to be secured. Modern usage, moreover, proposes that there is a state of affairs – insecurity – and the negation of that state of affairs – security – and by doing so thoroughly represses the complexity not only of the act of securing but also of the inextricable relation between security and insecurity. It offers, instead, a simple dialectical opposition together with the implied promise that insecurity can always be mastered in principle if not in current practice.

Asphaleia

In an essay written in honour of Ernst Junger, Heidegger refers to their shared preoccupation with 'basic words', amongst which he also includes security, and of how, in 'the basic words named, a kind of Language prevails other than scientific assertions'.[22] There is, then, not only a good Heideggerian precedent for returning to Greek words but also for paying some closer attention to security. It is nonetheless worth noting that *asphaleia* does not figure as one of those Greek words in which Heidegger finds disclosed that astounding early Greek insight into Being which so enthralled his own philosophical imagination; words whose history, he claims, has been so determinative of our civilisation. *Asphaleia* carries none of the disputatious baggage that, therefore, arises as a consequence of the genetic philosophic controversies which have surrounded *phusis, logos, techne*, and *aletheia*, for example. It, therefore, contains no substantial traditional philosophical valence that I know of. So, I do not present the word as if it has done the same sort of philosophical work in the tradition that Heidegger claims for *phusis* and the rest. But it might do something similar, because, while *asphaleia* has the distinction of being in a sense philosophically anonymous, it is nonetheless politically central and itself discloses that intrinsic duality which characterises its more philosophically charged counterparts. It did also figure briefly in Heidegger's reflections.

Just as, after the Latinisation of truth and its transformation into correctness, security is intimately connected with truth and certitude, so also the Greek word for security is intimately connected with truth. But, of course, according to Heidegger, through the word *aletheia* a different thought of truth pervaded the Greek understanding of truth; that is to say, the aletheic truth of disclosure. When thinking the relation between *sphallo, asphaleia* and truth we therefore have to keep in mind that this is truth thought in the aletheic way. Consequently, in the extended reading of *aletheia* which he gave in his Parmenides lectures, Heidegger notes that the stem of the Latin word *falsum* is 'fall' and that it is in turn related to the Greek *sphallo*, 'to overthrow, bring to a downfall, fell, make totter'. He notes also, however, that *sphallo* never became the 'genuine' counter-word to *aletheia*, the word for truth, even though it can be correctly translated as deceiving. The reason was that bringing to a fall or misleading, here, first becomes possible only on the basis of a certain 'putting forth, dissembling and concealing'. Hence, as he says, 'thought in the Greek way', *sphallo* is concerned with radically undermining what has been truly disclosed by putting something else up in its place, alleging that what is thus presented is what truly stands revealed. Conversely, therefore:

> *To asphales* means the un-falling, what remains standing in its abiding and enduring, i.e., in Greek, remains in its presencing into the unconcealed. *To asphales* is never the 'certain' and the 'secure' in the modern sense of *certitudo*.[23]

The Greek word for security is a compound that neatly conveys the duality of (in)security but in exactly the reverse order. It comes out as, not insecure. What I find most interesting about this is that it reinforces the point made when discussing the verb form in English: that security is an active process; something that has to be won, achieved, or imposed. And the direction is that from a state of insecurity towards that of having been secured.

Asphaleia is the privative of the verb *sphallo* – i.e. *a-sphaleia*. *Sphallo* means to err, to cause to fall or to fail, to bring down, trip-up (as in wrestling), to overthrow, defeat, baffle, disappoint or frustrate (for example, in respect of an oracle), or to make something or someone reel or stagger (as when drunk). It is translated into Latin as *fallo* – to fall. In the noun form, it is a fault, failing or error, a false step, or mistake. Hence the privative *asphaleia* is to avoid falling, error, failure, or mistake. It is to make something stand, steadfastness, assured from danger, safe, steady, fortified, to be furnished with a firm foundation, to be certain, or sure. The idea of struggle (*polemos*), as well as truth, is closely associated both with *sphallo* and *asphaleia*, and, through the strong connotation with phallus, of erection and potency.[24]

One of its most ancient uses, in *The Iliad*, is concerned with wrestling. In *The Odyssey* we have the connection with staggering. And in *The Odes* of Pindar it, and its cognates, are used in the sense of violent overthrow. Sophocles uses it in relation to the establishment and secure foundation of a city. Aristotle uses it as security in war and in respect of the positioning and lay-out of a city with a view to its defence. He also uses it in respect of the architectonics of political order; establishing a city on firm foundations 'according to the principles already laid down concerning the preservation and destruction of states'. In *Oedipus Rex* it is, amongst other things, used directly as certainty and truth. And Xenophon's *Memorabilia* uses it in terms of the sure means or steps to be taken in argument to secure the truth.[25]

The issue of truth therefore arises from the very beginning with security and is strongly associated with standing, under-standing, firm grounds, foundations and immutability. Yet, this truth is also the truth of aletheia, the truth of disclosure associated with the understanding of standing-out in the openness of Being. Moreover, the word itself simultaneously not only refers, of course, to its opposite – to falling and failing – and the need to overcome such conditions, but also and more disturbingly to their very interdependence; to the very duality of security itself and thereby to the struggle against the false standing – the *pseudos* – with which *sphallo* is intimately associated.

So, incidentally, does the deity (Poseidon) that the Greeks assigned to security.[26] Poseidon, ruler of the seas and god of horses, was also the securer. One of his other names (given by the people of Rhodes) was, in fact, *Asphalios* – the holder or stabiliser of the earth. And he popularly figured as 'safe Poseidon' the staff to be leaned upon. But Poseidon was also a deeply ambiguous figure because he was known, in addition, as the earth-shaker, the one who makes the earth tremble.[27] Poseidon, in short, is a precise figure of the very duality of (in)security,

who serves to recall the intimate relation between the secure and the insecure. He
is quite simply both at once. The fundamental duality of security is also carried-
over into, and signalled equally directly in, the Latin.

Securitas; Securus

The English word Security derives directly, of course, from the Latin *securitas/
securus*, which, in turn, is derived from the compound of *sine cura*. In this
Latinisation the connection between security and falling or failing is lost to the
word security, although it gains a further rich mixture of meaning that further
extends its already radically equivocal character. It is picked-up, however, in the
Latin *falsum*, which translates *sphallo*, and from which the English gets 'false'.

Sine cura comprises *sine*, meaning without, and *cura* from *curio* meaning
troubling; solicitude; carefulness; attention; pains; anxiety; grief and sorrow;
diligent as opposed to negligent; guardianship; concern for persons or things; to
have a care or be anxious about; later, oversight of certain state offices; task; or
duty. Hence *sine cura* (and sinecure): without solicitude; careless; free from cares;
untroubled; quiet; easy. *Securitas* is consequently defined as freedom from
concern; unconcern; composure; freedom from danger; safety; security. While
Cicero frequently also used *securitas* as a kind of synonym for the Stoic word
meaning free from mental perturbation, tranquillity or peace of mind (*euthumon*),
in the Augustan period it also came to mean a guarantee or security for a debt or
obligation. *Securitas* also acquired a certain political prominence, occurring in
imperial mottos and on emblems and coins. As, for example, with the motto
Securitas Publica – the 'safety', or immunity of the empire, in defence of which
the emperor toiled.[28]

The radical ambiguity of the notion of freedom from care which arises with
sine cura is, therefore, the location of the duality of security as it is carried-over
into the Latin. And it is compounded by the duality of the word *cura* itself –
referring both to states of mind and offices or responsibilities. Hence, to be free
from care was by no means an unambiguously advantageous, sensible, or indeed
safe, thing to be. Just as it is prudent to have certain cares or worries, so certain
offices, tasks and duties were things one ought to possess or discharge. Thus, in
the Augustan period and later, *sine cura* and *securitas* were used also to mean
careless; reckless; or negligent.

This usage was carried down historically until quite recent times. For example,
though ordinarily using security in a conventional way as something to be wished
for, Calvin occasionally also exploits the word's duality to distinguish security
from certainty. He does so because in the context of his preoccupation with
salvation and election it clearly becomes important – and for a variety of reasons
including, for example, the need to counter the presumption that one's conduct
no longer matters if one is truly elected – to reconcile the believer's profound
experience of doubt with the assurance of salvation. Certainty, then, is not a
subjective experience of security in the present, but the objective promise of

immortality in the future. Consequently '[t]he believer's doubt within his own human experience does not affect the integrity of the assurance of salvation that resides beyond all human experience'.[29] Seeking security, or deriving the comfort of security, from experience is therefore a false move. Consequently the only 'reliable' experience available to the believer, and which must therefore be cultivated, 'is his consciousness of his worthlessness'.[30] For it is this, signalled of course by the perturbations of doubt rather than the securities of believing oneself to be elected 'which refers him perpetually to the objective source of righteousness'.[31] Thus Calvin writes:

> When we teach that faith must be certain and sure (*securam*), we do not fantasise about some certitude (*certitudinem*) which is untouched by any doubt, nor a *securitatem* which is unassailed by any solicitude; rather what we say is that there is a perpetual contest in the faithful with their own lack of faith (*diffidentia*).[32]

In this context, therefore, security is used to denote an insecure, or baseless, state – a lack of solicitude; a carelessness of faith; a lack of proper concern – and differentiated from an objective certitude that is guarantee from without experience.

Using security to mean the very opposite of what it is now conventionally understood to mean – namely as 'a condition of false or misplaced confidence in one's position' – persisted down to the last century. James Der Derian, for example, notes that in *Macbeth*, Shakespeare declares (and in a way that is especially apposite to my general theme): 'Security is Mortals cheefest Enemie'; and that Edmund Burke condemned '[t]he supineness, neglect, and blind security of my friend, in that, and everything that concerns him'.[33] He refers also to the numerous citations in the *Oxford English Dictionary*, of sermons from the sixteenth to the nineteenth centuries, which all use security to convey the idea of careless, hubristic, overweening and even damnable over-confidence, reflecting and reinforcing the sense exploited by Calvin. And he records a sample of them: 'They . . . were drowned in sinneful security' (1575); '[t]his is a reflection which . . . should strike Terror and Amazement into the securest sinner' (1729); and '[i]t is an imaginary immortality which encloses him in sevenfold security, even while he stands upon its very last edge' (1876).[34] All this recalls, in addition, how in Heideggerian terms being without care is simply being in-human because care is the fundamental feature of the existential constitution of *Dasein*.

It is not so much the word – *asphaleia*; *securitas*; security – that is of greatest significance here, but that disclosure of the transactional, mutually constitutive exchange between security and insecurity, which endures throughout its changing composition in the very structure of the word itself. *A-sphaleia*/*securitas*/security indicates the thematics, analytics and economy (or rather transactional matrix) which is continuously at play and is also the source of the dynamic of security; of how, in fact, security and insecurity require one another. It is that unstable economy, not just of the plural but of the contradictory meanings already installed within the very word, that matters. It is precisely this, then, to which I want my fragment of an etymology to call attention. The truth of security is the radical ambiguity of human freedom. The double meaning is to be found in the word itself. And if we are to be true to the word, as all policers of the correspondence theory of truth continually insist that we must, we have no licence to ignore this dual economy in favour of one determinate meaning over another; security over insecurity, or *vice versa*. Both exist here. Together. Simultaneously. And that's the truth of it. The one final truth of it is signalled especially in the Greek word's privative rendering of security as not insecure. For if there is a co-belonging of security and insecurity there is also a radical dyssymmetry between them. Securing is what is done to a condition that is insecure. The not-secure of insecurity is the radical excess which continuously contours securing.

Security can, therefore, only be thought by incorporating the trace of insecurity – which in the Greek word has precedence – in the very articulation of security itself. That is to say, security only occurs by virtue of the interval between itself and its other. It is whatever it is only by virtue of the way insecurity is always already and simultaneously inscribed within security also. In short, security and insecurity are unequally co-determined. Hence my preference for the term (in)security.

The radical ambivalence of (in)security is consequently not a paradox. Neither is it a contradiction to be resolved through more careful securing. This ambivalence is inescapable and it provides the very dynamic behind the way in which security operates as a generative principle of formation for the production of political order. It is only because it is contoured by insecurity, and because in its turn it also insecures, that security can secure.

Neither does the term (in)security merely denote a position taken in regard to the occurrence of existence. It is not a product of consciousness nor a formal proposition. It is not a judgement about the pain of being 'colored with an effective content',[35] say, of fear, rage or despair; however much it may provoke such sentiments. Thus what (in)secures is not merely a particular form of life, nor simply death – for there is birth as well as death in (in)security – but the (in)security of existence itself. Existence is (in)security. The point which our politics of security – together with their attendant, refined and insistent discourses of danger – makes me want to add, however, is that grounding, and so confining our view of what politics is, in a *doxa* of danger is itself a dangerously self-immolative thing to do. What is politically relevant is not simply that the world is dangerous, and that it is full of people who otherwise constrained would want to kill me, but that this *doxa* – this site and sight of the world only ever opening up to us as a domain of fear – impacts upon the world itself in ways that are destined to destroy it; particularly when *doxa* becomes *techne* and the world is insistently fabricated after fear and not only apprehended that way. To see it differently of course requires us to undergo a different kind of experience with Language, and so also with our being, which demands a (political) vision and courage all of its own.

To link security to insecurity in this way is not, therefore, to fill a gap in thinking about security. It is to make a first step towards adequately posing the question concerning security itself. That first step is required in order ultimately to pose the question concerning the political, because I claim that the claim upon which the metaphysical tradition of political thought is premised is that security is the ground of (especially modern) politics, whereas I would argue that (in)security, namely the obligatory freedom of human being itself, is the opening which calls forth the prospect of a political life. To explore this thought further I return to the tragic.

Chapter 5

The political and the tragic

A mimesis opens the fiction of tone. It is the tragedy of 'Come' though it must be repeatable (*a priori* repeated in itself) in order to resonate.

(Jacques Derrida, *The Ends of Man*)

A philosophy of the limit provokes a questioning of the political at the limit not only of the mortality that human beings are, but also of both the thinking and the (inter)national politics to which we are now heirs. Given the dangers of our time, a philosophy of the limit brings the question of the limit – of both life and thinking, of the thinking life that we are – into question in a way which offers the prospect of opening-up thinking to some consideration of a non-eschatological response to the limit condition which delimits us; and thus to some continuing prospect of a future in which we might continue to live, love and think.

One way or another – including even those who in their way turn to 'God'[1] – philosophers of the limit have ensured that political thought can no longer turn to, or turn upon, metaphysics because it has lost its recourse to a transcendent omnipotent deity who grants man politics as an integral part of His plan of salvation, or a coherent *Logos* guaranteeing human reason. Political thought in the aftermath of the recovery of the question of Being – political thought thought in appreciation of the ontological difference – is political thought after the demise of metaphysics.[2] And that is political thought caught within tradition between tradition and a new beginning.[3] The impossibility of metaphysical foundations is now the starting point for political thought. In this sense, too, not only is it not nihilistic thought, it is thought designed to overcome the nihilism which is immanent in metaphysics.

Is an appreciation of human mortality, then, stripped of the metaphysical comforts of a transcendent being or the representative–calculative thought which goes by the name of rationality, capable of effecting a transformation of human being? Is an ethos which is nothing ethical, and, therefore, more than moral excuses, derivable from the shock of mortality alone? How might mortality bind human being to its freedom? How might the experience of mortality govern one's relations with others and Otherness? Can a sensibility of mortality give rise to a human solidarity which is not premised upon the supercession of difference which is the effacement of obligatory freedom? What kind of respect, if any, is derivable not only for human but for all beings from what might be called a civic solidarity of the shaken; a solidarity excited by a shared sensibility of the tragic mortality of human existence?[4] Is there a politics capable of discharging the debts which identity continuously incurs to the Otherness upon which it necessarily and always relies in bearing its freedom? Or, to put it another way, does this challenge – the challenge of that irremissible debt – now constitute the defining challenge of democratic politics in late modern times? How might the replies to these and related questions in-form a political community? Now. For perhaps the most important task facing those who are engaged in a political thought, which, as it seeks to discharge its responsibility to human freedom, nonetheless eschews recourse to metaphysical foundations which would foreclose that freedom, is to think what mortal politics could be now that mortality has become redoubled through the nuclearisation and cyberneticisation of late modern times.

It is important to add that while such thinking is neither a religious nor a secular thought, and so neither does it draw upon their attendant faiths, it nonetheless also entails a rethinking, rather than a rejection, of the reverence for beings and Being that is inspired by the experience of being; and of the sacred, which being such a peculiar (human) part of the event of Being evokes. Neither secular nor religious – categories that gained their contemporary currency through the way in which the dissolution of Christendom gave advent to Modernity – reverence or the sacred are at issue in it (not resolved dogmatically) either.[5]

Our metaphysical politics of security, I argue, are, however, impelled to make politics a matter of command; membership of a political community a matter of obedience; love synonymous with a policing order; order a function of discipline; and identity a narcissistic paranoia. Combined with the advances in science and technology, they have become deeply – potentially terminally – inimical to human flourishing. Not merely capable of species extinction – as the deterrent policies of the Cold War years first demonstrated – logically they come comprehensively to threaten it in consequence of the way they understand, organise, pursue, and legitimise the formation of political community and the purposes of political organisation. The dissolution of the Cold War has changed nothing here. Rather it has intensified the logic and disseminated it more pervasively. The capabilities have been proliferating globally in any event – Cold War or not – driven by the combination of technological, economic and military dynamics in association with which the (inter)national politics of security have been operating in modern times. Our civilisation is now quite capable of ending cataclysmically. I do not think that recognising this possibility necessarily results, however, in eschatological thought. On the contrary, that is why I am interested in the philosophy of the limit. The sensible thing to do in a world capable of effecting its own negation through its ability terminally to realise its limits as catastrophic ending, is to ally through deconstruction with that undecidability which continuously defers the terminal.

The philosophy of the limit therefore calls the very foundations of our civilisation into question not as a discovery, and not as a childish impiety, but simply by recognising that that that is what its own practices do. The philosophy of the limit is consequently not another voluntary schema of thought offering a superior technology of representation with more opaque, more beautiful or more epistemologically Byzantine excuses for human being. It is simply recognition.

And, yet, at one time, the philosophical project of deconstruction's foremost thinker, Heidegger, allied itself to the paradigmatic expression of the very self-immolative dynamic which distinguishes our civilisation. Heidegger's thinking is, therefore, also dangerous. But then how else could it be? Nothing is without danger, not even – not least – Language itself; that through which human being stands exposed in the (in)secure mortal freedom of its existence. Neither is the thought that has tried to overcome mortality with metaphysical illusions, nor the thought of mortality which has tried to think without the support of established metaphysical comforts. Their thinking cannot be made safe, I would maintain, precisely because they are thinkers of the mortal freedom of (in)security. 'To live', Nietzsche wrote, 'is ever to be in danger'.[6] To deny the danger in them is, therefore, not only to deny the very character of their thought but also to evade the most dangerous question of all, the question of how we belong together in that obligatory freedom in ways which remain responsive to its continuously changing demands. That question – which continuously and inescapably demands judge-ment, hence danger and violence too – is the question of the political. Although Heidegger's responses demonstrated how hard a question the question of the political is, Heidegger did not duck it. Rather, it is Heidegger's thought above all that is most dangerous in that it calls insistently and sometimes directly for a recovery of the political.

Here, with his very political fallibility, arises a particular reason why it does so. There is a pressing need to recover the question of the political as much from Heidegger-the-Nazi, who seems to corrupt it, as from Heidegger the philosopher who appears to elide it. A refurbished interrogation and understanding of the political is consequently one of the prizes to be prised-out of an engagement with Heidegger.[7] The preface for such an engagement, which is all I have been attempting here, must, I have been arguing, proceed through security by way of the tragic.

We cannot, therefore, go the route which Heidegger himself first took and against which his subsequent thinking was quite clearly and critically devoted. That is precisely the technological nemesis to which his own thought alerts us and from which the recovery of the political will always be required. The matter of Heidegger's 'silence' – that is to say, his refusal to repudiate the Nazi period publicly, to 'atone' for his membership of the Nazi Party, and his silence concerning the fate of European Jewry – is particularly relevant here. I could say that I do not have the space to give it all the thought and close attention it deserves, but in fact I do not know precisely what amount of space it would require. For this conventional genuflection to seriousness implies that somehow I do know, or could know. But I do not. And yet it is not a matter of me not knowing. I simply think it is not knowable. The question will never be answered and so it will never be settled. This is in fact what allows me to go on about it, and with it. Given the importance attached to silence in all of Heidegger's thought, this 'silence' cannot be mere omission.[8] In his lectures on Parmenides, for example, he says,

'to keep silent' is not merely to say nothing. Without something essential to say, one cannot keep silent. Only within essential speech, and by means of it alone, can there prevail essential silence, having nothing in common with secrecy, concealment, or 'mental reservations'.[9]

Manifestly, it is not a simple oversight either, because silence always resounds for Heidegger, and so perhaps it is also something even more than a 'radical failure of thought'.[10] For, in his thinking, Heidegger systematically and consistently elevated reticence and comportment even above thought. Or, rather, consonant with his radical hermeneutical phenomenology, and with his history of Being and its preoccupation with the hidden and the inconspicuous, Heidegger made of thought something which was fundamentally related to dwelling in a pious attentiveness to the mystery of Being. Hence, one might suspect that his association with the Nazis was no mere 'deficiency' of thought, but a consequence of his own 'disposition' or comportment.[11] And it is precisely this, though worked through his thought in detailed ways, which John Caputo concludes is Heidegger's scandal.[12]

Somehow Heidegger, here on this site and with respect to the site-ing of the political, seemed unwilling to think through the fundamental belonging together of dwelling *and* displacement: that we are all strangers native born, and so always already dwelling *en route*; that routes and roots are ineradicably intertwinned; hence, that to found and be a people (even, in his terms, with the assignment of the word) is an exclusionary practice; that indigeneity, however useful it may be as a device to protect some from the violence of Modernity and its modernisers, is a certain sort of violent claim; and that to circumscribe and inhabit a 'place' simultaneously also poses the question of the one who is thereby estranged from that place, or comes to that place as a stranger.

All of this, of course, is, nonetheless, however, precisely what his entire account of mortal existence also proclaims. For Heidegger, *par éminence*, is the philosopher of pathways. His very thought – especially where it concerns 'Homecoming', because homecoming (always already referring to an originary dispossession or being-out-of-place, rather than any simple-minded geographical repatriation) is a continuous cherishing re-calling of what it is to be human[13] – insists that displacement is a pre-condition of dwelling.[14] Homecoming, not staying but lingering a while, is only ever an episode in wandering. Moreover, and despite misguided criticisms that have been directed at him to this effect, while this exile in freedom is a continuous struggle to be, and to preserve the law of the possible which freedom entails, it is an exile without nostalgia.

Consequently, and though it nonetheless appears as if it also entails some failure of thought, this lacuna in Heidegger makes thought resound, and resounds to thought as well, in its own distinctive way; precisely because it always leaves the question of judgement open.[15] Heidegger seemed to make, take and accept no judgement upon himself. Did he evade judgement? More than that. Is *the* question – that is to say philosophy's question, the question of Being – itself a way of evading judgement? Or, on the contrary, but in ways with which we are unfamilar, does it not necessarily always already belong together with judgement, which it poses as a certain sort of *aporia* that summons the resoluteness entailed in de-cision? In noting the possibility of such a double evasion 'we' are, therefore, always confronted with having to say *what* it is we are judging, *whom* we are to judge, who *we* are who judge, what *judgement* is, on *what authority* and in *whose name* it is exercised, and whether it is *sufficient* merely to judge, when confronting Heidegger-the-Nazi.

His silence thus exposes how a 'we' is comprised by judgement (de-cision); how large an excess beyond judgement judgement, nonetheless, leaves-out for further account; and the violence against that remainder which judgement necessarily creates because there are no innocent alternatives (which is not the same as saying that all alternatives must therefore be equally 'guilty', or to explore what 'guilt' is).[16] It exposes, too, the way rhetorics of moral indignation and ritual purification provide an easy way out of the matter for thought – and so therefore of judgement and decision – which Heidegger-the-Nazi presents. While Being poses the *aporia* of judgement for human being in its very mortal freedom, does confining oneself to the question of Being become a way of evading judgement; of securing oneself through a subtle strategem from the intractable inescapable burden of judgement? Or, instead, does it effect a radically different disposition in and towards the *aporia* of judgement? Was Heidegger struggling all along, therefore, to escape the violent, dirty, debt-incurring, business of judgement whose aporetic difficulty his own thought of Being had nonetheless illuminated? Or, considering his reflections on silence as well as his silence, are 'we' more forcefully directed towards the burden of response-ability we carry in the freedom into which we are thrown after Heidgger – the heavy political mortgage of the twentieth century?

Did he intend or anticipate any or all, and more, of this? Of course I do not even pretend to know. But whatever reasons he may, or may not have had, for keeping silent, he must have done. He was too smart not to know. Do we, in any event, need to know that he knew for all the thoughts which his silence prompts to matter? For they do matter. Very much. And they matter, ultimately, more than Heidegger's life and thought, however much that life and thought forces us to endure this burden of judgement ourselves. Consequently, what is important for me in this affair is that, in the process of enduring the knowledge of Nazism as well as of Heidegger's association with it, it is possible for us to recognise 'ourselves' illuminated also in the *aporia* of judgement. Such a recognition is itself an assumption of response-ability for – which is the same as being open to, or freed as – a being-in-common that always and everywhere, in its openness, remains capable of Holocaust.

In respect of the political especially, I, therefore, have some sympathy with

Emmanuel Levinas' early position in relation to Heidegger. 'At the beginning our reflections are in large measure inspired by the philosophy of Martin Heidegger, where we find the concept of ontology and of the relationship which man sustains with Being', he wrote in one of his first essays. But 'they are also governed by a profound need to leave the climate of that philosophy, and by the conviction that we cannot leave it for a philosophy that would be pre-Heideggerian'.[17] Yet, even this is now no longer a satisfactory characterisation because the atmospherics of Heidegger's thought, as well as the atmospherics surrounding his thought, have changed substantially and in all sorts of ways since Levinas first polemicised against Heidegger.

Furthermore, Heidegger's 12-year membership of the Nazi Party enforces precisely that questioning attitude toward Heidegger which he himself was concerned not only to induce in respect of the Western tradition of thought, but also to establish as the way of thought itself. Does Heidegger's silence provide some clue to this thinker's unthought? Whatever the attractions of Heidegger the critical-eyed historian of the history of Being as metaphysics, Heidegger-the-Nazi would always prevent the simple adoption of that history as a kind of political manifesto. Ironically, his Nazi association serves the very path of thinking which Heidegger-the-philosopher sought to pioneer. The history of Being as metaphysics and the implications of that history will, therefore, always remain questionable, particularly in respect of the exclusive and unconditioned character of the destinal sending of it. At its thought-provoking best such questioning is precisely what Heidegger's own thought intends:[18] 'what he says about Nietzsche – that we must learn to read him with the same rigour that we read Aristotle – applies even more to himself'. We thereby gain 'a precise and sustained strategy of thinking, directed against withering principial referents, against the illusion of any legitimating first that could function as a rule for thinking and as an authority for conduct'.[19] Particularly against any temptation to present Heidegger, or his thought, as such an authority.

If it were not for his insistent sensibility to the liminality of limits which the belonging together of beginnings and ends constitutes, it might be argued that Heidegger himself is tempted into a version of tragic denial in what he once referred to as his eschatology of Being.[20] Heidegger, too, is obsessed with danger and a certain salvation from it.[21] Indeed, he has his own distinctive discourse of danger, special fears and way of fearing, preoccupied with anxiety, foundering failing, shattering, hardness, and struggle.[22] These all come to a pitch in an essay contained in the volume named after it; *The Question Concerning Technology And Other Essays*.[23] For Heidegger, human being is challenged to exert dominion over the forces of nature, including its own nature, in virtue of the way Being discloses itself in the history of metaphysics. This is what he means by technicity or technology. The danger of technology is precisely, therefore, that it will secure security – secure 'man' the subject as just another object in the process of securing all other things as objects – secure so effectively that it will secure us from ever even knowing that we have been so secured. And yet this very process of securing, he believes, is actually what may also alert us to its own danger; because human being is even more challenged technologically than the nature which it, in its turn, technologically suborns. In that very excess of challenge, and because human being is the only being which asks about Being and being, he argues, human being itself may ultimately be challenged beyond the age of technology which currently confines it; to question itself, in other words into a new receptivity to the taking place of the ontological difference of Being and being which it is.

But prior to this articulation of the end of philosophy in the event of technology, Heidegger is more originally distinguished by being, above all and in the first instance, also with Nietzsche, a 'philosopher of tragic insight'.[24] First, because the tragic articulates life as life which arises in virtue of the ontological difference. It is therefore attuned to the complex interplays – the very movement – of this event and of the way that it arises through Language itself. Second, because Heidegger's account of the advent of technicity is itself a kind of tragedy in that it too seeks to follow the movement of the ontological difference; one, indeed, which directly recalls the classical cadences of tragedy, especially, I would say, as these are exhibited in *Oedipus Rex*.[25]

The advent of technicity – like the ontological difference itself – is in no way an anthropological doing for Heidegger. Human being does not simply invent and employ technology and so attempt to master the earth. Being arrives for human being (is disclosed in and through human being – takes place in and through it) in the form of a technological challenging of human being to which human being perforce responds; technologically challenging itself and its habitat, ordering and reorganising both according to the demands of technology. Hence 'self-assertive man, whether or not he knows and wills it as an individual, is the functionary of technology'.[26] The underlying character of technology is that all beings, including human being itself, are posited beforehand as calculable entities and can, therefore, only ever present themselves, or be presented, as calculable; everything is reduced to forms of arithmetic because everything has to be counted com-mensurable, identifiable (hence political arithmetic too). The disclosure of Being in human being, in the form of this challenge to human being to render itself orderable and calculable, is a destiny – in Heidegger's terms the destinal sending of Being – into which human being is thrown, and which propels human being forward itself, in the modern age, as the subject/object of technology.

While destined, human being is not, however, compelled by this fate but thrown in this specific way into the *aporia* of its freedom. The human being 'becomes truly free', Heidegger writes, only insofar as it 'belongs to the realm of sending and so becomes one who listens, not one who simply obeys'.[27] One's individual fate is to encounter the burden of one's obligatory freedom in one's own singular way. Such freedom has nothing whatever to do, therefore, with the idea of the willing freedom associated with the reduction of human being to a subject. Rather, because 'Being does not simply, as it were, pass its judgement down,'[28] human being is freed to attend to the reception of Being to which its own existence belongs and attests. In so doing it may realise the fullness of the freedom to be that which it itself is.

All this is possible, according to Heidegger, precisely because, in *dis-closing* itself, Being simultaneously also reveals by concealing or being withdrawn, and human being is capable of attuning itself to the way in which, always arriving as some-thing, Being is never disclosed in this process as such at all. Concealment always accompanies unconcealment. There is, so to speak, always already consequently more to Being than the technological disclosive challenge it currently issues to and through human being. For technology, as the current mode of the disclosure of Being, hides as well as reveals Being. Indeed, it is the withdrawing amplified, intensified and subject to extension. Moreover, the very essence of human being is that it is the being for whom its own being is an issue. Challenged in its own being by the calculative predations of technology, it is capable of asking after the way its being has now become an issue for it through being technologised. Remember also, however, that Being and human being are not separate. They occur together because they belong together, locked in mutual disclosive need of one another; the play of the ontological difference. Hence, technology does not merely reveal and conceal – or, rather, reveal by concealing – Being. More precisely it simultaneously reveals and conceals the relationship of identity and difference of Being and human being which is, for Heidegger, the essence of human being. Obscuring this relation, the essence of technology endangers the very essence of human being – its freedom to be in questioning relation to Being – and is consequently the supreme danger.

Paying heed to this, human being may, therefore, find itself challenged beyond the securing confines of technology. In short, human being is challenged not determined, and in remaining steadfastly open to this challenge, by responding 'thoughtfully' to it rather than by merely embracing the determining trajectory it describes, and thereby forgetting its essential identity/difference with Being, it may thereby become receptive to Being in its own being differently; may come to recognise, acknowledge and live freely in response to the relationship of mutually disclosive need which it enjoys with, and by virtue of, Being, rather than according to the mere challenge of current technological disclosure. As with *Oedipus*, I will argue, so also with human being, each only becomes more fully the being which they are when, as listening overcomes seeing, each renews itself through its recovery or recollection of its indebtedness to the surplus in virtue of which its own free being occurs; for *Dasein* (through reflection) of Being; for *Oedipus* (through self-blinding) of the divine.

However, it is not a question for me of determining in detail whether Heidegger is a philosopher of tragic insight – his insistence upon the poetic confesses that he is – so much as exploring further the preliminary questions of what is meant by the tragic here, and of how it relates to the question of the political. Rather than provide a close reading of Heidegger's work to document the tragic in it, I think it is therefore necessary instead, or at least at first, to have a more developed understanding of the tragic. Although I will not have time to discuss it, how

Heidegger might be said to be a philosopher of tragic insight, and how his tragic insight may differ from that of the Greeks, would then become an important matter for discussion; not only for students of Heidegger, and for students of Heidegger's 'politics', but also for students of politics in general.

THE TRAGIC

The tragic is neither the aestheticisation of the political, nor mere fatedness and misfortune. ('The tragic artist is not a pessimist – it is precisely he who affirms all that is questionable and terrible in existence, he is Dionysian. . . .'[29]) Neither is it simply the mood evoked by the experience of 'the vanishing of the metaphysical ground as a tragic event'.[30] If we had not come to think that life can only be affirmed when it is subject to some final redemptive purpose, or grounded in some ultimate structure of meaning, then we would not be compelled to think of the tragic as something which fills the void when life is deprived of such comforts. This is precisely the trouble with the modern understanding of the tragic; that it fills the void or, worse, expresses the void, vacated by something else. Rather than filling a space voided by the dissolution of Christian or metaphysical faith, however, the tragic came before them and must necessarily always come before them; because it is openness to fortune and therefore fundamentally concerns, instead, the opening-up of a world in which faith may arise, but in which life can also be lived in recognition and appreciation of the belonging together of Being and beings in the openness afforded by the very difference between Being and beings.

This, too, was the world of the *polis* – as it was part constituted, portrayed and explored, through tragedy – where life was lived in truth as *aletheia*. If we, therefore, ask what political difference the ontological difference makes, which many commentators, like Richard Rorty for example, effectively do, the answer is the tragic.[31] The tragic is the ontological difference first experienced – not thought as such – as the possibility and practice of a mortal politics.

'For there to be tragic action', a recent classic study of tragedy concluded, 'it is necessary that a concept of human nature with its own characteristics should have already emerged and that the human and divine spheres should have become sufficiently distinct from each other for them to stand in opposition; yet at the same time they must continue to appear as inseparable.'[32] In consequence, the

> tragic sense of responsibility makes its appearance at the point when, in human action, a place is given to internal debate on the part of the subject [*sic*], to intention and premeditation, but when this human action has still not acquired enough consistency and autonomy to be entirely self-sufficient. The true domain of tragedy lies in that border zone where human actions are hinged together with the divine powers, where – unknown to the agent – they derive their true meaning by becoming an integral part of an order that is beyond man and that eludes him.[33]

(Human action never, of course, attains that consistency and autonomy which would make it self-sufficient, its very freedom to act and the character of its actions – which always, more or less unpredictably, set things in train – deny it this. The realm of the gods was also the Greek way of pointing towards, and expressing the divinity of, the beyond of mortality to which limited mortality is nonetheless linked.)

All this is directly related in addition, of course, to the question of security and insecurity, and to the radical ambiguity of (in)security as well. For within tragedy it becomes clear that it is not simply a question of insecure human being seeking security. Merely to see a recoil back and forth between security and insecurity is to miss the point altogether, because it misses something fundamental about human being itself which tragedy seeks to depict and celebrate. It is, therefore, to miss something which Martha Nussbaum explored so brilliantly that it is worth quoting her conclusion at length. 'There is a certain valuable quality in social virtue that is lost when social virtue is removed from the domain of uncontrolled happenings', she writes:

> There is no courage without the risk of death or of serious damage; no true love of city that does not say (with Alcibiades), 'Love of city is what I do not feel when I am wronged'; no true commitment to justice that exempts its own privileges from scrutiny.

In sum:

> This willingness to embrace something that *is* in the world and subject to its risks is, in fact, the virtue of the Euripidean child, whose love is directed at the world itself, including its dangers. The generous looks of such a child go straight to the world with love and openness; they do not focus upon the safe and the eternal, or demand these as conditions of their love. . . . any life that devoted itself entirely to safe activities would be, for a human being, impoverished. The *Hecuba* [for example] does not conceal from us the seductive dangers of romanticising risk itself. . . . [But] there are certain risks – including, here, the risk of becoming unable to risk – that we cannot close off without a loss in human value, suspended as we are between beast and god, with a kind of beauty available to neither.[34]

Being human being *is* tragic, and so we are (in)secure. That anxiety which is experienced in the duality of security and insecurity is the freedom – the very capacity to respond and so be responsible – of the human condition. In the tragic we not only find that we have been here before, but also that, in a sense, we have never truly been elsewhere because there is no escape from where we are at.

This juncture of the duality of human-ness that gives rise to the political and the democratic is what tragedy sought to speak about and provide an education in; for 'tragedy was born when myth began to be assessed from the citizen point of view'.[35] That is why the recovery of the political is not only something which must always already take place in the context of the specific, historical circumstances of human being – currently labelled 'Modernity' – it is also why that recovery must take place with, in and through the movement of democratic thought. Hence, while '[f]rom a political point of view, the questioning of modernity means the questioning of democracy'.[36] Democracy must also always remain a form of questioning which constantly recalls the political to mind and seeks to make space for it in the obligatory freedom of human being.

From within the *polis* the tragic, therefore, called into question the very demarcations that constituted it. The drama was a showing whose effect was to educate and individuate 'everyman' precisely because it derived its source material from

> the social thought peculiar to the fifth-century city, with all the tensions and contradictions that appear in it when the advent of law and the constitution of political life place in question the old religious and moral traditional values.[37]

When the 'hero' and the *polis* are thus publicly brought into question in Greek tragedy 'it is the individual Greek in the audience who discovers himself to be a problem in and through the presentation of the tragic drama'.[38] Nothing less than human being's civilising capacity and power is at issue in the tragic.[39] But because the tragic recognises Otherness to be immanent, as well as radical, it is compelled to find ways of responding to it with agonistic respect.

This sets the question of the political aside from all those, conventionally studied in terms of the (inter)national politics of security, of the structures, institutions, rationalities and technologies of our contemporary regimes of power and practices of rule.[40] In particular, it sets the question aside from the intense and pervasive cult of the subject which constitutes the (inter)national politics of Modernity, as such. While the cult of the subject seems to have arisen as a liberatory move within the dissolution of the Christian imaginary, it necessarily called into effect, and thereby entered into an intimate alliance with, the rationalising and reifying practices of rule of which 'we' are the inheritors. This was no mere accident. Neither was it a coincidence, nor the unfortunate pathology of an otherwise admirable development. It was integral and essential to what was a radical mutation in the symbolic order, and intensification of the logic of onto-theology, by which the very staging and sense of the political was fundamentally re-ordered. (Inter)national political Modernity, as the legatee of that mutation, is, itself, already mutating – through the rationalising, technologising, globalising velocity of its very own representational practices and dynamics – just as radically as the times which engendered it. That bequest from the dissolution of the Christian world is, in consequence of the very logics at work within it, rapidly fashioning a radically different political bequest to 'us'. *The (inter)national politics of Modernity must, therefore, become concerned not with living-out but with out-living the modern.* Out-living it through recalling and affirming, for example, the continuous disclosure of the excess of human (and other) being over appearance as this arises within and against the foreclosures threatened by the web of Modernity's technologising determinations. Such is a routine and mundane as well as a monumental task; though the mundane, for many in it, is often itself a monumental achievement. The need to engage in a contest for the political does not, therefore, arise somewhere else. Nor does it operate in some other time or place yet to come from out of the past or out of the future. It always already exists; here, now, for the future.

Tragedy, therefore, does not have to invent its characters or plots. It finds them already there in the human condition. Within the space, framework and interpretive dynamics of the tragic consciousness, human being is not represented as a model – however defined and determined – nor even as a problem, but as an excessive, abundant, temporal way of being. It is, therefore, a mortal riddle, never fully to be decoded, precisely because it is temporal; because being temporal it knows not from whence it came, and because being temporal it projects, that is to say, takes-up its freedom. Tragedy, therefore, always has history as its material.

But history here is not history in the historiographical sense of a series of facts and events more or less statically present in a once-present. It is history in the fundamental sense in which human being is temporal. '*Dasein* does not first become historical in repetition', Heidegger notes in *Being and Time*, 'but because it is historical as temporal, it can take itself over in its history by repeating'.[41] This historical sensibility, which is less 'historical' in the traditional sense and more radically temporal, recognises that what has taken place always already shapes and limits what comes to meet us, and how we are disposed to meet it; including also how we meet the 'past'. It thus recognises more than that we have a past and that that past is of antiquarian or independent interest to us. Rather, it recalls that, because of time, we are always already historical, shaped by the way the past unfolds through us as we project forward; and that the past is, therefore, always an issue for us in the present as we practise that projecting forward there in realising our potentiality-for-being. In sum, history is human being taking-up what it undergoes – the process, as Heidegger puts it, of its 'having its being to be' – and therefore always arising anew in the process.

Herein lies a fundamental problem, however, one that further illustrates the bind that we are in. Because tragedy is Greek, and we are not, strictly speaking we need a new name and new practices for that to which I have been using the tragic to draw attention. This lack is the gap that contemporary political thought has yet to bridge. That I have both to affirm and yet reject the tragic illustrates how 'we' are still suspended in the web of the political economy of the tradition of the 'West'; still ensnared in that historical, and historically specific, manifold problematic of identity which results in recurring cults of the subject (nation, people, state, class). 'We' shall not discover and elaborate for ourselves a sense of the political and of the tragic, therefore, as if we could, by seeking simply to re-adopt the Greek *polis* and Greek tragedy. Instead we can only do so by interrogating them for what they say about the very questions of origination and derivation themselves. The tragic may take history as its material, but Greek history is not (or not simply) our history, and Greek tragedy is not our tragedy. For one thing, metaphysics – and for another the fate of the Judeo-Christian God – intervene between then and now. In short, we lack a political genre to give single voice to the ineradicable duality of the mortal life – simultaneously necessitous and free – of human being as we encounter it in our present.[42] That lack is itself something which distinguishes us from the Greeks and is integral to our tragedy; part of which is the loss of the tragic sensibility itself.

Whereas in classical tragedy '[t]he nature of tragic action seems ... to be defined by the simultaneous presence of a "self" and something greater that is divine at work at the core of the decision and creating a constant tension between the two opposed poles',[43] in a way that seems powerfully to recall the ontological difference, it also forcefully reminds us that the ontological difference is a contemporary philosophical expression. The Greek understanding of reverence and of the divine is sufficient to indicate that the ontological difference was not experienced and thought by the Greeks in such terms. With the end of philosophy, therefore, arises not simply the death of God, but the depiction and exploration of the tragic – the mortal life of human being which exists in virtue of the very difference it bears within itself – without gods.[44]

Tragedy nonetheless constitutes the only powerful voice we currently possess for recalling the political difference which the ontological difference makes; as the mounting storm of technologising normalisation and representative–calculative thought threatens to efface any re-collection of it, thereby operating always to foreclose the opening of the political. While the tragic invokes 'a transformed relation to the essence of the old'[45] which asserts itself with such new vigour in our times, however, tragedy promises neither a new language, nor a novel set of assertive or prescriptive devices. Instead, through its very sensibility to human being, tragedy operates provocatively and evocatively to recall the tragic character of our mortal being to us despite and against the inroads which technology is making into it. Hence it remains an indispensable resource.

Mortal being, the condition of the condition known as tragic, is tragic not because we die or because we are fated and miserable, therefore, but because being temporal we live by virtue of death and are consequently always already differentiated, open and excessive creatures indebted to an excess that we can never master: Beings that know themselves to be and yet also to be had by, and so differ from, Being which they manifest. Destined to be some-thing, by the gratuitous gift of life itself, but not determined to be one thing or another, we are not just alive and not just dead (even, in a sense, when dead). We are always something more than either of them because we are always already both – living and dying – at the same time. The tragic, therefore, discloses an insight into existence as the mortality which is just this, a continuous adventure of freedom in an ethical frontier constituted by the opening of the ontological difference which constantly challenges us to decide how we should find the time and place to dwell freely in the freedom of our being, which is a being we share in common; with ourselves, each other, and the earth itself.[46]

There, too, in the opaque borderlands of this difference, knowledge and power constantly collide in a way that tragedy recognises: because there is no secure place in the tragic consciousness for a stable hierarchy of types of knowledge; for the architectonics of power; or for the contract they seek to conclude. Equally foreign to it is the enframing of the ineradicable duality of human being in terms of the endless either/ors of metaphysical thought. More even than this, because there is nothing which guarantees that the gift of life is benign, the tragic entertains the possibility of a fundamental indifference, or even antagonism, between truth and humanity and explores that very condition; the freedom of being human is the challenge, regularly evaded in ways too numerous to catalogue, of course, to discover ways of resolving the freedom of its (in)security. Hence the 'truth' of tragedy directly conflicts with that of philosophical truth; logic is confounded in the tragic precisely because it affirms the a-logicality of the duality of the human condition. The tragic effects what Krell would call a frontal ontology on the political,[47] exploring being as it experiences the experiencing of the ontological difference in its very own experience; out-facing, through its tropes and topologies, the vaunted ontic realism of our (inter)national politics of security. Tragedy thereby shifts the political into a different dimension of space, time and truth; where time has many cadences and the disclosive quality of truth retains a fundamentally obscure, divided and errant quality which finds its expression in many voices and is a challenge to mortal being itself. This is a dimension that specifically does not function according to the polarities of logic, the demands of adequation, and the policing impulse of a love that requires a why. Tragedy abounds, instead, in the boundary or limit; where limit is, however, liminality, the very occasioning of something.[48] Its world is a world of ambiguity and multiple disclosure where the validity or invalidity of a thesis is ultimately not the point. It is one where double arguments and duality proliferate and where differences encounter and counter, rather than simply negate, one another as they describe the struggle of being. Instead of being preoccupied with the formulation of rules that tell us what we must do, tragedy is concerned with depicting the predicament of the Being of a being which lives life in appreciation of the agonal freedom of the ontological difference.

In the tragic consciousness the very formulas, norms and boundaries employed to establish order are all themselves at issue. The very clarity of the world and the meaning of events is hidden behind a foreground which none of the characters can penetrate with certainty. But the figure of the so-called tragic 'hero' – breaking the laws that give order, unsecuring what secures, lacking stability of place and identity – is not simply the exceptional figure. Rather it is the figure that recalls the exceptional character of mortal being itself. Exhibiting a capacity for greatness, prone to excess, the tragic 'hero' is a figuration of the way in which for all human beings, their very being-ness, that is to say what it is to be human, has continuously to be recovered and reconstructed in ever changing circumstances. Where, classically, the 'hero' confronts the extreme polarities of mortal life and is the very device 'which springs the safe fastenings which hold together our logical, ordered world',[49] a heightened sense of the political – as the very mobile relationality of human being (capacity to respond to its being which is always and everywhere, necessarily, a being-in-common with others in Otherness in virtue of the fact that Otherness inheres within itself) in relation to the circumstances in which it finds itself – nonetheless arises. Precisely because the action and the character are a-political (city-less, cut off from the city, inhabiting and disrupting its boundaries) a sense of the political, as a movement in which the critical liminality of boundaries is experienced and respected to facilitate the disclosure of human being itself, is made available: a sensibility to precisely this arises – *polis*, not *stasis*.

Thus tragedy does not promise a release from the agonism integral to the freedom of human being, or from the violence which it always threatens. How could anything? It explores the prospects, instead, for practising life-affirming approaches to it. Danger, therefore, stalks the tragic consciousness as well; a special danger these days, in all sorts of ways, but especially since the *miasma* of Fascism has threatened profoundly to compromise the truth of the tragic itself, fundamentally impairing our capacity to recover a sense of it appropriate to our condition.

Yet, the tragic ultimately indicts rather than invites Fascism. First, because for the tragic the limit is liminality (creativeness) rather than terminality (the final solution). Second, however much it may have arisen in a time when the Greeks differentiated themselves from Barbarians, because tragedy does not locate the boundary between the civilised and the savage on the frontiers of society – at the limits of the inhabited/civilised world so that the immanent alterity of the human condition can then be dealt with by projecting it out and onto some outside – 'but brings it within the *polis* itself, within the very hearts of its rulers and citizens',[50] it thereby exposes how Fascism's self-immolative rage against others and Otherness is a war against alterity that is ultimately a self-loathing aimed at our very articulatedness.

Possessing yet also being possessed by existence, creative and yet created,

> that much that I did not make goes towards making me whatever I shall be praised or blamed for being; that I must constantly choose among competing and apparently incommensurable goods and that circumstances may force me to a position in which I cannot help being false to something or doing some wrong; that an event that simply happens to me may, without my consent, alter my life; that it is equally problematic to entrust one's good to friends, lovers, or country and to try to have a good life without them – all these I take to be not just the material of tragedy, but everyday facts of lived practical reason.[51]

The tragic is not, therefore, an excuse for evil, it is the setting in which evil arises as evil. The same goes for the good as well. We do not know securely what either is in advance, we have always to re-cognise what they are in our present circumstances. Not an escape from judgement or responsibility, the tragic is the condition that calls it up and apportions it while also acknowledging the creation of injustice and irresponsibility which judgement inevitably also entails.

Rather than displaying the dilemmas of human beings as 'pre-articulated', tragedy shows them 'searching for the morally [ethically] salient'.[52] Mortal life – free life – which is tragic life, forces each of us to be active in this way. That is to say, as an 'undecided being', to exit from the realm of undecided possibility into the contest over good and evil – neither of which we can escape because there is also, of course, a belonging together of good and evil (how else would we distinguish either?) which capacity is what constitutes freedom – and take-up that which we undergo, freedom itself, through the challenge of decision and judgement; which, because they are always concerned with the freedom of the human condition, are neither decisionistic nor arbitrary.[53] 'Interpreting a tragedy', Nussbaum continues, is, therefore, 'a messier, less determinate, more mysterious matter than assessing a philosophical example'. And truer. With both the mortal and the tragic 'even when the work has been interpreted it remains unexhausted, subject to reassessment in a way that example does not'.[54]

However much it addresses the general condition of mortality, the tragic has always to be set in the specific world in which mortals come to appearance. Tragedy, then, seeks to explore the meanings which constitute that world through the dynamics of what is meaningful in it, how and why they are meaningful, and how the condition of mortality works its way out there. Tragedy therefore historicises, contextualises and particularises as it seeks to address the condition of mortality. As it does so, it traces the history of a complex pattern of deliberation, exposes the roots of that conduct in a specific way of life, and seeks to work through or anticipate the consequences it will have for that way of life, and for the human beings who inhabit it. While involving us in that life, therefore, tragedy nonetheless also has a way of distancing us from its setting. Thus spacing things out, it thereby provides a space in which our experience is extended in ways that relate to our immediate concerns and partisan commitments, without allowing us merely to remain embroiled within them so that we get no other purchase on them than that provided by our immediate preoccupations with them.[55]

Given its basic *modus operandi*, including of course the fundamental require-ment to engage and communicate, how would the dramatist, then, pursuade an audience to engage with a drama that has no perspective? Of what interest could a view from nowhere be to people who are, however problematically, always already somewhere? There is no human point in operating from an Archimedean point. Hence the tragic implicitly disdains the argument that we cannot know how to proceed or judge unless we do have an Archimedean point from which to take our bearings and resolve our dilemmas. It knows that we do act, and have to act. It knows that, however inadequately, we always have reasons for acting. It knows, too, that we can never be fully in control of our actions, because much remains mysterious to us and there are always unintended, and often dreadful, consequences attached to what we do. And it knows, finally, that we have to take public responsibility for what we are and do, even though we are not fully in control of our actions and their outcomes, by virtue of the fact that as mortal beings we are open to Being and beings through our own being; and cannot, therefore, escape taking-up the burden of that which we undergo, namely, existence itself.

It appreciates also that because our actions are public and that the very publicness of them is what always already installs the critical distance within them which calls us forth from them so that we cannot remain solipsistically trapped by them. Here responsibility 'has nothing whatsoever to do with moral imperatives' arising out of a command ethic, but arises instead from human being's resolute openness which manifests itself in the desire to make manifest and answer 'before mankind for every thought', by affirming the life that is lived in 'that luminosity in which oneself and everything one thinks is tested'.[56] Once more, that responsibility is, then, the holding open of that openness which is the ability to respond. That indeed, precisely because we lack total control, we are destined to embrace such a world-creating responsibility; to hold open a time and place, a disposition, posture and stance, which insists on remaining open to all that we are. This, literally, from the perspective of tragedy, is the place and the function of the *polis*. In the process of doing so, tragedy claims, life is restored by a self-recognition through which humans can attain a certain greatness in that openness, for practical political questions emphatically do not admit of truth in the sense of simple correspondence or coherence.

Tragedy is, therefore, concerned precisely with the condition in which we do not and cannot know what is correct in advance, and with how, nonetheless, we creatively work-out and work with our disclosure in the truth of that condition in order to live the free manifold of life itself. And it can be this because correctness is ultimately not the point for it. Its truth, the truth of this occulting dis-closure, is a truth which antecedes correctness. For these very reasons, the tragic is not 'a form of playful imitation, nor does it resemble daemonic impersonation, it is a transmutation of life'.[57] It shows the transformative, restorative capacity operating within an existence that is free, not by writing a rule book but by offering, instead, the enacting of action, or the terrible movements, demands and responsibilities of that free life itself. Above all, tragedy is an exploration of the adventure in the freedom of repetition.

Of course, there is imitation in that performance, but the mimesis of tragedy is not passive reflection; neither is that entailed in the living of a political life.[58] It is not a mere process of 'repetition'. No repetition is ever in fact, of course, mere repetition: 'variation is not added to repetition in order to hide it, but is rather its condition or constitutive element, the interiority of repetition *par excellence*'.[59] Hence, the *mimesis* or repetition referred to is a process of active composition in which displacement and disruption also – and necessarily – take place. (As Deleuze noted: 'the power of difference and repetition ... [can] be reached only by putting into question the traditional range of thought'.[60]) That *mimesis* is one in which the ambiguities and strains of coping with the interactions of the inherent freedom and plurality of human being, and of the city (of the being capable of life in a *polis*), are explored.

Tragedy, then, offered a unique mode of learning which was itself a model of *politeia* because it literally called citizens forth into the specific situation – always a situation with others – in which they had to act. That is to say, through its moment of on-site in-sight, tragedy called the citizen forward into the situation where the political is itself always arising; the factical, contingent, temporal, spatial *mise en scène* and *mise en sens* of one of those moments of all of the moments in which human being continuously takes up that which it is undergoing in the politics of the *polis*. Such a moment – the undecidedness of freedom – is literally the moment where human being bears repeating; picks-up where it has been left-off and takes-over its temporal possibilities again, in that very situation and by virtue of that very situation. It is a moment which of necessity cannot be determined in advance for it only ever arises in virtue of the specific way in which it has been entered into. It is not, therefore, the abstracted kind of decision situation in which the options have been worked out beforehand, and are now present at hand ready for choice. It is the moment in which what is possible is resolutely worked out in the turn of the moment. There is, then, no application or mere repetition of models going on here, and neither is the outcome fully calculable in advance. This moment, enacted in tragedy, is the very moment of the political. Politics has its turn in the tragic.

As Franz Rosenzweig wrote,

> All criticism follows upon performance. The drama critic will have little to say *before* it, no matter how clever he may be, for his criticism is not supposed to testify to what cleverness he had prior to the performance but to that which the performance evokes in him. Similarly, a theory of knowledge that precedes knowledge has no meaning. For all knowing – whenever anything is really known – is a unique act, and has its own method.[61]

Showing, therefore, teaches us to look for the sake of seeing.[62] It gets us to think from somewhere rather than nowhere – namely the standpoint of someone else, thus allowing us not only to appreciate that other position, but also to recognise that it may legitimately be different and remain so – and so focuses our attention and judgement as spectators (which means we are integral and indispensable to the public-ness of the performance, bear witness to it) on the publicly available aspects and import of the play.[63] For showing also creates an audience which represents the world 'or rather the worldly space which has come into being', by virtue of the play.[64] Thus not only do people learn to speak and enact a politics through the tragic, a (political) people may be constituted this way.[65]

In this moment a world is created anew. It is a moment which, however, is neither making nor acting, in their metaphysical senses, neither creation *ex nihilo*, *techne*, nor the supposed mere repetition of tradition. It is something else which seems to combine aspects of all of these elements without being able to be reduced to any one, or any combination, of them. It seems to me to be, then, what Heidegger has tried to describe both in terms of resolute openness and in terms of those moments which found a 'people' or a 'State'. And yet, it is not as simple as either of these thoughts of his have been made out to be either; nor even as dangerously simple as he himself seemed to be inclined to make them sometimes when talking about the 'German' 'State' and 'people'. Take *Oedipus*, for example; both because

I want to come on to him next but also because – which is why I want to come on to him next – he seems to exemplify precisely this condition.

Oedipus appears to be a radical, a State-founder. He arrives as a stranger, and saves Thebes. But Thebes was there before he arrived – and it continues anew after his departure. Indeed, he was once a part of it, and there is some evidence for thinking that Sophocles creates a deliberate ambiguity in the play to intimate that *Oedipus* and the rest are covertly aware of this.

Oedipus, remember also, is both a native and a stranger born. The problematic which the play addresses is, therefore, neither simply that of how to found a polity (pure creation), nor is it simply that of how to ensure the continuation of a polity (supposed 'tradition'). Rather, it is the problematic of political renewal, the renewal of freedom and judgement posed by the *aporia* of freedom and judgement, and of the costs entailed in that process. Politics is not a simple matter of new foundation in *Oedipus*. Rather, *Oedipus'* guilt is a turn-up which precipitates a turn-around and a turn-over that recalls the liminality of limits which frees the *polis* to its freedom again.

This does not mean, however, that because *Oedipus* wins a certain restoration and transformation, with his public assumption of responsibility for remaining open to limits and difference, that he wins it for everyone; or that he wins it for Thebes forever. Neither does it mean that because he has won it once he might not have to win it again, and take the lesson to heart himself. Indeed, *Creon* is forced to remind him, at the very end of the play, that he no longer commands even though his instinct to hold-on to things seems as powerful as ever it was (in Greek the word to rule – *kratein* – means to grasp or hold-on to). It insists only that at a cost, and because – somehow both all alike and yet all different – human being is a possibility continuously open to a future, there is a real prospect of winning that renewal: 'In distinction from its goal, the principle of action can be repeated [and re-learnt] time and again, it is inexhaustible'.[66] Manifest in the world only through action, it lasts 'as long as action lasts but no longer'.[67] *Oedipus'* Dionysian affirmation of life, and freeing of the *polis*, is not won without cost – the cost of his own blood. Neither is it won once and for all for everyone. That yes to life, which is finally wrung from *Oedipus* – 'I am *Oedipus*' – has to be endlessly uttered. It has to be continuously recovered and repeated, in all the mundane, as well as the monumental, circumstances of life, through the resolute openness of which human being is capable precisely because it is mortal.[68] Gods do not need it, only mortals do. Gods, indeed, are not capable of it, only mortals are.

Neither committed to the will to truth, nor to the desire to mystify, tragedy is able to reflect upon how each seeks to reduce life's mysteries to its own ordering dynamics. In his recovery of reverence for the gods, for example, *Oedipus* renounces the exorbitant humanisation with which his calculative competence threatened him and so, uncannily, grows both more and less human. Or, rather, the already uncanny combination of being both more and less than we are is radically amplified once more in *Oedipus*. Tragedy is therefore not obliged, on the one hand, to confine the mysteries of life to the category of things not yet known but, living with and celebrating them, draw on them as a resource for life itself. And, while it classically consigned these mysteries to the realm of the gods, on the other hand it did not do so in order to propagandise on behalf of some final resolution of the human condition.

Moreover, tragedy necessarily employs an evocative style in the way that it addresses these issues precisely because it does not draw an *a priori* distinction between the parts of people that should be hailed and engaged in life and judgement; the head instead of the heart, or reason instead of passion. One way and another it seeks to address the whole ensemble; to call-up the articulated self and explore its predicaments neither as a rational nor as an emotional but as an articulated being. A carefully crafted show, as it asks us who and what we think we are, it is also deliberately designed to demand how we feel as well as what we think; appealing to the audience as both I and we, public and private (singular and plural, individual and collective) and to its experience of the expression and the jointedness – the articulation – of human being as an embodied being with Language. Literally, jointed.

Tragedy's point of departure, as I have argued, is consequently the unity, or at least simultaneity, of these distinctions; the radical duality of human being – creative yet created – which occurs as a consequence of being a being in Being, but not being Being. It is that very duality, of course, which makes human being uncanny. The uncanny is encountering the double, where the double is not the self-same but the duplication which exalts beyond the same.

I take tragedy, then, not only to be a systematic political and ethical reflection in its own right, but also one which is consistent with, while it nonetheless extends and develops, the bearing which the philosophy of the limit has on the question of the political. One that seeks to explore through content and style, as Martha Nussbaum argues, a specific interpretation of human excellence.[69] In a sense it is compelled, in both respects, to be more rigorously honest than a philosophical treatise or a work in political theory. It is less driven to lay claim to a uniform epistemology, coherence, systematicity, method, purity and comprehensiveness than such exercises are compelled to do by virtue of their metaphysics. While resort to such claims would necessarily subvert the very character of tragedy, the openness of the dramatic art itself would also expose such a move to critical appraisal.

Unlike much even of the best of theorising and philosophising, tragedy is not an argument for but rather an argument from the ontological difference, and the ethical and political complexity which it poses. Its superiority consequently inheres in its point of departure – difference, dissemination, duplication, gathering and iteration – and in its comportment towards the condition it explores, not in its claim to 'truth' and method.

That is why I would concur with Hannah Arendt's conclusion: 'No philosophy, no analysis, no aphorism, be it ever so profound, can compare in intensity and richness of meaning with a properly narrated story'.[70] For such a story 'reveals meaning without committing the error of defining it', and 'brings about consent and reconciliation with things as they really are'.[71]

Adopting and cultivating the tragic sensiblity is not, therefore, a matter of abandoning questions of agency, freedom, responsibility and judgement, or of preferring contingency, liberty, difference and excess over mastery, order, identity and modesty. It is a matter of addressing, and disposing ourselves towards, such issues differently. Moreover, although it is generally structured around the symmetries of these kinds of asymmetries, tragedy's portrayal of life surpasses the usual moral and political pieties of binary constrained choice simply because it does not start with the understanding of Being and human being that goes with binary distinctions. Neither is tragedy mere aestheticisation. An ethical and political exploration in its own right, it proceeds according to its own structures and dynamics and is propelled by an insight into the human condition which it shares directly with that of the philosophy of the limit.

Tragedy, however, is not philosophy. Rather, it is the art which complements the philosophy of the limit because it addresses and explores the question of how we should live through examination of life at the limit – *in extremis* – assailed by the possibility of a limitless violence against the very idea of limits itself.[72] Perhaps it is something like the art of which the philosophy of the limit would aspire to be.

More directly, from my perspective, tragedy is not preoccupied with any kind of political dilapidation and cultural disintegration. Neither is it concerned to specify what particular indispensable limit has to be met in order for social order to be established and maintained; as Hobbes does paradigmatically for modern politics, for example, in his account of the state of nature and his insistence that the fear of violent death at the hands of other men is the fundamental constraint which compels men to establish the social contract. Tragedy's distinctive concern is with the question of limits as such. In this sense it strives to preserve what Claude Lefort argues philosophy (I would say the philosophy of the limit) strives to preserve, namely:

> the experience of a difference which goes beyond differences of opinion . . . the experience of a difference which is not at the disposal of human beings, whose advent does not take place *within* human history, and which cannot be abolished therein; the experience of a difference which relates human beings to their humanity, and which means their humanity cannot be self-contained, that it cannot set its own limits, and that it cannot absorb its own origins and ends into those limits.[73]

For the fundamental principle operating in tragedy is that distinction and difference is integral to life, and that the loss of difference is profoundly inimical to human flourishing. The limit of the limit that is so threatening in tragedy is not a particular limit but the very loss of limits itself; limitlessness. It is very important to emphasise, however, that limitlessness arises as much when limits are treated terminally as when they are altogether effaced.

VIOLENCE AND THE TRAGIC

The mortal life of human being, I have argued with Heidegger, is distinguished by the ontological difference; the fundamental ineradicable distinction which obtains between Being and beings, despite their belonging together, which frees human being to be. The life which arises in virtue of the ontological difference – born of duplication – is a life which duplicates and re-duplicates that difference through, and throughout, its own free existence. Nothing we do turns us from beings into Being. Nothing we make or discover closes that gap either. We remain freed, mortal beings in Being; beings wherein the trace of the ontological difference is indelibly inscribed in the being-ness, as the being-ness, of our very being as mortal creatures. This, for Heidegger, is mortal freedom.

Itself not only tragic but also conflictual in the way that a break, a rendering, a *caesura*, tear, or a division sets-up a conflict because it frees things up, the originary struggle or *polemos* of the ontological difference is replicated in human being also. Human being bears that difference within itself because it comprises the freedom it affords. It struggles in this its freedom, the freedom of the ontological difference, precisely because freedom is not determination but an openness which has to be borne.

One has one's being to be. The struggle in life is, therefore, not simply a struggle for life. Much less is it a struggle between antecedently determined and conflictual features of human being. Rather, it is instead the struggle of life with its being, the striving of the striving to take-up that which it undergoes; the struggle of its occupation of, and its pre-occupation with and within, the freedom of its very being there. This is not human being's struggle to be, therefore, but, always already being, the struggle which the being of human being's freedom to be entails. Here, Heidegger's understanding of being in the free, active and verbal sense comes across most strongly. For where there is a life comprised by, and in virtue of, difference, there is always struggle less between its free constitutent parts as of this manifold openness with and within the freedom, marked by the ontological difference, into which it is thrown.[74] A being that bears this difference as its free composition is a being which is, therefore, continuously in danger of being overwhelmed by the violence into which that difference may degenerate. For violence incites reprisal and there is no necessary end to the cycle of violence which results, short of the extinction of human being. There is no principle of 'guaranteed effectiveness', as Girard puts it, for quelling violence.[75]

Only violence, it seems, can secure an end to violence, yet not even violence can do that securely because violence, of course, begets violence. Offered as the final guarantor, it is also the chief threat to order: 'the practice of violence . . . changes the world, but the most probable change is to a more violent world'.[76] It, like the being-in-common from which it arises is, therefore, also self-propagating.

The conundrum of violence is consequently not one problem amongst many, it is intimately related to the conundrum of being-in-common itself. For, in its freedom, human being is always potentially a violent mortal puzzle to itself, because the violence which it can always threaten itself with, in consequence of the very differential composition of the life that it is, cannot be mastered and overcome by greater violence. (Another way of saying that danger is inherent to the free (in)security of human being, and not an externality to be exterminated.) More to the point. Neither can it be mastered and overcome by regimes, either of normalising surveillance or of policing love, premised alike upon the violent, and violence-inducing, denial of violence and difference.[77] The political alone offers some way of addressing it short of the dissolution of all limits, particularly that threatened by those who dogmatically insist upon the violent, sovereign decidedness of their own limits.

The political arises precisely because we are condemned by our mortal life to be free. Because we are free we have to enact ourselves. In enacting ourselves, we violently articulate standards and judgements. Herein lies the possibility of a politics of freedom in which the function of politics is to preserve that dangerous and violent freedom, to sustain that capacity to invent standards and exercise judgement – and to enlarge it where possible – against existing standards and judgements, while keeping the question of the very violence entailed in judgement open. That is why the political is always concerned with the remainder or the surplus that politics as rule produces, or relies upon, but is always committed against.

The tragic challenge of being-in-common to being-in-common is, therefore, how to deal with a violence that is immanent; a possibility that inheres within its own being by virtue of the free differential composition of that being. One response to that challenge is to deny the tragic character of human being by indicting difference itself, and seeking to eradicate it. Integral to the tragic condition, therefore, is the desire to escape from it, resolving the *polemos* of life by turning upon the very freeing difference which constitutes it. Effacing difference in order to secure an end to the violence of a being that bears violence-threatening difference within itself, nonetheless, means embracing a project that seeks the dissolution of the very life it seeks to secure. Instead of securing an escape from violence, therefore, the eradication of difference paradoxically serves to institute that very cycle of limitless violence the logical outcome of which is the effacement of freedom and, ultimately, of human being itself. Tragedy's unique and indispensable contribution to the life of being-in-common is to resist, through exposing and exploring, that mortal threat to mortal life. It resists not by offering a facile solution to violence, however, but by differentiating violence from struggle, and by continuously holding open the question of violence entailed in the metaphysical means of trying to secure ourselves from it. Insisting that there is no such escape, it fixes our attention back on the issue of what Nietzsche calls the 'spiritualisation of enmity', or on what William Connolly Nietzscheanly calls agonistic respect; and, thereby, on the possibility of transformation in life.

Understanding human being as bearing the freeing difference of the ontological difference within itself necessarily results in a tragic sensibility. In this sense, the tragic is consequently more real. First, in that it is concerned with the radical phenomenal – that is to say not only with what comes to presence with human being and its worlds, to which difference and change are integral, but also with the way the inapparent thus becomes apparent in the phenomenal. Hence, and second, it is more real in that it recognises and acknowledges, through its preoccupation with limits, the continuous, inescapable and paradoxically ever-present beyond of phenomenal presencing. The tragic thus brutally exposes the crude naivety of realism's realism and of materialism's materialism.

Neither is it, therefore, preoccupied with the metaphysical questions of genesis *ab initio*, nor creation *ex nihilo*; or other states of nature fantasies. The problem of sovereignty, or of origin, is a false one; or falsely poses what the problem is. For there is no null point of departure. The 'origin' if it is to bear fruit – issue forth in anything at all – must always already be divided. Political experience is possible only because of that division. Because it is possible to know more than one political formation, to have to attend to more than one set of circumstances, and always to be encountering the new in politics, the tragic does not, therefore, imply an essentialist view of the political, nor does it seek to define a single determinate politics. Neither does tragedy ever articulate one. For the tragic, the political is always appearing. The task it sets is, therefore, to twist and turn not only to follow but also to preserve the very movement – the action itself – of that coming to presence, because it is the action, and the continuing capacity to act, that counts: 'the inspiring principle becomes fully manifest only in the performing act itself'.[78]

Tragedy is consequently not concerned with struggle, violence and innovation as inventions, or interventions, from outside, but with the advent of the new in consequence of the collision of incommensurables already encompassed within the divided beings that we are; the collision, ultimately, of the duplication and re-duplication of Being and being in human being itself, which is not the same as violence but, nonetheless, always threatens it.[79]

Because the very *caesura* of life is repeated throughout the self, society and logos, the unity of the logos itself is also at issue in this collision. But the effacement of difference alerts us to the fact that without differentiation there is no signification. If it is to have the capacity to mean at all, therefore, the logos must also be divided.

> The book is always born from a broken book. And the word, too, is born from a broken word. . . .[80]

The effacement of distinctions consequently also entails a crisis of meaning and threatens the destruction of Language. In the tragic, the fate of Language and the fate of being-in-common are thus inseparable. Language and reason, both, are consequently shown to break and rupture in tragedy, and to be divided against themselves. The reason is that Language is not simply the medium of the tragic. It does not merely represent. The tragic occurs through it. Integral to the tragic predicament of being-in-common, therefore, and at issue within it, Language discloses, and discloses the continuous replication of, the ontological difference. Divided within itself as well ('Babelization does not therefore wait for the multiplicity of languages. The identity of a language can only affirm itself as identity to itself by opening itself to the hospitality of a difference from itself or of a difference with itself'),[81] its phenomenality is ultimately also polyvalent, ambiguous and opaque. Hence, like the beings which live the tragic condition, Language too is tortured and cracked, stressed and strained to its limit and forced to yield more than it appears it is capable of yielding, in the advent of the new which the ontological difference perpetually precipitates through it.

At the core of the tragic is, therefore, the crisis of mortal human being – simultaneous moment of limit and judgement – as it confronts its own free differential composition and immanent violence. Rather than assuming an integrated self, potentially in control of an immanently ordered and structured world, the tragic concerns a being (and those structures in which that being is deeply implicated and for which its own creative powers are also partly responsible) as a being always threatened by the imminent dissolution of the bonds of its very being-ness. That is to say, of its being there; its being-in-common. Operating within that being, its 'civilisation' and 'civilising' capacity, tragedy does so in order to keep it in touch with the violence and creative and ethical complexity of its free existence and perdurance in a world that is ultimately not of its full making.[82] Tragedy therefore deals with a domain where the habitual divisions and binary oppositions between savage and civilised, right and wrong, order and disorder and, most fundamentally of all, between *polis*, *apolis* and *stasis* no longer rule by some metaphysical right. All the codes of inclusion and exclusion by which the human-ness of human being renews itself and takes on specific character and identity are at issue because human-ness itself is always an issue for human being.

Precisely because tragedy's starting point is, therefore, human being in its articulatedness – a being which bears difference within itself as part of its very composition as a being freed to be embodied with Language – tragedy is concerned with being-in-common. Neither a private nor a public but a plural being, that is both public and private at once,[83] being-in-common is capable of political life; a life that accepts and addresses the manifold ambiguities and possibilities of the plural interactions which necessarily result from its own differentiated differential constitution. It is, equally, capable of denying that life, however, and of seeking certainty and determination instead. The impulse to escape it, and the freedom to try, is integral to the tragic and to the political condition alike because it is integral to the free being of human being. Thus, as tragedy exposes and examines the general offensive against being-in-common which arises from the desire to escape its very own differential constitution, it illuminates the anti-politics of the political condition as well.[84]

Anti-political politics and tragic denial therefore always go together. Both human being and the 'city' are a *plethos*, a plurality. Each needs the difference which it comprises and each is resistant to being entirely composed of a single identity in which difference is effaced.[85] Yet, comprising difference, being-in-common is a plural being that can perish in the attempt to unify itself. Nowhere is the operation of such tragic denial more evident, or more evidently at issue, therefore, than in respect of political life; *politeia*, the life of the *polis*. And nowhere is tragic denial in the *polis* more profoundly explored in tragedy's great corpus of work than in Sophocles' masterpiece *Oedipus Rex*, where *Oedipus* first appears as bearing a solution to the human condition but ends rather as being fully exposed, as it, to it.

There are also few better explorations of the way 'language signifies beyond and against the explicit and even implicit attentions of the speaker'[86] than that provided by *Oedipus Rex*, and in particular by 'the linguistic maze' opened-up by the confrontation between *Oedipus* and *Teiresias*, the prophet who reverses *Oedipus'* words and reveals the duality at the heart of his being. It is as if the riot of double meaning which so pervades the entire significatory ensemble of the play is an insurrection of duplication and re-duplication against the terminal threat posed by the effacement of difference.[87] In particular it mocks the forensic univocity of *Oedipus* the calculative inquisitor, and radically subverts the imperial claim which he makes to truth and knowledge. *Oedipus'* transformation is, therefore, also the undergoing of a new experience of and with Language at the extremities of what can be borne and said. And, yet, the rendering of life and of Language is nonetheless also affirmed in the play, because the tragic concerns irrepressibility not pessimism, limit as the liminality of life's embarkations and re-embarkations rather than its termination.

LIMITS OF THE TRAGIC

We have especially to remember, therefore, not only that *Oedipus* is a representation of mortal human being – which, though deathbound like a beast and creative like a God, is neither beast nor God and therefore free, thus capable of its own particular kind of greatness – but also that his parricidal and incestuous pollution is a complex sign, too, of the mortal condition of a being divided within itself whose very condition of life is the capacity for duplication and re-duplication which it bears within itself. From the perspective of the political reading of the play which I present, incest represents the immanence and imminence of that endless cycle of reciprocal violence which threatens to overwhelm that being through effacing the difference which constitutes it.

Mortal being lives in duplication and re-duplication, directly participating in the begetting of itself in the *caesura*, replicated throughout its own being, in which its being arises. As with *Oedipus*, so with all human being, 'the sower is not only the sower' s/he is sown and is 'also the seed'.[88] Incest draws attention to the inherent duality of the human condition, however, by signifying a perversity which threatens the very composition of our being-in-common. For one of the features which distinguishes human being from other beings, and from Being, is the way human being is freed to take responsibility for the regulation of the self-producing procreative power of which it is a manifestation, by remaining open to, preserving and respecting, its own freeing duality. That way mortal being seeks the means of respecting the immanent alterity within its very own singularity, and so ensures its possibility of repetition, or new-found composition.

Thus, while *Oedipus* is the paradigmatic figure of the immanence of alterity in every human being, he is also a progenitor, as René Girard says, of 'formless duplications, sinister repetitions, a dark mixture of unnamable things'.[89] He threatens the very differential composition of the 'unstable arithmetic'[90] of the self itself, because his own example of scandalous equivalence – 'a slayer of distinctions'[91] – threatens the difference within the 'self'. *Oedipus*, therefore, violates the boundaries of self and other in his own self; husband and son; son and parricide; native and stranger. He 'collapses what should be distinct and plural [even in the self itself] into a perverse singularity'.[92]

Incest consequently does not only signify, as Euben notes, 'a political disease as much as a familial one'.[93] Because it effaces that viable system of relations of difference necessary for a being which bears freeing difference within itself, threatening to obliterate all distinctions including critically those co-joined within that self, it subverts the very possibility of such a being. It therefore signifies, in the strongest and most immediate way possible, the fundamental link between the loss of distinction and the violent chain of reciprocal violence which conducts a general offensive against the freedom, and hence the very possibility, of a political being-in-common.

Incest, then, is a paradigmatic representation of that non-difference which *Oedipus* threatens in all his relationships, including also those with other members of the *polis*; his persistent identification of himself with Thebes and of Thebes with himself is, for example, forcefully contested by *Creon*. Its fusion of singularity is, therefore, a cardinal offence against being-in-common, because the sovereign oneness which it symbolises fatally abuses the immanent alterity which is integral to the freeing differential constitution of mortal life. A fatal corruption of the intrinsic corruption (duality) of origination, incest subverts the entire social order because it assails the very condition of being-in-common.

We have to remember also that a limit is a polyvalent thing. That which allows something to be what it is, the limit also marks the point beyond which it cannot be. Moreover, the limit also always points beyond what is limited to the excess upon which anything relies, even though that supplement cannot be contained within the thing which is delimited. The limit here, then, is not only what makes politics possible, and so also impossible. It signifies as well that there is always something beyond politics with which the understanding and practice of politics has continuously to come to terms.

Free to be destructive, as well as capable, of politics, human being also signifies through its own existence something in excess of that existence indelibly traced within its existence. Something with which it nonetheless remains inextricably, if mysteriously, involved, and to which it remains irremissibly indebted. In the play, of course, that beyond is figured through what were themselves live political issues in fifth-century Athens: prophecy; the oracle; and the gods.[94]

Oedipus, then, and quite literally, is the limit. He is exasperating. He is violent and tempestuous. He rules and re-makes Thebes. He gathers it together in its time of extremity. Yet, he also threatens its utter destruction. It cannot contain him. For he is simultaneously also in excess of limits. Thus, he is the limit most of all in that his effacement of limits signals the limit beyond which mortal life, which is of course demarcated life or nothing, itself cannot be.

Figured in many ways, the limit in *Oedipus*-the-limit seems to be most obviously figured in relation to death. *Oedipus* was to be killed. *Oedipus* is a multiple killer. His wife/mother commits suicide. The Sphinx demanded human sacrifice. The plague, consequent upon his own being-ness, pollutes procreation itself.

Yet, the play's profound exploration of the limit does not stall at what seems most apparently limiting. Instead of violent death at the hands of other men, Sophocles teaches us to fear the loss of distinction and to reflect upon the vital connection between the possibility of political life and the maintenance of difference. Murder is the proximate instrument, but the obliteration of its own inherent Otherness is the ultimate threat, to being-in-common. Sophocles surpasses the sophisticated Hobbesian, as well as the naively realist, reading of the limit. Rather, our sensibility to limits is enhanced by this Oedipal figuration of the limitless.

The threat to the polity is, therefore, its very own creative medium – mortal human being. That is the sickness which afflicts the Thebans. For the plague does not merely demand tribute like the Sphinx.[95] Directly concerned with procreation, it is something integral to human being's procreative power which nonetheless fatally afflicts its capacity to reproduce and sustain itself as well.[96] Neither is it confined to *Oedipus*; a figure in whom the forceful inscription of the ontological difference is most pronounced (he does not know from whence he came, and he knows not where he is headed) and signified by his dis-jointed ankle. However much it is amplified and intensified within him into life-threatening proportions, the point is repeatedly made that this is what *Oedipus* shares with the other members of the *polis*. That sickness is the free capacity for being-in-common. There must be freedom for there to be tragedy, hence *Oedipus*' fate, partially predicted not totally determined, is to encounter the responsibilities of his own obligatory freedom in his own singular way.[97] Itself the condition of political life, being-in-common inevitably also entails the potential for self-destruction.[98]

THE TRAGIC EXTREMITY OF THE POLITICAL

In *Oedipus Rex*, then, we are presented with an exemplar of the limit engaged in the violent dissolution of limits who is, in turn, an exemplar of (political) human being. As the Chorus says, *Oedipus* is a paradigm (*paradeigma*). But he is not just political. Neither is he simply a-political. He is, of course, a double;

simultaneously both political and a-political. Reminding us that the haunting of the one in the other is always already installed within the self itself, *Oedipus* is thus haunted by himself. A paradigm of human being – 'of all mankind, and of the city which is man's greatest creation'[99] – *Oedipus'* greatness (neither perfect nor perfectible) is, however, not only signalled by his capacity for the political but also by the very limits of that capacity in the sense that he continuously oversteps the mark of the political. This a-politicality is inescapable because it is mortal being that must realise the possibility of a political life by the action which constitutes and sustains a political community. Capable of political life, of 'statute and limit', mortal being must nonetheless, of course, first create the statutes and limits of political life; which means that it must also always already be 'without statute and limit'.[100] Hence the struggle integral to it.

And in Thebes we are presented with a polity new-formed around the (a)political power – a form of political intelligence derived from the forensically calculative expertise which *Oedipus* employed to resolve the puzzle and remove the Sphinx – of its saviour and protector. When they find themselves not merely threatened but on the point of total dissolution – the plague appears to present a quite different order and magnitude of threat from that offered by the Sphinx – the Thebans appeal once more to that very same expertise. However under-standable, the appeal is bound to be frustrated because the soteriological credentials of any being-in-common are inherently compromised. But that does not mean that all is lost from the very beginning. *Oedipus* the saved,[101] is *Oedipus* the saviour,[102] is *Oedipus* the fell pollutant. Yet, is also *Oedipus*, finally, the transformed. What saves threatens, what threatens saves. But, saved in the sense of preserving itself in its openness, not in succeeding to some final solution to the human condition; and here, crucially, at least for those who know Heidegger, through human action.[103] Preserved for this fate, human being (being-in-common) is nonetheless elevated by its freedom to act in it and, by recognising and taking responsibility for it, retains the capability always of responding to it.

The play, then, is about the extremity which both creates and threatens the possibility of *politeia*. But it is equally concerned with how what lies beyond the *polis*, which is nonetheless also displayed in the mortal life of human being, limits the political as well. Thus, though they come close to it, neither the city nor *Oedipus* is deified but, rather, sanctified. Moreover, the threatening Otherness which *Oedipus* represents is not merely banished from the city, rather it is spiritualised in *Oedipus'* transformation from King to exile and sanctified interment at Colonus. The fate of the King, therefore, demarcates the liminal limit of the political and emphasises the fact that, despite the intricate and deep complicity of knowledge and politics, the question of the political is not exhausted by the question of the calculative knowledge of making; as it was newly understood, then, in terms of the rational analysis and manipulation of the representation of what comes to presence – of appearance – and as it has now traditionally come to be understood. That it is indeed threatened by its reduction to a certain *techne* because it originally concerns, instead, the question of the very creativity entailed by limits. For even as he comes to learn that he has been ignorant all along, *Oedipus* learns something new; acquires a different form of understanding.[104] Moreover, the (political) duality of *Oedipus'* (a)politicality is fundamentally played-out in terms of security and, specifically, in terms of the play on words which the Greek word for security (*asphaleia*) allows.

The strength of the play, read politically, is therefore precisely not that 'man' is a political animal. Neither is it that 'man' is an a-political animal (much less that he is an *animal rationale*). The point is that he is both at once and, more, that there is always already something beyond the *polis* as well that *politeia* must continuously respect. It is in that very ambiguity that the inherently liminal character of the political, and the challenges to it, continuously arise. Here we have the recognition of both the possibility and impossibility – the (im)possibility – of the *polis*,[105] in virtue of the identity and difference that inheres in both human being and *Logos*, explored through the character of knowing and being, and of the way that each (being, knowing, and their relationship) is integrally involved in the constitution and maintenance of a political community. It is a masterpiece not so much of political analysis as of the analysis of the whole ambiguous phenomenon of the political, as it liminally arises at the limit in respect of the dissolution of limits; one which surpasses in subtlety and range – while being concerned with many of the same essential questions of truth, appearance, prudence, machination, ground and calculation – even that provided, for example, by Machiavelli. It therefore ably advances a related and more general proposition, that there are many more provocative, and many more important, ways of thinking about the political, and about security and insecurity, than those to which the tradition specifically of International Relations and Strategic Studies would so rigidly and impoverishingly confine us.

While *Oedipus'* life and career describe a constant political passage, a journeying to and fro which revolves around the *polis*, his very talent for puzzle solving is indicative of the political intelligence which brought him to power because it once secured the *polis*, and he continues to rule through it. As Bernard Knox demonstrated so well, one of the dominant motifs of the play is that of a politico-legal inquiry.[106] One in which *Oedipus'* forensic intellectual skills and will to truth combine not only in pursuit of *Laius'* murderer and that of his own obscure genealogy, but also to smell conspiracy and betrayal. *Oedipus* the champion hermeneut is, however, an irresolvable hermeneutical puzzle to himself; 'an expert at decoding difficult messages, the hero cannot decode the meaning of his own name'.[107] The resolution of that puzzle precipitates a self-blinding which signifies the advent for him of a different kind of self-recognition. Language, knowledge and power – the complexities and mysteries of identity, appearance and misrecognition – are, therefore, all intermeshed in this account of the rise, fall and transformation of the securer of the *polis*. *Oedipus'* self-recognition is the acceptance of the riddle of human being; a being-in-common that is both friend and enemy to itself, united in its division and diversity, yet in receipt of that being by virtue of something whose necessarily absent trace it bears.

Oedipus thus continuously beats the bounds which comprise all that the political is, and entails, including fundamentally the very laws of consanguinity. He makes space for the *polis* through the play both of his presence and his absence. *Oedipus'* self-exclusion from the polity is consequently neither total nor is it irredeemable and exclusively sacrificial.[108] For, whereas ritual is conservative and confirmatory in regard to existing order, tragedy is polysemous, questioning and innovative; its unity a doubling and re-doubling renewal quite unlike the one-ness of the metaphysical impulse.[109] There is, therefore, neither sacrifice, understood in the Judeo-Christian sense, nor scape-goating, understood in the anthropological or sociological sense, here. What there is, is a precise figuration of Dionysian overcoming, or what Nietzsche described in his essay 'Homer's Contest', as the spiritualisation of otherness upon which the very *agon* of life itself depends.

Oedipus' will to know is precisely what trips him up. Yet, while he cannot forbear trying to master himself through the calculus of his knowing, the play's message is not as simple as insisting that the will to know must be denied. *Oedipus* cannot escape his doom by ceasing to question, as he is advised to do on no less than four occasions.[110] Failure at it, indeed the failure of it, is somehow also the path to a new understanding and transformation of the knower through a refining of his questioning capacity. Ignorance, rationalism's most despised heresy, but actually the liminal limit of knowing, has nevertheless to be learnt and understood in its own, and for its own, liminality; and precisely because it is liminal the limit of not knowing is not fixed.

Moreover, it is clear, in one sense, that *Oedipus* must also always have known the riddle of his being, for he has a bad foot. That foot always signalled something mysterious about his birth. As a Greek he would have known that the foot indicated that he was a foundling. More generally, of course, it corporeally signifies what we and he already know and flee – the foundling character of mortal being itself. What *Oedipus* therefore wanted from the Oracle was to know with certainty who he was. In consequence, he did not go there to discover the truth of his being. He went, instead, in the hope of finding a 'truthful' denial of what he already knew that would enable him to escape it. In the attempt to do just that he fulfilled the Oracle's prophecy of disaster.

His fall remains, however, essentially ambiguous and marginal; 'when the hero, revealed as homeless, most desires exile and homelessness, he is made to feel most fully his responsibilities to and his protection by an *oikos*'.[111] Indeed, his full acceptance of them is brutally signalled. Consequently, he is down but actually not (quite) out. Indeed he remains what he has always been, both within and without, hence outwith, the *polis*.[112] Even at the end he continues to be a question for it. More than that, it is precisely tragedy's *forte* that it poses the question more deeply still. Because it does so, we gain a greater understanding through it of the kind of issue that *Oedipus* represents to the *polis*; that of the question of limits and all its cognates including, for example, those of tolerance and tolerances – finely defined and refined openings and limits – which are so involved also with acceptance of responsibility.[113]

CONCLUSION: THE *POLOS* OF TRAGEDY

Instead of dissecting the dead tissue of the question of the political, therefore, tragedy offers the prospect of a radical hermeneutical phenomenology of the political, disclosing it in all its living form and force. In the process it educates politically because it is capable of radically shifting perspectives and so changing its audience's relation to the issues with which they are presented; the way it sees them, the way it approaches them, and the expectations which are engendered in respect of them. Integral to the political and religious life of the *polis*, tragedy was not just intensely but essentially concerned with movement: with reversals and revolutions; with rises and falls; speed and deliberation; comings and goings; setting things up and knocking them down; with the changing perspectives and moods of human being; with the changing landscapes and fear-scapes which they inhabit; with temporality itself; and, utimately, with the dance of the Chorus. If *Oedipus'* life revolved around the *polis*, the life of the *polis* (*politeia*) revolved around tragedy; hence *Oedipus Rex*. As Sallis notes:

> for Nietzsche one does not, in the face of tragedy, become a disinterested, pure will-less subject, but rather one is shaken, made to tremble at the edge of the abyss. . . . it is no mere, temporary masking of the source of human misery but rather a disclosure capable of leading one back from pessimism to affirmation.[114]

Tragedy depicted human being finding its way back to itself out of the depths of its shaken-ness. It was thereby capable of shifting the political world on its axis because, in a literal sense, it actually helped to comprise the very pivot of the political itself. It was not merely a means of political education but, in effect, a critical element of the very *polos* of the *polis*; that which made it *polis* and not *stasis*.[115] Through it, the ontological dualities of power and powerlessness[116] (which inevitably arise as a consequence of the ontological difference) are neither denied nor shifted on to something or someone else. Neither is the projection of the movement that they impart to life resisted. By turning them up, around, and over so that they could be explored and acknowledged, and by following that movement, tragedy was a means for effecting a solidarity of the shaken; holding them together in their very difference. It was itself, as Sallis calls it, a pivotal spacing; the clearing of a place, both in the imagination and in the living of a being that bears freeing difference within itself, for such a being-in-common to find a way to live freely with itself in its differences.

Here, then, political human being is explored at the limit in order to examine not only the violence and fragility of its very liminality, but also that play of Otherness within it which instigates the liminality. The question of the political is, thereby, posed and addressed not in terms of how can human being be ordered and domesticated, but in terms of what is required of a civilising movement through which human beings can accept and accommodate the freed uncanny thing that human being itself is, without betraying the uncanniness of that freedom.

Because it continuously insists on posing that question *in extremis*, because it arises in virtue of limits, the tragic thereby enlarges our political and ethical sensibility beyond the moralistic boundaries within which a politics confined to representational–calculative thought would secure it. It is for this reason, too, that it remains so desperately pertinent to the extremity of our own current world.[117] If the recovery of the political provoked by the philosophy of the limit requires a recovery of the tragic as well, then reading *Oedipus Rex* as a tragic masterpiece which explores the question of the political by exploring the question of limits in relation to the possibility of political life is one way of beginning to explore what is involved in that recovery.

Moreover this play offers itself as a perfect place to start because *Oedipus* was a 'Prince' and Thebes was a *polis*; a *polis* in a crisis and on the point of extinction. The play is as much concerned with the fate of the *polis*, therefore, as it is with that of this phenomenal human being – their fates being, of course, inseparable – and so, more precisely, with *politeia*. And that fate revolves around (in)security, because the threat to the existence of both *Oedipus* and Thebes is the pollution of *Oedipus* himself.[118] 'The menace which assails man's nature', Heidegger wrote, 'arises from that nature itself'. But, he reminds us, 'human nature resides in the relation of Being to man'.[119] The ontological difference is a parting between Being and being. Such a parting between may be a parting from, which, in the belonging together of Being and being, allows freedom to each; to human being, of course, but also to Being in as much as human being does not anthropomorphise it as a supreme being. A parting-between nonetheless always threatens to become a parting-against in which human being loses its relation to the Being of its own being and thus to Being altogether. This, set in the openness of the *polis*, is the tragedy of mortal human being, *Oedipus Rex*.

Chapter 6

Oedipus Asphaleos*

The tragedy of (in)security

> ... to bear a name is to claim an exact mode of collapse.
>
> (E.M. Ciaoran)

OPENING

Thebes is (in)secure because *Oedipus*, the figure of political man, simultaneously both threatens and secures it. Expelled as a baby from Thebes, *Oedipus* is a dispossessed foundling who does not know from whence he came, or where he is headed; a man without original name, identity or dwelling-place, fated to breach the most fundamental laws of the *oikos* (hearth) that form the basis of the *polis*.[1] Like all human kind, *Oedipus* is thrown free into a life which nonetheless has things in store for him.[2]

Given sanctuary and succour in Corinth he comes to political maturity there, but expels himself from the city in order to avoid fulfilling the prophecy that he will kill his father and marry his mother. His distinctive competence at calculating commensurabilities[3] – *Oedipus* seems to know how to weigh things up, to figure things out, and in consequence others come to count upon him – nonetheless returns him to the fold of the hearth and *polis* from which he was originally expelled; when he solves the riddle of the Sphinx, rescues Thebes, becomes its ruler and marries its Queen. A stranger to, yet native of, Thebes ('He passes for a stranger in the land But soon shall prove a Theban native born'[4]), in the same way that he is a stranger to himself, *Oedipus*-the-dispossessed by his own actions comes into his own and rules where once he was abandoned to his fate; and so fulfils his fate. That fate revealed, he seeks to have himself banished to the borders of the *polis* in order to relieve it of the pollution which he himself introduces into it.[5] But that assumption of responsibility which he freely undertakes, insisting that the deeds he did he chose to do, while it lifts the burden of contamination from Thebes does not dispense with the issue of it altogether. Rather, by taking responsibility for it, *Oedipus* more directly poses the issue – of how to respond appropriately to it – right back at the *polis*.

Consequently, as it bestows a kind of greatness upon him[6] so *Oedipus'* violent assumption of responsibility forces *Creon* and the rest to consider how they must now deal with him – the very excess (in which they themselves also share, even if now they appear to have been relieved of its immediate irruption in their midst), which also makes the *polis* possible. The plurality of the *polis* is thus preserved because *Oedipus'* assumption of responsibility, rather than effacing, confirms difference. Only through this self-transgression, or openness to difference, can the *polis* escape the danger 'of becoming mired in itself and of idolising the conditions of its existence [represented by *Oedipus* himself here] as something absolute or unconditional'.[7] The question of what responses are necessary to preserve the agonal unity of the *polis* is thereby kept open not only because his own continuing difference is asserted once more – the blinding brutally differentiates him from them – but also because they have to deal with that ineradicable sign of difference whose indelible trace he has left in their midst. In the event, that unity is realised as a prospect once more not through an act which simply draws the *polis* together, but from a radical and plural dispersion in which, as *Oedipus* marks himself off from it, he allows or effects a re-distribution of it in the space and time which his withdrawal – a singular act of political responsibility through which he exercises his freedom to act – precipitates. *Oedipus'* crisis is not a founding but a disseminating one.[8]

In no way whatsoever, therefore, does *Oedipus'* fall obviate the need to deal with his issue. That is to say with what he represents and with the legacy that he leaves behind him; specifically, for example, his daughters. More even than that, the *polis* remains agonistically tied – separate yet joined – to *Oedipus* himself. Cast to its borders, henceforth *Oedipus* not only journeys (as in a way he once always did) through the interstices between *polis* and *polis* – so that in *Oedipus at Colonus* he becomes a kind of 'international' issue between Thebes and Athens – but also between *politeia* and what lies beyond political life. For, without sight, *Oedipus* now lacks the capacity to see the world and to share his *doxa* (how the world discloses itself to him) with others in the constitution of what is integral to political life, namely a common world of appearance and common sense. Quite literally he has lost a common sense.[9] Yet, this loss of a common sense which amplifies what already distinguished him – his near god-like presence – is nonetheless also an action which, because in every action a person appears, serves to remind us that he is indeed mortal: racked with guilt, pain and suffering; moved still by love and concern; sensible of his terrible condition; solicitous for others; appreciative of the solicitousness extended to him in his down-fall by *Creon* and the Chorus; acting into the future up to the very end. ('Only in this humanised form does consciousness then become the outstanding characteristic of somebody who is a man and neither a god nor an animal'.[10]) Loss of his *doxa* recalls his original (ontological) estrangement. In as much as that estrangement is shared, loss of his *doxa* emphasises his being-in-common. His transformation is consequently a direct reflection upon the world of appearance which is the world of the *polis*; and upon the transformation of sight, *Oedipus* becoming more of a seer, required to see this. It is not, however, a Platonic denigration of that world. It is instead a stark reminder, first, of its fragility; second, of the immense effort required to sustain it as a political world; and, finally, of the surplus of Being and of meaning – the very excess and supplement – within which it resides, upon which it continuously draws, without which it could not be, to which it owes respect, and in virtue of its inescapable relation with which it possess this capacity for repetition. More than ever in his down-fall, therefore, *Oedipus* remains an issue for the *polis*. Indeed, he thereby serves to intensify and amplify all that is at issue in and for political life as a whole.

The threat to Thebes, then, is *Oedipus*. But *Oedipus*, of course, stands-out in that he stands for all. What is therefore 'rotten' in the state of Thebes, if we remain fully alive to *Oedipus* as the figuration of mortal human being, is mortality itself. Thebes' problem, then, is human being. For only human being is mortal. And only mortality is a being-in-common which – knowing that it lives and dies, cannot be one because of this reflection upon itself – bears the (in)security of life-engendering difference within itself.[11]

Oedipus is originally and continuously haunted by the spectre of his name – indeed that of his whole family[12] – which signifies the integral duality of his very existence. And what haunts this dual figure is the obligation entailed by his mortal freedom – here a necessarily political freedom, of course, because, as a being-with and a being-in-common, it is enacted directly through his being with others in Otherness – to give things their due, and to judge and be judged in that judging; in short, to submit to Justice and assume responsibility for this freedom which is, inescapably, his and his alone. Such responsibility is openness to the call of Justice – response to the Otherness whose absent presence is what stalks him in his doubleness. This call of Justice, which arises with him, is not only effected through him and enacted upon him, it is also discharged by him. To be just here, then, is to remain open – responsible – to the beyond of the living present whose possibility he corporeally endures. Being double, then, *Oedipus* is a temporal and corporeal creature whose temporality and corporeality are both out-of-joint. Born askew (consider the prophecy), then crippled in the vain attempt to wipe him out, his existence is nonetheless an opportunity to set things straight. But the man himself cannot stand straight. A true saviour would require two good feet and a secure ground to gain the purchase required to straighten-out a world as disjointed as this one. *Oedipus* has neither advantage. There will therefore be only so much that he can do to set the world to rights.

The critical difference which this difference makes – the very message of the play – is this. Precisely because mortal life – dying, and divided within itself – is a free and incomplete life, it is open to possibilities which only the debt of this difference can grant.[13] Blinded by his capacity to see through things, *Oedipus* could not see what was under his feet; the abyssal nature of the ground of his being, or transcendence, by which and through which he is able to come to presence at all.[14] Blinding himself because of the results of his determination to see things through, however, he henceforth commits himself to traversing the ground of his being with a new circumspection and insight.

'Only the testimony that is maintained through the tortures of an inquisition',[15] Rosenzweig writes, 'provides complete certainty'. And Pascal concurs: 'I believe only in those stories for which the witness would readily die'.[16] The world is, however, full of fools who will, of course, die for almost anything. And many witnesses are fools. Moreover, certainty never attends the doings of human being. But that person is also a fool who thinks *Oedipus* paid over the odds for the new understanding of the standing of which, as a mortal, he is capable. Moreover, *contra* Hegel, there is a radical and positive disjunction between *Oedipus'* previous knowing and his subsequent being, such that:

> The tragic event marks a revolution of time – a revolution that preserves the past (men and gods communicate in their infidelity so that 'the memory of those of the heavens should not fade' . . ., but in a radically altered form.[17]

Beginnings and ends belong together here, but not in any simple and symmetrical accord: 'what follows absolutely cannot resemble the initial situation'.[18]

Oedipus' fate is thus also fundamentally an expression of the Greek poet's understanding of the fate of all mortal being. Something which Heidegger summarised in the course of his reading of the opening chorus of *Antigone*, that understanding is worth quoting at length because it applies so well here:

> The sapient man enters into the very middle of the dominant order; he tears it open and violently carries being into the essent; yet he can never master the overpowering. Hence he is tossed back and forth between structure and the structureless, order and mischief, between the evil and the noble. . . . The *violent one*, the creative man, who sets forth into the un-said, who breaks into the un-thought, compels the unhappened to happen and makes the unseen appear – this violent one stands at all times in venture. . . . In venturing to master being, he must risk the assault of the non-essent, *me kalon*, he must risk dispersion, in-stability, disorder, mischief. The higher the summit of historical being-there, the deeper will be the abyss, the more abrupt the fall into the unhistorical, which merely thrashes around in issueless and placeless confusion.[19]

Not only is *Oedipus* consequently no mere personality, this figure of (political) human being is also a double. As such he necessarily, therefore, multiplies because, in assuming, he thereby also redistributes, the responsibility of the freedom into which he has been thrown.[20] *Oedipus* is, therefore, the familiarly unfamiliar in the midst of all that is familiar. He is that uncanny thing, the embodiment of the strangest of the strange, which we all know intimately. He, like all of us, is a mortal being. And that, in its essence, is simultaneously not only a manifestation of the awful power of Being, and a being that wields power like Being, but also a being which, in a certain way, itself brings Being to power. Limited and finite, mortal being is nonetheless that which, precisely because it is thus so bound-up with the power play of the way Being happens to beings, continuously surpasses the limits which would domesticate it even as it strives to domesticate itself and find a home for itself in its worlds.

Hence, *Oedipus'* condition is that of us all. After all, he is a stranger native born. Strange in our very at-homeness, at home in our very strangeness, we are a mortal threat to ourselves. So, born in Thebes, *Oedipus* is simultaneously a stranger to it. A calculative animal,[21] possessed of an uncanny knack for solving riddles, he does not know himself. The husband of his mother, and father to his siblings, he is a mortal threat to the city he saved. Supreme in the political craft or *techne* of puzzle solving (meaning making), his art projects him to power – rescuing the city from the threat of the Sphinx – but is also the chief means by which Thebes is brought to the point of disaster, because it propels *Oedipus* forward to know his own history and master his identity.[22] *Techne* cannot save Thebes because it is too deeply implicated in the city's mortal predicament. It is only when he is opened-up to a different truth, the truth (*aletheia*) to which *Teiresias* testifies – which is, simultaneously, the mysterious truth of his phenomenal duality – that *Oedipus* puts out his eyes and addresses the threat which he presents to the *polis*.

A play of the inter-play of *asphaleia* (security), *aletheia* (truth as disclosure) and *orthotes* (truth as correctness), *Oedipus Rex* is, therefore, fundamentally about what plagues a *polis* (*asphaleia*) and of the fate of knowledge as a kind of derelicted *techne* – the power-play of politics as optics; a technology of insight into riddles – thought necessary to secure it. While all readings of *Oedipus Rex* correctly stress the theme of sight, light and vision,[23] however, Euben has also noted that there appears to be 'some symbiosis between *Oedipus'* way of walking and his intellect, between his stoop and his stature'.[24] There is. That connection lies in the very word *asphaleia*. I, therefore, want to emphasise that because the play concerns the fundamental political question of *asphaleia* [human being's obligatory freedom or (in)security] its theme is more precisely played-out through the relation between stance and sight.

Oedipus Rex, in short, is a play about feet as much as about eyes. Intimately concerned, therefore, with the complex relation between standing straight and seeing straight which arises in virtue of the fact that temporality is the manifold of movement in which human existence stands out, and to which it must constantly compose itself, the play deliberately draws attention to and plays upon the question of stance, and of our stance, in relation to that experience and its political implications.[25] For, by emphasising neither sight nor standing alone but the relationship which necessarily obtains between them, the play insists that we confront questions of knowledge and power in terms of the judgement and responsibility which having to dispose and compose itself in the manifold movement of time demands of human being; namely a response to the call of Justice. It is not merely, then, a question of what we may see and know, but of where and how we stand in relation to ourselves, to each other and to the mystery of the obligatory freedom from whose burden of responsibility we can ultimately find no secure solution.

Oedipus Rex, then, is a play which is concerned with the abyssal ground of Being; with posture, comportment and standing. Moreover, *Oedipus* is always reliant as well upon some support or other, be it the crutch of disability or the mace of rule. The play is, therefore, also concerned with the original and radical needfulness of human being. But his response to that lack is nonetheless also the very means by which *Oedipus'* presence is supported and his standing is maintained. The King's very puissance depends upon an absence which calls for a prosthesis; which prosthesis metamorphoses through many guises in the course of the play until, ultimately, it becomes another human being. Preoccupied with the relationship to the ground – with the struggle to stand and with the inevitable prospect of tripping-up – the play insists upon the belonging together of standing and falling. All this is a way of referring to how the divided ground of the ontological difference – while nevertheless having to adopt a stance within it – necessarily affects the knowledge associated with light, vision, sight, perspective and perspicuity. Precisely because it exists in the manifold motion of ecstatic time, human being simultaneously confronts the question of how to stand within rather than against time, as well as how to see. Indeed, of course, how it stands radically affects what it sees, and what it seeks to see. Moreover, there is a wonderfully recursive symmetry in all this because these themes, compactly present from the outset in the riddle of the Sphinx itself, are not resolved by *Oedipus* as it first appears. Rather, they recur through the very fate which *Oedipus* bears.

Consequently the riddle, too, is a statement of the human condition in terms of *asphaleia*: of how it is a matter of being freed to find one's feet, of struggling to comport oneself, of having to rely upon some support in order to do so, and, finally, of the temporality of all human beings who, in their continuous effort to stand, are nonetheless always already destined to be brought down to earth by their very mortality. It also introduces us to *Oedipus'* great talent – the very thing which gives him standing – commensuration. For *Oedipus* sees that the common denominator of a creature that crawls on all fours, that has two legs and three legs, is human being itself. With an acute eye for equivalences, he thereby appears to solve the riddle of the Sphinx. But that riddle is not any riddle, it is the riddle of the human condition itself, the very mystery of human freedom. He is, therefore, fated, as a human being, not to solve it but to live it, and repeat it, in the actions by which he takes-up his response-ability for life.

In a sense the movement of the play revolves around a recognisably Machiavellian figure. Neither hereditary monarch nor elected ruler, *Oedipus* does not even possess citizenship. Even as he is depicted, in another play in Sophocles' trilogy, as a stranger at Colonus, so also *Oedipus* comes to Thebes as an outsider to whom a special place is given. Here, however, he appears as the very epitome of a self-determining, rationally guileful, political adventurer rather than a pariah. Acutely defensive of his genealogy, he is preoccupied with his name; not only in the sense that it simultaneously refers both to his impediment and his intelligence, but also because he is jealous alike of his political and analytical reputation. The spectre of the absence it specifies haunts him. Quick to detect plots against 'kingly' power, he is prepared to move with ruthless speed against them.[26] For a man with a bad foot he always moves with precipitate calculative haste, and is chided for it by the Chorus. But *Oedipus* is not the figure of The Prince, and his resoluteness is not *virtu.* The gulf that separates the two is located in the Greek understanding of the truth of disclosure. Whereas *virtu* is metaphysically grounded on the attempted self-assurance of man as subject (attempted, because Machiavelli was too smart not to appreciate that the attempt was likely to result in somewhat limited success), resoluteness is located in the tragic character of *Oedipus'* obligatory freedom. 'The distinguishing characteristic of modern resoluteness [*sic*]', Heidegger noted in the winter of 1942–3, 'is "the fanatical".'[27] Hence the story of *Oedipus* has a radically different ending than that of Fascist leadership.

Out-of-joint, plagued with a limp from when he was first cast-out into the world to make his fortune as fortune might dispense, *Oedipus* rises to power through a combination of murder and intelligence. Albeit unknowingly, he slays Thebes' King. Subsequently, he outwits the Sphinx. Killing furnishes him with the opportunity to take power, while knowledge provides him with his warrant. For *Oedipus*, knowledge and power go hand-in-hand.[28] His *forte* is, however, his political *techne*.[29] As an 'outsider' that skill comprises, typically, the abstract, new-found, forensic and analytical techniques which place a premium upon expert calculation and upon the practice as well as the divination of dis-simulation. He sees through things by weighing them up,[30] but that skill is productive and constructive as much as it is analytical. For as well as asking questions, as do all such methodological epistemic innovations, it produces answers and creates new power arrangements; his own rule in Thebes for one thing. *Oedipus*, a master of political calculation rather than prophetic divination is, thereby, also the harbinger and instrument of a new order. Via *techne* he makes the grade and thereby re-makes the *polis*. And he boasts of that fact when he rails against the ineffectualness of *Teiresias'* oracular art. It was *Oedipus* and not the prophet, he brags, who 'sussed' the Sphinx (Storr Translation, lines 380–400).

Through *Oedipus*, then, the inside and the outside are brought together. Or, better to say, through *Oedipus* the play of the demarcation of the inside and the outside occurs.[31] Because *Oedipus'* body is a threshold, it allows the passage to and fro of the political. The political comes and goes through him.[32] Moreover, when Thebes is threatened again, *Oedipus* is expected, and himself confidently expects, to maintain power by a similar alliance of violence and knowing. *Arche* for the Theban *polis* – not only their pilot but also their 'prop and stay' (Storr Translation, line 693), their very under-standing, their *hypostasis* – his own standing is nonetheless, of course, profoundly suspect. He both is and is not what he seems. Everything he says betrays itself as something else.

Oedipus, then, is profoundly (dis)abled. Don't ask what a people is, I suggested, ask how fear makes a people. Thebes is thus made in the image of *Oedipus'* fear. Both are ontologically threatened by the contamination which pollutes (obscures and afflicts) the very origin of their life. As the play progresses towards its climax, and the fear deepens with the increasing exposure of its origination in mortality itself, the Thebans – in the form of the Chorus – increasingly also come to fear *Oedipus'* fear. That fear becomes the anxiety which arises in the face of the very uncanniness with which they are also themselves always already afflicted.

Ostensibly, *Oedipus* appears to be the paradigm of a *Turannos*. A violent interloper who usurps power, he is an illegitimate upstart who continuously threatens more violence in the pursuit of his project to found a 'State', brooks no caution and can barely stand to be opposed or gainsaid. Dogmatically determined to discover *Laius'* murderer, and banish the culprit, he is equally determined to uncover his own origins no matter what the cost.

And yet, of course, he is also exactly the reverse. No one could be a more legitimate 'Prince' of Thebes than *Oedipus*. He is portrayed, in addition, as a deeply solicitous ruler and loving father who regularly consults his people. His genuine concern for their welfare is reciprocated through the astonishing esteem in which they hold him, and he identifies himself with them and the common good. (To such a degree that *Creon* is forced, in his own defence later, to contest the exclusive identification between himself and the *polis* which *Oedipus'* civic zeal is inclined to make.[33]) Moreover, he insists, twice crucially against *Creon's* alternative political inclination and advice, to make decisions openly. And he is also capable of deferring in his exercise of power. A mon-arch with a 'democratic temper', as he is described by Knox,[34] he even shares power with representatives of the previous regime; his wife/mother, *Jocasta*, and her brother (his uncle) *Creon*.[35] In every way the *arche* of the *polis*, its securing ground, is therefore depicted as divided within itself. *Difference and limits, not sovereignty, is the grounding question of the political here.* Moreover, *Oedipus* relents in his condemnation of *Creon*, conceding to the interventions of *Jocasta* and the Chorus: 'Then let him go, even if it does lead to my ruin, my death or my disgrace, driven from Thebes for life'.[36] And this is no lordly granting of a boon. It is the admission of a profound and doom-ladened political reversal in a mounting crisis of mutual incrimination in violence. For *Oedipus'* pollution is more than a contagion. It is something in which, the play continuously insists from the beginning, the Thebans themselves already share. Here, correctly, the origin – *a fortiori* the origin of power – is clearly nothing singularly original but always already contaminated: mixed, plural, divided, violent and impure.

Enjoying near god-like status, *Oedipus*, nonetheless, undergoes a supreme crisis and test of his skill. Thebes is threatened by a plague which has fallen upon its reproductive capacity and is fast destroying the life of the city. Smart, he may be, but that will not save the city now, precisely because the political clairvoyance which distinguished him, the very means by which he climbed to power – his 'sword of thought'[37] – is so deeply implicated in the city's impending doom. It offers no sure defence against the plague, therefore, because it is the very instrument, and he himself is the very occasion, of that pollution. The diagnostic and prescriptive political power which distinguishes him is a potentially fatal *pharmakos*.[38]

Unwittingly, and ironically, the Thebans appeal to the sure-footedness of this (dis)abled figure of a ruler to put the *polis* back on its feet and secure it there. But that he cannot do. Instead, by blinding himself, displaying his disability to the citizenry and insisting that the oracle's revelation and his own command be fulfilled by having himself removed to the boundary of the *polis*, *Oedipus* turns

Thebes towards the contamination – the (in)security or freedom of mortality itself – in which it dwells and with which it must always deal. The play therefore ends neither on a conclusive note nor in fact with *Oedipus'* banishment, but with an affirmation, instead, of his connection to the *polis* and of the positive undecidability of the human condition this side of death; for the law which tragedy expresses is a law which has to be engendered.[39] Although it, therefore, appears to have been resolved that *Oedipus* will be banished in accordance with the oracle's advice and the King's own curse,[40] in the final act of the play *Creon* escorts *Oedipus* back into the palace, the very epicentre of rule. And the last words – spoken by the Chorus – proclaim the fundamental (in)security of all mortal life: 'count no man happy till he dies, free of pain at last'.[41]

ACTION

Time, scene, sense

(In every respect, from dialogue through to staging, posture and blocking the opening of the play is arranged, unmistakably, so as to establish the connection between security and truth, standing and seeing, and the very possibility of political life.)

Dawn. Silence. The Royal Palace of Thebes. Many years after its deliverance from the scourge of the Sphinx, the city now assailed by a mortal plague. *Double* doors to the palace dominate the facade. Before and below them the altar of Apollo. Seated there are supplicants of all ages. At their head, a Priest of Zeus. Through the doors enters *Oedipus. Regal; he limps*. The Priest kneels. The King bids them, knowingly, to say why they are there sacrificing to the god and soliciting his aid. Unsteady on his own feet, *Oedipus* solicitously assists the Priest to his, and invites him to speak for the rest. A speech follows in which Sophocles anticipates and encapsulates, as Heidegger notes he does similarly in *Antigone*, the entire problematic of the play. He spends the rest of the drama catching-up with himself.[42]

The Priest replies that the *polis* is foundering in the blood red waves of a deathful blight that has afflicted all procreation. *Oedipus* is no god, but he is the first among men. An inter-face between men and gods, his god-like or god-inspired knowledge once saved them from the Sphinx. The Greek here is especially revealing. For the Priest literally says that, then, he lifted-up their lives ('*th'emin orthosai bion*'[43]); a phrase which directly invokes the connection between securing, standing and truth.[44] In bidding him do the same again – '*anorthoson polin*',[45] upraise or lift-up the *polis* – the Priest appeals directly to *Oedipus'* concern for his name and reputation. Praying that his reign should not have to be recorded as one which elevated Thebes only to see it fall and fail again, and reminding *Oedipus* that his own survival is at stake in that of the city, he asks the king to use the self-same knowledge to rescue it again now and secure it upon a rock; ('*stantes t'es orthon kai pesontes husteron, all' asphaleia tend' anorthoson polin*'[46]).

Because the plague threatens to empty the city of all life, the Priest, therefore, identifies the essence of *asphaleia*, that is the problem of rule for the *polis* ('*kratein*';[47] to grasp, hold firm, to support something), with which *Oedipus* is now confronted, not with *techne* or the provision of the engines of defence, battlements and warships, but with the very challenge of being-in-common; '*xunoikounton eso*'.[48] This, poor man, is the challenge *Oedipus* must now face if he is to put the city back on its feet and secure it there. The very expression of the challenge in this formula discloses the central theme of the play – the understanding of what political life is about and of how the *polis* realises it. For the *polis* is fundamentally allied to the disclosive truth of Being and replicates the *polemos*, or agonal bonding, which characterises Being, and the ontological difference between Being and beings. It concerns, then, the tragic freedom of (in)security which *Oedipus* – the figure of mortal human being – is destined to bear.

Being is 'essentially *xunon*, collected presence'. *Xunon* does not, however, mean 'universal' but, rather 'that which in itself collects all things and holds them together'. According to Fragment 114 of Heraclitus,

such a *xunon* is, for example, the *nomos* for the *polis*, the statute that puts together, the inner structure of the *polis*, not as universal, not something that hovers over all and touches none, but the original unifying unity of what tends apart.[49]

This unity is fundamentally different from that conceived as the product of a single sovereign supreme Being; a Being which promises redemption from division, that is to say, by mediating and adjudicating difference through the articulation of its unifying command. It is different, equally, from a unity of equivalences or of commensurability. *Xunon*,

is never a mere driving-together and heaping-up. It maintains in a common bond the conflicting and that which tends apart. It does not let them fall apart into haphazard dispersion. . . . It does not let what it holds in its power dissolve into an empty freedom from opposition, but by uniting the opposites maintains the full sharpness of their tension.[50]

'*Xunoikounton eso*', is, then, the agonal belonging-together or unity of Being and the being-with of being-in-common. This gathering together is, however, depicted in the play as a redistributive dispersal rather than a mere unity.

Oedipus' response, emphasising again as he did in his opening address that he knows what problem has brought them there, (the irony is inescapable – he does, and he does not), dedicates himself to the task by insisting on the identification of himself with his people. He bears the sickness they bear – in fact, the divided being of mortal being itself – but in him it attains a magnitude and intensity that outstrips its presence in them; ('*noseite pantes, kai nosountes, os ego ouk estin humon ostis ex' isou nosei*'[51]). All he is wanting, before rooting-out the problem, is the return of *Creon* from an embassy (*theoria*) to Delphi, on which *Oedipus* has already despatched him, to bring news of what the oracle says.

Creon, his consort's brother and co-ruler with *Oedipus* in Thebes, has a significantly different political temper from that which distinguishes the king. As he arrives he quickly demurs at announcing the oracle's message publicly ('If thou wouldst hear my message publicly, I'll tell thee straight, or with thee pass within'[52]). *Oedipus* commands a public declaration ('speak before all'[53]). The oracle reveals that the man who murdered the previous king (*Laius*) is responsible for the pollution and that he is still living in Thebes. If Thebes is to be saved, he must be driven from the city. And so by means of *Oedipus'* urgent cross-examination of *Creon*, the first account of *Laius'* murder is given. *Oedipus*, doubting that it was a random killing and suspecting some greater political motive behind the crime, is horrified to hear that a king's murderer, or murderers (a deliberate ambiguity is inserted at this point), was not pursued there and then. *Creon* explains that the City was preoccupied with meeting the demands of the Sphinx. *Oedipus* then commits himself, with all his renowned investigative skill and resource, to re-opening the enquiry and hunting down the killer; to expose the truth, bring everything to light, rid the city of its plague and save himself as well . . . for, as the limit, all these things are gathered together, dispensed and dispersed through *Oedipus*.

The opening closes with the same emphasis upon lifting and standing with which it began. *Oedipus'* confidence-inspiring commitment is a deliberately stirring response to the supplications of the Priests and people sitting and kneeling before him. He knows how to save them – literally put them back on their feet – and is confident he has the courage and skill required. Stand up, he tells them, or we fall/fail. With that, mobilising the supplicants, he also calls for the mobilisation of the whole city. And exits, limping, into the palace. The Priest echoes his words – 'let us stand up' ('*istomestha*')[54] – announces that *Oedipus* has volunteered what they came for (again the irony is evident), and prays that the god who sent the oracle will save them from the plague. The scene closes with representatives of the city rising to their feet and leaving the stage.

The Crisis of Truth

(The crisis of the *polis* is a crisis of security, is a crisis of the King and is also a crisis of truth. They are the same. The Chorus reels before its implications and the decisions it presents. It sets the scene for the way the crisis deepens and spreads in the encounters which now ensue between *Oedipus* and *Teiresias*; *Oedipus* and *Creon*; and *Oedipus* and *Jocasta*. In the process, *Oedipus'* politics of security dissolves into a letting-be as his fear is transformed into anxiety.)

A long hymn from the Chorus follows. Extolling the gods, and detailing how the plague blights all procreation, it calls upon them, bloodthirstily, to save the city. *Oedipus* returns and commends their praying, but recalls them to current practicalities. Describing himself as a stranger at the time to the crime, and to Thebes, he can nonetheless answer their prayers now and save them by discovering the secret of *Laius'* murderer; indeed, he implies (irony piled upon irony) the problem would never have arisen had he been around then. Should the murderer give himself up voluntarily, he would suffer nothing worse than exile. Anyone who knows the identity of the killer will be rewarded if he reveals it, banished if he does not. The killer himself is, however, violently cursed, and that curse unrestrainedly extends to anybody who impedes the investigation, even to *Oedipus'* own house should the culprit prove to be somehow connected with it.

And so the cold trail (trial) is picked-up once more, with *Oedipus* beginning by interrogating the Chorus. It knows nothing . . . except that the oracle itself must know, and that the only person who can see eye to eye with the oracle is the blind prophet *Teiresias*. He is, therefore, likely to have some special insight into the identity of the murderer. Seeing eye to eye with the oracle (*'oront' epistamai'*[55]) means, of course, that the prophet must be on the same level as it, shares its status. The issue is not, then, one of simple vision – *Teiresias* is, of course, blind – as of the seer's sight, of his standing and of his relation to the ground; which ground is the divided ground of mortality itself.

Presciently, however, and on *Creon's* insistence, *Oedipus* has seen to this – the trail (trial) is not as cold as it might seem – and in prospect now is a clash of sight and truth; of different forms of truth, of truth as the correspondence we claim to be able to see between things and the idea, or their true form, and of the disclosive truth of *aletheia* in which what is given for true also discloses a remainder that is always closed-off to us. Simultaneously, *Oedipus'* fear – of losing power, of discovering the truth and of discovering the truth of the truth – mount until, the truth disclosed and his being exposed, he is brought to the threshold of resolution through the radical anxiety which this exposure in disclosure brings about.

Teiresias has already been summoned to the palace. His entrance, led-in in an immemorial sign of wisdom by a boy, is announced by the Chorus. Here, it declares, is the one in whom truth is in-born (this time not *orthotes* or any of its cognates but *talethes*,[56] from *aletheia*). The blind man of truth (*aletheia*) and the sighted man of knowledge (*orthotes*) clash violently. Each as imperious as the other in this encounter, *Teiresias* at first seeks, nonetheless, to avoid the irruption that is now imminent by refusing to say what he knows and proclaiming that he and *Oedipus* (the same difference) should bear their respective burdens of humanness separately. This obduracy appears to endanger the city. Enraged, in keeping with the threats he has just made against any obstruction of justice, *Oedipus* precipitately accuses *Teiresias* of murdering *Laius*.

'Is that the truth?' scorns *Teiresias* (*'alethes'*[57]), and finally bursts-out that, on the contrary, *Oedipus* is the pollutant. The King condemns him for the accusation, insisting that his status will not protect the prophet from the consequences of issuing such a slander. *Teiresias* counters that he is indeed protected by the truth (*'talethes'*[58]) to which his own being bears witness. *Oedipus*, discerning a political conspiracy behind the prophet's astonishing declaration, and inadvertently hitting the point that being strong in the truth of disclosure (*aletheia*) is not acquired through some kind of *techne*,[59] wants to know who taught him this art (*'pros tou didachtheis? ou gar ek ge tes technes'*[60]). The passion grows as the argument proceeds. *Oedipus* always intensifies his insecurity as he seeks to secure knowledge about his origins (from his first bout with the drunken courtier in Corinth, through his response to the oracle's pronouncement, and now to a succession of clashes in Thebes, first here with *Teiresias* and soon with *Creon* and *Jocasta*).

For *Oedipus* the Prince, the master of political *techne*, there can be only one explanation for *Teiresias'* accusation. There is a conspiracy against his power, and *Creon*, who first advised sending for *Teiresias*, must be the prophet's co-conspirator. He has to move fast to nip this in the bud or else he will be outmanoeuvred. What seems to anger him most is not so much the threat to his survival – powerful and violent, despite his foot, he is clearly a fearless man – as the threat to his reputation and the insult to his pride. Who in hell do they think they are, full of envy for the crown he was freely given, arch manipulators (masters of *techne*, '*techne technes*') seeking to out-wit him in the battlefield of life ('*O ploute kai turanni kai techne technes huperpherousa to poluzelo bio*'[61]). *Creon* perhaps worst of all, repaying familial loyalty with political betrayal.

In a great burst of political invective *Oedipus* demonstrates his understanding of politics as *techne*, an art of making; a construction of calculative representations and judgements in which the very puzzle of representation itself – winess his defeat of the Sphinx – has been solved by *Oedipus* himself. He rails against the prophet accusing the old sage of being a master of political conspiracy rather than a true seer ('keen-eyed, but in his proper art stone-blind'; '*dedorke, ten technen d' ephu tuphlos*'[62]). Where was he, *Oedipus* asks, when the city needed someone to solve the riddle of the Sphinx? And what price his prophesying? Was it not *Oedipus'* calculative wit, unskilled in the prophetic arts, that did the trick? Yet, the play has already suggested, both through the Priest's appeal to *Oedipus* in the opening and now here in the form of the truth to which *Teiresias* bears witness, that the truth of the political is in some obscure way nothing 'political'; that the essence of the thing is not confined to the mundane practice of it. Indeed *Oedipus'* politics are the conveyance which bears him and Thebes towards doom. The political, then, is concerned, instead, with that tragic condition of human being itself – being-in-common; *xunoikounton* – to which the sighted *Oedipus* seems blind, and whose existence he threatens, but to whose truth *Teiresias* testifies; even, indeed, in his violent and intemperate opposition to *Oedipus*.

He bears his witness through lines 408 to 428 (Storr Translation) and simultaneously defends himself against *Oedipus'* charge of conspiracy, condemning the king's own blindness. His question to *Oedipus* – 'do you know your lineage?' ('*ar' oisth' aph' on ei*'[63]) – is both ontological as well as genealogical. For Thebes' problem – the political problem; the security problematic – does not come from outside. It is integral to the house of *Oedipus* (the house of *Laius* too, of course, because it is one and the same house) and so to all human dwelling; we are all children of '*Laius*' ill-starred race'.[64] With eyes of tragic denial the king currently sees right (truth as *orthotes*), but soon will see only endless night ('*Bleponta nun men orth', epeita de skoton*'[65]). After a further violent exchange, *Oedipus* dismisses *Teiresias* and returns to the palace. The prophet, however, closes the scene by depicting *Oedipus'* forthcoming fate. Playing not only on the images of blindness but also on those of standing and stooping, and of the transformation of *Oedipus'* crutch and murder weapon, quite literally his instrument of office, into a blind man's stick (each a *skeptron*; a *skeptron* was also, of course, the baton passed to an orator to authorise him to speak), *Teiresias* proclaims that his own truth and truth-telling power will be vindicated.

The *skeptron* simultaneously also draws attention to the hands in whose grasp (rule) it lies. For that grasp continuously betrays itself. Delivery, rule, murder and incest, all lie in those hands. Henceforth, *Oedipus* will feel his way groping (*prodeiknus*) with his staff, feeling his way forward – now not merely double but bent double by his existence – to another country. (Dis)abled, he nonetheless paid too much and too little attention previously to the treacherous ground of his being.

Exeunt *Teiresias* and *Oedipus*, the Chorus to survey the wreckage of their encounter. Threatened by the clash of truths they have just witnessed they are torn between their faith in the gods and their prudential loyalty to *Oedipus*. After all, *Teiresias* speaks for the gods. Yet, Thebes also flourished, took a positive hedonistic joy, in the truth that *Oedipus* once spoke ('*phanera gar ep' auto pteroess' elthe kora pote, kai sophos ophthe basano th' adupolis*'[66]). The crisis of truth and security – which is, of course, also the crisis of the *polis* – deepens dramatically as the rifts in the city's power base are further disclosed and *Creon* arrives; first, to discover how he has come to be charged with conspiracy and, then, to answer *Oedipus* for it.

Confirming with the Chorus that *Oedipus* has accused him of treason, *Creon* submits himself to their judgement. They reply that the charge was made in anger. *Creon* asks, in effect, was *Oedipus* seeing straight, or correctly, at the time ('*ex ommaton d' orthon te kax orthes phrenos kategoreito toupiklema touto mou*'[67]). The Chorus says it itself is blind to its King's acts, and is saved the embarrassment of having to mediate between the two by *Oedipus'* arrival. The King launches into *Creon*, violently repeating the charges and elaborating upon them. Once more it is as much the insult to his intelligence as the supposed threat to his life that fuels his rage. And again also, he reveals his understanding of politics; adding (anticipating Machiavelli, somewhat) the mobilisation of violence and a body of powerful supporters, for which *Creon* has foolishly failed to provide, to the ingredients essential to its making.

The ensuing argument, which takes the form of mutual interrogation, is almost entirely concerned at first with claims and counter-claims about who thinks and sees best. *Creon* concentrates on the notion of seeing and thinking straight or correctly ('*ouk orthos phroneis*'[68]). *Oedipus*, sensitive to this implicit slight, now talks more in terms of thinking well and having a care ('*ouk eu phroneis*'[69]). The contested nature of truth itself is at stake in the very language of this confrontation, and in it *Oedipus'* position begins to shift.

Creon is, however, no stranger to the intricacies of palace politics or the dynamics of public debate. Remember, his first instinct on returning from Delphi was to take *Oedipus* inside the palace and discuss the oracle's message privately.

His life is now on the line. A smooth and fast talker, he defends himself ably, with a clever move that shifts the grounds of the cross-examination to the question of what motive he could possibly have had for conspiring against *Oedipus*. He reminds *Oedipus*, and us, that Thebes is in effect ruled by a triple monarchy. *Oedipus* received power from the Queen, *Jocasta*, and shares it equally with her and *Creon*; albeit *Oedipus* carries the burden of rule and all the hopes and fears, of course, of the Theban people. No balanced, upright or sensible person (*'sophronein epistatai'*[70]), he says, would want the cares of office if, like *Creon*, they could enjoy its benefits without them. Enjoying power without responsibility, he argues, he has the best of both worlds. Would he not be mad to lust after responsibility as well?

What seems a quite plausible line of defence is, however, a classic and scandalous example of that sophistic evasion of responsibility through which power always seeks to see without being seen.[71] It is an elision of the entire question of how to keep open that capacity to respond – to, within and for the liminality of limits – which makes the *polis* possible. *Creon* is dis-claiming responsibility on the grounds that the desire to be there at the epicentre of the *polis* without being seen to be there proclaims his innocence. This is equivalent to saying that he wants to see without himself being seen. Such a manoeuvre is either impossible – how can you see without yourself also being in the field of vision and therefore available to be seen – or scandalous; in that it appeals to coversion (hiding oneself), or dissimulation (pretending that one is not there), to effect a spurious innocence. Alternatively it is radically impious, for is this not what the mysterious *phusis* of Being as such does? The implication that a ruler who does carry the burdens of office cannot be entirely, upright, balanced, sane and sensible – a slight on *Oedipus*, of course – completes the elision of responsibility by construing responsibility itself as unnatural.

Creon ends by protesting his innocence, appealing to the judgement of the oracle and admonishing *Oedipus*. In due time, he says, the king will learn how not to fall (*'all' en chrono gnosei tad' asphalos'*[72]). The Chorus concurs, urging caution on the king and advising him to look before he leaps (to conclusions) because those who move quickly are liable to fall; to fail; to miss the truth (*'phronein gar hoi tacheis ouk asphaleis'*[73]).

But *Oedipus'* very foundations are already crumbling under his feet. Or, rather, the abyssal ground of his being is beginning to open-up to him. The King's fear of being brought down is intense. If he stands still he fears that he will fall and fail. He seems impelled to secure both his standing as a King and as a man, for together they have been mortally impugned and threatened. (The plague, of course, is mortal. Neither *Teiresias* nor prophecy – the one apparently secure defence against the utter arbitrariness of life – can be trusted any longer either. And *Creon*, his former political ally, seems now to be his mortal enemy.) The more insecure he feels, the more he strives to secure himself. Compelled to find a more certain ground, his own grounds seemed good enough before and he is driven to rely upon them even more desperately now. The more threatened he is the more he resorts to the foundations of his political *techne*, and the more quickly he responds to the mounting tempo of events. Yet, the more he resorts to his *techne*, the faster he speeds to his downfall (*'otan tachus tis oupibouleuon lathra chore, tachun dei kame bouleuein palin ei d' esuchazon prosmeno, ta toude men pepragmen' estai, tama d' emartemena'*[74]). *Oedipus'* pursuit of the security of rule, and of the rule of security, accelerates him towards the very depths of political and human nemesis (*'arkteon g' omos'*[75]), his 'fear' becomes 'anxiety'.

As *Creon* and *Oedipus* continue to wrangle about who is more wise, and Creon protests that he is as much a Theban as *Oedipus*, *Jocasta* enters. Hailed by the chorus as the person who can straighten things out she upbraids them for causing such discord (literally an insurrection of language, *'stasis glosses'*[76]) and seeks to pacify and mediate; in short, to bring the situation under control. *Creon*, supported both by *Jocasta* and the Chorus, protests his innocence and gains a reprieve.

The Queen asks what caused the argument. The Chorus' reply is dark and enigmatic. Both protagonists are blamed, yet a wider state of confusion is also indicted. Refusing to take sides and recount the details of the dispute, the Chorus says that the *Logos* itself is not transparent enough to give an answer.[77] In a response which *Oedipus* himself says is strange, they describe the whole affair as an outbreak of the mystery and ambiguity which, it is implied, is somehow intrinsic to the *Logos* (*'dokesis agnos logon elthe, daptei de kai to me 'ndikon'*[78]).[79] There then follows the long dialogue between *Oedipus* and *Jocasta* in which the story of *Laius'* murder is told once again, *Jocasta* seeking to prove to *Oedipus* that he could not have been the murderer. In the process, further facts are revealed, *Oedipus* recounts his own genealogy again and, for the first time, tells the story of how he came to leave Corinth and journey to Thebes. In the process he is, of course, more deeply implicated in *Laius'* death and the decision is made to send for the slave who witnessed *Laius'* murder (the last, it has to be said, in a long line of people – first *Creon*, then *Teiresias*, next *Jocasta* and, now, this herdsman – who, having been called to resolve the problem and arrest the burgeoning crisis, serve only to advance it towards its dreadful conclusion).

Wracked by the conflict between their faith in the gods and their prudential commitment to *Oedipus*, the Chorus now call upon the Olympian deities to affirm the true order of things. Movement is already a principal motif of the play – *Oedipus'* limp, for example, contrasts with the intellectual agility and the precipitate political reflexes which also distinguish him – in doing so they do not simply emphasise this motif and develop it further, distinguishing between climbing, wrestling and dancing, rather they disclose how it is fundamental to the play's entire political message.

This differentiation of movements, distinguishing also between modes of struggle, elaborates the fundamental character of the tragic conception of the *polis* and recalls the defining fragile agonal unity of it; to which, as the play opened, the Priest appealed when he petitioned *Oedipus* to save Thebes. I can illuminate the political point which the play is now emphasising through this movement of movements by using Nietzsche's essay 'Homer's Contest', to which I referred in the previous chapter. For, there, Nietzsche explores the very point that the play is making here.

On the one hand struggle is seen as a means. It is subordinated to a finality determined outside the game, and its goal is identified with victory. On the other, struggle is regarded as an end in itself. The logic of the first ineluctably leads-on to the extermination of the opponent – their expulsion from the game. The second, designated as *agon*, is, so to speak, a double struggle concerned not only with the contest of a game – which always logically threatens extermination for one party or another – but simultaneously also with the struggle required to keep the very play of play itself in play. 'The core of the Hellenic notion of the struggle', Nietzsche wrote, is that it 'abominates the rule of one and fears its dangers; it desires as a protection against the genius, another genius'.[80] And he goes on to explore what might be called the law of agonistics rather than the law of the survival of the fittest. Here, according to Samuel Weber:

> It is a question of the *ostracism*, the exclusion that makes it possible for the agonistic field to define itself and, especially, to maintain itself – to stay in the game. Those who, by their superiority, would threaten the status of the joust [struggle] as a game are banished. And if ostracism thus becomes the indispensable condition for the continuation of the joust [struggle], it is because the latter is understood from the start as a movement not of identity but of otherness.[81]

For there to be a struggle, then, there has to be struggle. Moreover, mortal being is the being which, bearing difference within itself, is born of struggle (the *polemos* of the ontological difference). To efface struggle is thus to efface mortal being.

When an individual therefore threatens the very struggle of the *polis*, that individual has to be expelled from it for the struggle of the *polis* itself to continue. Politics here is not a promise of peace in the sense of the cessation of struggle. Neither is the war against Otherness and difference, which threatens in all struggles, depicted as external to the *polis*. The political life is not threatened from without by some external other which has to be eliminated but by the very dynamics of struggle of which the life of the *polis* is itself constituted. Similarly, the difference integral to the *polis* is not being translated into an external Otherness so that the *polis* can violently unify itself by making war on that other. The threat to the *polis* is, therefore, intrinsic not extrinsic, though it may deal with that threat by externalising it in another way – through ostracisation, for example. The very struggle which defines the *polis* is itself, therefore, always already ambivalently related to the Otherness upon which it is integrally dependent.

This insight defines the political imagination. Discovering how to respond to that insight in contingent and specific circumstances is what defines the challenge of political life. *Hubris* is the desire to withdraw from the game or transform it into technics. Ostracism alone, however, was not the device by which the play was kept in play. By itself ostracism is a crude mechanism which may easily degenerate into the illusion that the Otherness integral to the human condition can be successfully externalised. Rather, the Greeks sought to avoid *hubris* by spiritualising that irreducible Otherness; something which they recognised not only to be integral to the human condition, but also to the endless struggle to take-up that which it undergoes responsibly. Hence, *Oedipus* is not simply about to be expelled from Thebes. Sophocles is too sophisticated a dramatist for that, too sensibly immersed in his world to convey only the one-dimensional meanings of a unifocal insight into Being and beings, and so the very power of the tradition which he creatively mediates comes through most strongly here. A kind of sanctification also accompanies *Oedipus'* ostracism (a near divinisation which is depicted and accomplished in *Oedipus at Colonus*).

The ultimate law of Being, the destining of things, the Chorus now proclaims, is made elsewhere; on high Olympus. One needs tall legs or a high footing (*upsipodes*; there is no distinction between foot and leg here) to mount to that place. Pride, however, breeds the tyrant who, attempting to escape the abyssal ground of his being, seeks to scale and so command these heights; but fails/falls to his ruin because human being has neither the legs nor the feet for it. Such striving is not merely vain, it is dangerously irreverent. There are simply no secure footholds for human beings there (*'enth'ou podi chresimo chretai'*[82]). In contrast, however, the Chorus – representing the *demos* – does appeal to the gods to preserve a quite different sort of striving, the wrestling of the *polis* (*'to kalos d'echon polei palaisma mepote lusai theon aitoumai'*[83]). If it proves possible for the tyrant's pursuit of mastery to overcome the destinal freedom of being – resolving its (in)security by preserving himself from the bolts of the gods – however, then there is no requirement for the dance of the Chorus itself (*'ti dei me choreuein'*[84]).

Here the inter-facial relationship of the Chorus to the *polis* and to that which exceeds it – the gods – becomes evident in a way that also explains why and how it affirms the struggle of the *polis* over and against that of the tyrant. The (Dionysian) dance of the Chorus is radically opposed to the static singular preoccupation with standing straight and seeing straight whose dangerous implications have so far concerned the play; much less is it concerned with the final catastrophe of bringing things to a stand-still. Instead, it moves in celebratory step with the vital movement which infuses human being (the interplay of gods and mortals; of Being and being), for it is a movement which celebrates the agonal movement – *polemos* – of Being itself. Now, without that movement – the movement of the temporality which constitutes the very character of mortal life – there would be no need for, no possibility of, politics because there would be no burden of freedom for human beings to discharge through the composure with which they comport themselves to its silent call of Justice in the manifold of ecstatic existence. All would be predetermined, instead, by law or teleological ordinance. Without, in addition, the move which moves in conjunction with that movement, however, human being would not make space, or rather acknowledge the space in itself, for politics – witness the logic of closure entailed in the tyrant's hubristic ascent to mastery. The dance of the Chorus seems to follow Heraclitus' rule of 'acting according to presencing' – *poien kata physin*.[85]

Polis, then, is naturally opposed to *stasis* because the *polis* is the place where human beings preserve and practise their freedom – their openness to the agonal movement of Being; which endows them with their free capacity, as mortal beings, to act. It is consequently distinguished also by its own form of movement, or strife, which replicates that of Being and without which it would not be what it is. The Chorus calls it wrestling. And wrestling, *the* sport of the ancient Greeks, is a certain kind of 'institutionalisation of conflict'.[86] For it is concerned with moving, throwing and falling, with a ground that is continually shifting and with stances that are continually changing, with antagonists locked in struggle one with another in an open place according to rules and conventions. Above all, however, wrestling denotes the belonging together of standing and falling.

However, the dance of the Chorus does more than draw attention to the plural character of struggle. While expressing reverence for the agonal unity of Being and being, its dance is also a celebratory insistence upon the space for sanctioning and preserving the unifying strife of the *polis* as well. This *polemos*, manifested in the *polis*, is, then, a strife which in setting things apart and preserving them there actually allows them to make an appearance at all, as the individual things that they are, and to adopt a stand of their own. Whereas disjuncture inaugurates the political, Justice (the commission to put things in order and give them their due) is its project.[87]

The play of the word Chorus itself emphasises all this. The tragedy is in a sense both for, with and by the Chorus. Spelt with omikron for the first 'o' of the Greek word (*Choros*), the Chorus is no mere audience. As the people who dance, the Chorus is integral to the Dionysian rite of the tragic which was, in turn, integral to the life of the *polis*. Spelt with omega for that first 'o' (*Choros*), however, Chorus meant a place, a place of the dance. Finally, *Chora* means country – or that place politicised.[88]

The political significance of the Chorus is, therefore, two-fold. The dance of the Chorus – that movement which commits it to the movement of the ontological difference itself – makes space for the movement (the agonal wrestling) of the *polis*; because it recognises, in a sense institutionalises, the play of Being and being without which politics as the constitution of a shared public sphere and participation in the assumption of the demission of Justice would not even be a possibility. But, at the same time, its dance also recalls and reveres the beyond of the *polis*, that excess from whence human being has been projected into its freedom continuously to keep open the future possibility of giving things, including the *polis* itself, their due. The *hubris* of the tyrant, therefore, is the tragic denial which seeks to escape the bounding relations of movement, space and place which contrive a way for people to live the freedom of their disclosure together, and to take-up their responsibility for it.

The play now rapidly moves towards its climax. *Jocasta*, despite her disdain for oracles but alarmed by *Oedipus'* mounting disintegration, and so in a somewhat blasphemous fashion, returns to sacrifice to Apollo: how often, in extremity, we pray to a god in whom we do not believe. She receives the messenger newly arrived from Corinth. He is seeking political preferment from *Oedipus* by bringing him news of his 'father's' death, and the vacant throne which now awaits him in his old foster home. Having satisfied himself that there has been no coup in Corinth, *Oedipus* finds renewed hope; *Jocasta* too. The oracle was wrong. *Oedipus* could not have killed his father. The old man has just died of natural causes. The hope does not last long. The messenger's other news is, of course, that *Oedipus'* 'father' was not his father and that *Oedipus* was indeed a foundling. *Oedipus* resists to the last, however, still waiting for the testimony of the slave who had witnessed *Laius'* murder but who, it turns-out, was also charged with abandoning *Laius'* child to the mountain long before that. *Jocasta*, on the other hand, now concedes the inevitable and, after failing to prevent *Oedipus* from pursuing his will to know to the end, exits to commit suicide. The old man eventually arrives, the truth is told and *Oedipus*, too, learns his fate. Storming after *Jocasta* he discovers her dead. In the most untimely – and most unconsidered – of acts he puts out his eyes with the pins from her dress. *Oedipus'* blinding and *Jocasta's* death are reported, not seen.

The fall of *Oedipus*

(Mood and tempo change dramatically with the bloody release of tension. The main action is accomplished but the play is not spent. Horror and despair are joined also with love and affirmation. *Oedipus'* banishment seems determined, but his issue remains. His protestations to the contrary, desire of life, and his desire for the life of others, persist; only somewhat differently. He is recognisable still in his actions. More so. For his actions are even more responsible now than they were before. Enter *Oedipus* once more, then, through the double doors of the palace. Limping, and now also blinded, *Teiresias*-like he is led by a boy.)

The time of the play becomes that of the un-timely. That is to say, henceforth it concerns *Oedipus'* actions in time counter to his time, acting in time for the benefit of a time to come; which future will be a future without him.[89] Displaying and exemplifying the freedom of mortal being, *Oedipus'* blinding and banishment is no sacrifice. Rather it exemplifies that understanding of freedom which Nancy has explored in *The Experience of Freedom*.[90] It is sheer prodigality, a giving without measure other than the way it measures itself out in its own giving. *Oedipus*, the paradigm of mortal being, does this by making an example of himself, and by withdrawing from the scene. An example, Derrida has noted in several places, 'is first of all for others and beyond the self'.[91] Here, then, *Oedipus* gives powerful illustrative force to this point, and to Derrida's further observation that:

> Sometimes, perhaps always, whoever gives the example is not equal to the example he gives, even if he does everything to follow it in advance . . . he gives by giving what he has not and even what he is not.[92]

Moreover, precisely because the freedom he exemplifies is one that cannot be secured – it is not a property, condition or subsistent foundation – its further dissemination can only be either affirmed and facilitated, or denied. The free space of this freedom may, therefore, be freed-up from the inroads which the determination to secure it continuously makes upon it. Hence, it is only by withdrawing that *Oedipus* can effect the withdrawal of and from the determination (his very own securing rule of *techne*) which threatened freedom itself.

What now follows in the King's down-fall thus displays the structure of a very complex withdrawal in which *Oedipus* seeks precisely to give what he does not have and which he cannot give – namely time and freedom, or, more precisely, the freedom of time itself. And, precisely in trying to give time, he is also seeking to give others their space to be. Ultimately, of course, none of these are his to give. They are, instead, the very lack at the heart of their own differential constitution in Being which others must consequently assume for themselves. In any event, *Oedipus'* own time has run-out. In the process, his sight and standing are also transformed. For, losing his sight he becomes more of a seer, falling from power he learns to comport himself differently. None of this occurs in a flash, however – he pitches back and forth to the end – and none of it is accomplished without the cost of enormous pain and suffering.

Yet, how could he possibly free the *polis* and his family – daughters who are also sisters, sons who are also brothers – from the inheritance which he has bequeathed to them? In a sense this, too, seems to be an aspect of trying to give what is not within his gift. That may be so. But the play is not concerned with freedom conceived as something divorced from all that we have been. None of them will ever, can ever, be free from the legacy of *Oedipus*. It is integral to their very existence. Hence, it is no empty freedom of the will into which he helps precipitate them. *Oedipus* is about to leave them precisely in order to leave them not to any abstract general state of freedom, therefore, but to this their very own specifically situated and endowed freedom to be to actualise their possibility; to transform the necessity of their facticity into the possibility of their future. His leaving frees them to comport themselves to their being, of which his inheritance is, of course, an inalienable part. The scene now to be enacted consequently plays-out the way in which the freedom to be is dispersed once more – hence its prodigality – and redistributed amongst them, all through the withdrawal by which *Oedipus* gathers-up his own responsibility in the freedom that has been his alone.

Such a freeing assumption of the responsibility of freedom – the prodigal dispensation enacted here – commits no act of vengeance. *Oedipus* refuses to raise the stakes in what has been, and retains the potential to remain, a cycle of preemptive violence. Instead, he directs violence at himself, and leaves; leaving them all precisely to what belongs to them, and to their varied ability to assume responsibility for themselves and others in the freedom in which they, too, have to find their feet. No mere study in sacrifice, therefore, *Oedipus* discloses the structure, necessity and costs entailed in the assumption of the political responsibility integral to human freedom. At the end, then, the downed King yet 'stands'. But he is no longer revengeful against the 'it was', nor does he seek ballistic flight into some calculable future.

No fall is ever simple, and so *Oedipus* does not simply fall. He falls-back upon, that is to say returns and adheres to, the public space of the *polis* and discloses himself there again. In doing so he owns his own facticity in having been, comes alongside others in the present and effects the opening of a future. Uncannily, his fall is also somehow arrested in its very process. Arrested it simultaneously also arrests and secures the attention of the *polis*; ours too. Held-up, the fall elevates *Oedipus* and serves to sustain the *polis* and its membership as well. For, naturally, they are all implicated in and threatened by his down-fall. This is the crisis in the play; the limit as moment of judgement and resolution:

> at a certain point promise and decision, which is to say responsibility, owe their possibility to the ordeal of undecidability which will always remain their condition.[93]

Here it is, then, that *Oedipus* is decided. The scission between his being and Being is nonetheless withstood as – open, disclosed and disclosing towards beings – he withstands his responsibility as a human being in an act which allows the further dispersal of responsibility and freedom. It is precisely the fact that *Oedipus* ultimately does not hold on to power, or seek to draw everything together, but that he lets go and allows a redistribution and re-gathering to take place, which so distinguishes the play of political being that is being played-out here.

The Chorus is torn once more, this time between revulsion and the desire to learn from the spectacle it now beholds. Pity, love and respect, too, course through its response:

> I pity you but I can't bear to look.
> I've much to ask, so much to learn,
> so much fascinates my eyes,
> but you . . . I shudder at the sight.[94]

Its words touch *Oedipus*:

> Dear friends, still here?
> Standing by me, still with care for me,
> the blind man? such compassion, loyal to the last . . .[95]

Still, he insists on being cast out, banished from Thebes. He also longs for an escape from care[96] to live outside the caring/thinking (the Ancient Greek *phrono* covers both meanings), to be without the care of, mortal existence.

Indeed, he curses his fate while nonetheless owning it, 'it's mine alone, my Destiny – I am *Oedipus*',[97] and so he commits himself to it and takes responsibility for it; in particular for his blinding 'I did it all myself!'[98]

What is this fate, then, to which he has been condemned? Out-of-joint, it is to straighten things out and put them back on their feet. Compelled to be free, 'his mission to do justice to a demission of time'[99] or not, *Oedipus* executes his responsibility by effecting his withdrawal. The law he thus engenders does not derive from an economy of juridical revenge. The economy to which it gestures is one 'sheared free of retribution'. Consequently the payment of justice required by Justice – the debt he owes, and owns, in virtue of his freedom to be and to give things their due – is meted-out by *Oedipus* himself, upon himself and no one else. It is paid without expectation of return; no one inherits his eyes, they are gone for ever. It is also paid without calculation; they are gone for nothing. And, finally, it is paid outwith the calculus of accountability; no eye for an eye. Vengeance and the avenged have no purchase on or through this act. To the contrary, *Oedipus'* self-blinding disrupts the cycle of violence because, while it continues in the other plays and in other ways, it arrests rather than effects vengeance here.

The *polis* has now to witness the deliberation about his future, and to respond to his insistence that he be expelled from its midst in order to free it up. For it has options, so to speak, and, still standing-in for it, he itemises them. He could be hidden away. He might be immediately killed. He could be taken and cast into the sea. In any event its members should not fear him, for he alone bears the burden of his actions.

He is responsible. He takes-up that which he undergoes – the freedom of his mortal being – in this his new-found respect for them and for the fate which he bears amongst them; for having his being to be in, and in virtue of, the difference in which he and they stand-out exposed together. He chooses himself, even, in fact through, his self-mutilation. But, in making that choice, he is choosing for them also. Always already thrown into the midst of them, his relationship to them is ultimately not that of fear, or the anticipation of violent death at their hands and the security calculations and imperatives it provokes. It is in respect of, and so also exhibits a respect for, them. That is to say, he marks himself ('anything which bears the mark of their experience also bears the mark of an *ordeal*'[100]), and in marking himself thus he deliberately marks himself off from the rest, and from what he once was and thought himself to be. Yet, he still bears, and indeed also affirms, the name which has always marked him off from others. In doing so he henceforth determines not only his own, but also contributes directly to the determination of the *polis'* existence from out of that choice; which is his insistence upon standing-up and choosing his own end. Yet, that end is for freedom. Moreover, because that freedom is indissociable from being with them, it is the freedom of these others for which he now stands. He stands-up before and for them. However mutilating and awesome they may be, therefore, *Oedipus* comes across in his actions as an individual mortal being. But in this, as we shall see, he can only come across, and we only come across him, when he comes across with others in the space of the *polis*. He, therefore, literally comes across for the sake of others when he stands again as a fallen King.

In a sense, he has only ever come across for the sake of others. The whole play is about how this figure of mortal being comes across in taking-up responsibility for the sake of others. Yet, in the early part of the play he shoulders that responsibility by attempting insistently to stand-in for the *polis* and its members. In effect, he sought to substitute for them – remember *Creon*'s struggle to insist that *Oedipus* is not the only Theban – and failed/fell. He was also a stand-in for himself, of course, because he refused who he was.

So, how are *we* to understand this creature who was fated to mistake himself from the very beginning? What, then, is *Oedipus*' share or part of life, since the 'self' that he is is clearly not antecedent, or determined, here but 'given' only in his choosing it? Strictly speaking, of course, *Oedipus* is not, or does not possess, a 'self' in the sense that we have come to understand a 'self' as subject, subjectivity, subjectification and will. His share or part of life is, in Greek terms, his *daimon*. That is his lot – his part, his wager or his share of fortune which is being played-out.

Moreover, the responsibility of choice is the responsibility of self-disclosure, and self-disclosure is necessarily public. It is for the sake of others. But, *Oedipus*' for-the-sake-of-others undergoes a crucial shift here at the end of the play. He had tried to exorcise doubt about himself, and in himself – simultaneously trying to exorcise doubt about the *polis* in the *polis* – by resort to his *techne*. All he achieved, however, was the very intensification and ultimate exposure of the uncertainty, or (in)security, he was trying to overcome. Seeking to indemnify the *polis* he systematically inflated the premiums he was exacting upon himself and the *polis* in order to secure both; until the cost of them eventually outstripped that which he was trying to indemnify himself and the *polis* against – namely the very freedom of mortal being itself. No longer capable of securing certainty either of himself or for the *polis*, he nonetheless now exercises a commitment to himself and the *polis* in the public reappearance through which he takes-up his being again.

Where there is commitment, of course, certainty is absent and so inevitably there is also doubt in all this: doubt as to what now happens to him; doubt as to the future of his issue; and doubt as to the future of the *polis*. In nonetheless thus standing-up for himself and the *polis*, its people, and his family – by insisting that his fate was his own, by possessing it through the act of self-mutilation and, finally, removing their responsibility for it by insisting upon his own banishment – he lets himself and them be.

Oedipus is, therefore, free. Free in this sense. Not as an autonomous sovereign will antecedently given, but as thrown into a space wherein he has the capacity to act with and be-fore others; responsibly to keep open that freedom to act responsibly. Moreover, that is the freedom in which they all share. That is their being-in-common as differentially constituted in being. Specifically, then, his capacity for choice, his capacity to realise himself, is his capacity to choose for the sake of the others' freedom; that of the Otherness in himself; that of the others in the *polis*; and that, specifically also, of the daughters he is about to leave behind there. Here, at the end of the play, *Oedipus* acts and discloses himself so as to make the *polis*' free potentiality-for-being transparent to it. His last words to his daughters also enjoin them to pray for their existence; similarly making their free potentiality-for-being transparent to them. This crippled (mortal) being takes a certain stand – and so discloses himself as he is – to preserve their possibility, and not to fashion them into a final, determinate reality.

Recall that at the beginning of the play the priest begged the crippled *Oedipus* to secure them, to lift them up and found them upon a rock. It appeared as if the priest was asking *Oedipus* to stand-in for them, and that is what the King had tried to do throughout what followed; employing his securing *techne* – his eye for commensurabilities, his very calculative knowledge – as a substitute for both them and himself, eliding their having their being to be and the burden of freedom and responsibility which it imposes upon them all. Such a hubristic and tyrannical project, however, proved to be vain and impossible. This human being, the figure of all human beings as a near-god amongst them, did not have the legs for it. *Oedipus* the champion hermeneut could guarantee neither security nor 'truth'. If he above all was bound to fall and bound to err, securing security is an impossibility because truth itself cannot be secured.

At the end, however, *Oedipus* discovers a way of serving them better. Born of a *caesura* (his birth the very instigation also of another dreadful rift and dispersal), by the very painstaking, care-ridden act of taking responsibility for his own original contamination, *Oedipus* stands-up both for himself and for them.[101] No longer a stand-in, either for himself, or for the others, he lets himself and them finally be. So much for the thought that letting-be (*Gelassenheit*) amounts to a care-less benign neglect, or to 'a peculiar relaxed wilfulness, to the placid self-abandonment to a fundamental mood'.[102] Here it requires nothing less than the King's disfigurement and utter ruination. At the cost of his vision, and of his old standing, *Oedipus* eschews the project of securing himself and them – standing-in for himself and for them – for that of re-disclosing of their freedom to them. He stands-up before the *polis* and *withstands* his fate. This move – his new comportment – invites them to stand-up for themselves and assume their own burden of responsibility for the freedom of their being. All this illuminates, as well, the character of the transcendence of human being.[103] Sophocles' brilliance is, therefore, no more brilliant than the end he contrives here. For, in this very act of letting-them-be, *Oedipus* in every respect leaves them all standing.

That, then, is why they have nothing to fear in encountering his 'pollution'. They are all human beings; all mortals. And this is an account of what is entailed in that freedom, both individually and politically. Its essence is concerned with the limit but it is not limited nor is it limitless. It is neither confined to what currently is, nor is it infinite; for where there are no limits there is no beyond, and where there is no beyond there is no future. It is precisely the fragile play of the liminality of the limit. Being human is not something, therefore, which anybody or anything else can do for you. It is not something, the play seems to say, for which you can ultimately find a substitute. It is something you undergo. And, although all human beings undergo it, this particular existence which you yourself are is only something which you yourself undergo. That is your fate, your destiny. Equally, being human is not a contagion. Neither, therefore, can you catch it, for you always already have it to be.

Human being is, instead, therefore, a gratuitous gift. As you take it up and persevere with it, your givenness individualises. Individualises not in the sub-jectivising sense of an atomistic subject who engages in empty speculation about there not being any other subjects in the world, but in the decisively embodied and situated sense of recognising that it itself is the only one which has its being to be, that it can be responsible for itself, take care of the potentiality that it is, and of the possibilities of its being there in the world. For this individual – this human being, this being *there* – exists as and for its possibility. All of which necessarily entails a struggle also, however, within and against its everydayness. While you enjoy it, there is, therefore, no escaping the responsibility that is conferred upon you by this donating, and in which you yourself participate in the living that you do. Each mortal bears his or her own responsibility, therefore, for how they discharge of the life – and the debt – into which they have been thrown, and ultimately no-one can bear that of another. Bearing in mind that this mortal life is a being-in-common, however, the responsibility it invokes nonetheless involves the Otherness which it integrally comprises, and the others with which it necessarily shares its being there. You cannot live another's life, and another cannot live yours. Yet, the life that you have necessarily involves you in a responsibility for, and with, others without living their lives for them; and precisely because this responsibility is not an identification with them, nor an assimilation of them to what you may think you may be, but an openness which commits you to responsiveness to them as they present themselves to you, because you yourself are such an open being, by virtue of your very own openly granted differential constitution in openness. A responsibility arises, from out of your own openness, then, to allow them to be rather than to substitute for them.

Assuming your own freedom to be – to stand-up – consequently requires that you comport yourself before others. And there is a way of standing-up before others which is simultaneously also a way of standing-up for others. That is to say, you present yourself in a way which allows them to present themselves also. To stand-up before others in a way that also stands-up for others – rather than standing-in for them – expresses a solicitude for them which tries not to intrude upon their freedom to be, because it allows them to assume their own freedom by taking responsibility for it through the comportment which they adopt. There is a profoundly difficult and subtle art entailed in this delicate and constantly adaptive task of finding one's feet in a way which also allows others the space to find theirs with you. That is to say, of letting others be to assume the responsibility by which they take-up their freedom to be with you. With you, because the freedom of a creature whose essential openness constitutes it as a relational being, must also be relational. With you also means, however, for and against you; because there is no escaping the fact that we are all in this together even if, even as, we think of it as a brutal state of nature. This art, too, helps define the political project which is the public space of the *polis*.

At which juncture *Creon* enters; newly empowered by the course of events. Once again he displays his aversion to the publicness of *Oedipus'* actions.

Notwithstanding *Oedipus'* earlier valorisation of technique, and his immediate concern on *Creon's* arrival to figure-out how he can now win his trust because the *affaire Oedipus* is still not fully resolved[104] (of course, it never truly is), *Creon's* instinct for rule is significantly different from the political instincts of his previous co-regent. *Oedipus* had insisted that he be brought out of the palace, his sin exposed to public intelligence ('He cries, "Unbar the doors and let all Thebes behold the slayer of his sire, his mother's—"'[105]). After briefly assuring *Oedipus* that he has not come to criticise or mock, *Creon*, however, immediately upbraids the guards for allowing the shame and horror which *Oedipus* has come to represent to be exposed to public view. *Creon*, on the contrary, therefore, considers this pollution to be a private and not a public matter: an obscenity and not both an obscenity and a political disaster; an offence against the gods and not both an offence against the gods and the polity:

> You there,
> have you lost all respect for human feelings?
> At least revere the Sun, the holy fire
> that keeps us all alive [the altar of Apollo before which all this takes place].
> Never expose a thing
> of guilt and holy dread so great it appals
> the earth, the rain from heaven, the light of day!
> Get him into the halls – quickly as you can.
> Piety demands no less. Kindred alone
> should see a kinsman's shame. This is obscene.[106]

My point does not deny the boundary between the public and the private, of course, nor that between the sacred and the profane. Rather, it emphasises that the public and the private, like the sacred and the profane, are mutably-bound together. It insists upon this inescapable, and inescapably contingent, duality. *Oedipus* the persistent boundary crosser consequently teaches us these things. Most especially, along with their very necessity, he also teaches us the desperate plurality, permeability and mutability of the limits which delimit us. He thereby calls attention to the domains, and to the fragility of those domains, which limits delimit, precisely because his boundary beating problematises them for us. Thus he is even here, still, making an issue of the constitution of the public and the private, the sacred and the profane, by the way in which to the very end he cuts (decides) back and forth within and between them. *Creon*, however, not only seems to treat them as fixed and unproblematic, his partiality is always exercised anti-politically towards privacy rather than disclosure.

And more than this. Even at the end *Oedipus* is free to act and does so in a very special way. This action is not an extension of the past, another imitation of it, and it is not an exercise of the will – the idea of the freedom of the will was, of course, unknown to the Greeks. It is not teleologically driven either. It is not a means to an end, and it does not aim at progress towards a positive future in whose name the present may be sacrificed. Neither, finally, is it merely a private and individual act.

Oedipus does not seek to retreat back into the supposed automaticity of 'tradition' (the time of the before) and he does not flee forward and outwards into the making of 'history' (a ballistically calculated future of successive nows). He falls back once more upon public appearance, and returns to the time and the place of this event – the futural crisis of the here and now – as it is provided-for through the *polis*. He thereby takes-up his political responsibilities as he lays down his power; or, rather, he takes-up his political responsibilities *by* laying down his power. His public response to the historical possibilities he shares with other mortals, here at the play's end, frees the historical space of destining to be something different from what it has been hitherto. That is the whole point of his disclosing himself again publicly, and in doing so he both affirms the public space of the *polis* – through his continuing courage to exercise the freedom for action which mortal life bestows upon human being – and takes-up, though now differently, that which he is undergoing (his very mode of being) while freeing others to do the same.

Here he is again, then, seen in action in the space whose purpose is to allow such action, thus confirming its central significance in ensuring mortality's freedom of action; that freedom and action which together constitute the very possibility of a free political life:

> Because we are plural, action in politics is not a matter of lonely heroes but of interaction between peers; because we are plural even the most charismatic leader cannot do more than lead what is essentially a joint enterprise; because we are plural, human beings are at their most glorious not when their individuality is lost in Spartan comradeship on the battlefield, but when they are revealing their unique identities on the public stage.[107]

Oedipus' response to the repeated possibilities opened-up by time – the conjunction of traditions, discourses, practices, happenings and events in which we are always already immersed in a destined way – indeed to repetition itself – is one which ultimately disavows any notion of slavish continuity or identity with the past even as it freely acknowledges its indebtedness to the past. His very actions, however destined they are by the way in which he is inescapably thrown into a world which he did not make and cannot master, no matter how hard he has responded to the way in which he is challenged technologically to do so, disrupts identity and continuity. Just as it was his destiny from the very outset to have the prospect of any simple routinisation of life pre-empted, so the living-out of that destiny, his very action in coming before the *polis* (self-blinded, and so newly sighted and newly sited) disrupts the routine of life once more. This free and critical response to the occurrence, and to the recurrent repetition, of the specific and unique is itself specific and unique.[108] It leads, in the realisation of the possibility of something else unexpected and unpredictable, not only to the repetition of the *polis* but also to that of *Oedipus* himself: his release from the destiny bequeathed to him towards another; Thebes' release from the irruption of that destiny, and its projection into another.

This action does not ultimately rely and does not appeal to any authorisation of repeatable historical possibilities founded upon myth, nor upon the projection of a past into a future as the extension of automatic processes and of repeatable occurrences – a succession of nows – that come to pass as if human beings did not act; and as if nothing unexpected occurred in virtue of the fact that they do act, and in virtue of the fact that even as they act other things happen which are unaccountable in terms of those actions. Just as tragedy is itself more than mere 'mimicry', so also the action which it enacts is itself more than 'mere' repetition and identification with past practices.[109] In thus 'cultivating and sustaining the strife between what is assigned to him as a task and what has been given him as his endowment',[110] *Oedipus'* act re-enacts the very agonism of the *polis* and the freeing act of political responsibility itself. It seems a perfect expression of Heidegger's understanding of resoluteness:

> Here, then, it is a matter of decision – and of incision – in our lives, a matter of cutting away what has prevailed hitherto, what has by now run its course, from what still 'remains'. Obviously, the cut is made by the thought of return, which transforms everything.[111]

And, yet. *Oedipus'* resoluteness, this point at which he gathers himself together by gathering together all the trammelled strands of his history, is also a new dispensation; a re-dispersal and redistribution of himself, of the beings he has been with, and of the place in which they have shared that being-in-common which has been shared-out amongst them there.

Because there is difference, and not a sovereign point of departure, a multiplying process of duplication and re-duplication 'which animates and inspires all human activities and is the hidden source of production of all great and beautiful things',[112] there is renewal in and through the human freedom repeatedly to act. Whatever impels the chain of infinite improbabilities which produces human being also animates human being itself. However improbable it may, therefore, seem, in the depths particularly of a nemesis such as this, the play affirms, things can and do begin again. But so long as this 'source' does not appear, is not manifested, 'freedom is not a worldly, tangible reality'.[113] (That freedom is what the celebratory dance of the Chorus is concerned to bring before us and keep in view.) It, therefore, requires a space and a place where it can make its appearance. Evident, first, in human being itself, it nonetheless requires the confirmation, amplification, celebration and perspective which the very public space of the *polis* – the very space in which human being can show itself and where 'freedom can manifest itself and become a [mundane] reality'[114] – also provides (and remember also that if people cannot appear they cannot fully be; visibility and equality are, therefore, intimately related here). It does so because freedom ultimately concerns not merely being-in-common's capacity to act but also the 'I-can', and not 'I-will', of being-in-common. It, therefore, necessarily entails that public action in respect of Otherness with others required of the 'I-can', wherein lies the prospect of calling something new into being which did not exist before, rather than the mere solipsistic dreaming of the 'I-will'.[115]

Here *Oedipus'* struggle – his striving – is the struggle of the *polis* as well. It is not a willing – a struggle that is representational in that it is always thought to be related to that for which it strives – this striving is a striving to reach beyond himself because as a mortal human being, simultaneously living and dying and so bearing difference within himself and on his way to death as we all are, he is always already beyond himself. And so it is a striving ultimately towards himself.[116] In this, as with the striving of the *polis* of which the Chorus sang earlier, he not only gathers himself together but also initiates a new dispersal of freedom and responsibility amongst them. It is not a matter of asking why he should do this. *Oedipus*, like Angelus Silesius' rose or Meister Eckhart's understanding of human being, is without a why:

> If you were to ask a genuine man who acted from his own ground, 'Why do you do what you are doing?' If he were to answer rightly, he would say no more than, 'I do it because I do it'.[117]

Oedipus does what he does because that is what it is to be mortal; that is what he is as a mortal.

Here is the human being, then. Fully extended at its extremity, gathered together in its extremity by its extremity, it is nonetheless also redistributed through that extremity. Here it is repeating itself through the capacity for repetition which originally frees the being that it enjoys, because – like it or not – it bears the indelible trace of that mortal freedom in its very corporeality.

Hence, the being-in-common of mortal life is neither simply private, nor simply public, but simultaneously both a public and a private and, therefore, plural and initiatory plenitude of being; in that, life showing-up in it, that life has the freedom (initiative) also to show itself because it has to deal with Otherness and act with others. To act is to have the freedom to begin again, the same but different, to have the capacity to break into the automaticity of things and in so doing take responsibility for oneself in respect of the Otherness of which one is constituted; to revere, also, and take joy in that mystery of being.

This act of judgement, this judgement on himself so publicly disclosed, is based upon no political standard or model – *Creon* forcefully objects to it. Neither is it a re-presentation of an external standard or *eidos* according to which *Oedipus* is finally compelled to judge himself – he insists that it was not the gods who required it, he did it himself. Incest is an abomination in the eyes of mortals and gods, of course, but *Oedipus* is not compelled to this judgement and this disclosure here in virtue of the operation of some universal law which tells him what must be done. Incest is his inheritance, his secret. He has had to read it, to interpret and interrogate it, because it was never transparent to him or anyone else. Even here, at the end, it retains its fundamentally enigmatic and opaque character. Through it he has not only been decided, he has also had to decide. This radically ambiguous and fluid condition – of simultaneously being decided and of having to decide so as to keep the possibility of the future open – he withstands now as the play approaches its climax. The choice, in which he tears himself away, effects another rent or opening. Law, then, is missing and must be engendered.[118] That is what *Oedipus'* final acts do. In so doing they establish another ineradicable difference or dissension, serving notice of a further terrible severance – *Oedipus'* banishment – which acknowledges the excessiveness of the indeterminate (witness *Oedipus'* new-found reverence, for example) that actually sustains the openness of the play, because it engenders a new accord between the determinate world of mortals and the indeterminate Being of their world.

Neither, finally, is *Oedipus'* judgement upon himself a private thing. It cannot be. Rather, because the ability to judge one's situation depends upon the radical excess of judgement, it is something that must be given perspective. It must, therefore, 'free itself from the private and idiosyncratic view and engage in the "enlarged mentality", which always finds itself in and among the perspectives of others'.[119] Hence, as *Oedipus'* being is a being-in-common, it has to be public.

This freedom, then, with which the *polis* is integrally involved because it is the place in which it is exercised and amplified, is the sheer capacity of the repetition which initiates a new beginning. *Oedipus'* action is glorious, if bloody, precisely because this freely chosen public display of his terrible condition re-affirms the publicness of the public world, re-engenders the *polis*, and restores to it its function not to be a reflection of him but the ultimately formless – in that sense 'empty', to extend a thought of Claude Lefort – place where people are free to assume their freedom and stand as what they are. The political in the political life of the *polis* is, therefore, not given as such either. That is to say, it is not simply present and presentable. It is the absent presence towards which mortals are pulled in their resolute public and responsible actions. What is not given has, therefore, in this way and with this kind of effort, to be continuously engendered. Ultimately, *Oedipus'* destiny is not to kill his father and marry his mother. *Oedipus'* destiny – remembering that it is the destiny of all mortal beings – is to engender and re-engender the freedom of the political in moments of dread. Incorporating the terrible discordance of disjointed temporality within his own mortal corporeality – he is not only the situated, he is the embodied site of disjuncture – *Oedipus* is challenged to exercise the resoluteness to judge himself with and in response to others. From being the body which threatened difference, because of the incestuous way in which it was gathered together in him, however, *Oedipus* now becomes the body in which and through which difference is re-distributed; meted-out. This is *Oedipus* the limit at the limit acting as the threshold once more, trying to do what, in Shakespearian language, is mete. His actions at the play's end are an example of that resoluteness; a resoluteness which

> must esteem what is of worth and significance, . . . must judge what is of worth in its historical possibilities from within the terrible discordance between

the determinate and the indeterminate which characterizes the very moment of resoluteness itself.[120]

In effect *Oedipus'* final act does this through the dispersal of a last political will and testament. In doing so, and while still exhibiting much of his earlier practice, he now exhibits a significantly different understanding of the political than that of securing calculability which largely impelled him hitherto. Once more he demands his banishment – the city must be rid of him – and *Creon* demurs until the gods are consulted again and clarify what ought to be done. He then commands, corrects himself and begs, *Creon* to bury *Jocasta* properly. His sons will be of no concern to *Creon*. Being already men, they will be able to fend for themselves.[121] His two younger daughters will, however, require *Creon's* wardship and he pleads for it. *Creon*, out of mercy and pity, knowing also *Oedipus'* deep love for them and anticipating his wish, has already had them brought-out to say their last goodbyes.

Hear *Oedipus'* goodbye to them:

> You little ones, if you were old enough
> to understand, there is much I'd tell you.
> Now, as it is, I'd have you say a prayer.
> Pray for life my children,
> live where you are free to grow and season.
> Pray god you find a better life than mine,
> the father who begot you.[122]

Oedipus, whose life from first to last has been an obscenity of a life ultimately daunted and diminished by life, nonetheless speaks every loving father's last words to the daughters he cherishes, in an astonishing affirmation of life. Pray for life and live a life in which your being can flourish! Even at the end he enacts his life in letting life be for them. What can this life be that, despite the life which he has had, he wants with all his being for them? Not the particular life that he or any of them has led thus far, of course, but the very donation – giving, receiving, gathering and sending-on – of life from which life itself springs, of which it is also constituted, and of which they are an instance; a measure of whose mysterious unfulfilment they have to live for themselves. He asks them to pray for that infinite improbability of givenness – that very potentiality-for-being – of which they themselves are an instance. In loving that very mystery of life which they themselves are – native and strangers to himself, as he has been to Thebes – *Oedipus* can do no other than express his love of the existence of life itself:

> The will of love takes precedence over the will of the ground, and this precedence and eternal decidedness – that is, the love of being for being – this decidedness is the innermost core of absolute freedom.[123]

Hence as his love desires for them to explore and celebrate their participation in it, so, too, it must affirm life. Here, then, love breaks the surface of the play and juts forth directly into the *polis* with *Oedipus* teaching us more, once more, about the motions and e-motions of our free being-in-common.

We can progress no further now without addressing in detail the relationship between love, the freedom of mortal life and the idea of politics which the tragedy of the *polis* presents. But that must wait for another time and perhaps also another text. Suffice it to repeat, for the moment, that love of them positively enjoins *Oedipus* to affirm life, because if he did not affirm life he could not love them. He *has* to affirm life if he loves them, for how could he love them – the living which they are – if he did not love living itself. And so love he does. In doing so he re-engenders the law of the inviolability of the possible; to let only their death be their uttermost possibility, and to displace all attempts to make this un-presentable present, so that they can be free to exist in their potentiality-for-being this side of death, until death must ultimately claim them too. His love is a love which strives to let the possibilities of their Otherness be. He directs an unconditional yes at them. He wants for them to be what they are in their essence: a specific, unique, radically open potentiality-for-being, engendered by him yet also, of course, strangers to him, and free of him; sharing his exile-without-nostalgia as other human beings. His final words, I suggest, say this to them in this his own dread moment of resolute judgement: 'I love you, I want you to be what you are in your essence'.[124] Love, then, is the unconditional affirmation of this very possibility which each of us individually is, the freedom to be.

So far addressed through the play's preoccupation with knowledge and power, standing and seeing, grounds and heights, the mystery of life here, therefore, assumes a different masque as the face of the play metamorphoses into a visage of love. Love not as an explanation, causation or justification – a reason – as if it stood outside the life which it affirms. Love not as a goal.[125] But love itself as the struggle of life, for life, with life and the nothing:

> According to the old saying of Heraclitus, struggle is the basic principle and moving force of being. But the greatest struggle is love – which provokes the deepest contest precisely in order to be and display itself in its reconciliation.[126]

Love, then, as integral to the movement of the free being that human being is; itself another expression of its struggle to be. Love, another name for being-in-common as it articulates its desire for the difference of which it is constituted, and that it shares with others, exulting in the prospect which its differential constitution in a world of openness excites. Love which, coming in many tempers and guises, finds one form of exemplification in the love of one's child; that uncanny, infinite improbability of yet another singular instance of identity/difference.[127]

But do not mistake this love for a peaceful reconciliation, or a reconciliation which brings peace, neither for a release that brings tranquillity. There is a force in this 'I love you, I want you to be'. Do not be fooled into thinking, therefore, that the only violence of any consequence is the violence which elides the other, effaces and defaces the other; as if, if we could, facing up to rather than effacing the other, we might bring an end to violence. For in this releasing love also lies the power and latent force of an injunction – 'an injunction that is itself disjointed'.[128] Issuing from someone who is himself out-of-joint, this injunction effects another disjunction. *Oedipus*, with love, and through love, releases them to their inheritance of life. That injunction insists, albeit lovingly, that the other can be no other than other, come what may; and exhorts it to remain so. Ultimately, he says, you can (must) be no other than other because that is what you are; haunted, as am I, by an Otherness which I recognise but can never know, and I love you for it. Smitten as he is with love, *Oedipus* smites back in the same currency:

> Pray for life my children, live where you are free to grow and season. Pray god you find a better life than mine, the father who begot you.

In being loved, and finding love, these lines suggest, you do not find peace. Instead, the struggle of your being is refreshed.

This, therefore, is not the struggle-free love of a happy ending. Love does not gather everything together in unison and unity here. An expression of their being-in-common, of their belonging together in virtue of difference, this love also effects a new scission or severance in which the possibility of the being of these *other* beings – specifically his daughters – takes place. It consequently also splits asunder, severs and divides, allowing for a further duplication of difference. For only in division does the possibility of possibilities and their multiplication occur. There is violence in it precisely, therefore, because it is an acceptance of this mortal freedom. Moreover, it is not a freedom which is paternally, or patriarchally, granted by *Oedipus*, despite his being their father. His off-spring are being wrenched from his grasp, and it is not a freedom, in any event, that is within his gift. Instead, it is an antecedent freedom which, in extremity, he now recognises that he shares in common with them. This 'I love you, I want you to be' therefore says: stand up – for yourself and before others – take up the burden of freedom afresh and live it out more fully.

Just as he tries to give that which he does not have – the bearings of their latitude to be – so *Oedipus*' love amounts to an impossible command. Freeing them of himself is not possible. He cannot efface what he is and what has happened. He cannot, in fact, withdraw what has already been given, and nothing can free them of the inheritance into which they have come.[129] In short, they cannot be delivered of their existence. But, is it possible to have it delivered over to them, freely to assume it as best they might, in a freeing way? Perhaps this is what *Oedipus* is trying to do. They alone can bear their inheritance. But, in the way in which he himself comports himself towards its handing-on – saying something like 'grieve for me, therefore, keep me enough to use me as you must'[130] – *Oedipus* tries to contribute somehow to their free reception and assumption of it. Ultimately, however, it is impossible because (irrespective of the awfulness of the inheritance which he leaves to them) there is nothing he, or they, can do to secure compliance with a command to find and enjoy a better life. And, yet, that is precisely the forceful insistent desire of love for the loved one. For its otherness, and the Otherness it bears, to thrive.

Clutching his daughters to him, yet clamouring again to be driven from Thebes, *Oedipus* seems finally to get his wish as *Creon* appears to consent. Only the gods can grant this, says *Creon*. The gods must abhor *Oedipus*, says *Oedipus*. Well then, *Creon* replies, *Oedipus'* wish must be quickly granted. Do you mean that you consent? demands *Oedipus*. To which *Creon* responds: 'When I speak I mean it so'.[131]

If the play has taught anything, however, it has taught us to mistrust the plain spoken. Especially, the plain spoken when it is spoken by someone as sophistically 'savvy' as *Creon*. These near concluding lines are, therefore, amongst the most ambiguous of the play. The gods have not yet been consulted again; and even if they should be there is no guarantee that their *theorema*, the divine saying, would be anything other than equivocal. It most usually was! It seems reasonable to say that *Oedipus* is an abhorrence in their sight, but their purpose in respect of him has not been clarified. Indeed, when was it ever clear? If *Oedipus'* logic is correct, then nothing can stand in the way of his exile. We know about *Oedipus'* logic, however; the vaulting, vaunting *hubris* of the tyrant. We know also about the ways of the gods. Ultimately we do not know. So, *Oedipus* might be wrong. He has been wrong in everything else. If he is, what then? To precisely what, therefore, does *Creon* assent when he speaks so plainly? To leaving the question open still for the oracle's advice? If so, why did he not simply say so? His reply is a 'plain' politician's reply. Even in this respect the issue of *Oedipus* remains to be settled. His daughters wrenched from his grasp – *Creon* admonishing that *Oedipus* continues to seek to hold fast (*kratein*) again as once before, when he fell through trying to hold tight to the rule (*kratein*) of truth and the truth of rule – *Oedipus* and *Creon* exit through the double doors of the palace, back into the divided centre of rule from which *Oedipus* issued at the very beginning of the play.

'At the extreme limit of distress', Hölderlin noted in respect of *Oedipus*, 'there is in fact nothing left but the conditions of time and space'.[132] It seems, then, as though nothing much is destined for this derelict mortal being any more. If there was a motivating fear in the play (and I think, on the contrary, the entire disposition of the play amounts to an astonishing exploration and affirmation of human being's free capacity to undertake that which it undergoes, in the irresponsible clearing of space and time), I would say that that fear is the fear of the loss of destiny. Which is the same as saying what I said at the beginning about the tragic. The supreme danger to which the tragic alerts us is the loss of destiny or limits. For destiny is the very liminal freedom which happens within limits because of limits; between the limits of birth and death. And so I somewhat demur from the poet's reading.

Precisely because of his responsible actions, *Oedipus'* fate at the close of the play is on the way to being accomplished rather than finished. Of course, he is cast-down. Of course, he is cast-out. But, in the process, *Oedipus* assumes a spirituality which elevates him. As he finally passes-out of life and is buried, at Colonus, the body of *Oedipus Rex* is bequeathed as a treasure not only to Athens but also to us. For, after all, the play is a play; though we are haunted by it.[133] It is the play of the play which bears repeating; that is to say, transports the message of repeatability itself. Millennia later, therefore, repeating the accomplishment of *Oedipus'* fate we are recalled to the burden of human freedom. Thus, *Oedipus'* destiny is never, in fact, brought to a close.

Directing the audience to look upon this spectacle, the Chorus reminds them of the envy they once felt at *Oedipus'* ability to hold-on to the truth and master the world through his *techne*, and urges them to reflect now upon the downfall which this has wrought. But that is not its conclusion. Rather, its final message is that there is no conclusion. There is no simple moral, no final accounting, no summary last look of ultimate understanding. You cannot hold on securely to the last *scène/sens* played here either.

> *oste thneton onta keinen ten taileutaian idein*
> *hemeran episkopounta meden' olbizein, prin an*
> *terma tou biou perase meden algeinon pathon.*[134]

Wait. Keep watching. What you see now is not the end of things. It is also another beginning. For there is, of course, a liminal belonging together of beginning and ends.

ENDING

In this final scene *Oedipus* comes finally to know his facticity in not having known – and ultimately for all human being it is a matter of not being able to know – his own original provenance. Whereas that had once been a problem which he had set before himself to be resolved, it is now understood as a condition which effects a transformation in his very being. He does not know from whence he came or where he is finally headed, even as he necessarily always projects ahead of himself in the living that he does. This lack is not an add-on to his being. Integral to him, it is what constitutes him as a differentially constituted duality. Thrown into existence he must necessarily, therefore, bear the consequences both of his choices and his non-choices because he did not have any choice in the matter of his birth, nor in its patrimony which he has just lived-out. Hence he is deeply indebted to that which he undergoes – his very being (t)here – but for which, at least in the usual sense of the term, he was not responsible. He is indebted, moreover, not because of this or that situation or event whose account he might settle, but originally and forever. And, yet, here at the play's end, he comes to understand that he must assume this 'archi-debt', respond to and take responsibility for it, and thereby transfigure it without ever being able finally to discharge it altogether.

That transformation effects a similar shift in his solicitude for others. His earlier concern to stand-in for the Thebans was ultimately one of power and domination. Standing-up for and before them in the *polis* at the end of the play, however, it becomes a solicitude which 'leaps ahead and liberates'.[135] Liberates in the sense not of relieving them of all care (most especially of the particular care which having been with him has given to them) but of freeing them for it by not obstructing that freedom through putting himself in their place.

Heidegger's inconspicuous law of the possible, which demands that one act so that the possibility of the impossible not be made actual, is operating here.[136] In a world radically endangered by politics of security now capable of making the impossible happen, human being must learn politically how to follow this inconspicuous law of the possible or finally realise its own impossibility. That is the challenge which, successfully met, might inaugurate a new *mise en forme* (*mise en scène/mise en sens*) of the political. Failed, it is capable now, in our world, of accomplishing the end of the world; the very closure which it is *Oedipus'* destiny both to threaten and yet, ultimately also, to forestall.

Conclusion

Imagination at the call of ethico-political responsibility

Are we not ready to recognize in the power of the imagination, no longer simply the faculty of deriving 'images' from our sensory experience, but the capacity for letting new worlds shape our understanding of ourselves?

(Paul Ricoeur, 'Metaphor and the Central Problem of Hermeneutics')

Those who advocate an alliance of the poetic with the political, as I have been doing here, do so in order to expand our political imagination. I have also been trying to employ the poetic in a way which is not exclusively indebted to Heideggerian insight. For the poetic is something which can be seen to operate elsewhere as well; in the way that biblical poetry, for example, functions discordantly in relation to the rules of discourse. Using key words to amplify meaning, disclose unexpected assimilations, and 'hitherto unseen interconnections which cannot be reduced to a single meaning',[1] is therefore not the preserve of tragedy, either, but a possibility that inheres within Language itself. That possibility is, of course, one to which other poetic idioms are also attuned. For a word is not a mere tool, even to those who most insist that Language is only a conveyance or means of communication.

Those who advocate an alliance of the poetic with the political do so in order to emphasise, also, that the political is ultimately a *how*, and not a *what*. In consequence, it cannot be grasped in a concept nor fixed with a definition. Instead of the endless insistence on what one is, therefore, the political is concerned with how one is. Specifically, it is an attunement to the call of Justice that demands a certain composure towards others in the Otherness in which human beings stand-out together. That is why political 'style', for example, may be more than mere fashion.

As a *how* the political is consequently also always taking place, and necessarily taking place in a space of undecidability which allows decisions to be taken without being certain about what decisions are correct. That taking place is the continuous interruption of the conditioned – the decided – by the unconditioned – the not decided – in the form of a challenge to give things their due. Such a taking place requires the resolution which engenders the law that is precisely not already given.

This is also how I would interpret destiny and fate. Not as that which is specifically preordained, but the inescapability of having to assume the responsibility of engendering the law that is not already given – of having to decide and be decided – for one's own time, and in the very specificity of one's own topos of encounter. Such is possible only because the self *is* that open topos of ethical encounter – plural, divided and shared – where this *how* takes place.

Such a taking place necessarily also both allows and requires what William Connolly calls revisionary practices of the (political) self. These are concerned with responding to the continuous insurrectionary call of Justice that arises within the self, as well as between selves, to the self. Such practices, while depending upon the possibility of imagining and knowing ourselves differently, recall the very reality of having imagined and known ourselves differently. They do so in order to keep open the possibility that we may continue to imagine and know ourselves differently. It is how this responsibility is assumed – not the *essentia* of a what – which ultimately decides the question of identity. Hence, the more unity, uniformity and immutability demanded of the self, the more ethical dissolution and irresolution is produced; and the more the self is fragmented into competing egotistical solipsisms, incarcerated within equally fragmented and dessicated worlds.

Those who fear this alliance, however, do so out of a radical mistrust of the limitlessness which espousal of the poetic imagination appears sometimes to imply. As Richard Kearney puts it: 'Poetic licence applies only to poetics, not to the ethical world of action beyond the text'. Kearney goes on to note that a certain Post-modern strand in philosophy has tended also to accord priority to poetics over ethics. This tempts their critics, he suggests, to charge some, like Foucault, with an aesthetic of 'deliberate irresponsibility', or to charge others, such as Derrida, with an indecisive 'indifference'. Whatever the accuracy of such claims, and I think they are disputable, no one could level such charges at the tragic.

I want to use Kearney's observations about the poetic now, however, to effect a move from a play about the political life to make one final point about the play of political life itself, and the role of imagination within it. For he makes his points in an argument about the relation between the poetic, the ethical and, ultimately, the political, which – inspired by his reading of Paul Ricoeur's hermeneutics – is designed to ally the operation of imagination to the antecedent ethical claims of the other. He does so in a way that is designed to challenge the very exercise of the political imagination of Modernity; as well as of some of its Post-modern critics. He seeks, thereby, to expand certain aspects of political Modernity beyond the (inter)national political limits that it sets for itself. He does so, especially, where those limits work to effect terminal political impasses whose anchorings, in unreconstructed narratives of the self and of the past, foreclose the possibility of reclaiming politically habitable futures for ourselves as other selves. But he does so in ways which do not deny the irremissible debt that we simultaneously owe to both past and future, to both self and other.[2]

In practice this is a project I espouse, albeit I would pursue it through the tragic rather than the narrative imagination; and I think that there are differences between them. I recognise also, of course, that it is something which needs carrying forward not only in respect of the discourse of the political, but also at the level of the constitutional question of the organisation of the public space of (inter)national political life, as well as in relation to political decision itself; where the tragic topos of encounter of political life appears in all its historical tropographical specificity and detailed policy complexity. It also requires a powerful preliminary chain of argument, however, which raises the question of the political out of the habitual ways not just of how we think about it, but of how we think as such. For thinking is one of the principal resources upon which we call, both when we rehearse traditional accounts of the political as well as when we challenge them at our limits, including the limits of our imagination.

I have tried to sketch-out certain links in that chain of argument here, while drawing attention, in addition, to the rift between poetry and thought which also delimits thinking. Thinking is not, of course, all that there is to how we are. 'We are human before being learned', Levinas reminds us, 'and remain so after having forgotten much'.[3] The role of imagination within the play of political life, I therefore want to argue, is related to what Levinas has called the source of 'the must'. The poetic, especially in the form of tragedy, recalls that 'must'. By articulating, in all its aporetic difficulties, the burden of its very undecidability, the poetic contributes towards replenishing the ethical energy which 'the must' demands of us, in a world in which we are habitually preoccupied with the oneself and the everyday.

These are some of the reasons, therefore, why I make no excuse for pitching this particular adventure into the question of the political at the level of the discourse about the political, nor for resorting to a device – namely a tragedy – which seems so distant from the practical institutional and policy questions which ordinarily preoccupy (inter)national political debate. Its very strangeness is meant to challenge the thought that we already know very well in modern times what the political is – and what some of its key words mean – as well as what being political demands of human being. And, indeed, that this knowledge is precisely what will save us from ourselves.

My pugnaciousness concerning the seriousness of the poetic's relation to political thought, while intended to challenge the fatal hubris of that assumption, is not intended, however, to diminish the significance of institutional and policy questions. But, the cultivation of political imagination is not only a complex thing, requiring intervention at the institutional as well as the decisional level, it is critically reliant also upon the transformation of the vocabulary of politics itself. Such a project is one in which the poetic has special significance and responsibilities.

If our existing vocabulary of politics were adequate to the local–global challenge which humankind now faces – that of politically out-living the modern – there would be no need to argue for a retrieval of politics and a revivification of political imagination. Yet, who now confidently embraces the fatal (inter)national embrace of political Modernity? If the political is, however, in need of re-imagining through that struggle over political vocabulary which amounts to a challenge to the way we think the political as such, this raises the related question of the imagination, and of its relation to the question of limits which has so preoccupied this text. How, then, does the imagination – to which the poetic so powerfully appeals – operate? Specifically, how does it operate in respect of limits; the taking place of the ethico-political encounter of human being with its being, with other beings and with Being?

Recognising the inevitable role played by the imagination in respect both of history and ethical responsibility, and while detailing and extolling the positive need for it in enlarging our ethico-political sensibilities, Kearney invokes Ricoeur to insist also that: whereas 'imagination knows no censure *in itself*', the summons of responsibility to others, and I would add to Otherness, 'has to come from beyond *itself* – that is, from others'. Narrative, he argues, permits – that is to say, it does not necessarily enjoin – the structuring of imagination in a way which propels it beyond its egotistical circle 'to a relation of analogy, empathy, or apperception (*Paarung*) with others'.[4] The point is well taken and chimes, to a degree, with the thrust of what I have been arguing here. I think the tragic, however, does this more powerfully.

For tragedy teaches that the other is the limit of the self, just as Otherness is the limit of the self-same. I would, therefore, force Kearney some steps further. Neither imagination nor ethical responsibility, I would argue, given what I have already said about limits, can function without limits. Each, quite literally, must take place. The configuration of its taking place is its very delimitation, and that delimitation is a political struggle. Without taking place what could the ethical, or imagination, be? Is not, then, the taking place the point? Equally the point, is it not, for the appearance of the inapparent as for the appearance of things? And is this taking place of the political not something which preeminently takes place in the very space of the *inter* of International Relations?

Taking place, of course, though the point bears constant repetition, never precludes taking place differently. To the contrary. It is the condition of possibility of taking place differently. Attunement to the possibility of taking place differently, the art of making way for new possibilities of being, is a positively superior – and intensely political – attunement to the very character of taking place as such.

People *may*, therefore, do what they like in their fantasies. Certainly they *can* never act with impunity in the world no matter how immune they may think they are. But, *pace* Ricoeur, not even imagination is limitless. Rather, I would say, the imagination is distinguished as that faculty which is most attuned to the full power of liminal intimation, whose limits derive from the very surplus that they always already give away *as* limits. It is that inescapable liminality of limits which provides for the very possibility of things' taking place differently at all. Similarly, the call of the ethical is heard only because, resounding throughout human being, it sounds-out human being-there.

The issue again, then, is less limitlessness or the absence of limits. It is, once more, their figuration and one's composure *in respect* of them. The limit so necessary to the exercise both of imagination and ethical responsibility does, however, derive ultimately from the call of the other in the Otherness that we inhabit together. This is the condition that allows us to say 'we' the human, while keeping the openness of the human open to its very responsibility as responsiveness to its being.

Now, if Heidegger's thesis about the so-called end of philosophy is not only persuasive, when construed as a philosophy of the limit, but also profoundly important for the way in which we think the political, then we are merely brought to this limit and enjoined continuously to seek through it ways beyond its particular historical taking place. Here, this place is the place of the (inter)national politics of political Modernity, which International Relations claims for its distinctive competence. It is a place now, I claim, which we are challenged to out-live. International Relations may be reconfigured as the place where we can think differently about the taking place of this project.

Liminally responsive to the way of the limit, the poetic does not merely inhabit that way, however; it makes way for it. The one houses the other. But, this is a fragile habitation, itself concerned with the fragile. Fragility – 'that is to say, what is perishable through natural weakness and what is threatened under the blows of historical violence'[5] – as a source of 'the must', nonetheless, therefore, obliges us. In making us experience a situation that is, but should not be – a definition of the human as fragile possibility, as much as of its multitudes of abject beings – it invokes our care. Such a care is distinguished as much by a generous ethic of cultivation as it is by traditional accounts of authorship and responsibility. *For the fragile calls-out as possibility, and we are called to be responsible selves as much by how hospitably we respond to that call, as by the extent to which we acknowledge authorship of our actions.* Indeed, cultivating the possibility of that which is fragile – including, above all, making way for the political life's response to the call of Justice – imposes much greater demands upon us, because it entails much greater risks. Knowing that we are fallible, and that the world is a world of wrong-doing, standing-up for the possible by making way for it to be – however much that requires acknowledging also an indebtedness to what has been – is no mere retrospective. It is the wager we take upon the future of life itself. Fragility, therefore, does en-join us. As we share in it, it also enjoins us to let its possibilities and accomplishments flourish. Out-living the modern invokes the art of letting other possibilities of being be. That letting-be is a delicate, but nonetheless material and empowering, political art.

Such an art is easily lost, overlooked or snuffed-out in the daily struggle to be. The way of the limit is, I have argued, the way of the ethico-political project of political life as well. Hence, the affinity I detect between the poetic and the political. Hence, too, their affinity with the fragile, and the indispensable bond between the poetic imagination and the ethical energy required to sustain the fragility of the very ethos of political life itself; namely the obligatory freedom of human being. Its very fragility in being attuned to the fragile call of the other, in the Otherness we share, requires the political to draw sustenance from its affinity with the poetic imagination. In doing so, it may furnish new figurations of politics and new inscriptions of political time that stand-up for Justice. Nowhere, it seems to me, is this call more fragile, yet nowhere does it issue more loudly, than in the *inter* of the (inter)national politics of late modern times. There, I believe, out-living the modern becomes the name for a new ethico-political project of human being.

Notes

INTRODUCTION

1 W. Connolly, *The Ethos of Pluralization*, Minneapolis: Minnesota University Press, 1995, p. xvi.

1 SECURITY, PHILOSOPHY AND POLITICS

1 W. Leibniz, *Philosophical Writings*, G. H. R. Parkinson, ed., London: Everyman, 1973, p. 93.
2 The phrase was formulated by Cyprian. See S. Wolin, *Politics and Vision*, London: George Allen and Unwin, 1961; especially the chapter on 'The Early Christian Era: Time and Community'.
3 See for example P. I. Kaufman, *Redeeming Politics*, Princeton, New Jersey: Princeton University Press, 1990.
4 See especially *The History of Sexuality; Volume One. An Introduction*, Harmondsworth: Peregrine Books, 1987, pp. 3–13, and 'Part Five. Right of Death and Power over Life'. And see also *Volume Two. The Use of Pleasure*, Harmondsworth: Penguin Books, 1987; and *Volume Three. The Care of the Self*, Harmondsworth: Penguin, 1988.
5 The Foucault quote comes from *The History of Sexuality. Volume One*, p. 14.
6 See J. der Derian and M. J. Shapiro, eds, *International/Intertextual. Postmodern Readings of World Politics*, Lexington, Mass.: Lexington Books, 1989.
7 M. Foucault, *Power/Knowledge. Selected Interviews and Other Writings*, New York: Pantheon Books, 1980, p. 164.
8 For a useful review of conceptual history and its relation in particular to political theory, see M. Richter 'Conceptual History (*Begriffsgeschichte*) and Political Theory', *Political Theory*, vol. 14, no. 4, 1986; Richter 'Reconstructing the History of Political Languages: Pocock, Skinner, and the *Geschichtliche Grundbegriffe*', *History And Theory. Studies In The Philosophy Of History*, vol. xxix, no. 1, 1990; and R. Koselleck 'Begriffsgeschichte and Social History', *Economy And Society*, vol. 11, no. 4, 1982. For an example of the general approach, see T. Ball, J. Farr and R. L. Hanson, eds, *Political Innovation and Conceptual Change*, Cambridge: Cambridge University Press, 1989.
9 For two reflective studies see M. Pearton, *The Knowledgable State. Diplomacy, War and Technology since 1830*, London: Burnett Books, 1982; and C. Dandeker, *Surveillance, Power and Modernity. Bureaucracy and Discipline from 1700 to the Present Day*, Cambridge: Polity Press, 1990.
10 Nietzsche, *The Gay Science*, trans. W. Kaufmann, New York: Vintage Books, 1974,

#355. This is a recurring issue in Nietzsche. See in addition, for example, *Twilight of the Idols and the Anti-Christ*, Harmondsworth: Penguin Books, 1990, where he reiterates the point at length on p. 61.

11 E. Levinas 'Philosophy and Awakening', in E. Cadava, P. Connor and Jean-Luc Nancy, eds, *Who Comes After the Subject*, London: Routledge, 1991, p. 215.

12 See L. P. Thiele 'The Agony of Politics: The Nietzschean Roots of Foucault's Thought', *American Political Science Review*, vol. 83, no. 3, 1990; and the reply by J. S. Johnson 'Reading Nietzsche and Foucault: A Hermeneutics of Suspicion', *American Political Science Review*, vol. 85, no. 2, 1991.

13 The inspiration for posing the question this way comes from the opening sentence – 'Do we *truly* need a *true* sex?' – which Foucault uses to introduce the remarkable *Herculine Barbin. Being the Recently Discovered Memoirs of a Nineteenth Century French Hermaphrodite*, New York: Pantheon Books, 1980.

14 M. Heidegger, *Nietzsche. Volume I: The Will to Power as Art*, San Francisco: Harper Collins, 1979, p. 26.

15 Foucault's final interview in the spring of 1984 confirmed the dual importance of Nietzsche and Heidegger in his thinking. 'Nietzsche and Heidegger', he said 'that was a philosophical shock'. M. Foucault 'Final Interview', *Raritan*, vol. 5, no. 1, 1985, pp. 8–9.

16 M. Foucault 'Truth and Power', in P. Rabinow, ed., *The Foucault Reader*, Harmondsworth: Penguin Books, 1984, p. 74.

17 'Such half wayness', Heidegger writes in his rigorous way, 'only secures the technological world all the more in its metaphysical predominance'. While he goes on insistently, and I think correctly, to ask 'But what authority has decided that nature as such must forever *remain* the nature of modern physics, and that history must forever appear only as subject matter for historians?' he leaves us struggling with the more proximate questions of what to do which Foucault at least addressed and explored through his attacks upon specific regimes of truth. See M. Heidegger 'The Principle of Identity', *Identity and Difference*, trans. J. Stambaugh, New York: Harper and Row, 1969, p. 40.

18 Heidegger wrote of this new and global predicament: 'No prophetic gestures are needed in order to realise that such a global dwelling is going to face encounters for which the partners on neither side [of Eastern and Western traditions of thinking] are at all prepared'. Quoted in F. Dallmayr, *The Other Heidegger*, Ithaca: Cornell University Press, 1993, p. 73.

19 A point cogently made by J. Caputo in his *Radical Hermeneutics. Repetition, Deconstruction and the Hermeneutic Project*, Bloomington: Indiana University Press, 1987. For a critical account of the implications of Heidegger's questioning of Being for the question of the political see R. Wolin, *The Politics of Being. The Political Thought of Martin Heidegger*, New York: Columbia University Press, 1990.

20 The relationship between the two is a fundamental theme in Hannah Arendt's work. For an exploration of this point see for example M. Canovan 'Socrates or Heidegger? Hannah Arendt's Reflections on Philosophy and Politics', *Social Research*, vol. 57, no. 1, Spring, 1990.

21 I use the bracketed term (inter)national in order to emphasise the radical interdependency, and mutually constitutive relationship, that obtains in contemporary politics between so-called domestic and foreign affairs. R. B. J. Walker, *Inside Outside: International Relations as Political Theory*, Cambridge: Cambridge University Press, 1993; and D. Campbell, *Writing Security*, Manchester: Manchester University Press, 1992, both take-up and develop this point. The idea of 'nation' is equally problematic, of course.

22 My adaptation to politics of Heidegger's point about philosophy. See M. Heidegger

'The End of Philosophy and the Task of Thinking', trans. J. Stambaugh, *On Time and Being*, New York: Harper and Row, 1972, p. 57.

23 Heidegger 'Letter on Humanism' in D. F. Krell, ed., *Martin Heidegger. Basic Writings*, San Francisco: Harper, 1977. Others have noted just how much the early humanist thought of the Renaissance, of Vico for example, is more consonant with Heidegger's own thinking than either Heidegger or his critics have sometimes allowed. See E. Grassi, *Heidegger and the Question of Renaissance Humanism: Four Studies*, Binghampton: State University of New York, Medieval and Renaissance Texts and Studies, January 1983.

24 I introduce this point, first, noting Nietzsche's observations on 'What preserves the species', in *The Gay Science*, p. 79; and, second, noting also Heidegger's argument about the destinal sending of Being while reserving my position for the moment in respect of both.

25 I formulate this point by adapting R. Schurmann's argument in *Heidegger. On Being and Acting: From Principles to Anarchy*, Bloomington: Indiana University Press, 1990, pp. 25–6.

26 A point Foucault increasingly began to explore in his work. See for example H. Dreyfus and P. Rabinow, *Michel Foucault, Beyond Structuralism and Hermeneutics*, Brighton: Harvester Press, 1982; G. Burchell, C. Gordon and P. Miller, *The Foucault Effect. Studies in Governmentality*, Brighton: Harvester Wheatsheaf, 1991.

27 These themes are pursued in D. Campbell and M. Dillon, eds, *The Political Subject of Violence*, Manchester: Manchester University Press, 1993.

28 The phrase comes from T. B. Strong, *Friedrich Nietzsche and The Politics of Transfiguration*, Berkeley: University of California Press, 1988, p. 25.

29 The 'end of philosophy' or 'end of metaphysics' referred to here is used in the sense which occurs throughout Heidegger's work, and subsequently discussed by Derrida. See for example M. Heidegger, *The End of Philosophy*, trans. J. Stambaugh, New York: Harper and Row, 1973. The finitude of metaphysics is not, however, its death, as Derrida has been at pains to point out; recently countering any suggestion of an 'apocalyptic tone'. See his 'On a Newly Arisen Apocalyptic Tone in Philosophy', especially the version reprinted in P. Fenves, *Raising The Tone Of Philosophy*, Baltimore: The Johns Hopkins University Press, 1993. See also R. Bernasconi, *The Question of Language in Heidegger's History of Being*, Atlantic Highlands, New Jersey: Humanities Press, 1985. An excellent review of the end of philosophy thesis, modified by Derridean and Levinasian readings, is provided by S. Critchley in *The Ethics of Deconstruction*, Oxford: Basil Blackwell, 1992. My view amounts to endorsing Critchley's interpretation and what D. Cornell calls the philosophy of the limit in her book, *The Philosophy of the Limit*, London: Routledge, 1992. See also D. Wood, *Philosophy at the Limit*, London: Unwin Hyman, 1990, for an excellent summary introduction to these issues.

30 Heidegger, *Parmenides*, Bloomington: Indiana University Press, 1990, p. 82.

31 W. E. Connolly, *The Augustinian Imperative. A Reflection on the Politics of Morals*, London: Sage, 1993, p. 153.

32 D. J. Schmidt 'Changing the Subject: Heidegger, "the" National and Epochal', in *Heidegger and the Political. The Graduate Faculty Philosophy Journal*, vol. 14, no. 2 – vol. 15, no. 1, 1991, p. 442.

33 Campbell and Dillon, eds, *The Political Subject of Violence*. Richard Kearney has written two rich and thought-provoking studies of imagination: *The Wake of Imagination*, London: Hutchinson, 1988; and *Poetics of Imagining from Husserl to Lyotard*, London: HarperCollins, 1991.

34 The defining cultural moment was not Hiroshima but World War One. A point newly explored recently by M. Eksteins, *Rites of Spring. The Great War and the Birth of the Modern Age*, London: Bantam Press, 1989.

35 The dual exhaustion of philosophy and politics is something which exercised all of Hannah Arendt's thought. For an elucidation of this point, see J. Kohn, 'Thinking/ Acting', *Social Research*, vol. 57. no. 1, Spring, 1990.

36 A classic contemporary example is B. Buzan, *People, States and Fear*, 2nd edn, Hemel Hempstead: Harvester Wheatsheaf, 1991.

37 For a detailed illustration see my *The Falklands, Politics and War*, London: Macmillan, 1989.

38 For a discussion and summary of crisis management see *The Falklands, Politics and War*.

39 Quoted in J. Marshall, *Swords and Symbols. The Techniques of Sovereignty*, London: Oxford University Press, 1939.

40 Arendt 'What is Freedom', p. 148.

41 *Ibid.*, p. 151; a 'form' because Heidegger might well accuse Arendt of that same anthropocentrism which he believed characterised all Western thought.

42 C. Lefort, *Democracy and Political Theory*. Cambridge: Polity Press, 1988, p. 4.

43 Arendt 'Truth and Politics', *Between Past and Future*, p. 228. 'Security remained the decisive criterion, but not the individual's security against "violent death", as in Hobbes (where the condition of all liberty is fear) [though he is concerned to inculcate that fear in order to maintain the discipline required for the State], but a security which should permit an undisturbed development of the life process of society as a whole'. Arendt 'What is Freedom?' p. 150.

44 One author who devoted an entire career to thinking the difference between the two and to mapping the operation of liminality was V. Turner. See the following four examples: *The Anthropology of Performance*, New York: PAJ Publications (A Division of The Performing Arts Journal, Inc.), 1987; *From Ritual to Theater: The Human Seriousness of Play*, New York: The Performing Arts Journal, 1982; *Dramas, Fields and Metaphors. Symbolic Action In Human Society*, Ithaca: Cornell University Press, 1974; and *The Ritual Process. Structure and Anti-structure*, London: Routledge and Kegan Paul, 1969.

45 M. A. Gillespie, *Hegel, Heidegger and the Ground of History*, Chicago: Chicago University Press, 1984; D. F. Krell, *Intimations Of Mortality. Time, Truth, and Finitude in Heidegger's Thinking of Being*, University Park, Pennsylvania: The Pennsylvania State University Press, 1986; and D. J. Schmidt, *The Ubiquity of The Finite. Hegel, Heidegger and the Entitlements of Philosophy*, Cambridge, Mass.: The MIT Press, 1988.

46 M. Canovan, *Hannah Arendt. A Reinterpretation of her Political Thought*, Cambridge: Cambridge University Press, 1992, p. 214.

47 Which is not to say that Heidegger was the only influence on her thought, nor that the essence of her thinking was entirely consonant with that of his; especially in respect, for example, of her central emphasis on human action and his fundamental hostility to the anthropocentrism of Western thought. There are, of course, many secondary studies and commentaries on all aspects of Arendt's thought. See in addition to Canovan's study, M. P. D'Entreves, *The Political Philosophy of Hannah Arendt*, London: Routledge, 1994.

48 H. Arendt, *The Life Of The Mind. Volume 1. Thinking*, London: Secker and Warburg, 1978, p. 176.

49 Quoted in J. Stambaugh, *Thoughts On Heidegger*, Boston: University Press of America, 1991, pp. 139–40.

50 *Ibid.*, p. 177.

51 More generally, see the essays on this theme in Dallery and Scott, with P. Holley Roberts, eds, *Ethics and Danger, Essays On Heidegger and Continental Thought*, Albany: SUNY, 1992.

52 D. Schmidt 'Changing The Subject: Heidegger, "the" National and Epochal', p. 443.

53 M. Heidegger, *Parmenides*, pp. 52–3.

54   Peg Birmingham seems to me to be one of the very few to understand what this moment
     of political fallibility for Heidegger was, and was for Heidegger. See her essay 'The
     Time of the Political', *The Graduate Faculty Philosophy Journal, Heidegger and the
     Political*, vol. 14, no. 2 – vol.15, no. 1, 1991. She has also addressed the more general
     question of whether Heidegger's work allows for a practical philosophy in 'Ever
     Respectfully Mine: Heidegger on Agency and Responsibility', in Dallery and Scott,
     with P. Holley Roberts, eds, *Ethics and Danger, Essays On Heidegger and Continental
     Thought*. There she specifically pursues the thought that Heidegger is challenging the
     two basic tenets of modern liberal political theory: the inviolability of the subject; and
     the right to self-preservation.
55   See J. Sallis, *Delimitations. Phenomenology and the End of Metaphysics*, Bloomington:
     Indiana University Press, 1986, ch. 7 on the question of the influences in Heidegger's
     thinking.
56   Nietzsche, *The Gay Science*, p. 121. The renewal of ontology in contemporary
     philosophy has nothing in common, of course, with 'realism'. Quite the contrary. In
     Heidegger it specifically gives rise to a profound critique of realism's impoverished
     understanding of the real. See especially M. Heidegger, *The End Of Philosophy*, trans.
     J. Stambaugh, London: Souvenir Press, 1975; and also M. Heidegger 'The Problem of
     Reality in Modern Philosophy', *Journal of the British Society for Phenomenology*, vol.
     4, no. 1, January 1973.
57   See a stimulating set of essays on just this theme in W. E. Connolly's *Identity/
     Difference*, Ithaca: Cornell University Press, 1991.
58   'What counts is the idea of the overflowing of objectifying thought by a forgotten
     experience from which it lives.' E. Levinas, *Totality and Infinity*, trans. A. Lingis,
     Dordrecht: Kluwer Academic Publishers, 1991, p. 28. 'Isn't the liveliness of life', he
     asks in another place, 'excessiveness, a rupture of the containing by the uncontainable,
     a form that ceases to be its proper content already offering itself in the guise of
     experience'. Levinas, in Cadava *et al.* eds, *op. cit.*, p. 210.
59   I mean hermeneutics in the sense of the radical hermeneutics which Caputo describes.
     See Caputo, *Radical Hermeneutics*.
60   Here I am adapting Connolly's general account of the investigative purpose of
     genealogical inquiry from *The Augustinian Imperative*, p. 138.
61   *The Augustinian Imperative*, p. 138.
62   Nietzsche, *The Gay Science*, p. 109.

2   RADICAL HERMENEUTICAL PHENOMENOLOGY

1   H. Morgenthau 'Death in the Nuclear Age', in J. Riemer, ed., *Jewish Reflections On
    Death*, New York: Schocken Books, 1974, p. 46.
2   A point made by Pierre Bourdieu, for example, in *The Political Ontology of Martin
    Heidegger*, Stanford: Stanford University Press, 1991.
3   For an important and recent discussion of this wider point in relation not only to
    Heidegger but also to the connection between Philosophy and Politics in Nazi Germany
    as a whole, see H. Sluga, *Heidegger's Crisis. Philosophy and Politics in Nazi Germany*,
    Cambridge, Mass.: Harvard University Press, 1993.
4   For a rare philosophical discussion of this issue see G. Fried 'Heidegger's *Polemos*',
    Journal of Philosophical Research', vol. xvi, 1990–91, pp. 159–95.
5   M. Haar 'The Question of Human Freedom in the Later Heidegger', *The Southern
    Journal of Philosophy, Spindel Conference 1989. Heidegger and Praxis*, T. J. Nenon,
    ed., vol. XXVIII Supplement; and Haar, *Heidegger and the Essence of Man*, trans. W.
    Mcneill, Albany: SUNY Press, 1993.
6   Jean-Luc Nancy, *The Experience of Freedom*, Stanford, California: Stanford University

Press, 1993. See also Nancy, *The Inoperative Community*, Minneapolis: University of Minnesota Press, 1991; and Nancy, *The Birth to Presence*, Stanford, California: Stanford University Press, 1993.

7 Simon Critchley has begun to explore this thought under the term 'democracy to come', in *The Ethics of Deconstruction, Derrida and Levinas*; and in 'Derrida's Specters of Marx', *Philosophy and Social Criticism*, vol. 21, no. 3, 1995.

8 Heidegger, describing what he calls the Greek way of thinking limits, in M. Heidegger, *Parmenides*, p. 82. Limit thought liminally is, however, what deconstructs the end so that this is not a philosophy of the end in an apocalyptic tone, to note Derrida's point, but of the end of ends; a philosophy not simply of gathering but of the persistent and essential creativity of the double move of both gathering and dispersal. See especially the reading of *Oedipus Rex* below. Derrida's corrective to the apocalyptic tone he claims to detect in accounts of the end of philosophy thesis in general, and that of Heidegger's in particular, is to be found in 'Of an Apocalyptic Tone Recently Adopted in Philosophy', trans. J. P. Leavey, *Oxford Literary Review*, vol. 6, no. 2, 1984, pp. 88–97.

9 For a discussion of this point in respect of Marx and Nietzsche, see H. Caygill 'The Return of Nietzsche and Marx' in Paul Patton, ed., *Nietzsche, Feminism and Political Theory*, London: Routledge, 1993, pp. 189–203.

10 See for example M. Heidegger, *The End of Philosophy*; and M. Heidegger 'The End of Philosophy and the Task of Thinking', in M. Heidegger, *On Time and Being*, New York: Harper Torch Books, 1972.

11 M. Heidegger, *Basic Questions of Philosophy. Selected 'Problems' of 'Logic'*, Bloomington: Indiana University Press, 1994, pp. 115–16.

12 *Ibid.*, p. 116.

13 *Ibid.*

14 H. Rapaport, *Heidegger and Derrida. Reflections on Time and Language*, Lincoln: University of Nebraska Press, p. 34.

15 Heidegger, *Basic Questions of Philosophy*, p. 32.

16 *Ibid.*, p. 35.

17 *Ibid.*

18 Heidegger broaches the question of the essence of the political in *An Introduction to Metaphysics*, New Haven: Yale University Press, 1987; and in *Parmenides*.

19 M. Haar, *Heidegger and the Essence of Man*, p. 151. See M. Heidegger, *Nietzsche, Volumes I–IV*, San Francisco: HarperCollins, 1991. See especially *Volume II: The Eternal Recurrence of the Same*, where Heidegger asserts that the end of metaphysics requires a return to the question of the essence of tragedy. I agree with Thomas Davis, specifically to 'the going-under of the tragic hero', as *Gelassenheit*. See Davis 'The Deinon of Yielding', in A. B. Dallery and C. E. Scott with P. Holley Roberts, eds, *Crises in Continental Philosophy*, Albany: SUNY Press, 1990, p. 165.

20 Gerald Bruns, however, argues that there is, instead, a darkly comic sensibility at work in Heidegger. That whereas tragedy is knowing too late the limits of knowing – see below, precisely, my reading of *Oedipus Rex* – comedy is risking not knowing, to leave things open and see where the play might take us. Heidegger is on the side of that risk says Bruns. See Bruns, *Heidegger's Estrangements. Language, Truth and Poetry in the Later Writings*, New Haven: Yale University Press, 1989. See also William Richardson, *Heidegger: Through Phenomenology to Thought*, The Hague: Martinus Nijhoff, 1963 for further support of this point.

21 See especially E. Husserl, *Cartesian Meditations*, trans. D. Cairns, The Hague: Martinus Nijhoff, 1960.

22 As Bernasconi, for example, notes so clearly, it is this which distinguishes his hermeneutics from Gadamer's: 'the truth lay not in what was said explicitly in the text as something directly accessible to antiquarian scholarship, but in the unsaid which

emerges only in a questioning dialogue with it'. See Bernasconi, *The Question of Language in Heidegger's History of Being*, p. 4.

23 See H. Dreyfus and P. Rabinow, *Michel Foucault. Beyond Structuralism and Hermeneutics*. Such hermeneutics would have to be distinguished from what Caputo, for example, calls radical hermeneutics in *Radical Hermeneutics. Repetition, Deconstruction and the Hermeneutic Project*.

24 Heidegger, *Being and Time*, trans. J. Macquarrie and E. Robinson, Oxford: Blackwell, 1988, p. 58.

25 *Ibid.*, p. 59.

26 *Ibid.*

27 *Ibid.*

28 J. Derrida, *Specters of Marx*, trans. P. Kamuf, London: Routledge, 1994. See also S. Critchley's discussion in 'Specters of Marx'.

29 M. Heidegger 'Phenomenological Interpretations with Respect to Aristotle (Indication of the Hermeneutical Situation)', trans. M. Baur, *Man and World*, vol. 25, 1992, pp. 355–93. The significance of this essay was first explored in English in T. Sheehan's 'Heidegger's Interpretation of Aristotle: *Dynamis* and *Ereignis*', *Philosophy Research Archives*, vol. 4, 1978. Aristotle's importance is also explored in the following: R. Bernasconi 'Heidegger's Destruction of *Phronesis*', *The Southern Journal of Philosophy, Spindel Conference 1989. Heidegger and Praxis*; R. A. Makkreel 'The Genesis of Heidegger's Phenomenological Hermeneutics and the Rediscovered "Aristotle Introduction" of 1992', *Man and World*, vol. 23, 1990, pp. 305–20; F. Volpi '*Being and Time*: A Translation of *The Nicomachean Ethics*?'; Kisiel and van Buren, eds, *Reading Heidegger From The Start*; and W. Brogan 'The Place Of Aristotle In Heidegger's Phenomenology', *ibid*. However, the most comprehensive account of the early influences on Heidegger's thought, including that of Aristotle, is to be found in T. Kisiel, *The Genesis of Heidegger's Being and Time*, Los Angeles: University of California Press, 1993.

30 J. Taminiaux, *Heidegger and the Project of Fundamental Ontology*, trans. M. Gendre, Albany: SUNY Press, 1991, p. 54.

31 Heidegger 'My Way To Phenomenology', *Time and Being*, p. 79.

32 For Derrida's own account of the word 'deconstruction' see 'Letter to a Japanese Friend', in D. Wood and R. Bernasconi, eds, *Derrida and Differance*, Evanston: North Western University Press, 1988. Bernasconi analyses Derrida's adoption of the Heideggerian term 'destruction' in 'Seeing Double: Destruktion and Deconstruction', in D. P. Michelfelder and R. E. Palmer, eds, *Dialogue and Deconstruction*, Albany: State University of New York Press, 1989, pp. 233–50.

33 M. Heidegger, *Nietzsche. Volume 3. The Will to Power as Knowledge and as Metaphysics*, quoted in Fried 'Heidegger's *Polemos*', pp. 167–68.

34 *Ibid.*, p. 167.

35 R. Bernasconi 'Repetition and Tradition: Heidegger's Destructuring of the Distinction Between Essence and Existence in *Basic Problems of Phenomenology*', in Kisiel and van Buren, eds, *Reading Heidegger From The Beginning. Essays in His Earliest Thoughts*, pp. 123–36.

36 Heidegger 'The Origin of the Work of Art', in *Poetry, Language and Thought*, p. 71.

37 H. Blumenberg's account in *The Legitimacy of the Modern Age*, Cambridge, Mass.: The MIT Press, 1983.

38 See M. Dillon, ed., *Tradition*. Special Edition of the *Journal of The British Society for Phenomenology*, October 1995, especially the essays by Dillon and Bernasconi.

39 See especially M. Heidegger, *The Principle of Reason*, trans. R. Lilly, Bloomington: Indiana University Press, 1991. The move comes particularly with the play Heidegger makes on the German word *erhören*. This may be translated as 'to hear', but the literal

translation does not cover all the work which Heidegger gets out of the word in these lectures.

40 See Dillon, ed., *Tradition*.
41 M. Heidegger 'The End of Philosophy and the Task of Thinking', in Heidegger, *On Time and Being*, New York: Harper, 1972, p. 69.
42 See especially the essays in *Poetry, Language and Thought*; also those in *On The Way To Language*. See also Heidegger, *Identity and Difference*. Gerald Bruns has a sensitive discussion of *Ereignis* in *Heidegger's Estrangements*, pp. 165–73. See also T. Sheehan 'Heidegger's Interpretation of Aristotle: *Dynamis* and *Ereignis*, in *Philosophy Research Archives*, vol. 4, 1978, pp. 278–301; and T. Prufer 'Glosses on Heidegger's Architectonic Word-Play: Lichtung and Ereignis, Bergung and Wahrns', *Review of Metaphysics*, vol. 44, 1990–91, pp. 607–12.
43 See for example Heidegger, *Time and Being*; and also *Parmenides*.
44 Caputo 'Demythologising Heidegger: *Aletheia* and the History of Being', *Review of Metaphysics*, vol. 41, March 1988, pp. 519–46. For another account of *aletheia* see David Farrell Krell 'On the Manifold Meaning of *Aletheia*: Brentano, Aristotle and Heidegger', *Research in Phenomenology*, vol. 5, 1975, pp. 77–94. The 'Justice' to which he refers and to which I also subscribe here and later is that 'Justice' which Derrida discusses and elaborates in his essay 'Force of Law: The Mystical Foundation of Authority', in D. Cornell, *et al.*, eds, *Deconstruction and the Possibility of Justice*, London: Routledge, 1992.
45 J. Grondin 'The Ethical and Young Hegelian Motives in Heidegger's Hermeneutics of Facticity', in Kisiel and van Buren, eds, *Reading Heidegger From The Beginning. Essays in His Earliest Thoughts*, p. 355.
46 Heidegger, *The Concept of Time*, trans. W. McNeil, Oxford: Blackwell, 1992, p. 9E.
47 M. Heidegger, *Logic: The Question of Truth*, Bloomington: Indiana University Presss, 1995.
48 Heidegger, *The Concept of Time*, p. 12E.
49 Heidegger, *The Essence of Reasons*, trans. T. Malick, Evanston: Northwestern University Press, 1969, p. 115.
50 Heidegger, *Nietzsche. Volume IV: Nihilism*, p. 141.
51 Already, around the time of the composition of *Being and Time*, Heidegger began to distance himself from his identification with the project of phenomenology.
52 H.-G. Gadamer 'Martin Heidegger's One Path', in Kisiel and van Buren, eds, *Reading Heidegger From The Beginning*, p. 20.
53 Heidegger, *The Essence of Reasons*, p. 89.
54 Caputo's attacks are deliberately polemical. Others, no less well-aimed and no less ethically charged, are delivered in a different tone. See for example R. Bernasconi 'Habermas and Arendt on the Philosopher's "Error": Tracking the Diabolical in Heidegger', *Graduate Faculty Philosophy Journal*, vols 14–15, 1991, pp. 3–25.
55 For an excellent extended account of this point see J. Hodge, *Heidegger and Ethics*, London: Routledge, 1995.
56 Of all contemporary writers Paul Virilio, Michael Shapiro and James Der Derian seem to me to capture these best. See for example P. Virilio, *Pure War*, New York: Semiotext(e); and *Popular Defence and Ecological Struggles*, New York: Semiotext(e), 1990. M. Shapiro, *The Politics of Representation. Writing Practices in Biography, Photography, and Policy Analysis*, Madison: Wisconsin University Press, 1988; and Shapiro, *Reading The Postmodern Polity. Political Theory as Textual Practice*, Minneapolis: Minnesota University Press, 1992. See also J. Der Derian, *Anti-Diplomacy. Spies, Terror, Speed and War*, Oxford: Basil Blackwell, 1992.
57 The phrase comes from Cornell, *The Philosophy of the Limit*.
58 M. Heidegger, *Kant and the Problem of Metaphysics*, Bloomington: Indiana University Press, 1990, p. 185.

59 Which refers to the essential character of a polity; the very 'constitution of the social space, of the *form* of society, of the essence of what was once termed "the city"'. Claude Lefort writes: 'The political is thus revealed, not in what we call political activity, but in the double movement whereby the mode of institution of society appears and is obscured'. C. Lefort, *Democracy and Political Theory*, p. 11.

60 Which refers to the practices of rule and of policy making, and of all the 'empirical' and calculative operations which go with them. See also Fred Dallmayr, *The Other Heidegger.* 'Whereas politics in the narrower sense revolves around day-to-day decision-making and ideological partisanship', writes Dallmayr, '"the political" refers to the frame of reference within which actions, events, and other phenomena acquire political status in the first place . . . Heidegger's promising contributions to political thought are located at the level of ontology or paradigmatic framework (the political) rather than of practical policy and ideology (which is the level of the Nazi involvement)'. p. 9. The distinction is discussed and disputed, at least in terms of the way in which it was presented by Jean-Luc Nancy and Philippe Lacoue-Labarthe in the early 1980s, and in ways that require much further discussion, by Simon Critchley. See his *The Ethics of Deconstruction*, pp. 201–19.

61 Though ordinarily a much more subtle thinker, this is what Samuel Ijsseling appears to do, for example, in 'Heidegger and Politics', in Dallery *et al.*, eds, *Ethics and Danger. Essays On Heidegger and Continental Thought.*

62 The foremost exponent, in modern political theory, of this understanding of politics has, of course, been Heidegger's student Hannah Arendt. See for example *The Human Condition*, Chicago: Chicago University Press, 1958. Arendt figures as a prominent influence below, especially Chapters 4 and 5.

63 M. Heidegger 'Phenomenological Interpretations with Respect to Aristotle (Indication of the Hermeneutical Situation)', trans. M. Bauer, *Man and World*, vol. 25, 1992, pp. 359–60.

64 J. Derrida, *Aporias*, Stanford: Stanford University Press, 1993, p. 16; a contrasting form of responsibility with that which derives from a command ethic. See also A. White, *Within Nietzsche's Labyrinth*, London: Routledge, 1990, which I also read as largely concerned with exploring this notion of freedom and the fear it evokes.

65 And therefore to say that Hannah Arendt, for example, is an exponent of such a 'radical' politics.

66 It would seem that this point should also extend to Emmanuel Levinas; for whom, also, the 'attributes of God are given not in the indicative [consider, later, the oracles for example], but in the imperative'. E. Levinas, *Difficult Freedom. Essays on Judaism*, p. 17. But whether or not I would thus extend it remains an outstanding issue not only for me but more importantly – because of Levinas' fundamental opposition to it – to the thought upon which I am drawing here. For Levinas, too, is opposed to the way modern philosophy fails to think human solidarity, in thinking 'that each exists for oneself and that everything is permitted,' *ibid.*, p. 20. See also *Otherwise than Being or Beyond Essence*, London: Kluwer Academic Publishers, 1991; *Collected Papers*, London: Kluwer Academic Publishers, 1993; and *Outside the Subject*, trans. M. B. Smith, Stanford: Stanford University Press, 1993. Levinas haunts what follows recalling the question of the political incessantly to the question of the ethical.

67 H. Arendt, *The Origins of Totalitarianism*, London: Andre Deutsch, 1986.

68 Rather than, say, confining the poetic to the ironic in the way that Richard Rorty does. See R. Rorty, *Irony, Contingency and Solidarity*, Cambridge: Cambridge University Press, 1989. In Rorty, the ironic then becomes the strategy by which the very radicalness of the philosophical destructuring of metaphysics which Heidegger initiated – and which, Rorty notes, also threatens the metaphysical foundations of Liberalism – can be contained. The curious thing about exploring the implications of Heidegger's thought is, however, that his membership of the Nazi party continuously undermines

any and every device by which you may be tempted to rest comfortably with the cruelties that might be integral to it. The thought itself has continuously to be rethought in response to the cruelty of the system to which Heidegger was once willing to commit himself. No refuge of moral smugness is available in the region of Heidegger's thought. An *Auseinandersetzung* with Heidegger is positively compelled by him, for his thought and his commitments are not glibly dissociable.

69   I am elaborating a point T. Kisiel makes. See his 'The Language of the Event: The Event of Language', in J. Sallis, ed., *Heidegger and the Path of Thinking*, Pittsburgh: Duquesne University Press, 1970.

70   M. Heidegger 'A Letter on Humanism', trans. F. Capuzzi in D. F. Krell, ed., *Martin Heidegger: Basic Writings*, pp. 232–3.

71   Peter Euben discusses whether Plato, too, might be thought to be engaged in a kind of tragedy, and so problematises the simplistic notion that he was crudely anti-poetic. See his 'Introduction' to P. Euben, ed., *Greek Tragedy and Political Theory*, London: University of California Press, 1986.

72   Heidegger 'The Origin of the Work of Art', *Poetry, Language and Thought*, p. 63.

73   G. Bruns 'On The Tragedy Of Hermeneutical Experience', *Research in Phenomenology*, vol. 18, 1988, pp. 191–201.

74   Gasche claims that this is what deconstruction aims to do as well: R. Gasche, *Inventions of Difference*, Cambridge, Mass.: Harvard University Press, 1994.

75   *Ibid.*, p. 193.

76   On Antigone, see C. Douzanis and R. Warrington, *Justice Miscarried: Ethics, Aesthetics and the Law*, London: Harvester Wheatsheaf, 1994.

77   Heidegger, *The Concept of Time*, p. 11E.

78   Heidegger, *The Concept of Time*, p. 10E.

79   Heidegger, quoted in Haar, *Heidegger and the Essence of Man*, p. 8.

80   *Ersatz*, because it was the product of manipulatory representation and objectification designed explicitly for political consumption: 'What is constant in things produced as objects merely for consumption is: the substitute – *Ersatz*', Heidegger 'What are Poets for?' in M. Heidegger, *Poetry, Language and Thought*, trans. A. Hofstadter, New York: Harper and Row, 1971, p. 130.

81   Here, while I admire his inspiring thinking, at one time with and now increasingly passionately against Heidegger, I would also recover resoluteness from John Caputo's suspicion of it. Amongst other work, see the following: '*Sorge* and *Kardia*: The Hermeneutics of Factical Life and the Categories of the Heart', in T. Kisiel and J. van Buren, eds, *Reading Heidegger From The Beginning. Essays in His Earliest Thoughts*; 'Heidegger's Kampf: The Difficulty of Life', *Graduate Faculty Philosophy Journal*, vols 14–15, 1990–91, pp. 61–83; *Against Ethics: Contributions to a Poetics of Obligation with Constant Reference to Deconstruction*, Bloomington: Indiana University Press, 1993; and *Demythologising Heidegger*, Bloomington: Indiana University Press, 1993.

82   Heidegger, *On Time and Being*, p. 25.

83   Heidegger, *The Essence of Reasons*, p. 105.

84   Caputo, *Demythologising Heidegger*, p. 167.

85   An issue acutely observed and discussed by Michael Shapiro in his essay 'The Ethics of Encounter: Unreading/Unmapping the Imperium', ISA, Chicago, February 1995.

86   One could argue this point from the modern Hobbesian understanding of the state to its foremost twentieth-century exponent Carl Schmitt. See for example Schmitt, *The Concept of the Political*, New Brunswick, New Jersey: Rutgers University Press, 1976.

87   See *The Basic Questions of Philosophy*, Chapter 5.

88   M. Heidegger, *The Concept of Time*, especially p 13E.

89   See F. Dastur 'Three Questions to Jacques Derrida', in A. B. Dallery and C. E. Scott, with P. Holley Roberts, eds, *Ethics and Danger. Essays On Heidegger and Continental Thought*, p. 31.

90 Joseph Conrad, *Heart of Darkness. A Case Study in Contemporary Criticism*, R. C. Murfin, ed., New York: St. Martin's Press, 1989, p. 64.

91 *The Order of Things*, London: Tavistock/Routledge, 1989, p. 332.

92 *The Order of Things*, p. 332.

93 Heidegger, *The Basic Questions of Philosophy*, p. 132.

94 Haar, *Heidegger And The Essence Of Man*, p. 43.

95 Heidegger, *Being and Time*, p. 330.

96 Heidegger, *The Essence of Reasons*, pp. 119–31.

97 *Ibid.*, p. 331.

98 Heidegger, *The Basic Questions of Philosophy*, p. 133.

99 This move recurs throughout Heidegger's thought but it is especially evident in the lectures on Parmenides. See Heidegger, *Parmenides*.

100 Especially in M. Heidegger, *Nietzsche. Volume I: The Will To Power As Art*; and M. Heidegger 'The Origin of the Work of Art', in *Poetry, Language and Thought*. Robert Bernasconi complains that the 'secret kinship' between thinking and poetry is something which Heidegger proclaimed rather than explored. See Bernasconi, *The Question of Language in Heidegger's History of Being*, p. 30. My suggestion is that kinship is there to be explored in tragedy.

101 G. Bruns, *Heidegger's Estrangements*.

102 Heidegger, *The Basic Questions of Philosophy*, p. 133.

103 M. Haar discusses this point in his exemplary and challenging interpretation of Heidegger. See *Heidegger and the Essence of Man*; especially Chapter 5, in the section entitled 'The Limit of the Requisitioning of Man: The Absence of Distress', pp. 132–7.

104 Bruns, *Heidegger's Estrangements*, p. 168. Foucault knew this better than almost any other contemporary thinker. His testament to it was the simple, yet explosive, *Herculine Barbin. Being The Recently Discovered Memoirs of a Nineteenth-Century French Hermaphrodite*. Connolly provides a rich and thought-provoking reading of this text to reflect upon the question of evil, in 'Voices from the Whirlwind', from his *The Augustinian Imperative*.

105 M. Heidegger 'On the Way to Language', in *On the Way to Language*, pp. 123–4.

106 See for example Heidegger, *The Concept of Time*, especially pp. 11E–22E.

107 The movement essential to temporality is brought out most forcefully by Heidegger in his discussion of 'The Anaximander Fragment', in M. Heidegger, *Early Greek Thinking*, trans. D. F. Krell, New York: Harper and Row, 1984.

108 Heidegger, *The Concept of Time*, p. 14E.

109 Heidegger, *The Concept of Time*, p. 20E.

110 See how Derrida plays on the ear in J. Derrida, *The Ear of the Other. Otobiography, Transference, Translation*, Lincoln: University of Nebraska Press, 1988.

111 For Heidegger's account of the 'real', see his essay: 'The Problem of Reality in Modern Philosophy', *Journal of the British Society for Phenomenology*, vol. 4, no. 1, January 1971, pp. 64–71. See also *The Essence of Reasons*, p. 27, note 14.

112 This is the theme of Campbell/Dillon, eds, *The Political Subject of Violence*.

113 On this point see especially Dallmayr, *The Other Heidegger*; and Fynsk, *Heidegger. Thought And Historicity*, Ithaca: Cornell University Press, 1993.

114 Quoted in R. J. S. Manning, *Interpreting Otherwise than Heidegger. Emmanuel Levinas' Ethics as First Philosophy*, Pittsburgh: Dusquesne University Press, 1993, p. 215n. This does not mean, as Levinas seems to imply, that the question of responsibility and of obligation is absent from Heidegger's thought.

115 Heidegger, *Nietzsche. Volumes I–IV*.

116 Though I have Peg Birmingham to thank for the initial idea. See what she has to say about 'critical mimesis' in Birmingham 'The Time of the Political', *Graduate Faculty Philosophy Journal. Heidegger and the Political*.

117 E. Levinas 'De L'Evasion', *Recherches Philosophiques*, 5, 1935–36, p. 391.

118 Bernasconi, *The Question of Language in Heidegger's History of Being*, p. 94.
    Bernasconi was wise enough also to note how telling silence can be.
119 G. Bruns, *Heidegger's Estrangements*, pp. 12–13.
120 See for example T. Eagleton, *Literary Theory: An Introduction*, Minneapolis:
    Minnesota University Press, 1983.
121 F. Dallmayr, *Politics and Praxis: Exercises in Contemporary Political Theory*,
    Cambridge, Mass.: MIT Press, 1984, p. 104.
122 Which is not to say that the Holocaust was not distinctive. It was. I think of it as being
    distinctive in the way that Zygmunt Bauman, for example, thinks of it as distinctive.
    See Bauman, *Modernity and the Holocaust*, Cambridge: Polity Press, 1989.
123 Caputo has the keenest eye for danger in Heidegger and offers a trenchant account of
    it. See especially his essay 'Spirit and Danger', in Dallery, *et al.*, eds, *Ethics and
    Danger*.
124 I owe this beautiful phrase to Adorno *via* Dennis Schmidt. See D. Schmidt 'Economies
    of Production', in A. B. Dallery and C. E. Scott with P. Holley Roberts, eds, *Crises
    in Continental Philosophy*, p. 154.
125 See for example Heidegger's discussion of *aletheia* in *Parmenides*, p. 26.
126 Heidegger, *The Basic Questions of Philosophy*, p. 136.
127 Descartes' Meditations are not only a determined and sustained search for security,
    which he calls certainty, they also disclose the extraordinary lengths to which he was
    willing to go, in working on his own being, to secure it. See R. Descartes, *Discourse
    on Method and The Meditations*, Harmondsworth: Penguin Books, 1968.

3 THE *TOPOS* OF ENCOUNTER

 1 R. Schurmann 'Ultimate Double Binds', *Graduate Faculty Philosophy Journal.
    Heidegger and the Political*, vol. 14, no. 2–vol. 15, no. 1, 1991, pp. 213–36.
 2 I think, above all, that this is what is going on in Heidegger 'The Anaximander
    Fragment', *Early Greek Thinking. The Dawn of Western Philosophy*. In respect of
    'overdose', see how I derive this thought from *dosis*, the Greek word for tradition, in
    Dillon '*Dosis*', Dillon, ed., *Tradition*. Special Edition of the *Journal of the British
    Society for Phenomenology*.
 3 'The Anaximander Fragment', p. 44.
 4 For an account of where and how Levinas indebted to Heidegger also differs from
    him, see for example R. J. S. Manning, *Interpreting Otherwise than Heidegger*,
    Pittsburgh: Dusquesne University Press, 1993.
 5 See the reflections in J. Derrida 'Force of Law: The Mystical Foundation of Authority'.
 6 Schurmann 'Ultimate Double Binds', p. 214.
 7 Levinas, *Existence and Existents*, trans. A. Lingis, Dordrecht: Kluwer, 1988, pp. 21–2.
 8 Levinas, *Existence and Existents*, p. 20.
 9 Levinas, *Existence and Existents*, p. 67.
10 Levinas, *Existence and Existents*, p. 29.
11 Levinas, *Existence and Existents*, p. 78.
12 Levinas, *Existence and Existents*, p. 78.
13 Levinas, *Existence and Existents*, p. 79.
14 Schurmann 'Ultimate Double Binds', p. 232.
15 Heidegger, quoted in V. Foti, *Heidegger and the Poets. Poiesis/Sophia/Techne*,
    Atlantic Highlands, New Jersey: Humanities Press, 1992, p. xv.
16 Heidegger, quoted in Schurmann 'Ultimate Double Binds', p. 222.
17 Here, in his approach to translation in general and in the translation of the
    Anaximander Fragment in particular, Heidegger practises this form of giving things
    their due by granting them more than it appears that they actually require. Translation,

for Heidegger, is trans-porting ourselves into the world opened-up by the fragment. Granting it more than its due is granting, first, that – despite its very age, strangeness and fragmentedness – there is possibly something to be heard here and, second, that more is possibly available in the fragment than a mere literal translation, or a reading through the optic of the tradition which draws it into a region dominated by the spheres of questioning of subsequent metaphysics, would allow. To give it a hearing grants it more than its due. To attend to its possibilities beyond the confinement of a traditional reading is consonant with the same just response. Without this generosity we are likely to grant the fragment very little if anything at all. Being true to the fragment is entering into the possibilities it helps to disclose as a threshold, rather than secure repository, of meaning. Heidegger 'The Anaximander Fragment.'

18   Heidegger 'Moira (Parmenides VIII, 34–41)', *Early Greek Thinking*, p. 87.
19   Heidegger, *Parmenides*, p. 138.
20   Heidegger, *Basic Questions of Philosophy*.
21   'That is to say, a "being in itself", does not make thinking mandatory, nor does "Being for itself", necessitate thought. Neither, taken separately, will ever let it be known to what extent Being calls for thinking. But because of their duality ... thinking comes to presence.' Heidegger 'Moira', p. 89.
22   Heidegger, *Parmenides*, p. 149.
23   Heidegger, *Parmenides*, p. 149.
24   See how B. Honig argues this point in *Political Theory and the Displacement of Politics*, Ithaca: Cornell University Press, 1993.
25   For a more extensive treatment, see Heidegger 'The Origin of the Work of Art', *Poetry, Language, Thought*; and for a condensed account see Heidegger, *Parmenides*, p. 115.
26   Heidegger, *An Introduction To Metaphysics*, pp. 191–2.
27   I am adapting and extending here what C. Lefort says about what happens to the place of power as a consequence of the democratic revolutions of the modern age, *Democracy and Political Theory*. For a discussion of this point, and more generally for an outstanding collection of essays on the implications for political philosophy of what I have been calling the philosophy of the limit, see B. Flynn, *Political Philosophy At The Closure Of Metaphysics*, London: Humanities Press, 1992. See also P. Brook, *The Empty Space*, Harmondsworth: Pelican Books, 1984; and A. Artaud, *The Theatre and its Doubles*, London: Calder, 1989.
28   W. Benjamin, *The Origins of German Tragic Drama*, trans. J. Osborne, London: Verso Books, 1992.
29   Heidegger, *An Introduction To Metaphysics*, p. 205.
30   Levinas, *Existence and Existents*, p. 17.
31   Heidegger, *Parmenides*, p. 150.
32   See Heidegger 'The Question Concerning Technology', and 'The Turning', in *The Question Concerning Technology and Other Essays*, trans. W. Lovitt, New York: Harper, 1977.
33   See for example Heidegger 'What Are Poets For?' in *Poetry, Language, Thinking*; and *What Is Called Thinking*, trans. J. Glenn Gray, New York: Harper and Row, 1968.
34   P. Birmingham 'Logos and the Place of the Other', p. 34.
35   Heidegger, *Parmenides*, pp. 51–2.
36   Heidegger 'The Anaximander Fragment', p. 25.
37   Heidegger, *Parmenides*, p. 45.
38   Heidegger, *Parmenides*, p. 50.
39   Heidegger, *Parmenides*, p. 50.
40   Heidegger, *Parmenides*, p. 41.
41   Heidegger, *Parmenides*, p. 40.
42   Heidegger, *Parmenides*, pp. 44–5.

43 Heidegger, *Parmenides*, p. 45.
44 Heidegger, *Parmenides*, p. 42. In fact in these extremely dense passages there is a definite ambiguity or obscurity in the relation between *imperium* and truth. For, although Heidegger specifically says that the 'imperial . . . is nevertheless not the basis of the essential transformation of *aletheia* into *veritas* as *rectitudo*, but is its consequence', (p. 42), he also says, slightly later in the text, 'the essential domain of the *imperium* is decisive for *verum* and *falsum* and their opposites' (p. 48). I hesitate to try to sort this out, but given the priority he ordinarily attaches to truth I allow it the priority here.
45 See for example P. I. Kaufman, *Redeeming Politics*, Princeton, New Jersey: Princeton University Press, 1990.
46 Heidegger, *Parmenides*, p. 48.
47 Heidegger, *Parmenides*, p. 50.
48 Heidegger, *Parmenides*, pp. 51–2.
49 Heidegger, *Parmenides*, p. 53.
50 See A. H. Hinsley's classic account of the history of sovereignty, *Sovereignty*, Cambridge: Cambridge University Press, 1989; and his more elaborate *Power and the Pursuit of Peace*, Cambridge: Cambridge University Press, 1988. The story can be further traced in great detail in Q. Skinner, *The Foundations of Modern Political Thought. Volume One, The Renaissance. Volume Two, The Age of Reformation*, Cambridge: Cambridge University Press, 1988.
51 Heidegger, *Parmenides*, p. 60.
52 Heidegger, *Parmenides*, p. 57.
53 Heidegger, *Parmenides*, p. 57. Heidegger gives considerable attention to the different forms of untruth and of concealment, see especially pp. 61–5.
54 Heidegger, *Parmenides*, p. 57.
55 Heidegger 'The Origin of the Work of Art', *Poetry, Language, Thought*, pp. 17–81.
56 Heidegger, *Parmenides*, p. 18.
57 Heidegger, *Parmenides*, p. 26.
58 Heidegger, *Parmenides*, p. 26.
59 Heidegger, *Parmenides*, p. 17.
60 Heidegger, *Parmenides*, p. 17.
61 Heidegger, *Parmenides*, p. 90.
62 Heidegger, *Parmenides*, p. 90.
63 Schmitt, *The Concept of the Political*, p. 26.
64 Schmitt, *The Concept of the Political*, p. 27.
65 Schmitt, *The Concept of the Political*, p. 47.
66 Schmitt, *The Concept of the Political*, p. 27.
67 W. E. Connolly's exemplary reading of Hobbes inspired this point. Connolly, *Political Theory and Modernity*, Oxford: Basil Blackwell, 1988.
68 'The Greeks think and poeticise and "deal" *within* the essence of *aletheia* and *lethe*, but they do not think and poeticise *about* this essence and they do not deal with it.' Heidegger, *Parmenides*, p. 87.
69 Heidegger, *Parmenides*, p. 89.
70 See in particular how he criticises culture in *Parmenides*, p. 70.
71 Heidegger, *Parmenides*, p. 137.
72 M. Blanchot, *The Infinite Conversation*, Minneapolis: Minnesota University Press, 1993. See my discussion of this in Dillon 'Sovereignty and Governmentality', *Alternatives*, Fall, 1995.
73 See also note 85 below, and chapters 5 and 6.
74 See especially Heidegger, *Parmenides*, p. 117.
75 P. Birmingham 'Logos and the Place of the Other', *Research in Phenomenology*, vol. xx, 1990, p. 36.

76 Heidegger, *Parmenides*, pp. 67–8.
77 See also Heidegger, *On The Way To Language*.
78 I take this quotation from J. T. Hospital's novel, *The Last Magician*, London: Virago, 1992, with thanks to Bob Mckinlay for drawing it to my attention in a valiant effort to raise my artistic standards.
79 Heidegger, *Parmenides*, p. 69.
80 Heidegger, *Parmenides*, p. 68.
81 Heidegger, *Parmenides*, p. 68.
82 I confess that I steal the lovely phrase 'telling silence' from R. Bernasconi, *The Question of Language in Heidegger's History of Being*.
83 Caputo 'Demythologising Heidegger: *Aletheia* and the History of Being', p. 520.
84 For an extended discussion of space see Heidegger 'Building, Dwelling, Thinking', in *Poetry, Language, Thought*.
85 There is a major problem or clutch of problems here. For only the ancient Greeks, according to Heidegger, had the word in this sense (*Parmenides*, p. 68). Those who did not they called barbarians. This did not mean that barbarians did not have a language, nor did it simply mean that their tongue was foreign to the Greeks, he says, but that they did not 'dwell' in this disclosive power of the word. The question therefore arises as to how those with the word are to speak with and comport themselves towards those who do not or, rather, towards those whose way of being is differently constituted. The start point is an interrogatory disposition towards one's own constitution rather than an imperial disposition towards others because you can only speak, in the first instance, out of your own make-up. Remember, however, that that make-up is itself an interrogatory – radically hermeneutic phenomenological – one. This, in part, I take to be the point of Heidegger's 'A Dialogue on Language', in *On the Way to Language*.
86 Heidegger, *Parmenides*, p. 89.
87 Heidegger, *Parmenides*, pp. 89–90.
88 *Pace* Derrida, of course, whose struggle with Heidegger has concerned precisely the emphasis which Derrida puts on dissemination as against the emphasis which he accuses Heidegger, justifiably, of putting on gathering. See for example J. Derrida, *Writing and Difference*, London: Routledge and Kegan Paul, 1981; *Dissemination*, Chicago: Chicago University Press, 1981. Nonetheless, it is both; in Heidegger as well as in politics.
89 Heidegger, *Being and Time*, p. 205.
90 'This latter must not be understood as a sequence of written propositions and rules, although the word pertains so originally to the "constitution" that what is written down does not merely present a subsequent "formula" or "formulation".' Heidegger, *Parmenides*, p. 95.
91 Here is the source of Heidegger's own, albeit rethought and rarified, security project and discourse of danger – the oblivion of Being; the supreme danger of the destitution of technology; and the soteriological prospect of a new dispensation of Being – which he works out here in *Parmenides* as well as in his essays on Technology and on 'The Turning'.
92 See how M. Shapiro makes this argument in 'The Ethics of Encounter: Unreading/ Unmapping the Imperium', ISA, Chicago, February 1995, pp. 10–14.
93 See the interview 'Ethics and Politics', in S. Hand, ed., *The Levinas Reader*, Oxford: Basil Blackwell, 1989.
94 Birmingham 'Logos and the Place of the Other', p. 39.
95 Bearing in mind not only Derrida's reading, *Of Spirit*, but also what Heidegger himself says here: 'The concept of "spirit" and "culture" no matter how they are defined are representations belonging to modern thought'. *Parmenides*, p. 91.
96 Heidegger, *Parmenides*, p. 96.

97 Heidegger, *Parmenides*, pp. 105–6.
98 See how interest became allied to subjectivity in the evolution of the modern understanding of politics and economics in A. O. Hirschman, *The Passions and the Interests. The Political Argument for Capitalism before its Triumph*, Princeton: Princeton University Press, 1977.
99 Birmingham 'Logos and the Place of the Other', p. 39.
100 Heidegger, *Being and Time*, p. 344.
101 Birmingham 'Logos and the Place of the Other', p. 44.
102 For more extended, thought-provoking and differing accounts of this idea of 'community' see the following: M. Blanchot, *The Unavowable Community*, trans. P. Joris, Barrytown, New York: Station Hill Press, 1988; Nancy, *The Inoperative Community*; Miami Theory Co-op, eds, *Community at Loose Ends*, Minneapolis: Minnesota University Press, 1991; and A. Lingis, *The Community of Those who Have Nothing in Common*, Bloomington: Indiana University Press, 1994.
103 Heidegger, *Being and Time*.
104 MERIDIAN: '2 . . . the point at which the sun attains its highest altitude . . . b. The point or period of highest development or perfection, after which decline sets in, culmination, full splendour. 4. a . . . the great circle (of the celestial sphere) which passes through the celestial poles and the zenith of any place on the earth's surface. b . . . The great circle (of the earth), what lies in the plane of the celestial meridian of a place and which passes through that place and the poles; also often applied to that half of this circle that extends from pole to pole through the place. 5. A locality or situation considered as separate and distinct from others and as having its own particular character; the special character or circumstances by which one place, person, set of persons, etc., is distinguished from another'. *Oxford English Dictionary*.
105 Heidegger, *Parmenides*, p. 95.
106 No one challenges Heidegger more powerfully on this critical point, or in a more powerful way, I think, than V. Foti, *Heidegger and the Poets*.

4 INTERLUDE: (IN)SECURITY

1 See especially the essays in Heidegger, *On the Way to Language*. For a discussion of Heidegger and Language see for example: J. J. Kockelmans, *On Heidegger and Language*, Evanston: Northwestern University Press, 1972; R. Bernasconi 'The Transformation of Language at Another Beginning', *Research in Phenomenology*, vol. 13, 1983, pp. 1–23; J. Sallis 'Toward the Showing of Language', *Southwestern Journal of Philosophy*, vol. 4, 1973, pp. 75–83; Sallis 'Language and Reversal', *Southwestern Journal of Philosophy*, Winter 1970, pp. 381–97; and K. Haries 'Heidegger and Hölderlin: The Limits of Language', *The Personalist*, vol. xlvi, 1963, pp. 5–23.
2 G. Agamben, *Language and Death. The Place of Negativity*, Minneapolis: Minnesota University Press, 1991, p. 91.
3 Agamben, *Language and Death*, p. 89.
4 Agamben, *Language and Death*, p. 85.
5 Agamben, *Language and Death*, p. 95.
6 For a breath-takingly Stalinist statement to this effect see A. James 'System or Society?', *Review of International Studies*, vol. 19, 1993.
7 Quoted in J. Sallis, *Crossings. Nietzsche and the Space of Tragedy*, Chicago: Chicago University Press, 1991, p. 10.
8 M. Heidegger 'The Anaximander Fragment', in *Early Greek Thinking*, p. 16.

9 Nietzsche, in the 'Preface' to *Daybreak. Thoughts on the Prejudices of Morality*, trans. R.J. Hollingdale, Cambridge: Cambridge University Press, 1990, p. 4.

10 *Ibid.*

11 W. E. Connolly, 'Suffering, Justice and the Politics of Becoming', Private paper, The Johns Hopkins University, 1995, p. 43n.

12 Quoted in G. L. Ormiston's introduction to J.-F. Lyotard, *Phenomenology*, trans. B. Beakley, New York: The State University of New York Press, 1991, p. 13.

13 Lyotard 'Answering the question: What is Post Modernism?' *The Postmodern Condition: A Report On Knowledge*, Minneapolis: Minnesota University Press, 1984, quoted in *ibid.*, p. 14.

14 'You see', Foucault wrote, 'what I want to do is not the history of solutions, and that's the reason why I don't accept the word *alternative*. My point is not that everything is bad, but that everything is dangerous, then we always have something to do.' Quoted in J. Der Derian 'The Value of Security', in Campbell/Dillon, eds, *The Political Subject of Violence*, p. 97.

15 'What man walks more strangely than *Oedipus*?' Euben, *The Tragedy of Political Theory*, p. 102.

16 The phrase comes from G. Steiner, *After Babel. Aspects of Language and Translation*, London: Oxford University Press, 1975.

17 See H. Arendt, *The Human Condition*. 'The freedom of political action is the freedom of a plurality, and the freedom of plurality entails an inescapable contingency: action's futility, boundlessness and uncertainty of outcome.' p. 195. See the discussion in D. R. Villa 'Beyond Good And Evil. Arendt, Nietzsche, and the Aestheticization of Political Action', *Political Theory*, vol. 20, no. 2, 1992.

18 Heidegger, *Basic Concepts*, trans. G. E. Aylesworth, Bloomington: Indiana University Press, 1993, p. 83.

19 Heidegger, *Parmenides*, p. 27.

20 This is one reason why I introduce the ugly but nonetheless more accurate term (in)security. See also Chapter 2.

21 'The experience of the uncanny fosters anxiety', writes Connolly. 'And anxiety readily becomes translated into those pangs of guilt through which a moral economy reinstates the equivalences that had just been disturbed. . . . If you experience the uncanny, what you thought was in place now seems to be filled with that which displaces or disturbs it. So you lose secure bearings.' *The Augustinian Imperative: A Reflection On The Politics Of Morality*, London: Sage, 1993, p. 133. Later, he adds 'The most productive and dangerous effect of the uncanny is the feeling of anxiety it foments. Anxiety is a fluid mood of estrangement from an uncertain object'. p. 136.

22 Heidegger, *The Question of Being*, trans. W. Kluback and J. T. Wilde, New Haven, Connecticut: College and University Press, 19??, p. 67.

23 Heidegger, *Parmenides*, p. 39.

24 All entries taken from H. G. Liddell and R. Scott, *Greek–English Lexicon*, Oxford: Clarendon Press.

25 As note 24.

26 Walter Otto notes that, while in Homer the dominion of Poseidon is wholly limited to the sea, he was once conceived to be much more powerful than he appears in the *Iliad*. Formerly not merely a great God, but an all-embracing one who figures both as a creator and destroyer, the shrinkage of his legendary prowess 'is proof of a greater change in thought'. *The Homeric Gods. The Spiritual Significance of Greek Religion*, New York: Octagon Books, 1954, p. 28.

27 *Oxford Classical Dictionary*, Oxford: Clarendon Press, 1966, p. 721.

28 Entry, *Securitas*, E. A. Andrews, *Latin–English Lexicon*, London: Sampson, Low, Marston, Low and Searle, 2nd edn, 1875, p. 1380.

29 R. C. Hancock, *Calvin and the Foundations of Modern Politics*, Ithaca: Cornell University Press, 1989, p. 131. See also H. Hopfl, *The Christian Polity Of John Calvin*, Cambridge: Cambridge University Press, 1985.
30 *Ibid.*, p. 130.
31 *Ibid.*
32 John Calvin, *Institutionis Christianae Religionis*, 2nd edn, 1539, III.2.17.
33 Der Derian 'The Value of Security', in Campbell/Dillon, eds, *The Political Subject of Violence*, pp. 97–8.
34 *Ibid.*
35 E. Levinas, *Existence and Existents*, London: Kluwer, 1988, p. 21.

5 THE POLITICAL AND THE TRAGIC

1 Levinas' tragic is not the one operating here. See especially Levinas, *Difficult Freedom*.
2 'The pillars of the best known truths', Arendt wrote, 'today lie shattered; we need neither criticism nor wise men to shake them any more. We need only look around to see that we are standing in the midst of a veritable rubble heap of such pillars. . . . long ago it became apparent that the pillars of truth have also been the pillars of political order'. Arendt 'On Humanity In Dark Times', in *Men In Dark Times*, New York: Harcourt Brace, 1983, p. 10.
3 W. Marx's description of the predicament of our age; see his *Towards a Phenomenological Ethics. Ethos and the Life-World*, Albany: SUNY Press, 1992. And a way of characterising how Arendt saw the question of the political particularly, for example, in *Between Past and Future*. There, in her essay on 'What is Authority', she concludes: 'For to live in a political realm with neither authority nor the concomitant awareness that the source of authority transcends power and those who are in power, means to be confronted anew, without the religious trust in a sacred beginning and without the protection of traditional and therefore self-evident standards of behaviour, by the elementary problems of human living together'. p. 141.
4 Marx also attempts to address such questions in *Is There a Measure On Earth?* Chicago: Chicago University Press, 1987. The idea of the solidarity of the shaken is taken from J. Patocka. See E. Kohak, *Jan Patocka, Philosophy and Selected Writings*, Chicago: University of Chicago Press, 1989.
5 Caputo broaches this topic, for example in *The Mystical Element In Heidegger's Thought*, New York: Fordham University Press, 1986.
6 F. Nietzsche 'Schopenhauer as Educator', in *Untimely Meditations*, trans. R. J. Hollingdale, Cambridge: Cambridge University Press, 1989.
7 Canovan writes: 'The specter of Heidegger the Nazi haunts Arendt's reflections [on the profoundly agonistic relationship between politics and philosophy], forcing her again and again to tear up her attempted resolution and to start again'. 'Socrates or Heidegger? Hannah Arendt's Reflections on Philosophy and Politics', p. 162. Perhaps the point of that relationship is precisely that the agonism of it is and should remain irresolvable. See also D. F. Krell's *Daimon Life*, Bloomington: Indiana University Press, 1992; H. Ott, *Martin Heidegger: A Political Life*, London: Harper Collins, 1993; Habermas' introduction to V. Farias, *Heidegger and National Socialism*; P. Lacoue-Labarthe, *Heidegger, Art and Politics*, Oxford: Basil Blackwell, 1990; and, in particular, D. Janicaud, *L'ombre de cette pensée: Heidegger et la question politique*, Grenoble: Jerome Millon, 1990.
8 See also G. Kovacs' essay 'On Heidegger's Silence', *Heidegger Studies*, vol. 5, 1989. Silence, reticence and stillness are also the words and themes which pervade

his major, so far untranslated, work, *Beiträge zur Philosophie*, Frankfurt am Main: Klosterman. This, significantly enough, was written throughout the Nazi period.

9 M. Heidegger, *Parmenides*, p. 75.

10 Which is one of the ways Krell approaches it. See 'The Silence', in *Daimon Life*, pp. 138–42. R. Bernstein also explores the relationship between Heidegger's philosophy and 'his politics' in 'Heidegger's Silence: *Ethos* and Technology'. See Bernstein, *The New Constellation*, Cambridge: Polity Press, 1991.

11 Comportment can neither be divorced from Heidegger's own specific historical situatedness, nor from his earliest thinking. With respect to the former, see Ott's recent biography, *Heidegger: A Political Life*. With respect to the latter, see T. Kisiel, *The Genesis of Heidegger's Being and Time*.

12 See, especially, Caputo 'Heidegger's Scandal: Thinking and the Essence of the Vicitm', in J. Margolis and T. Rockmore, eds, *The Heidegger Case*, Philadelphia: Temple University Press, 1992; and Caputo, *Demythologising Heidegger*.

13 Dallmayr, *The Other Heidegger*, p. 72.

14 Although Levinas, too, emphasises Heidegger's supposed emphasis upon dwelling when elucidating his own reading of Judaism; in which, for Levinas, 'the world becomes intelligible before a human face and not, as for a great contemporary philosopher [Heidegger] who sums up an important aspect of the West, through houses, temples and bridges'. *Difficult Freedom*, p. 23. Levinas argues, with some reason, against Heidegger – but, ultimately, I think distortingly in respect of the ontological constitution of *Dasein* – that 'Man, after all, is not a tree, and humanity is not a forest.' However, as I read him, Heidegger is concerned more with the pathways than the forest, and with the tree as an illustration of the operation of the principle of ground as it functions in the abyssal circumstances of the ontological difference. As ever, Heidegger is always trying to say more than one thing at once. Levinas concludes that the freedom he espies through Judaism 'relegates the values to do with roots and institutes other forms of fidelity and responsibility. . . . promotes more human forms, for they presuppose a conscious commitment; freer forms for they allow us to glimpse a human society and horizon vaster than those of the villages where we were born'. *Difficult Freedom*, p. 23. Does the ontological constitution of *Dasein* necessarily militate aginst such a vision? Cannot pagans enfold the ethic of the 'nomad' into their attempts at building and dwelling? Heidegger's account of *Dasein*'s coming-into-its-own, for example, is definitely not that of a narrow egoism: 'Only by coming-into-its-own is *Dasein* sufficiently enabled truly to shoulder solicitude "for others"'. He continued, in order to emphasise the point, 'this coming-into-its-own never denotes an isolated ego conception but rather acceptance of one's belonging to the truth of being'. Elswhere, (and at the height of Nazism) the point is driven home again when, in the *Beiträge*, he argues against the many disguises of egocentrism. The most dangerous and obnoxious of these, he wrote, occurs precisely 'where the worldless ego has seemingly abandoned and surrendered itself to something else which is "greater" than it and into which it is fused as an integral part. The dissolution of the "I" into the "life" of the people involves an overcoming of the ego – but one that neglects the first precondition of such an overcoming, namely, reflection on self-hood and its essential being.' Quoted in Dallmayr, *The Other Heidegger*, pp. 61 and 63. Does Levinas, then, deny the modest, fragile and difficult promise of the political? Does he mistake or diminish the burden of responsibility for the other, which the very idea of the political fundamentally entails, and which Hannah Arendt, for example, recognised as a necessary requisite for keeping the good from being extinguished in the fires which totalitarianism continuously prepares for them?

15 Many have been tempted to argue that this is another instance of the philosophical overdetermination of philosophy in the age-old consideration of the relationship

between philosophy and politics. But how could that be? Heidegger accords systematic priority to comportment, to the dependency of a mode of thinking on a mode of living, throughout his thought. Schurmann makes this especially clear in *Heidegger. On Being and Acting. From Principles to Anarchy.* See Chapter XIII.

16　I have explored the idea of guilt and of betrayal in '*Paradosis*'. See also G. Bataille, *Guilty*, trans. B. Boone, intro. D. Hollier, Venice, California: The Lapis Press, 1988.

17　Levinas, *Existence and Existents*, p. 19.

18　Dennis Schmidt emphasises from the beginning, for example, that 'it is doubtful whether philosophy has ever had such a unity that would justify talk about "the tradition" as if it were a whole cut of the same seamless cloth'. And insists that: 'Talk of the "tradition" does not mean that the long history of efforts to wrestle with phenomena, and to reflect upon the capacity and powers of reflection, has been reduced to a unified effort. . . . Speaking about the "tradition of metaphysics" is not the last gasp of historicism but one of the ways in which contemporary thinkers have sought to simultaneously establish and loosen the history of the discourse that is philosophy . . . The point is this: despite its richness and depths, despite its honesty and efforts, depite its complexity and conflicts, it has become increasingly difficult for contemporary thinkers to hold onto what can be found in the history as vital, tenable, and answering needs of today.' Schmidt, *The Ubiquity of the Finite*, pp. ix–x.

19　Schurmann, *op. cit.*, p. 17.

20　His own term for his work in *Early Greek Thinking*. It is this quasi-eschatology which Derrida terms 'Heideggerian hope' in 'Différance'. See *Margins of Philosophy*, p. 27. Krell also provides an important discussion of eschatology in chapter 7 of *Intimations of Mortality*.

21　Caputo's work on Heidegger is particularly sensitive to Heidegger's sensibility to danger, and to the danger of that sensibility. See especially *The Mystical Element in Heidegger's Thought*; and *Radical Hermeneutics*. An excellent collection of essays on the broader theme of danger and 'continental thought' is to be found in Dallery and Scott, eds, *Ethics and Danger*. In the event, I do not think that Heidegger does present an eschatology because for him the end as death is not a possibility that can be actualised: 'Death as possibility gives nothing to be "actualised", nothing *Dasein*, as actual, could itself be'. *Being and Time*, p. 307. Death is the non-relational, absolute exteriority. It is the non-integratable. Because finality, the limit, death, is non-relational, Heidegger seems therefore to be allowing for thinking finality without totality. See Birmingham 'The Time of the Political'.

22　See Krell, *Daimon Life*.

23　Heidegger, *The Question Concerning Technology*; and 'What Are Poets For?' in *Poetry, Language and Thought*.

24　See Krell's introduction to Heidegger, *Early Greek Thinking*, especially pp 9–10. For a more extended discussion of Heidegger and the tragic, see Fynsk, *Heidegger. Historicity and Thought*.

25　Heidegger has often been mistakenly charged with a nostalgia for the Greek *polis*, as has Arendt. The charge is silly – neither of them have an understanding either of history or of human being that could possibly generate nostalgia – and, of course, it misses the point of their interest entirely; which is to rethink what the political might be. Where Heidegger is concerned the following observation from his lectures on Parmenides indicates that neither did he entertain any illusions about it: '. . . the frightfulness, the horribleness, the atrociousness of the Greek *polis*. Such is the rise and the fall of man in his historical abode of essence – *epipolis* – *apolis* – far exceeding abodes, homeless, as Sophocles (Antigone) calls man. It is not by chance that man is spoken of in this way in Greek tragedy. For the possibility, and the necessity, of "tragedy" itself has its single source in the conflictual essence of *aletheia*.' Heidegger, *Parmenides*, 1982, p. 90.

26 'What Are Poets For?' in Heidegger, *Poetry, Language, Thought*, p. 116.

27 Heidegger quoted in Kockelmans, *On the Truth of Being*, p. 239.

28 Bernasconi, *The Question of Language in Heidegger's History of Being*, p. 9.

29 Nietzsche, *Twilight of the Idols*, p. 49.

30 One of the ways Krell seems to characterise it in his introduction to Heidegger's *Early Greek Thinking*.

31 Heidegger acknowledges and explores this everywhere he refers to poetic thinking. But see specifically, for example, *An Introduction to Metaphysics*, pp. 144–65.

32 J.-P. Vernant and P. Vidal-Naquet, *Myth and Tragedy in Ancient Greece*, New York: Zone Books, 1988, pp 46–7.

33 *Ibid.*

34 M. Nussbaum, *The Fragility of Goodness. Luck and Ethics in Greek tragedy and Philosophy*, Cambridge: Cambridge University Press, 1989, p. 420.

35 Vernant and Vidal-Naquet, *Myth and Tragedy*, p. 305. 'The true material of tragedy is the social thought peculiar to the city-state, in particular the legal thought that was then in the process of being evolved.' *Ibid.*, p. 7. See also E. Hall, *Inventing the Barbarian*, Oxford: Clarendon Press, 1989, which discusses tragedy, democracy and the invention of the barbarian in the context of the panhellenism stimulated by the threat from the Persian empire. Set in the very heart of the *oikos*, the family, the *polis*, and the relations between them, tragedy is preoccupied with the phenomenon of this being-in-common, how it appears and what joins it together in its dividedness; the very flexing and rendering of the hyphenation. It is this that makes of democratic politics a tension between the 'legitimacy of limits and conventions essential' to it, and 'the exposing and opposing of the modern drift toward rationalization, normalization, and dependency'. Connolly, *Politics and Ambiguity*, pp. 107–8.

36 Lefort, *Democracy and Political Theory*, p. 55. Lefort added, at another point: 'If we are to interpret the political, we must break with the scientific view in general' (p. 10).

37 Vernant and Vidal-Naquet, *op. cit.*, p. 88.

38 *Ibid.*, p. 186.

39 Segal, *Tragedy and Civilisation*.

40 Whereas, for example: 'Decision and responsibility are understood as two connected levels in tragedy and thus have an ambiguous, enigmatic character; they are seen as questions that, in default of any fixed and unequivocal answers, always remain open'. Vernant and Vidal-Naquet, *op. cit.*, p. 81. Which, again, is not to say that judgements cannot and are not made about them; only that those judgements are necessarily contingent and provisional. See for example my *The Falklands, Politics and War*.

41 Heidegger, *Being and Time*, p. 438.

42 See for example J. Schwarz 'Human Action and Political Action in *Oedipus Tyrannos*', Euben, *Greek Tragedy and Political Theory*, London: University of California Press, 1986.

43 Vernant and Vidal-Naquet, *op. cit.*, p. 75.

44 See G. Stenstad 'The Last God – A Reading', *Research in Phenomenology*, vol. XXIII, 1993, for a discussion of this issue.

45 Heidegger 'Letter to Richardson'. in W. J. Richardson, *Heidegger. Through Phenomenology to Thought*.

46 For an excellent inquiry into Heidegger and earth see Haar, *The Song of the Earth*. See also L. McWhorter, ed., *Heidegger and the Earth. Essays in Environmental Philosophy*, Kirksville, Missouri: The Thomas Jefferson University Press, 1992.

47 Krell, *Intimations of Mortality*, p. 45.

48 Krell, *Daimon Life*.

49 Segal, *op. cit.*, p. 11.
50 *Ibid.*, p. 30.
51 Nussbaum, *The Fragility of Goodness*, p. 5.
52 *Ibid.*
53 See for example the discussion in Dallmayr, *The Other Heidegger*, pp. 116–17.
54 *Ibid.*, p. 14.
55 Arendt analyses this, in terms which appropriate Kant, as 'representative thinking'. See Villa 'Beyond Good and Evil'.
56 Arendt 'Karl Jaspers: A *Lauditio*', *Men in Dark Times*, p. 75.
57 A. Lesky, *Greek Tragedy*, London: Ernest Benn, Ltd., 2nd edn, 1967, p. 40.
58 J. Sallis, *Crossings*, Chicago: Chicago University Press, 1991, calls tragedy, after Nietzsche, 'a mimetic supplement of the reality of nature'. p. 83. Sallis later argues, in his subtle reading of Nietzsche's *The Birth of Tragedy*, that in this way tragedy, too, offers a form of metaphysical comfort which is why Nietzsche later rejects it in the interests of laughter: 'Let it be said, then, that tragedy exposes one to the abyss, disclosing the abyss by way of a double *mimesis*; and yet, that tragedy, in its very disclosure of the abyss, protects, saves, even heals one from the destructive consequences that such exposure can have. Tragedy leads one back, leaves one finally comforted, by letting the horrible turn into the sublime'. p. 93.
59 G. Deleuze, *Difference and Repetition*, London: Athlone Press, 1994, p. xvi.
60 *Ibid.* See also Lyotard, *The Inhuman*, Cambridge: Polity Press, 1991.
61 Rosenzweig quoted in S. A. Handelman, *Fragments of Redemption. Jewish Thought and Literary Theory in Benjamin, Scholem and Levinas*, Bloomington: Indiana University Press, 1991, p. xvii.
62 'Recognising that it is the nature of the universe to be in conflict, and accepting a problematical view of the world, the spectator himself, through the spectacle, acquires a tragic consciousness.' Vernant and Vidal-Naquet, *Myth and Tragedy*, p. 114.
63 See Arendt 'Truth and Politics', *Between Past and Future*.
64 Arendt 'On Humanity in Dark Times', in *Men in Dark Times*, p. 7.
65 An adaptation of a point made about Euripides by Nietzsche in *The Birth of Tragedy*, New York: Anchor Books, 1956, p. 71. It was, therefore, a 'democratic *paideia* complete in itself'. William Arrowsmith quoted in Euben, *Greek Tragedy and Political Theory*, p. 23.
66 Arendt 'What is Freedom', p. 152.
67 *Ibid.* Taminiaux explores these points further in an excellent essay on the relation between art and the political which is contained in Jacques Taminiaux, *Poetics Speculation and Judgement*, trans. and ed. by M. Gendre, New York: SUNY Press, 1993, Chapter 1. In effect Taminiaux argues that, paid by the city to attend the theatre, tragedy inculcated *phronesis* (that type of knowledge specifically adjusted to human affairs) in its citizens. The Greek word for theatre, *theatron*, means, of course, a place for seeing. And prior to Plato *theoria* meant beholding a spectacle, not solitary contemplation of Ideas beyond the common world of appearances.
68 Or, as Haar puts it: 'The very height of truth requires a lofty affirmation'. Haar, *The Song of the Earth*, p. 105. See in addition Nietzsche, *The Birth of Tragedy*, pp. 65–7 where Nietzsche suggests that 'Dionysus *remains* the sole dramatic protagonist and that all of the most famous characters of the Greek stage, Prometheus, *Oedipus*, etc., are only masks of that original hero'; and also the discussion of Dionysian affirmation in P. Valadier 'Dionysus Versus the Crucified', in D. B. Allison, ed., *The New Nietzsche*, Cambridge, Mass.: The MIT Press, 4th Printing, 1990.
69 Nussbaum, *The Fragility of Goodness*.
70 Arendt 'On Humanity in Dark Times', in *Men in Dark Times*, p. 22. See also the discussion in Canovan, *Hannah Arendt. A Reinterpretation of Her Political*

Philosophy, p. 96; and S. Benhabib 'Hannah Arendt and the Redemptive Power of Narrative', *Social Research*, 57/1, Spring 1990.

71   Quoted in Canovan, *Hannah Arendt. A Reinterpretation Of Her Political Thought*, p. 96. Canovan notes that this 'reality' is the reality of the human condition as Arendt conceives of it.

72   See for example L. Ayleen, *Greek Tragedy and the Modern World*, London: Methuen, 1964, p. 2. What follows is, however, heavily indebted to R. Girard's *Violence and the Sacred*, trans. P. Gregory, Baltimore: The Johns Hopkins University Press, 1977; especially his brilliant analysis of what he terms sacrificial crisis, reciprocal violence and, to some degree also, of his reading of *Oedipus Rex*. I adapt and modify all this a little, but fundamentally depart from his thesis in taking exception to what he says, *en passant*, about Nietzsche and Heidegger. I argue against Girard that the philosophy of the limit is actually integrally related to all he has to say about the tragic and about the violence entailed in the effacement of difference.

73   Lefort, *Democracy and Political Theory*, p. 222.

74   And the ever present possibility of monstrosity. Neither god nor beast, human being itself appears in the tragic imagination as a monstrosity. Neither one thing nor the other, a hybrid, it is cross-bred. See for example Sallis, *Crossings*.

75   Girard, *Violence And The Sacred*, p. 26. Girard makes the point that 'while acknowledging the differences, both functional and mythical, between vengeance, sacrifice and legal punishment, it is important to recognise their fundamental identity'. By that he means a judicial system abrogates to itself and institutionalises the act of reprisal, thus substituting public vengeance for private vengeance to cap the cycle of reciprocal violence: 'whether it is through sacrificial killing or legal punishment, the problem is to forestall a series of reprisals', p. 25. I think he fails to consider how much sacrifical killing is, however, retained within rational-legal systems. And he does not consider the endless cycle of reciprocal violence which threatens in relations between contending sovereignties; within and without the state.

76   Arendt 'On Violence', in *Crises of The Republic*, New York: Harcourt Brace Jovanovich, 1972, p. 177.

77   I am following Arendt's differentiation of power from violence, as well as her account of authority, here. See Arendt, *The Human Condition*; Arendt, *On Violence*, New York: Harcourt Brace, 1970; and Arendt 'What is Authority?' *Between Past and Future*.

78   Arendt 'What is Freedom', p. 152.

79   An absolutely crucial question arises here which requires much more attention than I can currently give to it. It is the question of whether *polemos* is the same as violence and, more generally, of the distinguishing of different forms of struggle. Heidegger notes the problem in his lectures on Parmenides. There, while introducing the discussion of the conflictual essence of truth, he says: 'Presumably, "conflict" here means something other than mere quarrel and fight, other than blind discord, other than "war", and other than "competition" as well. Perhaps these are only variations and initial appellations of the conflict, the primordial essence of which we may surmise in the essence of truth in the sense of *aletheia* and which we will come to know one day. Perhaps the word of Heraclitus, so often misused and always truncated . . . [*polemos* translated as war] has in common with Greek thinking only the empty verbal sound'. And, later, he repeats his fundamental view of truth: 'The primordial essence of truth is conflictual. What "conflictual" means here remains a question.' But he does not explore the point further. See Heidegger, *Parmenides*, pp. 17–18 and p. 26.

80   Jabes, quoted in Handelman, *Fragments of Redemption*, p. 344.

81   Derrida, *Aporias*, p. 10.

82   Segal, *Tragedy and Civilisation*, p. 42. It does so in a way that allows us to appreciate

Nietzsche's dictum that 'We have art that we may not perish of life'. Segal writes at greater length: 'We have the tragic art that we may not forget the dimensions of life that our structures cannot encompass. Tragedy pushes back the structures and reopens the powerful possibility of seeing life as chaos. Without that paradoxically pleasurable pain of tragedy, our order and our structures would become sterile, self-enclosed, solipsistic, arrogant with the *hybris* of their own intellectual power', p. 42.

83 The public/private distinction, together with all of the connotations that it has for us, is, of course, essentially a function of liberal individualist thought. Nonetheless, even for the ancients there was an understanding of the distinction between personal and collective life. For a discussion of this point see R. Mulgan 'Aristotle and the Value of Political Participation', *Political Theory*, vol. 18, no. 2, 1990.

84 C. Farrar writes: 'The *polis*, and particularly the democratic *polis*, was intentionally un-natural. The *polis* was designed to enable order to emerge from the un-ordered, to make it possible for men to be more than their conditions or resources would suggest they are capable of being.' See her essay 'Ancient Greek Political Theory and Democracy', in John Dunn, ed., *Democracy: The Unfinished Journey, 508 BC to AD 1993*, Oxford: Oxford University Press, 1992, p. 34.

85 Taminiaux, *Poetics, Speculation and Judgement*, pp. 8–9.

86 Girard 'Teiresias and the Critic', in R. Macksey and E. Donato eds, *The Structuralist Controversy: The Languages of Criticism and the Sciences of Man*, Baltimore: The Johns Hopkins University Press, 1972, p. 17.

87 'No literary genre of antiquity made such full use of the double entendre as did tragedy and *Oedipus Rex* contains more than twice as many ambiguous expressions as Sophocles' other plays (fifty according to the count made by Hug in 1872). However, the problem is not so much one of quantity as of nature and function.' Vernant and Vidal-Naquet, *Myth and Tragedy*, p. 113. In *Oedipus Rex*, they confirm, the ambiguity and duality is meant to be immanent within meaning and human being themselves.

88 B. Knox, *Oedipus at Thebes*, New Haven: Yale University Press, 1957, p. 116.

89 Girard, *Violence and the Sacred*, pp. 74–5.

90 Zeitlin, quoted in Euben, *The Tragedy of Political Theory*, p. 97.

91 Girard, *Violence and the Sacred*, p. 74.

92 Euben, *The Tragedy of Political Theory*, p. 98.

93 *Ibid*.

94 In Levinas, the status of that beyond which is, of course, always integral to the present of human being is the unlimited ethical call of the other which calls-up the self to be a self. See especially *Totality and Infinity*; and *Otherwise than Being*.

95 Though Euben makes the interesting point that the Sphinx too is in its own way like *Oedipus*, part human part beast. *The Tragedy of Political Theory*, p. 113n.

96 H. Musurillo, *The Light and the Darkness*, Leiden: E. J. Brill, 1967, pp. 81–2.

97 See Knox 'The Last Scene', M. J. O'Brian, ed., *Twentieth Century Interpretations of Oedipus Rex*, Englewood Cliffs, New Jersey: Prentice Hall, 1968; and the last chapter of Knox's classic book, *Oedipus at Thebes*. The same point is well emphasised in Schwartz 'Action in *Oedipus Tyrannos*', in Euben, ed., *Greek Tragedy and Political Theory*.

98 Girard, *Violence and the Sacred*, p. 55. And hence, although in the play the plague is sent by the gods, this is entirely consistent with the reading here; because, of course, human being also arrives from the beyond of human being as does the plague which it bears.

99 *Ibid*., p. 195.

100 Heidegger, *An Introduction to Metaphysics*, pp. 152–3.

101 'I was saved for some dreadful evil'. p. 138.

102 'I saved the city I don't care what happens to me.' Line 443.

103 For Heidegger it is not man, or even human being, that is saved in the turning which the advent of the age of technology makes possible. It is the event of presencing. This is what makes sense of his apparent disinterest in the concrete future of humankind. But that neither dismisses nor resolves the question of the relationship between *Dasein* and the event of the saving turn which he detects in technology. Rather, it poses it in a certain way, which is why he calls for a different sort of thought: 'Neither the political, nor the economical, nor the sociological, nor the technical and scientific, nor even the religious or metaphysical perspectives are adequate to thinking what is happening in this age of the world'. Heidegger, quoted in Schurmann, *Heidegger. On Being and Acting*, p. 208.

104 *Ibid.*, pp. 48–9.

105 I think that this is also one way of describing what Arendt is addressing in a previously unpublished essay 'Philosophy and Politics', *Social Research*, 57, 1990.

106 *Ibid.*

107 Segal, *Tragedy and Civilisation*, p. 241. 'No figure in Greek drama more powerfully and tragically embodies the paradoxes of man's civilising power than *Oedipus* . . . *Oedipus* sums up all that man can attain by mind alone. And yet this solver of riddles does not know the most fundamental thing about himself. He lacks the basic information about his origins that gives man his human identity and sets him apart from the undifferentiated realm of nature and the anonymous undifferentiated realm of the beasts.' *Ibid.*, p. 207.

108 Contra, Girard, *Violence and the Sacred*. See in contrast Knox 'The Last Scene'; and the last chapter of his *Oedipus at Thebes*.

109 Segal, *Tragedy and Civilisation*, pp. 40–1.

110 Knox, *Oedipus at Thebes*, p. 12: once by the shepherd; once by *Teiresias*; and twice by *Jocasta*.

111 Segal, *Tragedy and Civilisation*, p. 208.

112 For a stimulating collection of essays on the theme of inside/outside as it arises in international political theory, see R. B. J. Walker, *Inside/Outside: International Relations as Political Theory*.

113 And, of course, Sophocles explores these issues further in the other two of the three Theban plays: *Oedipus at Colonus* and *Antigone*.

114 Sallis, *Crossings*, p. 99.

115 Heidegger, *Parmenides*.

116 The phrase is taken from Euben, *The Tragedy of Political Theory*, p. 122.

117 Here I want to acknowledge while also emphasising what Peter Euben noted in his editor's introduction to an excellent collection of essays on the theme of the tragic and the political: that 'Greek tragedy was about boundaries of space, time and place, about being inside and outside. It was also about how such boundaries, divisions, and oppositions are born, maintained and justified.' *Greek Tragedy and Political Theory*, p. 37.

118 It is this which radically distinguishes my reading of *Oedipus Rex* as a tragedy of (in)security from that, for example, of W. Kaufmann, *Tragedy and Philosophy*, Princeton: Princeton University Press, 1968.

119 Heidegger 'What Are Poets For?' p. 115.

6 *OEDIPUS ASPHALEOS:* THE TRAGEDY OF (IN)SECURITY

* I wish to record my thanks to Costas Constantinou for his help not only with the reading of *asphaleia* but also with the reading of *Oedipus Rex*.

1 Which is not to say that there is an identity of *polis* and *oikos*. Quite the contrary,

of course. The tension between the two was a constant question in Greek thought and life. See for example the discussions both in J. Taminiaux, *Poetics, Speculation and Judgement*, and in Vernant and Vidal-Naquet, *Myth and Tragedy*.

2 Much of the debate about the supposed conflict between freedom and determination – by the gods through the oracle – in *Oedipus Rex* is conducted within the context of an understanding of subjective freedom which simply does not obtain in the imagination at work in tragedy. Specifically, the subjective understanding of freedom does not understand the workings of the belonging together of freedom and un-freedom. In consequence it always finds itself locked into irresolvable debates over structure and agency, conditioning and free will.

3 This is what the riddle of the Sphinx amounts to: to make commensurable what appears initially to be incommensurable, ultimately equating difference with identity. Knox points-out, as part of the general argument about the way the play is a microcosm of Periclean Athens, that mathematical as well as medical and legal forms of reasoning are 'inextricably woven into the texture of the play's taut and suggestive language'. Knox, *Oedipus at Thebes*, p. 147.

4 *Teiresias*, lines 452–3, from the translation by F. Storr, *Sophocles in Two Volumes. Oedipus The King. Oedipus at Colonus. Antigone*, London: Heinemann, 1962, p. 43. I make use of two translations in this chapter. The first, by Storr, is the one I have relied upon most because it provides the joint English–Greek text. The other, by R. Fagles, is *Sophocles. The Three Theban Plays. Oedipus Rex*, trans. Harmondsworth: Penguin Books, 1984. I have used this when the English translation seems less antiquated and more direct.

5 Schwartz discusses the historical references to Athens' plague which preceded the play in his essay 'Action in *Oedipus Tyrannos*', in Euben, ed., *Greek Tragedy and Political Theory*.

6 I am deliberately using the term which Arendt uses in *The Human Condition*. This assumption of responsibility for his acts is constitutive of what *Oedipus* is.

7 Heidegger speaking against the subjectivist interpretation of a 'people' in the *Beiträge zur Philosophie*. Quoted in Dallmayr, *The Other Heidegger*, p. 103.

8 I draw this distinction from Schurmann, *Heidegger. On Being and Acting: From Principles to Anarchy*, p. 273.

9 Sight is not, however, our only common sense.

10 Arendt, talking about Socrates but I think it can be said to apply to *Oedipus* also; quoted in Kohn 'Thinking/Acting', *Social Research*, vol. 57, no. 1, Spring 1990, p. 128.

11 '*Oedipus*' destiny is in a way our own, because we carry with us the same curse that the oracle pronounced against him.' Vernant and Vidal-Naquet, *Myth and Tragedy*, p. 86.

12 C. Lévi-Strauss notes how the entire run of his family – *Labdacus, Laius, Oedipus* – all refer to lameness. See *Structural Anthropology*, New York: Basic Books, 1963, pp. 213–19.

13 It therefore differs significantly from how Benjamin characterises German *Trauerspiel* which, he said, 'is taken up entirely with the hopelessness of the earthly condition'. Quoted in Handelman, *Fragments of Redemption*, p. 129.

14 'When Heidegger says "transcendence constitutes selfhood", he is not saying anything that would be compatible with mystics, American transcendentalists, or the like. For Heidegger views transcendence as an inhabiting of ontological difference through which the categories of metaphysics are violently demolished.' H. Rapaport, *Heidegger and Derrida*, p. 12.

15 Quoted in Handelman, *Fragments of Redemption*, p. 263.

16 *Ibid.*

17 Fynsk quoting Hölderlin's interpretation of *Oedipus*. See Fynsk, *Heidegger. Thought and Historicity*, p. 181.

18 Hölderlin quoted in Fynsk, *ibid.*, p. 188. My reading of *Oedipus* would follow what Fynsk describes as Hölderlin's rather than Heidegger's reading here.

19 Heidegger, *An Introduction to Metaphysics*, p. 161.

20 This point is brilliantly brought out and developed by Vernant and Vidal-Naquet in Chapter V of *Myth and Tragedy*.

21 'Man is the calculative animal. All this holds true, in various transformations and yet unanimously, throughout the entire history of Western thought.' Heidegger quoted in Schurmann, *Heidegger. On Being and Acting: From Principles to Anarchy*, p. 192. Schurmann adds: 'Man is the calculative animal insofar as in all metaphysical economies – whether Greek or technological – the relations that link entities have been fixed in reference to him and therefore remain, more than ever, equalising'. p. 193. Hence, in metaphysical thought, justice, for example, becomes technological equalisation.

22 Taminiaux shows how *techne* is distinct from *phronesis* in a way that has a direct bearing on all this. '*Techne* and *phronesis* are essentially different. To be sure, both are classified as dianoetic virtues, both include a deliberation, and they both refer to the perishable. But whereas *techne* deliberates only about the adequate means for predefined ends, *phronesis* deliberates about its proper aim, well-doing in general, that is, the good life, which is not an intelligible Idea, but what is worth being done here and now, in relation to *kairos*. It is always in relation to a concrete situation that one has to decide about what is just or unjust, noble or vile, wise or mad, beautiful or ugly. Because it is tied to *kairos*, practical wisdom is fully temporal and concerns the irreversible process and quality of particular existences, whereas a failure in matters of *techne* does not prevent the process of fabrication from starting all over again and does not affect the very existence of the artisan.... Its teaching takes place in the consideration of examples, for instance, the memorable ones that the poet relates better than the historian.' *Poetics, Speculation and Judgement*, pp. 8–9. See also Heidegger 'The Question Concerning Technology', in the collection of his essays entitled *The Question Concerning Technology.*

23 And regularly point out that his name which literally means swollen-foot also, through *oida*, gestures towards the sight of true knowledge as well of course.

24 Euben, *The Tragedy of Political Theory*, p. 103.

25 If by virtue of living in time you are inevitably a mobile being whose horizon is constantly changing, and if you do not stand straight what, then, do you have to do in order to be able to see straight? Answer: bring everything to a stand-still. *Oedipus* seems to recognise this and more: "Now I've exposed my guilt, horrendous guilt, could I train a level glance at you my countrymen? Impossible! No, if I could just block off my ears, the springs of hearing, I would stop at nothing – I'd wall-up my loathsome body like a prison, blind to the sound of life, not just the sight. Oblivion – what a blessing ... for the mind to dwell a world away from pain".' Fagles Translation, p. 243, lines 1516–23.

26 Both *Creon* and *Teiresias*, of course, come to be accused of such plotting. But earlier in the play, when the story of *Laius'* death is first recounted to him, he is just as quick to suspect a conspiracy behind that murder also.

27 See how Heidegger specifically differentiates resoluteness from *virtu* when discussing *aletheia*, in *Parmenides*, pp. 75–6.

28 The Foucauldian undertones are, of course, very powerful here. Euben addresses them specifically in *The Tragedy of Political Theory*. And Knox's *Oedipus at Thebes* goes as far as to talk of *Oedipus Rex* in terms of the catastrophe of enlightenment thinking; although the enlightenment is that of fifth-century Athens the wider connotation is evident.

29 I think Knox is quite wrong to characterise this as a kind of brilliant amateurism: *Oedipus at Thebes*, pp. 72–3. Athens was 'the school of Hellas'. It was a rigorous and 'professional' *techne*.

30 Knox, *Oedipus at Thebes*, and Lesky, *Greek Tragedy*, rigorously document this.

31 As Euben says: 'Greek tragedy was about boundaries of space, time and place, about being inside and outside'. See his 'Introduction' to *Greek Tragedy and Political Theory*, p. 37.

32 There is something about *Oedipus* which serves to recall what Derrida has called the 'absolute *arrivant*'. 'Such an *arrivant*', Derrida tells us, in a way that directly recalls the poet's attempt to disclose the character of the political through *Oedipus*, 'affects the very experience of the threshold, whose possibility he thus brings to light before one even knows whether there has been an invitation, a call, a nomination, or a promise'. It, therefore, arrives with and through *Oedipus*, though he does not fully compass it. Derrida, *Aporias*, pp. 34–5.

33 Storr Translation, line 630. E. Hall gives an excellent historical account of the background to the emergence of the *Tyrannoi* in Greece, and of the populistic character of their rule. See Hall, *Inventing the Barbarian*.

34 Knox, *Oedipus at Thebes*, p. 25.

35 Knox documents these points in detail in *Oedipus at Thebes*, especially pp. 22–3.

36 Fagles Translation, lines 669–71.

37 Fagles Translation, line 195.

38 See also Vernant and Vidal-Naquet, *Myth and Tragedy*, p. 131.

39 *Ibid.*, p. 339. Hence: 'Decision and responsibility are understood on two different levels in tragedy and thus have an ambiguous, enigmatic character; they are seen as questions that, in default of any fixed and unequivocal answers, always remain open'. *Ibid.*, p. 81. Derrida has pursued this conundrum in many of his writings as the thought of duty, or 'over-duty'. He summarised it in a recent work, *Aporias*, as follows: 'Duty must be such an over-duty, which demands acting without duty, without rule or norm (therefore without law) under the risk of seeing the so-called responsible decision become again the merely technical application of a concept and therefore of a presentable knowledge'. And, of course, recognises the aporia involved: '. . . who would call a decision that is without a rule, without norm, without determinable or determined law, a decision? Who will answer for it as if for a responsible decision, and before whom? Who will dare call duty a duty that owes nothing, or, better (or, worse), that *must owe nothing*?' He concludes: 'It is necessary, therefore, that the decision and responsibility for it be taken, interrupting the relation to any *presentable* determination but still maintaining a presentable relation to the interruption and to what it interrupts'. He then asks the philosophical question 'Is that possible?' Tragedy answers that it happens all the time; that the bearing of such a duty is the law of the tragic; and that the law of the tragic is the condition of mortal life. The exercise of this impossible duty is precisely what is being enacted at this point in the play.

40 And, in *Oedipus At Colonus*, of course, he is; though only to journey to the borderlands of another *polis*.

41 Fagles Translation, final line of the play, p. 251.

42 This point is prompted by Heidegger's reading of the opening chorus of *Antigone*. See *An Introduction to Metaphysics*, p. 148.

43 Storr Translation, line 39.

44 Remember: *asphaleia* is security; *sphalo* is to limp or stumble and also to mistake the truth, to err; *orthos* is [to stand] straight; and *orthotes* is truth as correspondence.

45 Storr Translation, line 46.

46 Storr Translation, lines 50–1.

47 Storr Translation, lines 54 and 55.

48 Storr Translation, line 57.
49 Heidegger, *An Introduction to Metaphysics*, p. 131.
50 *Ibid.*, p. 134.
51 Storr Translation, lines 60–1.
52 Storr Translation, lines 91–2.
53 Storr Translation, lines 93–4. Fagles Translation, and accompanying stage direction, make the point more explicitly: 'If you want my report in the presence of these people ... *pointing to the Priests while drawing Oedipus toward the palace.* I'm ready now, or we might go inside', p. 163; as does that by Stephen Berg and Diskin Clay, *Oedipus the King*, New York: Oxford University Press, 1978: 'Here? Now? In front of all these people? Or inside privately?', p. 27.
54 Storr Translation, line 147.
55 Storr Translation, line 284.
56 Storr Translation, line 299.
57 Storr Translation, line 350.
58 Storr Translation, line 356.
59 In Heidegger's terms it would come through the experience of *angst*. See for example, *Being and Time*.
60 Storr Translation, line 358.
61 Storr Translation, lines 380–1.
62 Storr Translation, line 389.
63 Storr Translation, line 415.
64 Storr Translation, line 1225.
65 Storr Translation, line 419.
66 Storr Translation, lines 508–10.
67 Storr Translation, lines 528–9. Note again the cognates of *orthotes* and the play on standing. For, if *Oedipus* cannot stand straight, how can he see straight unless he immobilises everything, including himself?
68 Storr Translation, line 550.
69 Storr Translation, line 552.
70 Storr Translation, line 589.
71 See Derrida, *Specters of Marx*, trans. P. Kamuf, London: Routledge, 1995, p. 8; and also Merleau-Ponty, *The Visible and the Invisible*.
72 Storr Translation, line 613.
73 Storr Translation, line 617.
74 Storr Translation, lines 618–21.
75 Storr Translation, line 628.
76 Storr Translation, line 634.
77 Storr Translation, lines 685–6.
78 Storr Translation, lines 681–2.
79 '*logos* is *in itself and at the same time* a revealing and a concealing'. Heidegger '*Logos* (Heraclitus, Fragment B 50)', in *Early Greek Thinking*, p. 71.
80 I have taken this point – and the slightly amended Nietzsche quotation – from Samuel Weber's 'Afterword' to Lyotard and Thebaud, *Just Gaming*, pp. 105–7.
81 *Ibid.*, p. 106.
82 Storr Translation, line 879.
83 Storr Translation, line 881.
84 Storr Translation, line 895.
85 Schurmann discusses this Heraclitean observation in *Heidegger. On Being and Acting: From Principles to Anarchy*, 'Conclusion'.
86 Lefort's interpretation of how modern democracy, together with its representation of power in such a way as 'to show that power is an *empty place*', inaugurates a new *mise en forme* of the political. *Democracy and Political Theory*, p. 223.

87 Nowhere is this point better brought out than in Aeschylus' trilogy *The Oresteia*.

88 Heidegger writes: 'The Greeks had no word for 'space'. This is no accident; for they experienced the spatial on the basis not of extension but of place (*topos*); they experienced it as *chora*, which signifies neither place nor space but that which is occupied by what stands there. The place belongs to the thing itself. Each of all the various things has its place. . . . But in order that this should be possible, "space" must be free from all the modes of appearance that it might derive from anywhere. For if it were similar to any of the modes of appearance that enter into it, it would, in receiving forms of antithetical or totally different essence, manifest its own appearance and so produce a poor realization of the model. That wherein the things in process of becoming are placed must precisely not present an aspect and appearance of its own.' *An Introduction to Metaphysics*, p. 66. I do not have the space to develop this understanding of *chora* and, more importantly, explore its implications for understanding the *polis*. But, disturbing and intriguing, they recall Lefort's observations on democratic politics and the empty place of power. See Lefort, *Democracy and Political Theory*.

89 See Nietzsche, *Untimely Meditations*, trans. R. J. Hollingdale, Cambridge: Cambridge University Press, 1989.

90 Nancy, *The Experience of Freedom*.

91 See Derrida, *Specters of Marx*; *The Other Heading, Reflections on Today's Europe*, trans. P.-A. Brault and M. Nass, Bloomington: Indiana University Press, 1992; and *Given Time: I. Counterfeit Money*, trans. P. Kamuf, Chicago: Chicago University Press, 1991.

92 Derrida, *Given Time*, p. 34.

93 Derrida, *Specters of Marx*, p. 75.

94 Fagles Translation, p. 239.

95 *Ibid*., p. 240.

96 '*phrontid*' exo'. Storr Translation, line 1390.

97 Fagles Translation, line 1497.

98 Fagles Translation, line 1471.

99 Derrida's observation on Hamlet which operates with equal force here. See *Specters of Marx*, p. 20.

100 Lefort, *Democracy and Political Theory*, p. 223.

101 This giving of himself has the structure of the gift that Cixous calls feminine; a 'giving for'. See 'Sorties', in H. Cixous, *The Newly Born Woman*, Manchester: Manchester University Press, 1986.

102 K. Held 'Fundamental Moods and Heidegger's Critique of Contemporary Culture', in J. Sallis, ed., *Reading Heidegger*, Bloomington: Indiana University Press, 1993, p. 292. See also Dallmayr's description of *Gelassenheit* as 'a broadly ontological perspective . . . in which different elements or modalities of being are related without mutual intrusion and by granting each other space in the interstices of presence and absence, arrival and departure'. Dallmayr, *The Other Heidegger*, p. 10. This seems to me to capture very well what is going on at this point in the play, but neither Dallmayr nor Held really addresses the sheer effort involved in letting-be, or the price it exacts; both of which are evident here at the end of *Oedipus Rex*.

103 This move of *Oedipus* recalls the leap of thought to which Heidegger continuously refers especially in his later work. 'It is a strange, or even uncanny thing', he says in *What is Called Thinking?* 'that we first have to leap in order to attain the very ground on which we find ourselves', p. 41. (I prefer Michel Haar's translation of these lines, here, over those of the English translation. See Haar, *Heidegger and the Essence of Man*, p. 96.)

104   'Oh no, What can I say to him? How can I ever hope to win his trust?' Fagles Translation, lines 1553–4.

105   Storr Translation, line 1290. Only subsequently does he clamour to be driven from the public gaze.

106   Fagles Translation, lines 1558–66.

107   Canovan's eloquent summary of Arendt's political sensibility which seems so fitting a summary of *Oedipus'* actions at this point as well. Canovan, *Hannah Arendt. A Reinterpretation of Her Political Thought*, p. 205.

108   Derrida, of course, explores in detail how this structure continuously operates: 'Repetition and first time, but also repetition and last time, since the singularity of any first time makes of itself also a last time. Each time it is the event itself, a first time is also a last time'. *Specters of Marx*, p. 10.

109   'A mimesis opens the fiction of tone. It is the tragedy of 'Come' that it must be repeatable (*a priori* repeated in itself) in order to resonate.' Derrida 'The Ends of Man', in *Margins of Philosophy*.

110   Heidegger, *Nietzsche. Volume I*, p. 311.

111   Quoted in Peg Birmingham 'The Time of the Political', p. 34. I have relied heavily on Peg Birmingham's excellent essay in the preceding analysis.

112   Arendt 'What is Freedom', *Between Past and Future*, p. 169.

113   *Ibid.*

114   Arendt 'Freedom and Politics', in A. Hunold, ed., *Freedom and Serfdom*, Dordrecht: Reidel, 1961, p. 192.

115   Arendt, *The Life of the Mind. Volume 2. Willing*, New York: Harcourt Brace Jovanovich, 1977.

116   Heidegger writes in *The Basic Problems of Phenomenology*, Translation, Introduction and Lexicon by A. Hofstadter, Bloomington: Indiana University Press, 1982: '*Dasein* understands itself by way of its own most peculiar capacity to be, of which it is expectant. In thus comporting toward its own most peculiar capacity to be, *it is ahead of itself*. Expecting a possibility, I come from this possibility toward that which I myself am ... *Dasein*, expecting its ability to be, *comes toward itself*. In this coming-toward-itself, expectant of a possibility, the *Dasein* is *futural* in an original sense'. p. 265.

117   Meister Eckhart quoted in Schurmann, *Heidegger. On Being and Acting: From Principles to Anarchy*, p. 260.

118   Perhaps this is also why *Creon* is so ambivalent about *Oedipus'* exile at the end of the play. See below.

119   P. Birmingham 'The Time of the Political', p. 40.

120   *Ibid.*, p. 41.

121   Antigone shows in a later play how she can, in a sense, stand-up for herself too. The issue of male and female is relevant here but is not one I have the space to take-up.

122   Fagles Translation, lines 1658–60.

123   Heidegger's summary of Schelling's thought which, as Dallmayr says, 'is not alien to Heidegger's thought'. Quoted in Dallmayr, *The Other Heidegger*, p. 117.

124   I trust Peg Birmingham will forgive the way I have woven her into my own text throughout the preceding section without always acknowledging precisely where and how. My debt to her essay must, however, be very evident.

125   Love has, of course, been a central concern of philosophers thoughout the tradition. Naturally, it found its first systematic treatment in Plato. See *The Phaedrus*, Harmondsworth: Penguin Books, 1973; and *The Symposium*, Harmondsworth: Penguin Books, 1951. For some classic surveys of the tradition's treatment of love from classical through Christian times, see for example: A. Nygren, *Agape and Eros*, London: SPCK, 1953; A. Soble, *Eros, Agape and Philia. Readings in the*

Philosophy of Love, London: Paragon House, 1989; G. Outka, *Agape. An Ethical Analysis*, New Haven: Yale University Press, 1972; I. Singer, *The Nature of Love. Volume 1. From Plato to Luther*, Chicago: Chicago University Press, 1984; and N. K. Badhwar, ed., *Friendship. A Philosophical Reader*, Ithaca: Cornell University Press, 1993.

126 Heidegger quoted in Dallmayr, *The Other Heidegger*, p. 128.

127 The theme of love and friendship is discussed in Arendt, *Men in Dark Times*, especially the essay on Lessing; and in Derrida 'The Politics of Friendship', *The Journal Of Philosophy*, 1988. See also J. M. Cooper 'Aristotle On The Forms of Friendship', *Review of Metaphysics*, vol. 30.

128 Derrida, *Specters of Marx*, p. 16.

129 'That which we *are* as having been', Heidegger explains 'has not gone by, passed away, in the sense in which we say that we could shuffle off our past like a garment. The *Dasein* can as little get rid of its [past as] bygones as escape its death. In every sense and in every case everything we have been is an essential determination of our existence.' *The Basic Problems of Phenomenology*, pp. 265–6.

130 Derrida, *Given Time: I Counterfeit Money*, Chicago: Chicago University Press, 1991, p. 57.

131 Storr Translation, line 1521. The Fagles Translation has it as: 'I try to say what I mean; it's my habit', line 1671.

132 Quoted in Lyotard, *The Inhuman*, p. 114.

133 'A masterpiece', Derrida reminds us 'always moves by definition in the manner of a ghost'. *Specters of Marx*, p. 53.

134 Storr Translation, Lines 1526–30.

135 *Being and Time*, p. 159.

136 Again I am indebted to Peg Birmingham; especially 'Ever Respectfully Mine: Heidegger on Agency and Responsibility', in Dallery and Scott, eds, *Ethics and Danger*, p. 121.

CONCLUSION: IMAGINATION AT THE CALL OF ETHICO-POLITICAL RESPONSIBILITY

1 The quotation is from Ricoeur's reference to R. Alter's account of biblical poetry in P. Ricoeur 'Love and Justice', *Philosophy and Social Criticism*, vol. 21, nos. 5/6, 1995, p. 25.

2 In addition to the Kearney references already cited, see also 'Narrative Imagination: Between Poetics and Ethics', *Philosophy and Social Criticism*, vol. 21, nos. 5/6, 1995, pp. 173–90; and *Transitions. Narratives in Modern Irish Culture*, Dublin: Wolfhound Press, 1987.

3 E. Levinas, *Outside the Subject*, Stanford: Stanford University press, 1993, p. 3.

4 Kearney 'Narrative Imagination', p. 185.

5 Ricoeur 'Fragility and Responsibility', *Philosophy and Social Criticism*, vol. 21, nos. 5/6, 1995, p. 15.

Bibliography

Agamben, G: *Language and Death. The Place of Negativity*, Minneapolis: Minnesota University Press, 1991.

Allison, D. B. ed.: *The New Nietzsche*, Cambridge, Mass.: The MIT Press, 4th Printing, 1990.

Anderson, B: *Imagined Communities*, revised edition, London: Verso, 1991.

Arendt, H: *Between Past and Future. Eight Exercises In Political Thought*, Harmondsworth: Penguin, 1977.

—— *Crises of The Republic*, New York: Harcourt Brace Jovanovich, 1972.

—— *Lectures On Kant's Political Philosophy*, R. Beiner, ed., Chicago: University of Chicago Press, 1982.

—— *Men In Dark Times*, New York: Harcourt Brace, 1983.

—— *On Violence*, New York: Harcourt Brace, 1970.

—— *The Human Condition*, Chicago: University of Chicago Press, 1958.

—— *The Life Of The Mind. Volume 1. Thinking*, London: Secker and Warburg, 1978.

—— *The Life Of The Mind. Volume 2. Willing*, New York: Harcourt Brace Jovanovich, 1977.

—— *The Origins of Totalitarianism*, London: André Deutsch, 1986.

Ayleen, B: *Greek Tragedy and the Modern World*, London: Methuen, 1964.

Badhwar, N ed.: *Friendship. A Philosophical Reader*, Ithaca: Cornell University Press, 1993.

Bataille, G: *Guilty*, trans. B. Boone, intro. D. Hollier, Venice, Calif.: The Lapis Press, 1988.

Bauman, Z: *Modernity and the Holocaust*, Cambridge: Polity Press, 1989.

Beiner, R: 'Hannah Arendt and Leo Strauss. The Uncommenced Dialogue', *Political Theory*, vol. 18, no. 2, 1990.

Benhabib, S: 'Hannah Arendt and the Redemptive Power of Narrative', *Social Research*, 57/1, Spring 1990.

Bernasconi, R: 'Habermas and Arendt on the Philosopher's "Error": Tracking the Diabolical in Heidegger', *Graduate Faculty Philosophy Journal*, vols 14–15, 1991.

—— 'Heidegger's Destruction of *Phronesis*', *The Southern Journal of Philosophy, Spindel Conference 1989. Heidegger and Praxis*.

—— 'The Transformation of Language at Another Beginning', *Research in Phenomenology*, vol. 13, 1983.

—— *The Question of Language in Heidegger's History of Being*, Atlantic Highlands, New Jersey: Humanities Press, 1985.

Bernstein, R: *The New Constellation*, Cambridge: Polity Press, 1991.

Bhabha, H ed.: *Nation and Narration*, London: Routledge, 1990.

Birmingham, P: 'The Time of the Political', *The Graduate Faculty Philosophy Journal, Heidegger and the Political*, vol. 14, no. 2–vol.15, no. 1, 1991.

Blanchot, M: *The Infinite Conversation*, Minneapolis: Minnesota University Press, Theory and History of Literature, vol. 82, 1993.

Bourdieu, P: *Homo Academicus*, Cambridge: Polity Press, 1988.

—— *The Political Ontology of Martin Heidegger*, Stanford: Stanford University Press, 1991.

Brown, N: *Redefining National Security*, Washington, D.C.: Worldwatch Institute, Paper, no. 14, 1977.

Bruns, G. L: 'On The Tragedy Of Hermeneutical Experience', *Research in Phenomenology*, vol. 18, 1988.

—— *Heidegger's Estrangements. Language, Truth and Poetry in the Later Writings*, New Haven: Yale University Press, 1989.

Burchell, G., Gordon, C. and Miller, P: *The Foucault Effect. Studies in Governmentality*, Brighton: Harvester Wheatsheaf, 1991.

Campbell, D: *Writing Security*, Manchester: Manchester University Press, 1992.

Campbell, D. and Dillon, M. eds: *The Political Subject of Violence*, Manchester: Manchester University Press, 1993.

Canovan, M: 'Socrates or Heidegger? Hannah Arendt's Reflections on Philosophy and Politics', *Social Research*, vol. 57, no. 1, Spring 1990.

—— *Hannah Arendt. A Reinterpretation of her Political Thought*, Cambridge: Cambridge University Press, 1992.

Caputo, J: 'Demythologising Heidegger: *Aletheia* and the History of Being', *Review of Metaphysics*, vol. 41, March 1988.

—— 'Heidegger's Kampf: The Difficulty of Life', *Graduate Faculty Philosophy Journal*, vols 14–15, 1990–91.

—— 'Heidegger's Scandal: Thinking and the Essence of the Victim', in J. Margolis and T. Rockmore, eds, *The Heidegger Case*, Philadelphia: Temple University Press, 1992.

—— *Against Ethics: Contributions to a Poetics of Obligation with Constant Reference to Deconstruction*, Bloomington: Indiana University Press, 1993.

—— *Demythologising Heidegger*, Bloomington: Indiana University Press, 1993.

—— *Radical Hermeneutics. Repetition, Deconstruction and the Hermeneutic Project*, Bloomington: Indiana University Press, 1987.

—— *The Mystical Element in Heidegger's Thought*, New York: Fordham University Press, 1986.

Cixous, H: *The Newly Born Woman*, Manchester: Manchester University Press, 1986.

Connolly, W: *The Ethos of Pluralisation*, Minneapolis: Minnesota University Press, 1995.

—— *Identity/Difference*, Ithaca: Cornell University Press, 1991.

—— *Political Theory and Modernity*, Oxford: Basil Blackwell, 1988.

—— *Politics and Ambiguity*, Madison: University of Wisconsin Press, 1987.

—— *The Augustinian Imperative. A Reflection on the Politics of Morals*, London: Sage, 1993.

Conrad, J: *Heart of Darkness. A Case Study in Contemporary Criticism*, ed. R. C. Murfin, New York: St. Martin's Press, 1989.

Cooper, J: 'Aristotle On The Forms Of Friendship', *Review Of Metaphysics*, vol. 30.

Cornell, D: *The Philosophy of the Limit*, London: Routledge, 1992.

Cornell, D., Rosenfeld, M. and Carlson, D. G. eds: *Deconstruction and the Possibility of Justice*, London: Routledge, 1992.

Critchley, S: 'Derrida's Specters of Marx', *Philosophy and Social Criticism*, vol. 21, no. 3, 1995.

—— *The Ethics of Deconstruction, Derrida and Levinas*, Oxford: Basil Blackwell, 1992.

D'Entreves, M. P: *The Political Philosophy of Hannah Arendt*, London: Routledge, 1994.

Dallery, A. B. and Scott, C. E. with Holley Roberts eds: *Crises in Continental Philosophy*, Albany: SUNY Press, 1990.

—— *Ethics and Danger, Essays On Heidegger and Continental Thought*, Albany: SUNY Press, 1992.

Dallmayr, F: *Politics and Praxis: Exercises in Contemporary Political Theory*, Cambridge, Mass.: MIT Press, 1984.

—— *The Other Heidegger*, Ithaca: Cornell University Press, 1993.

Dandeker, C: *Surveillance, Power and Modernity. Bureaucracy and Discipline From 1700 To The Present Day*, Cambridge: Polity Press, 1990.

Deleuze, G: *Difference and Repetition*, London: Athlone Press, 1994.

Der Derian, J. and M. J. Shapiro, eds: *International/Intertextual. Postmodern Readings Of World Politics*, Lexington, Mass.: Lexington Books, 1989.

Der Derian, J: *Anti-Diplomacy. Spies, Terror, Speed and War*, Oxford: Basil Blackwell, 1992.

Derrida, J: 'Of an Apocalyptic Tone Recently Adopted in Philosophy', trans. J. P. Leavey, *Oxford Literary Review*, vol. 6, no. 2, 1984.

—— 'Force of Law: The Mystical Foundation of Authority', in D. Cornell, *et al.*, eds, *Deconstruction and the Possibility of Justice*, London: Routledge, 1992.

—— 'Onto-theology of National Humanism (Prologomena to a Hypothesis)', *Oxford Literary Review*, vol. 14, 1992.

—— 'Psyche: Inventions of the Other', trans. C. Porter, in L. Waters and W. Godzich, eds, *Reading de Man Reading*, Minneapolis: Minnesota University Press, 1989.

—— 'The Politics of Friendship', *The Journal Of Philosophy*, 1988.

—— *Aporias*, Stanford: Stanford University Press, 1993.

—— *Given Time: I. Counterfeit Money*, trans. P. Kamuf, Chicago: University of Chicago Press, 1991.

—— *Margins of Philosophy*, trans. A. Bass, Chicago: University of Chicago Press, 1982.

—— *Of Spirit*, Chicago: University of Chicago Press, 1987.

—— *Specters of Marx*, trans. P. Kamuf, London: Routledge, 1994.

—— *The Ear of the Other. Otobiography, Transference, Translation*, Lincoln: University of Nebraska Press, 1988.

—— *The Other Heading. Reflections on Today's Europe*, trans. P.-A. Brault and M. Nass, Bloomington: Indiana University Press, 1992.

Descartes, R: *Discourse on Method and The Meditations*, Harmondsworth: Penguin Books, 1968.

Dillon, M. ed.: *Tradition*. Special Edition of the *Journal of The British Society for Phenomenology*, October 1995.

Dreyfus, H. and Rabinow, P: *Michel Foucault. Beyond Structuralism and Hermeneutics*, Brighton, Sussex: The Harvester Press, 1982.

Dunn, J. ed.: *Democracy: The Unfinished Journey, 508 BC to AD 1993*, Oxford: Oxford University Press, 1992.

Eagleton, T: *Literary Theory: An Introduction*, Minneapolis: Minnesota University Press, 1983.

Eksteins, M: *Rites of Spring. The Great War and the Birth of the Modern Age*, London: Bantam Press, 1989.

Euben, P. ed.: *Greek Tragedy and Political Theory*, London: University of California Press, 1986.

Fenves, P: *Raising The tone of Philosophy*, Baltimore: The Johns Hopkins University Press, 1993.

Foucault, M: 'Final Interview', *Raritan*, 1985, vol. 5, no. 1.

—— *Herculine Barbin. Being the Recently Discovered Memoirs of a Nineteenth-Century French Hermaphrodite*, introduced by M. Foucault, trans. R. McDougal, New York: Pantheon Books, 1980.

—— *The History Of Sexuality. Volume One. An Introduction*, Harmondsworth: Penguin Books, 1987.

—— *The History of Sexuality. Volume Two. The Use Of Pleasure*, Harmondsworth: Penguin Books, 1987.
—— *The History of Sexuality. Volume Three. The Care of The Self*, Harmondsworth: Penguin, 1988.
—— *The Order of Things*, London: Tavistock/Routledge, 1989.
Fried, G. 'Heidegger's *Polemos*', *Journal of Philosophical Research*, vol. xvi, 1990–91, pp. 159–95.
Fynsk, C: *Heidegger. Thought and Historicity*, Ithaca: Cornell University Press, 1993.
Gasché, R: *Inventions of Difference. On Jacques Derrida*, Cambridge: Mass.: Harvard University Press, 1994.
Gillespie, M. A: *Hegel, Heidegger and the Ground of History*, Chicago: University of Chicago Press, 1984.
Girard, R: *Violence and the Sacred*, trans. P. Gregory, Baltimore: The Johns Hopkins University Press, 1977.
Gordon, C. ed.: *M. Foucault, Power/Knowledge. Selected Interviews and Other Writings*, New York: Pantheon Books, 1980.
Grassi, E: *Heidegger and the Question of Renaissance Humanism: Four Studies*, Binghampton: State University of New York, Medieval and Renaissance Texts and Studies, January 1983.
Haar, M: *Heidegger And The Essence Of Man*, trans. W. McNeill, Albany: SUNY Press, 1993.
—— *The Song of the Earth. Heidegger and the Grounds of the History of Being*, Bloomington: Indiana University Press, 1993.
Hall, E: *Inventing The Barbarian*, Oxford: Clarendon Press, 1989.
Hancock, J: *Calvin and the Foundations of Modern Politics*, Ithaca: Cornell University Press, 1989.
Handelman, S. A: *Fragments of Redemption. Jewish Thought and Literary Theory in Benjamin, Scholem and Levinas*, Bloomington: Indiana University Press, 1991.
Harries, K: 'Heidegger and Hölderlin: The Limits of Language', *The Personalist*, vol. xlvi, 1963.
—— 'Heidegger's Conception of the Holy', *The Personalist*, vol. 47, no. 2, Spring 1966.
Heidegger, M: 'The Problem of Reality in Modern Philosophy', *Journal of the British Society for Phenomenology*, vol. 4, no. 1, January 1971.
—— 'Phenomenological Interpretations with Respect to Aristotle (Indication of the Hermeneutical Situation)', trans. M. Bauer, *Man and World*, vol. 25, 1992.
—— *On Time and Being*, New York: Harper Torch Books, 1972.
—— *An Introduction to Metaphysics*, New Haven: Yale University Press, 1987.
—— *Basic Concepts*, trans. G. E. Aylesworth, Bloomington: Indiana University Press, 1993.
—— *Basic Questions of Philosophy. Selected 'Problems' of 'Logic'*, Bloomington: Indiana University Press, 1994.
—— *Being and Time*, Oxford: Basil Blackwell, 1988.
—— *Early Greek Thinking*, trans. D. F. Krell, New York: Harper and Row, 1984.
—— *Identity and Difference*, trans. J. Stambaugh, New York: Harper and Row, 1969.
—— *Kant and the Problem of Metaphysics*, Bloomington: Indiana University Press, 1990.
—— *Logic: The Question of Truth*, Bloomington: Indiana University Presss, 1995.
—— *Nietzsche. Volumes I–IV*, San Francisco: HarperCollins, 1991.
—— *On The Way To Language*, trans. P. D. Hertz, San Fransisco: HarperCollins, 1971.
—— *Parmenides*, Bloomington: Indiana University Press, 1992.
—— *Poetry, Language and Thought*, trans. A. Hofstadter, New York: Harper and Row, 1971.
—— *The Basic Problems of Phenomenology*, Translation, Introduction and Lexicon by A. Hofstadter, Bloomington: Indiana University Press, 1982.

—— *The Concept of Time*, trans. W. McNeil, Oxford: Basil Blackwell, 1992.
—— *The End of Philosophy*, London: Souvenir Press (Educational and Academic) Ltd., 1975.
—— *The Essence of Reasons*, Evanston, Ill.: Northwestern University Press, 1969.
—— *The Metaphysical Foundations of Logic*, trans. M. Heim, Bloomington: Indiana University Press, 1992.
—— *The Principle of Reason*, trans. R. Lilly, Bloomington: Indiana University Press, 1991.
—— *The Question Concerning Technology and Other Essays*, New York: Harper Torch Books, 1977.
—— *The Southern Journal of Philosophy, Spindel Conference 1989. Heidegger and Praxis*, T. J. Nenon, ed., vol. XXVIII Supplement.
Hodge, J: *Heidegger and Ethics*, London: Routledge, 1995.
Höpfl, H: *The Christian Polity Of John Calvin*, Cambridge: Cambridge University Press, 1985.
Husserl, E: *Cartesian Meditations*, trans. D. Cairns, The Hague: Martinus Nijhoff, 1960.
Johnson, J. S: 'Reading Nietzsche and Foucault: A Hermeneutics of Suspicion', *American Political Science Review*, vol. 85, no. 2, 1991.
Kaufman, I: *Redeeming Politics*, Princeton, New Jersey: Princeton University Press, 1990.
—— *Tragedy and Philosophy*, Princeton: Princeton University Press, 1968.
Kearney, R: *Poetics of Imagining from Husserl to Lyotard*, London: HarperCollins, 1991.
—— *The Wake of Imagination*, London: Hutchinson, 1988.
Kisiel, T: 'The Language of the Event: The Event of Language', in J. Sallis, ed., *Heidegger and the Path of Thinking*, Pittsburgh: Duquesne University Press, 1970.
—— *The Genesis of Heidegger's Being and Time*, Los Angeles: University of California Press, 1993.
Knox, B: *Oedipus at Thebes*, New Haven: Yale University Press, 1957.
Kocklemans, J. J: *On the Truth of Being*, Bloomington: Indiana University Press, 1984.
Kohak, E: *Jan Patocka, Philosophy and Selected Writings*, Chicago: University of Chicago Press, 1989.
Kohn, J: 'Thinking/Acting', *Social Research*, vol. 57. no. 1, Spring, 1990.
Koselleck, R: 'Begriffsgeschichte and Social History', *Economy and Society*, vol. 11, no. 4, 1982.
Kovacs, G: 'On Heidegger's Silence', *Heidegger Studies*, vol. 5, 1989.
Krell, D. F: 'On the Manifold meaning of *Aletheia*: Brentano, Aristotle and Heidegger', *Research in Phenomenology*, vol. 5, 1975.
—— *Daimon Life*, Bloomington: Indiana University Press, 1992.
—— ed.: *Martin Heidegger: Basic Writings*, New York: Harper and Row, 1977.
—— *Intimations Of Mortality. Time, Truth, and Finitude in Heidegger's Thinking of Being*, University Park Pennsylvania: The Pennsylvania State University Press, 1986.
Kristeva, J: *Strangers To Ourselves*, trans. L. S. Roudiez, London: Harvester Wheatsheaf, 1991.
Lacoue-Labarthe, P: *Heidegger, Art and Politics*, Oxford: Basil Blackwell, 1990.
Lefort, C: *Democracy and Political Theory*, Cambridge: Polity Press, 1988.
Leibniz, G. W:*Philosophical Writings*, G.H.R. Parkinson, ed., London: Everyman, 1982.
Lesky, A: *Greek Tragedy*, London: Ernest Benn Ltd., 2nd edn, 1967.
Levinas, E: 'De L'Evasion', *Recherches Philosophiques*, 5.
—— 'Philosophy and Awakening', in E. Cadava, P. Connor and Jean-Luc Nancy, eds, *Who Comes After the Subject*, London: Routledge, 1991.
—— *Collected Papers*, London: Kluwer Academic Publishers, 1993.
—— *Difficult Freedom. Essays on Judaism*, London: Athlone Press, 1990.
—— *Existence and Existents*, trans. A. Lingis, Dordrecht: Kluwer Academic Publishers, 1988.

—— *Otherwise than Being or Beyond Essence*, London: Kluwer Academic Publishers, 1991.

—— *Outside the Subject*, trans. M. B. Smith, Stanford: Stanford University Press, 1993.

—— *Totality and Infinity*, trans. A. Lingis, London: Kluwer Academic Publishers, 1991.

Lingis, A: *Deathbound Subjectivity*, Bloomington: Indiana University Press, 1989.

Loscerbo, J: *Being and Technology. A Study in the Philosophy of Martin Heidegger*, The Hague: Martinus Nijhoff, 1981.

Lyotard, J.-P., and Thebaud, J.-L: *Just Gaming*, Manchester: Manchester University Press, 1985.

—— *Heidegger and 'The Jews'*, Minneapolis: Minnesota University Press, 1990.

—— *Phenomenology*, trans. B. Beakley, New York: The State University of New York Press, 1991.

—— *The Inhuman*, Cambridge: Polity Press, 1991.

—— *The Postmodern Condition: A Report on Knowledge*, Minneapolis: Minnesota University Press, 1984.

Macksey, R. and Donato, E. eds: *The Structuralist Controversy: The Languages of Criticism and the Sciences of Man*, Baltimore: The Johns Hopkins University Press, 1972.

Makkreel, R. A: 'The Genesis of Heidegger's Phenomenological Hermeneutics and the Rediscovered "Aristotle Introduction" of 1992', *Man and World*, vol. 23, 1990.

Manning, R. J. S: *Interpreting Otherwise than Heidegger. Emmanuel Levinas' Ethics as First Philosophy*, Pittsburgh: Dusquesne University Press, 1993.

Marshall, T: *Swords and Symbols. The Techniques of Sovereignty*, London: Oxford University Press, 1939.

Marx, W: *Is There a Measure On Earth?* Chicago: University of Chicago Press, 1987.

—— *Towards a Phenomenological Ethics. Ethos and the Life-World*, Albany: State University of New York Press, 1992.

Michelfelder, D. P. and Palmer, R. E. eds: *Dialogue and Deconstruction*, Albany: State University of New York Press, 1989.

Morgenthau, H: 'Death in the Nuclear Age', in J. Riemer ed., *Jewish Reflections on Death*, New York: Schocken Books, 1974.

Mulgan, R: 'Aristotle and the Value of Political Participation', *Political Theory*, vol. 18, no. 2, 1990.

Musurillo, H: *The Light and the Darkness*, Leiden: E. J. Brill, 1967.

Nancy, J.-L: *The Birth to Presence*, Stanford, California: Stanford University Press, 1993.

—— *The Experience of Freedom*, Stanford, California: Stanford University Press, 1993.

—— *The Inoperative Community*, Minneapolis: University of Minnesota Press, 1991.

Nietzsche, F: *Daybreak. Thoughts on the Prejudices of Morality*, trans. R. J. Hollingdale, Cambridge: Cambridge University Press, 1990.

—— *The Birth of Tragedy*, New York: Anchor Books, 1956.

—— *The Gay Science*, trans. W. Kaufmann, New York: Vintage Books, 1974.

—— *Twilight Of The Idols and The Anti-Christ*, Harmondsworth: Penguin Books, 1990.

—— *Untimely Meditations*, trans. R. J. Hollingdale, Cambridge: Cambridge University Press, 1989.

Nussbaum, M: *The Fragility of Goodness. Luck and Ethics in Greek Tragedy and Philosophy*, Cambridge: Cambridge University Press, 1989.

Nygren, A: *Agape and Eros*, London: SPCK, 1953.

O'Brian, F. ed.: *Twentieth Century Interpretations Of Oedipus Rex*, Englewood Cliffs, New Jersey: Prentice Hall, 1968.

Ott, H: *Martin Heidegger: A Political Life*, London: HarperCollins, 1993.

Oudemans, Th: 'Heidegger: Reading Against The Grain', in Kisiel, T. and van Buren, J. cds: *Reading Heidegger From The Beginning. Essays in His Earliest Thoughts*, Albany, New York: SUNY Press, 1994.

Outka, G. *Agape. An Ethical Analysis*, New Haven: Yale University Press, 1972.

Pearton, M: *The Knowledgable State. Diplomacy, War and Technology Since 1830*, London: Burnett Books, 1982.
Prufer, T: 'Glosses on Heidegger's Architectonic Word-Play: Lichtung and Ereignis, Bergung and Wahrns', *Review of Metaphysics*, vol. 44, 1990–91.
Rabinow, P. ed.: *The Foucault Reader*, Harmondsworth: Penguin Books, 1984.
Rapaport, H: *Heidegger and Derrida. Reflections on Time and Language*, Lincoln: University of Nebraska Press.
Richardson, W: *Heidegger: Through Phenomenology to Thought*, The Hague: Martinus Nijhoff, 1963.
Richter, M: 'Conceptual History (*Begriffsgeschichte*) And Political Theory', *Political Theory*, vol. 14, no. 4, 1986.
—— 'Reconstructing The History Of Political Languages: Pocock, Skinner, And The *Geschichtliche Grundbegriffe*', *History And Theory. Studies In The Philosophy Of History*, vol. xxix, no. 1, 1990.
Rockmore, T: *On Heidegger's Nazism and Philosophy*, London: Harvester Wheatsheaf, 1992.
Rorty, R: 'Heidegger, Contingency and Pragmatism', in H. L. Dreyfus and H. Hall, eds, *Heidegger: A Critical Reader*, Oxford: Basil Blackwell, 1992.
—— *Irony, Contingency and Solidarity*, Cambridge: Cambridge University Press, 1989.
Rosen, S: *Nihilism*, New Haven: Yale University Press, 1971.
—— *The Question of Being. A Reversal of Heidegger*, New Haven: Yale University Press, 1993.
Sallis, J: 'Language and Reversal', *Southwestern Journal of Philosophy*, Winter 1970.
—— 'Meaning Adrift', *Heidegger Studies*, vol. 1, 1988.
—— 'Toward the Showing of Language', *Southwestern Journal of Philosophy*, vol. 4, 1973.
—— *Crossings. Nietzsche and the Space of Tragedy*, Chicago: University of Chicago Press, 1991.
—— *Delimitations. Phenomenology and the End of Metaphysics*, Bloomington: Indiana University Press, 1986.
—— ed.: *Heidegger and the Path of Thinking*, Pittsburgh: Duquesne University Press, 1970.
—— ed.: *Reading Heidegger*, Bloomington: Indiana University Press, 1993.
Schmidt, D: 'Changing the Subject: Heidegger, "the" National and Epochal', *Heidegger and the Political. The Graduate Faculty Philosophy Journal*, vol. 14, no. 2–vol. 15, no. 1, 1991.
—— *The Ubiquity of The Finite. Hegel, Heidegger and the Entitlements of Philosophy*, Cambridge, Mass.: The MIT Press, 1988.
Schmitt, C: *The Concept of the Political*, New Jersey: Rutgers University Press, 1976.
—— *Political Theology*, Cambridge, Mass.: The MIT Press, 1988.
—— *The Crisis of Parliamentary Democracy*, Cambridge, Mass.: The MIT Press, 1988.
Schurmann, R: *Heidegger. On Being and Acting: From Principles to Anarchy*, Bloomington: Indiana University Press, 1990.
Shapiro, M: *Reading The Postmodern Polity. Political Theory as Textual Practice*, Minneapolis: Minnesota University Press, 1992.
—— *The Politics of Representation. Writing Practices in Biography, Photography, and Policy Analysis*, Madison: Wisconsin University Press, 1988.
Sheehan, T: 'Heidegger's Interpretation of Aristotle: *Dynamis* and *Ereignis*', in *Philosophy Research Archives*, vol. 4, 1978.
Singer, I: *The Nature of Love. Volume 1. From Plato to Luther*, Chicago: University of Chicago Press, 1984.
Sluga, H: *Heidegger's Crisis. Philosophy and Politics in Nazi Germany*, Cambridge, Mass.: Harvard University Press, 1993.

Soble, A: *Eros, Agape and Philia. Readings in the Philosophy of Love*, London: Paragon House, 1989.

Stambaugh, J: *Thoughts On Heidegger*, Boston: University Press of America, 1991.

Steiner, G: *After Babel. Aspects of Language and Translation*, London: Oxford University Press, 1975.

Stenstad, G. 'The Last God – A Reading', *Research in Phenomenology*, vol. XXIII, 1993.

Strauss, L: *Spinoza's Critique of Religion*, New York: Schocken Books, 1965.

Strong, T. B: *Friedrich Nietzsche and The Politics of Transfiguration*, Berkeley: University of California Press, 1988.

Taminiaux, J: *Heidegger and the Project of Fundamental Ontology*, trans. M. Gendre, Albany: SUNY Press, 1991.

—— *Poetics Speculation and Judgement*, trans. and ed. by M. Gendre, New York: State Univerity of New York Press, 1993.

Thiele, P: 'The Agony of Politics: The Nietzschean Roots of Foucault's Thought,' *American Political Science Review*, vol. 83, no. 3, 1990.

Ullman, R: 'Redefining Security', *International Security*, vol. 8, no. 1, Summer 1983.

Vattimo, G: *The Adventure of Difference. Philosophy after Nietzsche and Heidegger*, Oxford: Polity Press, 1993.

Vernant, J.-P. and Vidal-Naquet, P: *Myth and Tragedy in Ancient Greece*, New York: Zone Books, 1988.

Villa, D: 'Beyond Good And Evil. Arendt, Nietzsche, and the Aestheticization of Political Action', *Political Theory*, vol. 20, no. 2, 1992.

Virilio, P: *Popular Defence and Ecological Struggles*, New York: Semiotext(e), 1990.

Voti, V: *Heidegger and the Poets. Poiesis/Sophia/Techne*, Atlantic Highlands, New Jersey: Humanities Press, 1992.

Walker, R. B. J: *Inside Outside: International Relations as Political Theory*, Cambridge: Cambridge University Press, 1993.

Weber, S: 'Upsetting The Set Up: Remarks on Heidegger's Questing After Technics', *Modern Language Notes*, vol. 104, no. 5, December 1989.

White, A: *Within Nietzsche's Labyrinth*, London: Routledge, 1990.

Wolin, S: *Politics and Vision*, London: George Allen and Unwin, 1961.

Wood, D: *Philosophy at the Limit*, London: Unwin Hyman, 1990.

Wood, D. and Bernasconi, R. eds: *Derrida and Différance*, Evanston: Northwestern University Press, 1988.

Wright, Q: *A Study Of War Volume Two*, Chicago: University of Chicago Press, 1942.

Zimmerman, M. E: *Heidegger's Confrontation with Modernity. Technology, Politics, Art*, Bloomington: Indiana University Press, 1990.

Index